Complexity and Contradiction in Architecture

Robert Venturi

with an introduction by Vincent Scully

The Museum of Modern Art, New York

in association with

the Graham Foundation for Advanced Studies in The Fine Arts, Chicago

Distributed by Doubleday & Company, Garden City, New York

© The Museum of Modern Art, 1966
11 West 53 Street, New York, N.Y. 10019
Library of Congress Catalog Card Number 66-30001
Printed in the U.S.A.
Reprinted 2019

To my mother and the memory of my father.

Acknowledgments

Most of this book was written in 1962 under a grant from the Graham Foundation. I am also indebted to the American Academy in Rome for the Fellowship, ten years ago, which enabled me to live in Italy.

The following people helped me: Vincent Scully, through his crucial appreciation and criticism when I really needed them; Marion Scully, through her skill, patience and understanding in making the text clearer; Philip Finkel-pearl, through his talking with me over the years; Denise Scott Brown, by sharing her insights into architecture and city planning; Robert Stern, through concrete enrichments to the argument; Mrs. Henry Ottmann and Miss Ellen Marsh of the staff of The Museum of Modern Art, through their cooperation in collecting illustrations.

R. V.

Chapter

This remarkable study is the first in a series of occasional papers concerned with the theoretical background of modern architecture. Unlike other Museum publications in architecture and design, the series will be independent of the Museum's exhibition program. It will explore ideas too complex for presentation in exhibition form, and authors will represent no single professional group.

Mr. Venturi's book is published by the Museum in collaboration with The Graham Foundation for Advanced Studies in the Fine Arts. It is a particularly appropriate volume with which to inaugurate the series, as the author was originally enabled to work on the text through the aid of a Graham Foundation grant.

Like his buildings, Venturi's book opposes what many would consider Establishment, or at least established, opinions. He speaks with uncommon candor, addressing himself to actual conditions: the ambiguous and sometimes unattractive "facts" in which architects find themselves enmeshed at each moment, and whose confusing nature Venturi would seek to make the basis of architectural design. It is an alternative point of view vigorously championed by Vincent Scully of Yale University, whose introduction contrasts the frustrations of abstractly preconceived architectural order with Venturi's delight in reality—especially in those recalcitrant aspects most architects would seek to suppress or disguise. Venturi's recommendations can be tested immediately: they need not wait on legislation or technology. Problems in the architecture he seeks to supplant are so far from being resolved that, whether or not we agree with his results, we are impelled to grant him an attentive hearing.

Arthur Drexler
Director
Department of Architecture and Design

This is not an easy book. It requires professional commitment and close visual attention, and is not for those architects who, lest they offend them, pluck out their eyes. Indeed, its argument unfolds like a curtain slowly lifting from the eyes. Piece by piece, in close focus after focus, the whole emerges. And that whole is new—hard to see, hard to write about, graceless and inarticulate as only the new can be.

It is a very American book, rigorously pluralistic and phenomenological in its method; one is reminded of Dreiser, laboriously trodding out the way. Yet it is probably the most important writing on the making of architecture since Le Corbusier's *Vers une Architecture,* of 1923. Indeed, at first sight, Venturi's position seems exactly the opposite of Le Corbusier's, its first and natural complement across time.* This is not to say that Venturi is Le Corbusier's equal in persuasiveness or achievement—or will necessarily ever be. Few will attain to that level again. The experience of Le Corbusier's buildings themselves has surely had not a little to do with forming Venturi's ideas. Yet his views do in fact balance those of Le Corbusier as they were expressed in his early writings and as they have generally affected two architectural generations since that time. The older book demanded a noble purism in architecture, in single buildings and in the city as a whole; the new book welcomes the

* Here I do not forget Bruno Zevi's *Towards an Organic Architecture,* of 1950, which was consciously written as a reply to Le Corbusier. One cannot, however, regard it as a complement to the other or as an advance upon it, since it was hardly more than a reaction against it in favor of "organic" principles which had been formulated by architects other than Zevi and had indeed passed their peak of vitality long before. They had found their best embodiment in the work of Frank Lloyd Wright before 1914 and their clearest verbal statement in his writings of that period.

contradictions and complexities of urban experience at all scales. It marks, in this way, a complete shift of emphasis and will annoy some of those who profess to follow Le Corbusier now, exactly as Le Corbusier infuriated many who belonged to the Beaux-Arts then. Hence the books do in fact complement each other; and in one fundamental way they are much the same. Both are by architects who have really learned something from the architecture of the past. Few contemporary architects have been able to do this and have instead tended to take refuge in various systems of what can only be called historical propaganda. For Le Corbusier and Venturi, the experience was personal and direct. Each was thus able to free himself from the fixed patterns of thought and the fashions of his contemporaries, so carrying out Camus' injunction to leave behind for a while "our age and its adolescent furies."

Each learned most from very different things. Le Corbusier's great teacher was the Greek temple, with its isolated body white and free in the landscape, its luminous austerities clear in the sun. In his early polemics he would have his buildings and his cities just that way, and his mature architecture itself came more and more to embody the Greek temple's sculptural, actively heroic character. Venturi's primary inspiration would seem to have come from the Greek temple's historical and archetypal opposite, the urban façades of Italy, with their endless adjustments to the counter-requirements of inside and outside and their inflection with all the business of everyday life: not primarily sculptural actors in vast landscapes but complex spatial containers and definers of streets and squares. Such "accommodation" also becomes a general urban principle for Venturi. In this he again resembles Le Corbusier, in so far as they are both profoundly visual, plastic artists whose close focus upon individual buildings brings with it a new visual and symbolic attitude toward urbanism in general—not the schematic or two-dimensionally diagrammatic view toward which many planners tend, but a set of solid images, architecture itself at its full scale.

Yet again, the images of Le Corbusier and Venturi are diametrically opposed in this regard. Le Corbusier, exercising that side of his many-sided nature which professed Cartesian rigor, generalized in *Vers une Architecture* much more easily than Venturi does here, and presented a clear, general scheme for the whole. Venturi is more fragmentary, moving step by step through more compromised relationships. His conclusions are general only by implication. Yet it seems to me that his proposals, in their recognition of complexity and their respect for what exists, create the most necessary antidote to that cataclysmic purism of contemporary urban renewal which has presently brought so many cities to the brink of catastrophe, and in which Le Corbusier's ideas have now found terrifying vulgarization. They are a hero's dreams applied en masse—as if an Achilles were to become the king. That is why, one supposes, Venturi is so consistently anti-heroic, compulsively qualifying his recommendations with an implied irony at every turn. Le Corbusier used irony too, but his was as sharp as a steel-toothed smile. Venturi shrugs his shoulders ruefully and moves on. It is this generation's answer to grandiose pretensions which have shown themselves in practice to be destructive or overblown.

Like all original architects, Venturi makes us see the past anew. He has made me, for example, who once focused upon the proto-Wrightian continuities of the Shingle Style, revalue their equally obvious opposite: the complicated accommodations of inside and outside with which those architects themselves were surely entranced. And he has even called attention once more to the principle of accommodation in Le Corbusier's early plans. So all inventive architects bring their dead to life again as a matter of course. It is appropriate that Le Corbusier and Venturi should come together on the question of Michelangelo, in whose work heroic action and complex qualification found special union. Venturi fixes less than Le Corbusier upon the unified assertion of Michelangelo's conception in St. Peter's but, like Le Corbusier, he sees and, as the fenestration of his Friends' Housing for the Aged shows, can build in accordance with the other: the sad and mighty discordances of the apses, that music drear and grand of dying civilizations and the fate of mankind on a cooling star.

In that sense Venturi is, for all his own ironic disclaimers, one of the few American architects whose work seems to approach tragic stature in the tradition of Furness, Louis Sullivan, Wright, and Kahn. His being so suggests the power of successive generations, living in one place, to develop an intensity of meaning; so much of it is carried in Philadelphia: from Frank Furness to the young Sullivan, and on through Wilson Eyre and George Howe to Louis Kahn. Kahn is Venturi's closest mentor, as he has been for almost all the best young American architects and educators of the past decade, such as Giurgola, Moore, Vreeland, and Millard. The dialogue so developed, in which Aldo Van Eyck of Holland has also played an outstanding role, has surely contributed much to Venturi's development. Kahn's theory of "institutions" has been fundamental to all these architects, but Venturi himself avoids Kahn's structural preoccupations in favor of a more flexibly function-directed method which is closer to that of Alvar Aalto. Unlike his writing, Venturi's design unfolds without strain. In it he is as facile as an architect of the Baroque and, in the same sense, as scenographic. (His project for the Roosevelt Memorial, probably the best, surely the most original of the entries, shows how serene and grand that scenographic talent can be.) There is none of Kahn's grim struggle in him, no profound agony of structural and functional opposites seeking expression. He is entirely at home with the particular and so offers the necessary opposition to the technological homogenizers who crowd our future. There is surely no quarrel here with Le Corbusier, or even with Mies, despite the universal regularity of the latter's forms. Many species of high quality can inhabit the same world. Such multiplicity is indeed the highest promise of the modern age to mankind, far more intrinsic to its nature than the superficial conformity or equally arbitrary packaging which its first stages suggest and which are so eagerly embraced by superficial designers.

The essential point is that Venturi's philosophy and design are humanistic, in which character his book resembles Geoffrey Scott's basic work, *The Architecture of Humanism*, of 1914. Therefore, it values before all else the actions of human beings and the effect of physical forms upon their spirit. In this, Venturi is an Italian architect of the great tradition—whose contact with that tradition came from art history at Princeton and a fellowship at the American Academy in Rome. But, as his Friends' Housing shows equally well, he is one of the very few architects whose thought parallels that of the Pop painters—and probably the first architect to perceive the usefulness and meaning of their forms. He has clearly learned a good deal from them during the past few years, though the major argument of this book was laid out in the late fifties and predates his knowledge of their work. Yet his "Main Street is almost all right," is just like their viewpoint, as is his instinct for changes of scale in small buildings and for the unsuspected life to be found in the common artifacts of mass culture when they are focused upon individually. The "Pop" in Le Corbusier's "Purism," as in that of the young Léger, should not be forgotten here, and it takes on renewed historical significance as its lesson of exploded scale and sharpened focus is learned once more. Again one has the feeling that Le Corbusier, painter and theorist that he was, would have best understood Venturi's alliance of visual method with intellectual intention.

It is significant in this regard that Venturi's ideas have so far stirred bitterest resentment among the more academic-minded of the Bauhaus generation—with its utter lack of irony, its spinsterish disdain for the popular culture but shaky grasp on any other, its incapacity to deal with monumental scale, its lip-service to technology, and its preoccupation with a rather prissily puristic aesthetic. Most of the Bauhaus design of the twenties, in buildings and furniture alike, can be distinguished by exactly those characteristics from Le Corbusier's more generous and varied forms of the period. Two strains in modern architecture seem to separate here, with Le Corbusier and Venturi now seen as working the same larger, more humane, architects' rather than "designers' " vein.

Venturi's projected City Hall for North Canton, Ohio, shows how his architecture also has a connection with the late work of Sullivan and so with the deepest untapped force of American vernacular experience as a whole. This is surely Venturi's largest achievement in American terms, that he opens our eyes again to the nature of things as they are in the United States—in the small town no less than in New York—and that out of our common, confused, mass-produced fabric he makes a solid architecture; he makes an art. In so doing he revives the popular traditions, and the particularized methodology, of the pre-Beaux Arts, pre-International Style, period. He thus completes that renewed connection with the whole of our past which Kahn's mature work had begun.

It is no wonder that few of the present crop of redevelopers can yet endure him. They, too, are much in the American grain, village boys with their noses pressed against the window of the candy store and with money to burn for the first time. So they are generally buying junk, fancy trash readymade by an army of architectural entrepreneurs, who portentously supply a spurious simplicity and the order of the tomb: the contemporary package, *par excellence*. Venturi looks both too complicated and too much like everyday for such people, who, in their architectural forms as in their social programs, would much prefer to gloss over a few of reality's more demanding faces. Hence, precisely because he recognizes and uses social phenomena as they exist, Venturi is the least "stylish" of architects, going always straight to the heart of the matter, working quickly without either fancy pretenses or vaporish asides. Although he has learned from Mannerist architecture, his own buildings are in no sense "mannered," but surprisingly direct. After all, a television aerial at appropriate scale crowns his Friends' Housing, exactly as it fills— here neither good nor bad but a fact—our old people's lives. Whatever dignity may be in that, Venturi embodies, but he does not lie to us once concerning what the facts are. In the straightest sense, it is function that interests him, and the strong forms deriving from functional expression. Unlike too many architects of this generation, he is never genteel.

It is no wonder that Venturi's buildings have not found ready acceptance; they have been both too new and, for all their "accommodation" of complexity, too truly simple and unassuming for this affluent decade. They have refused to make much out of nothing, to indulge in flashy gestures, or to pander to fashion. They have been the product of a deeply systematic analysis in programmatic and visual terms and have therefore required a serious reorientation in all our thinking. Hence the symbolic image which prepares our eyes to see them has not yet been formed. This book may help in that regard. I believe that the future will value it among the few basic texts of our time—one which, despite its anti-heroic lack of pretension and its shift of perspective from the Champs-Elysées to Main Street, still picks up a fundamental dialogue begun in the twenties, and so connects us with the heroic generation of modern architecture once more.

Vincent Scully

Preface

This book is both an attempt at architectural criticism and an apologia—an explanation, indirectly, of my work. Because I am a practicing architect, my ideas on architecture are inevitably a by-product of the criticism which accompanies working, and which is, as T. S. Eliot has said, of "capital importance . . . in the work of creation itself. Probably, indeed, the larger part of the labour of sifting, combining, constructing, expunging, correcting, testing: this frightful toil is as much critical as creative. I maintain even that the criticism employed by a trained and skilled writer on his own work is the most vital, the highest kind of criticism . . ." [1] I write, then, as an architect who employs criticism rather than a critic who chooses architecture and this book represents a particular set of emphases, a way of seeing architecture, which I find valid.

In the same essay Eliot discusses analysis and comparison as tools of literary criticism. These critical methods are valid for architecture too: architecture is open to analysis like any other aspect of experience, and is made more vivid by comparisons. Analysis includes the breaking up of architecture into elements, a technique I frequently use even though it is the opposite of the integration which is the final goal of art. However paradoxical it appears, and despite the suspicions of many Modern architects, such disintegration is a process present in all creation, and it is essential to understanding. Self-consciousness is necessarily a part of creation and criticism. Architects today are too educated to be either primitive or totally spontaneous, and architecture is too complex to be approached with carefully maintained ignorance.

As an architect I try to be guided not by habit but by a conscious sense of the past—by precedent, thoughtfully considered. The historical comparisons chosen are part of a continuous tradition relevant to my concerns. When Eliot writes about tradition, his comments are equally relevant to architecture, notwithstanding the more obvious changes in architectural methods due to technological innovations. "In English writing," Eliot says, "we seldom speak of tradition. . . . Seldom, perhaps, does the word appear except in a phrase of censure. If otherwise, it is vaguely approbative, with the implication, as to a work approved, of some pleasing archeological reconstruction. . . . Yet if the only form of tradition, of handing down, consisted in following the ways of the immediate generation before us in a blind or timid adherence to its successes, 'tradition' should be positively discouraged. . . . Tradition is a matter of much wider significance. It cannot be inherited, and if you want it you must obtain it by great labour. It involves, in the first place, the historical sense, which we may call nearly indispensable to anyone who would continue to be a poet beyond his twenty-fifth year; and the historical sense involves perception, not only of the pastness of the past, but of its presence; the historical sense compels a man to write not merely with his own generation in his bones, but with a feeling that the whole of the literature of Europe . . . has a simultaneous existence and composes a simultaneous order. This historical sense, which is a sense of the timeless as well as of the temporal and of the timeless and temporal together, is what makes a writer traditional, and it is at the same time what makes a writer most acutely conscious of his place in time, of his own contemporaneity. . . . No poet, no artist of any kind, has his complete meaning alone." [2] I agree with Eliot and reject the obsession of Modern architects who, to quote Aldo van Eyck, "have been harping continually on what is different in our time to such an extent that they have lost touch with what is not different, with what is essentially the same." [3]

The examples chosen reflect my partiality for certain eras: Mannerist, Baroque, and Rococo especially. As Henry-Russell Hitchcock says, "there always exists a real need to re-examine the work of the past. There is, presumably, almost always a generic interest in architectural history among architects; but the aspects, or periods, of history that seem at any given time to merit the closest attention certainly vary with changing sensibilities." [4] As an artist I frankly write about what I like in architecture: complexity and contradiction. From what we find we like—what we are easily attracted to—we can learn much of what we really are. Louis Kahn has referred to "what a thing wants to be," but implicit in this statement is its opposite: what the architect wants the thing to be. In the tension and balance between these two lie many of the architect's decisions.

The comparisons include some buildings which are neither beautiful nor great, and they have been lifted abstractly from their historical context because I rely less on the idea of style than on the inherent characteristics of specific buildings. Writing as an architect rather than as a scholar, my historical view is that described by Hitchcock: "Once, of course, almost all investigation of the architecture of the past was in aid of its nominal reconstruction—an instrument of revivalism. That is no longer true, and there is little reason to fear that it will, in our time, become so again. Both the architects and the historian-critics of the early twentieth century, when they were not merely seeking in the past fresh ammunition for current polemical warfare, taught us to see all architecture, as it were, abstractly, false though such a limited vision probably is to the complex sensibilities that produced most of the great architecture of the past. When we re-examine—or discover—this or that aspect of earlier building production today, it is with no idea of repeating its forms, but rather in the expectation of feeding more amply new sensibilities that are wholly the product of the present. To the pure historian this may seem regrettable, as introducing highly subjective elements into what he believes ought to be objective studies. Yet the pure historian, more often than not, will eventually find himself moving in directions that have been already determined by more sensitive weathervanes." [5]

I make no special attempt to relate architecture to other things. I have not tried to "improve the connections between science and technology on the one hand, and the humanities and the social sciences on the other . . . and make of architecture a more human social art." [6] I try to talk about architecture rather than around it. Sir John Summerson has referred to the architects' obsession with "the importance, not of architecture, but of the *relation* of architecture to other things." [7] He has pointed out that in this century architects have substituted the "mischievous analogy" for the eclectic imitation of the nineteenth century, and have been staking a claim for architecture rather than producing architecture.[8] The result has been diagrammatic planning. The architect's ever diminishing power and his growing ineffectualness in shaping the whole environment can perhaps be reversed, ironically, by narrowing his concerns and concentrating on his own job. Perhaps then relationships and power will take care of themselves. I accept what seem to me architecture's inherent limitations, and attempt to concentrate on the difficult particulars within it rather than the easier abstractions about it "... because the arts belong (as the ancients said) to the practical and not the speculative intelligence, there is no surrogate for being on the job." [9]

This book deals with the present, and with the past in relation to the present. It does not attempt to be visionary except insofar as the future is inherent in the reality of the present. It is only indirectly polemical. Everything is said in the context of current architecture and consequently certain targets are attacked—in general, the limitations of orthodox Modern architecture and city planning, in particular, the platitudinous architects who invoke integrity, technology, or electronic programming as ends in architecture, the popularizers who paint "fairy stories over our chaotic reality" [10] and suppress those complexities and contradictions inherent in art and experience. Nevertheless, this book is an analysis of what seems to me true for architecture now, rather than a diatribe against what seems false.

1.

Nonstraightforward Architecture:

A Gentle Manifesto

I like complexity and contradiction in architecture. I do not like the incoherence or arbitrariness of incompetent architecture nor the precious intricacies of picturesqueness or expressionism. Instead, I speak of a complex and contradictory architecture based on the richness and ambiguity of modern experience, including that experience which is inherent in art. Everywhere, except in architecture, complexity and contradiction have been acknowledged, from Godel's proof of ultimate inconsistency in mathematics to T. S. Eliot's analysis of "difficult" poetry and Joseph Albers' definition of the paradoxical quality of painting.

But architecture is necessarily complex and contradictory in its very inclusion of the traditional Vitruvian elements of commodity, firmness, and delight. And today the wants of program, structure, mechanical equipment, and expression, even in single buildings in simple contexts, are diverse and conflicting in ways previously unimaginable. The increasing dimension and scale of architecture in urban and regional planning add to the difficulties. I welcome the problems and exploit the uncertainties. By embracing contradiction as well as complexity, I aim for vitality as well as validity.

Architects can no longer afford to be intimidated by the puritanically moral language of orthodox Modern architecture. I like elements which are hybrid rather than "pure," compromising rather than "clean," distorted rather than "straightforward," ambiguous rather than "articulated," perverse as well as impersonal, boring as well as "interesting," conventional rather than "designed," accommodating rather than excluding, redundant rather than simple, vestigial as well as innovating, inconsistent and equivocal rather than direct and clear. I am for messy vitality over obvious unity. I include the non sequitur and proclaim the duality.

I am for richness of meaning rather than clarity of meaning; for the implicit function as well as the explicit function. I prefer "both-and" to "either-or," black and white, and sometimes gray, to black or white. A valid architecture evokes many levels of meaning and combinations of focus: its space and its elements become readable and workable in several ways at once.

But an architecture of complexity and contradiction has a special obligation toward the whole: its truth must be in its totality or its implications of totality. It must embody the difficult unity of inclusion rather than the easy unity of exclusion. More is not less.

2.   *Complexity and Contradiction vs.*

Simplification or Picturesqueness

Orthodox Modern architects have tended to recognize complexity insufficiently or inconsistently. In their attempt to break with tradition and start all over again, they idealized the primitive and elementary at the expense of the diverse and the sophisticated. As participants in a revolutionary movement, they acclaimed the newness of modern functions, ignoring their complications. In their role as reformers, they puritanically advocated the separation and exclusion of elements, rather than the inclusion of various requirements and their juxtapositions. As a forerunner of the Modern movement, Frank Lloyd Wright, who grew up with the motto "Truth against the World," wrote: "Visions of simplicity so broad and far-reaching would open to me and such building harmonies appear that . . . would change and deepen the thinking and culture of the modern world. So I believed." [11] And Le Corbusier, co-founder of

Purism, spoke of the "great primary forms" which, he proclaimed, were "distinct . . . and without ambiguity."[12] Modern architects with few exceptions eschewed ambiguity.

But now our position is different: "At the same time that the problems increase in quantity, complexity, and difficulty they also change faster than before,"[13] and require an attitude more like that described by August Heckscher: "The movement from a view of life as essentially simple and orderly to a view of life as complex and ironic is what every individual passes through in becoming mature. But certain epochs encourage this development; in them the paradoxical or dramatic outlook colors the whole intellectual scene. . . . Amid simplicity and order rationalism is born, but rationalism proves inadequate in any period of upheaval. Then equilibrium must be created out of opposites. Such inner peace as men gain must represent a tension among contradictions and uncertainties. . . . A feeling for paradox allows seemingly dissimilar things to exist side by side, their very incongruity suggesting a kind of truth."[14]

Rationalizations for simplification are still current, however, though subtler than the early arguments. They are expansions of Mies van der Rohe's magnificent paradox, "less is more." Paul Rudolph has clearly stated the implications of Mies' point of view: "All problems can never be solved. . . . Indeed it is a characteristic of the twentieth century that architects are highly selective in determining which problems they want to solve. Mies, for instance, makes wonderful buildings only because he ignores many aspects of a building. If he solved more problems, his buildings would be far less potent."[15]

The doctrine "less is more" bemoans complexity and justifies exclusion for expressive purposes. It does, indeed, permit the architect to be "highly selective in determining which problems [he wants] to solve." But if the architect must be "committed to his particular way of seeing the universe,"[15] such a commitment surely means that the architect determines how problems should be solved, not that he can determine which of the problems he will solve. He can exclude important considerations only at the risk of separating architecture from the experience of life and the needs of society. If some problems prove insoluble, he can express this: in an inclusive rather than an exclusive kind of architecture there is room for the fragment, for contradiction, for improvisation, and for the tensions these produce. Mies' exquisite pavilions have had valuable implications for architecture, but their selectiveness of content and language is their limitation as well as their strength.

I question the relevance of analogies between pavilions and houses, especially analogies between Japanese pavilions and recent domestic architecture. They ignore the real complexity and contradiction inherent in the domestic program—the spatial and technological possibilities as well as the need for variety in visual experience. Forced simplicity results in oversimplification. In the Wiley House, for instance (1), in contrast to his glass house (2), Philip Johnson attempted to go beyond the simplicities of the elegant pavilion. He explicitly separated and articulated the enclosed "private functions" of living on a ground floor pedestal, thus separating them from the open social functions in the modular pavilion above. But even here the building becomes a diagram of an oversimplified program for living—an abstract theory of either-or. Where simplicity cannot work, simpleness results. Blatant simplification means bland architecture. Less is a bore.

The recognition of complexity in architecture does not negate what Louis Kahn has called "the desire for simplicity." But aesthetic simplicity which is a satisfaction to the mind derives, when valid and profound, from inner complexity. The Doric temple's simplicity to the eye is achieved through the famous subtleties and precision of its distorted geometry and the contradictions and tensions inherent in its order. The Doric temple could achieve apparent simplicity through real complexity. When complexity disappeared, as in the late temples, blandness replaced simplicity.

Nor does complexity deny the valid simplification which is part of the process of analysis, and even a method of achieving complex architecture itself. "We oversimplify a given event when we characterize it from the standpoint of a given interest." [16] But this kind of simplification is a method in the analytical process of achieving a complex art. It should not be mistaken for a goal.

1

An architecture of complexity and contradiction, however, does not mean picturesqueness or subjective expressionism. A false complexity has recently countered the false simplicity of an earlier Modern architecture. It promotes an architecture of symmetrical picturesqueness—which Minoru Yamasaki calls "serene"—but it represents a new formalism as unconnected with experience as the former cult of simplicity. Its intricate forms do not reflect genuinely complex programs, and its intricate ornament, though de-

2

pendent on industrial techniques for execution, is dryly reminiscent of forms originally created by handicraft techniques. Gothic tracery and Rococo rocaille were not only expressively valid in relation to the whole, but came from a valid showing-off of hand skills and expressed a vitality derived from the immediacy and individuality of the method. This kind of complexity through exuberance, perhaps impossible today, is the antithesis of "serene" architecture, despite the superficial resemblance between them. But if exuberance is not characteristic of our art, it is tension, rather than "serenity" that would appear to be so.

The best twentieth-century architects have usually rejected simplification—that is, simplicity through reduction —in order to promote complexity within the whole. The works of Alvar Aalto and Le Corbusier (who often disregards his polemical writings) are examples. But the characteristics of complexity and contradiction in their work are often ignored or misunderstood. Critics of Aalto, for instance, have liked him mostly for his sensitivity to natural materials and his fine detailing, and have considered his whole composition willful picturesqueness. I do not consider Aalto's Imatra church picturesque. By repeating in the massing the genuine complexity of the triple-divided plan and the acoustical ceiling pattern (3), this church represents a justifiable expressionism different from the willful picturesqueness of the haphazard structure and spaces of Giovanni Michelucci's recent church for the Autostrada (4). Aalto's complexity is part of the program and structure of the whole rather than a device justified only by the desire for expression. Though we no longer argue over the primacy of form or function (which follows which?), we cannot ignore their interdependence.

3

The desire for a complex architecture, with its attendant contradictions, is not only a reaction to the banality or prettiness of current architecture. It is an attitude common in the Mannerist periods: the sixteenth century in Italy or the Hellenistic period in Classical art, and is also a continuous strain seen in such diverse architects as Michelangelo, Palladio, Borromini, Vanbrugh, Hawksmoor, Soane, Ledoux, Butterfield, some architects of the Shingle Style, Furness, Sullivan, Lutyens, and recently, Le Corbusier, Aalto, Kahn, and others.

4

Today this attitude is again relevant to both the medium of architecture and the program in architecture.

First, the medium of architecture must be re-examined

if the increased scope of our architecture as well as the complexity of its goals is to be expressed. Simplified or superficially complex forms will not work. Instead, the variety inherent in the ambiguity of visual perception must once more be acknowledged and exploited.

Second, the growing complexities of our functional problems must be acknowledged. I refer, of course, to those programs, unique in our time, which are complex because of their scope, such as research laboratories, hospitals, and particularly the enormous projects at the scale of city and regional planning. But even the house, simple in scope, is complex in purpose if the ambiguities of contemporary experience are expressed. This contrast between the means and the goals of a program is significant. Although the means involved in the program of a rocket to get to the moon, for instance, are almost infinitely complex, the goal is simple and contains few contradictions; although the means involved in the program and structure of buildings are far simpler and less sophisticated technologically than almost any engineering project, the purpose is more complex and often inherently ambiguous.

3.   *Ambiguity*

While the second classification of complexity and contradiction in architecture relates to form and content as manifestations of program and structure, the first concerns the medium and refers to a paradox inherent in perception and the very process of meaning in art: the complexity and contradiction that results from the juxtaposition of what an image is and what it seems. Joseph Albers calls "the discrepancy between physical fact and psychic effect" a contradiction which is "the origin of art." And, indeed, complexity of meaning, with its resultant ambiguity and tension, has been characteristic of painting and amply recognized in art criticism. Abstract Expressionism acknowledges perceptual ambiguity, and the basis of Optical Art is shifting juxtapositions and ambiguous dualities relating to form and expression. Pop painters, too, have employed ambiguity to create paradoxical content as well as to exploit perceptual possibilities.

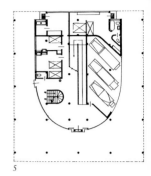

5

In literature, too, critics have been willing to accept complexity and contradiction in their medium. As in architectural criticism, they refer to a Mannerist era, but unlike most architectural critics, they also acknowledge a "mannerist" strain continuing through particular poets, and some, indeed, for a long time have emphasized the qualities of contradiction, paradox, and ambiguity as basic to the medium of poetry, just as Albers does with painting.

Eliot called the art of the Elizabethans "an impure art,"[17] in which complexity and ambiguity are exploited: "in a play of Shakespeare," he said, "you get several levels of significance"[18] where, quoting Ben Jonson, "the most heterogeneous ideas are yoked together by violence."[19] And elsewhere he wrote: "The case of John Webster . . . will provide an interesting example of a very great literary and dramatic genius directed towards chaos."[20] Other critics, for example, Kenneth Burke, who refers to "plural interpretation" and "planned incongruity," have analyzed elements of paradox and ambiguity in the structure and meaning of other poetry besides that of the seventeenth century metaphysical poets and those modern poets who have been influenced by them.

6

7

Cleanth Brooks justifies the expression of complexity and contradiction by their necessity as the very essence of art: "Yet there are better reasons than that of rhetorical vainglory that have induced poet after poet to choose ambiguity and paradox rather than plain discursive simplicity. It is not enough for the poet to analyze his experience as the scientist does, breaking it up into parts, distinguishing part from part, classifying the various parts. His task is finally to unify experience. He must return to us the unity of the experience itself as man knows it in his own experience. . . . If the poet . . . must perforce dramatize the oneness of the experience, even though paying tribute to its diversity, then his use of paradox and ambiguity is seen as necessary. He is not simply trying to spice up, with a superficially exciting or mystifying rhetoric the old stale

8

stockpot. . . . He is rather giving us an insight which preserves the unity of experience and which, at its higher and more serious levels, triumphs over the apparently contradictory and conflicting elements of experience by unifying them into a new pattern." [21]

9

And in *Seven Types of Ambiguity* William Empson "dared to treat what [had] . . . been regarded as a deficiency in poetry, imprecision of meaning, as poetry's chief virtue . . ." [22] Empson documents his theory by readings from Shakespeare, "the supreme ambiguist, not so much from the confusion of his ideas and the muddle of his text, as some scholars believe, as simply from the power and complexity of his mind and art." [23]

Ambiguity and tension are everywhere in an architecture of complexity and contradiction. Architecture is form *and* substance—abstract *and* concrete—and its meaning derives from its interior characteristics and its particular context. An architectural element is perceived as form *and* structure, texture *and* material. These oscillating relationships, complex and contradictory, are the source of the ambiguity and tension characteristic to the medium of architecture. The conjunction "or" with a question mark can usually describe ambiguous relationships. The Villa Savoye (5) : is it a square plan or not? The size of Vanbrugh's fore-pavilions at Grimsthorpe (6) in relation to the back pavilions is ambiguous from a distance: are they near or far, big or small? Bernini's pilasters on the Palazzo Propaganda Fide (7) : are they positive pilasters or negative panel divisions? The ornamental cove in the Casino Pio V in the Vatican (8) is perverse: is it more wall or more vault? The central dip in Lutyens' façade at Nashdom (9) facilitates skylighting: is the resultant duality resolved or not? Luigi Moretti's apartments on the Via Parioli in Rome (10) : are they one building with a split or two buildings joined?

10

11

The calculated ambiguity of expression is based on the confusion of experience as reflected in the architectural program. This promotes richness of meaning over clarity of meaning. As Empson admits, there is good and bad ambiguity: ". . . [ambiguity] may be used to convict a poet of holding muddled opinions rather than to praise the complexity of the order of his mind." [24] Nevertheless, according to Stanley Edgar Hyman, Empson sees ambiguity as "collecting precisely at the points of greatest poetic effectiveness, and finds it breeding a quality he calls 'tension' which

12

we might phrase as the poetic impact itself."[25] These ideas
apply equally well to architecture.

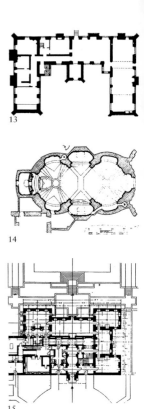

13

14

15

4.   *Contradictory Levels:*

The Phenomenon of "Both-And" in Architecture

Contradictory levels of meaning and use in architecture involve the paradoxical contrast implied by the conjunctive "yet." They may be more or less ambiguous. Le
Corbusier's Shodan House (11) is closed yet open—a cube,
precisely closed by its corners, yet randomly opened on its
surfaces; his Villa Savoye (12) is simple outside yet complex inside. The Tudor plan of Barrington Court (13) is
symmetrical yet asymmetrical; Guarini's Church of the Immaculate Conception in Turin (14) is a duality in plan and
yet a unity; Sir Edwin Lutyens' entrance gallery at Middleton Park (15, 16) is directional space, yet it terminates at a
blank wall; Vignola's façade for the pavilion at Bomarzo
(17) contains a portal, yet it is a blank portico; Kahn's
buildings contain crude concrete yet polished grantite; an
urban street is directional as a route yet static as a place. This
series of conjunctive "yets" describes an architecture of
contradiction at varying levels of program and structure.
None of these ordered contradictions represents a search
for beauty, but neither as paradoxes, are they caprice.

Cleanth Brooks refers to Donne's art as "having it
both ways" but, he says, "most of us in this latter day,
cannot. We are disciplined in the tradition either-or, and
lack the mental agility—to say nothing of the maturity of
attitude—which would allow us to indulge in the finer
distinctions and the more subtle reservations permitted by
the tradition of both-and."[26] The tradition "either-or" has

characterized orthodox modern architecture: a sun screen is probably nothing else; a support is seldom an enclosure; a wall is not violated by window penetrations but is totally interrupted by glass; program functions are exaggeratedly articulated into wings or segregated separate pavilions. Even "flowing space" has implied being outside when inside, and inside when outside, rather than both at the same time. Such manifestations of articulation and clarity are foreign to an architecture of complexity and contradiction, which tends to include "both-and" rather than exclude "either-or."

If the source of the both-and phenomenon is contradiction, its basis is hierarchy, which yields several levels of meanings among elements with varying values. It can include elements that are both good and awkward, big and little, closed and open, continuous and articulated, round and square, structural and spatial. An architecture which includes varying levels of meaning breeds ambiguity and tension.

16

Most of the examples will be difficult to "read," but abstruse architecture is valid when it reflects the complexities and contradictions of content and meaning. Simultaneous perception of a multiplicity of levels involves struggles and hesitations for the observer, and makes his perception more vivid.

Examples which are both good and bad at the same time will perhaps in one way explain Kahn's enigmatic remark: "architecture must have bad spaces as well as good spaces." Apparent irrationality of a part will be justified by the resultant rationality of the whole, or characteristics of a part will be compromised for the sake of the whole. The decisions for such valid compromises are one of the chief tasks of the architect.

17

In Hawksmoor's St. George-in-the-East (18) the exaggerated keystones over the aisle windows are wrong in relation to the part: when seen close-up they are too big in relation to the opening they span. When seen farther back, however, in the context of the whole composition, they are expressively right in size and scale. Michelangelo's enormous rectangular openings in the attic story of the rear façade of St. Peter's (19) are wider than they are high, so that they must be spanned the long way. This is perverse in relation to the spanning limitations of masonry, which dictate in Classical architecture that big openings, such as these, be vertically proportioned. But because one usually expects vertical proportions, the longitudinal spanning ex-

18

presses validly and vividly their *relative* smallness.

The main stair in Frank Furness' Pennsylvania Academy of the Fine Arts in Philadelphia (20) is too big in relation to its immediate surroundings. It lands on a space narrower than its width, and faces an opening narrower than its width. Furthermore, the opening is bisected by a post. But this stair is ceremonial and symbolic as well as functional, and it relates to the hall immediately beyond the opening, to the whole building, and to the great scale of Broad Street outside. The outer thirds of Michelangelo's stair in the Laurentian Library vestibule (21) are abruptly chopped off and lead virtually nowhere: it is similarly wrong in the relation of its size to its space, and yet right in relation to the whole context of the spaces beyond.

Vanbrugh's end bays in the central pavilion of the entrance façade of Blenheim Palace (22) are incorrect because they are bisected by a pilaster: this fragmentation produces a duality which decreases their unity. Their very incompleteness, however, reinforces by contrast the center bay and increases the overall unity of this complex composition. The pavilions which flanked the château at Marly (23) contained a similar paradox. The compositional duality of their two-bay façades lacks unity, but reinforces the unity of the whole complex. Their own incompleteness implied the dominance of the château itself and the completeness of the whole.

19

The basilica, which has mono-directional space, and the central-type church, which has omnidirectional space, represent alternating traditions in Western church plans. But another tradition has accommodated churches which are both-and, in answer to spatial, structural, programmatic, and symbolic needs. The Mannerist elliptical plan of the sixteenth century is both central and directional. Its culmination is Bernini's Sant' Andrea al Quirinale (24), whose main directional axis contradictorily spans the short axis. Nikolaus Pevsner has shown how pilasters rather than open chapels bisect both ends of the transverse axis of the side walls, thereby reinforcing the short axis toward the altar. Borromini's chapel in the Propaganda Fide (25) is a directional hall in plan, but its alternating bays counteract this effect: a large bay dominates the small end; a small bay bisects the center of the long wall. The rounded corners, as well, begin to imply a continuity of enclosure and a central-type plan. (These characteristics occur in the courtyard of San Carlo alle Quattro Fontane too.) And the diagonal

20

22

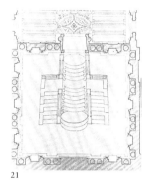

21

23

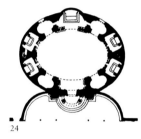

24

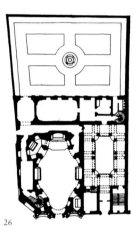

26

25

27

gridlike ribs in the ceiling indicate a multidirectional structure as much like a dome as a vault. Hagia Sophia in Istanbul is equivocal in a similar way. Its central dome on the square bay with pendentives implies a central type church, but its two apses with half-domes begin to set up a longitudinal axis in the tradition of the directional basilica. The horseshoe plan of the Baroque and neo-Baroque opera house focuses on the stage and the center of the auditorium. The central focus of the elliptical plan is usually reflected in the ornamental ceiling pattern and the enormous central chandelier; the focus toward the stage in the directional distortion of the ellipse and partitions between the surrounding boxes as well as in the interruption of the stage itself, of course, and the seating in the pit. This reflects the dual focus in the program of the gala theatre: the performance and the audience.

28

Borromini's San Carlo alle Quattro Fontane (26) abounds in ambiguous manifestations of both-and. The almost equal treatment of the four wings implied in the plan suggests a Greek cross, but the wings are distorted toward a dominant east-west axis, thus suggesting a Latin cross, while the fluid continuity of the walls indicates a distorted circular plan. Rudolf Wittkower has analyzed similar contradictions in section. The pattern of the ceiling in the articulations of its complex mouldings suggests a dome on pendentives over the crossing of a Greek cross (27). The shape of the ceiling in its overall continuity distorts these elements into parodies of themselves, and suggests rather a dome generated from an undulating wall. These distorted elements are both continuous and articulated. At another scale, shape and pattern play similarly contradictory roles. For example, the profile of the Byzantine capital (28) makes it seem continuous, but the texture and vestigial patterns of volutes and acanthus leaves articulate the parts.

29

The pedimented porch of Nicholas Hawksmoor's St. George, Bloomsbury (29), and the overall shape of its plan (30) imply a dominant axis north and south. The west entrance and tower, the interior configuration of balconies, and the east apse (which contained the altar) all suggest an equally dominant counter axis. By means of contrary elements and distorted positions this church expresses both the contrasts between the back, front, and sides of the Latin cross plan and the duo-directional axes of a Greek cross plan. These contradictions, which resulted from particular

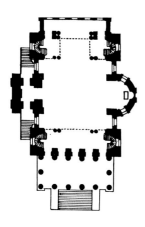

33

31

34

35

36

37

32

site and orientation conditions, support a richness and tension lacking in many purer compositions.

The domed basilica of Vierzhenheiligen (31) has a central altar under a major dome in the nave. Nikolaus Pevsner has vividly contrasted its series of domes, which are distorted and superimposed on the Latin cross plan, with the conventional placing of a single dome at the crossing. This is a Latin cross church, which is also a central-type church because of the unusual position of the altar and the central dome. Other late Baroque churches juxtapose the square and the circle. Bernardo Vittone's elements—ambiguously pendentives or squinches—in the nave of S. Maria di Piazza in Turin (32) support what is both a dome and a square lantern. Hawksmoor juxtaposes mouldings in rectangular and elliptical patterns on the ceilings of some of his churches. They create contradictory expressions of both central and directional-type churches. In some rooms of the Palazzo Propaganda Fide (33) a straddling arch in the corners allows the space to be rectangular below and continuous above. This is similar to Wren's ceiling configuration in St. Stephen Walbrook (34).

38

In the ceilings of his secular chambers (35) Sir John Soane glories in spaces and structures both rectangular and curvilinear, and domed and vaulted. His methods include complex combinations of vestigial structural shapes resembling squinches and pendentives, oculi, and groins. Soane's Museum (36) employs a vestigial element in another dimension: the partition in the form of suspended arches, meaningless structurally yet meaningful spatially, defines rooms at once open and closed.

39

The façade of the cathedral at Murcia (37) employs what has been called inflection to promote largeness yet smallness. The broken pediments above the shafts are inflected toward each other to help suggest an enormous portal, appropriate spatially to the plaza below and symbolically to the region beyond. Storied orders within the shafts, however, accommodate the scale of the immediate conditions of the building itself and its setting. Bigness and smallness are expressed at once in a characteristic Shingle Style stair through distortion in width and direction. The risers and treads remain constant, of course, but the widening of the run at the bottom accommodates the spacious living-room hall below, while the narrower run at the top relates to the narrower hall above.

40

Precast concrete construction can be continuous yet

fragmentary, flowing in profile yet surfaced with joints. The contours of its profiles between columns and beams can designate the continuity of the structural system, but the pattern of its grouted joints can designate the fragmented method of its erection.

The tower of Christ Church, Spitalfields (38), is a manifestation of both-and at the scale of the city. Hawksmoor's tower is both a wall and a tower. Toward the bottom the vista is terminated by the extension of its walls into kinds of buttresses (39) perpendicular to the approaching street. They are seen from only one direction. The top evolves into a spire, which is seen from all sides, spatially and symbolically dominating the skyline of the parish. In the Bruges Town Hall (40) the scale of the building relates to the immediate square, while the violently disproportionate scale of the tower above relates to the whole town. For similar reasons the big sign sits on top of the Philadelphia Savings Fund Society building, and yet it is invisible from below (41). The Arc de Triomphe also has contrasting functions. Seen diagonally from the radial approaches other than the Champs Elysées, it is a sculptural termination. Seen perpendicularly from the axis of the Champs Elysées, it is spatially and symbolically both a termination and a portal. Later I shall analyze some organized contradictions between front and back. But here I shall mention the Karlskirche in Vienna (42), whose exterior contains elements both of the basilica in its façade and of the central-type church in its body. A convex form in the back was required by the interior program; the urban space required a larger scale and a straight façade in front. The disunity that exists from the point of view of the building itself is contradicted when the building is seen in relation to the scale and the space of the neighborhood.

The double meanings inherent in the phenomenon both-and can involve metamorphosis as well as contradiction. I have described how the omni-directional spire of the tower of Christ Church, Spitalfields, evolves into a directional pavilion at its base, but a perceptual rather than a formal kind of change in meaning is possible. In equivocal relationships one contradictory meaning usually dominates another, but in complex compositions the relationship is not always constant. This is especially true as the observer moves through or around a building, and by extension through a city: at one moment one meaning can be perceived as dominant; at another moment a different meaning

41

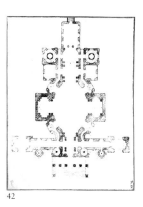

42

seems paramount. In St. George, Bloomsbury (30), for instance, the contradictory axes inside become alternatingly dominant or recessive as the observer moves within them, so that the same space changes meaning. Here is another dimension of "space, time and architecture" which involves the multiple focus.

5.   *Contradictory Levels Continued:*

The Double-Functioning Element

The "double-functioning"[27] element and "both-and" are related, but there is a distinction: the double-functioning element pertains more to the particulars of use and structure, while both-and refers more to the relation of the part to the whole. Both-and emphasizes double meanings over double-functions. But before I talk about the double-functioning element, I want to mention the multifunctioning building. By this term I mean the building which is complex in program and form, yet strong as a whole—the complex unity of Le Corbusier's La Tourette or the Palace of Justice at Chandigarh in contrast to the multiplicities and articulations of his Palace of the Soviets project or the Armée du Salut in Paris. The latter approach separates functions into interlocking wings or connected pavilions. It has been typical of orthodox Modern architecture. The incisive separations of the pavilions in Mies' design for the urban Illinois Institute of Technology can be understood as an extreme development of it.

Mies' and Johnson's Seagram Building excludes functions other than offices (except on the ground floor in back), and by using a similar wall pattern camouflages the fact that at the top there is a different kind of space for mechanical equipment. Yamasaki's project for The World Trade Center in New York even more exaggeratedly simplifies the form of an enormous complex. The typical office skyscrapers of the '20's differentiate, rather than camouflage, their mechanical equipment space at the top through architecturally ornamental forms. While Lever House includes differently-functioning spaces at the bottom, it exaggeratedly separates them by a spatial shadow joint. In contrast, one exceptional Modern building, the P.S.F.S. (41), gives positive expression to the variety and complexity of its program. It integrates a shop on the first floor and a big bank on the second with offices above and special rooms at the top. These varieties of functions and scales (including the enormous advertising sign at the top) work within a compact whole. Its curving façade, which contrasts with the rectangularity of the rest of the building, is not just a cliché of the '30's, because it has an urban function. At the lower pedestrian level it directs space around the corner.

The multifunctioning building in its extreme form becomes the Ponte Vecchio or Chenonceaux or the Futurist projects of Sant' Elia. Each contains within the whole contrasting scales of movement besides complex functions. Le Corbusier's Algerian project, which is an apartment house and a highway, and Wright's late projects for Pittsburgh Point and Baghdad, correspond to. Kahn's viaduct architecture and Fumihiko Maki's "collective form." All of these have complex and contradictory hierarchies of scale and movement, structure, and space within a whole. These buildings are buildings and bridges at once. At a larger scale: a dam is also a bridge, the loop in Chicago is a boundary as well as a circulation system, and Kahn's street "wants to be a building."

There are justifications for the multifunctioning room as well as the multifunctioning building. A room can have many functions at the same time or at different times. Kahn prefers the gallery because it is directional and nondirectional, a corridor and room at once. And he recognizes the changing complexities of specific functions by differentiating rooms in a general way through a hierarchy of size and quality, calling them servant and major spaces, directional and nondirectional spaces, and other designations more generic than specific. As in his project for the Trenton Community Center, these spaces end by paralleling in a more complex way the pre-eighteenth century configurations of rooms en suite. The idea of corridors and rooms each with a single function for convenience originated in the eighteenth century. Is not Modern architecture's characteristic separation and specialization of program functions within the building through built-in furniture an extreme manifestation of this idea? Kahn by implication questions such rigid specialization and limited functionalism. In this context, "form evokes function."

The multifunctioning room is a possibly truer answer to the Modern architect's concern with flexibility. The room with a generic rather than a specific purpose, and with movable furniture rather than movable partitions, promotes a perceptual flexibility rather than a physical flexibility, and permits the toughness and permanence still necessary in our building. Valid ambiguity promotes useful flexibility.

The double-functioning element has been used infrequently in Modern architecture. Instead, Modern architecture has encouraged separation and specialization at all scales—in materials and structure as well as program and space. "The nature of materials" has precluded the multifunctioning material, or, inversely, the same form or surface for different materials. Wright's divergence from his master began, according to his autobiography, with Louis Sullivan's indiscriminate application of his characteristic ornament to terra cotta, iron, wood, or brick. To Wright, "appropriate designs for one material would not be appropriate for another material." [28] But the façade of Eero Saarinen's dormitory at the University of Pennsylvania includes among its materials and structure vine-covered grade, brick wall, and steel grille—yet the curving profile of its form is continuous. Saarinen overcame the current obsession against using different materials in the same plane or the same material for two different things. In Robert Rauschenberg's painting, *Pilgrim* (43), the surface pattern continues from the stretcher canvas to the actual chair in front of it, making ambiguous the distinction between the painting and the furniture, and on another level, the work of art in a room. A contradiction between levels of function and meaning is recognized in these works, and the medium is strained.

43

44

But to the structural purist, as well as the organicist, the double-functioning structural form would be abhorrent because of the nonexact, ambiguous correspondence between form and function, and form and structure. In contrast, in the Katsura Villa (44) the bamboo rod in tension and the wood post in compression are similar in form. To the Modern architect, I think, the two would seem sinisterly similar in section and size despite the current inclination toward traditional Japanese design. The Renaissance pilaster (as well as other structural elements used in a nonstructural way) can involve the phenomenon both-and at several levels. It can be at the same time physically structural or not, symbolically structural through association, and compositionally ornamental by promoting rhythm and also complexity of scale in the giant order.

45

Besides specializing forms in relation to materials and structure, Modern architecture separates and articulates elements. Modern architecture is never implicit. In promoting the frame and the curtain wall, it has separated structure from shelter. Even the walls of the Johnson Wax Building are enclosing but not supporting. And in detailing, Modern architecture has tended to glory in separation. Even the flush joint is articulated, and the shadow joint predominates. The versatile element which does several things at once is equally rare in Modern architecture. Significantly the column is favored over the pier. In S. Maria in Cosmedin's nave (45) the column form results from its dominant, precise function as a point support. It can direct space only incidentally in relation to other columns or elements. But the alternating piers in the same nave are intrinsically double-functioning. They enclose and direct space as much as they support structure. The Baroque piers in the chapel at Frésnes (46), residual as form and redundant as structure, are extreme examples of double-functioning elements which are structural and spatial at once.

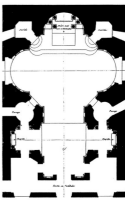
46

Le Corbusier's and Kahn's double-functioning elements may be rare in our architecture. The brise-soleils in the Unite d'Habitation in Marseilles are structure and porches as well as sunscreens. (Are they wall segments, piers, or columns?) Kahn's clusters of columns and his open piers "harbor" space for equipment, and can manipulate natural light as well, like the rhythmically complex columns and pilasters of Baroque architecture. Like the open beams in the Richards Medical Center (47), these elements are neither structurally pure nor elegantly minimum in section. Instead, they are structural fragments inseparable from a greater spatial whole. It is valid to sense stresses in forms which are not purely structural, and a structural member can be more than incidentally spatial. (However, the columns and the stair towers in this build-

47

ing are separated and articulated in an orthodox manner.)

Flat plate construction consists of concrete slabs of constant depth and varied reinforcement, with irregularly placed columns without beams or caps. To maintain a constant depth, the number of reinforcing bars changes to accommodate the more concentrated structural loads in the constant, beamless section. This permits, in apartment houses especially, a constant ceiling profile for the spaces below in order to accommodate partitions. Flat plates are structurally impure: their section is not minimum. The demands of structural forces are compromised because of the demands of architectural space. Form follows function here in a contradictory way; substance follows structural function; profile follows spatial function.

In some Mannerist and Baroque masonry construction the pier, pilaster, and relieving arch about evenly make up a façade, and the resultant structure, like that of the Palazzo Valmarana (48), is bearing wall and frame at once. The relieving arches in the Pantheon (49), in this case not originally part of the visual expression, similarly generate a wall structurally double-functioning. In this context the Roman basilica, Gaudí's Sagrada Familia (50), and Palladio's Il Redentore (51) are totally different from the Gothic basilica (52). In contrast to the segregated flying buttress, the Roman countervault spans as well as buttresses, and Gaudí's subtle invention of the tilted pier-buttress supports the weight of the vault as well as buttresses the thrust in one continuous form. Palladio's buttresses are also broken pediments on the façade. A flying buttress at S. Chiara in Assisi forms a portal for the piazza as well as a support for the building.

The double-functioning element can be a detail. Mannerist and Baroque buildings abound in drip mouldings which become sills, windows which become niches, cornice ornaments which accommodate windows, quoin strips which are also pilasters, and architraves which make arches (53). The pilasters of Michelangelo's niches in the entrance of the Laurentian Library (54) also look like brackets. Borromini's mouldings in the rear façades of the Propaganda Fide (55) are both window frames and pediments. Lutyens' chimneys at Grey Walls (56) are literally sculptural entrance markers as well, a dado at Gledstone Hall (57) is an extension of a stair riser in the same room, and the stair landing at Nashdom is also a room.

The balloon frame, which has been traced by Siegfried

48

49

50

42

51

52

53

54

55

56

57

43

Giedion, *becomes* on all levels. Structurally and visually it evolves from a separate frame to a skin which is both structural and sheltering: to the extent that it is made up of 2 x 4's, it is frame; to the extent that the 2 x 4's are small, close together, and braced and meshed by diagonal siding, it becomes skin. These intricate characteristics are evident in the way penetrations are made in it and in the way it is terminated. The balloon frame is another element in architecture which is several things at once. It represents a method between two pure extremes, which has evolved from each of them until it has characteristics of both.

Conventional elements in architecture represent one stage in an evolutionary development, and they contain in their changed use and expression some of their past meaning as well as their new meaning. What can be called the vestigial element parallels the double-functioning element. It is distinct from a superfluous element because it contains a double meaning. This is the result of a more or less ambiguous combination of the old meaning, called up by associations, with a new meaning created by the modified or new function, structural or programmatic, and the new context. The vestigial element discourages clarity of meaning; it promotes richness of meaning instead. It is a basis for change and growth in the city as manifest in remodeling which involves old buildings with new uses both programmatic and symbolic (like palazzi which become museums or embassies), and old street patterns with new uses and scales of movement. The paths of medieval fortification walls in European cities became boulevards in the nineteenth century; a section of Broadway is a piazza and a symbol rather than an artery to upper New York state. The ghost of Dock Street in Philadelphia's Society Hill, however, is a meaningless vestige rather than a working element resulting from a valid transition between the old and the new. I shall later refer to the vestigial element as it appears in Michelangelo's architecture and in what might be called Pop architecture.

The rhetorical element, like the double-functioning element, is infrequent in recent architecture. If the latter offends through its inherent ambiguity, rhetoric offends orthodox Modern architecture's cult of the minimum. But the rhetorical element is justified as a valid if outmoded means of expression. An element can seem rhetorical from one point of view, but if it is valid, at another level it enriches meaning by underscoring. In the project for a gateway at Bourneville by Ledoux (58), the columns in the arch are structurally rhetorical if not redundant. Expressively, however, they underscore the abstractness of the opening as a semicircle more than an arch, and they further define the opening as a gateway. As I have said, the stairway at the Pennsylvania Academy of the Fine Arts by Furness is too big in its immediate context, but appropriate as a gesture towards the outside scale and a sense of entry. The Classical portico is a rhetorical entrance. The stairs, columns, and pediment are juxtaposed upon the other-scale, real entrance behind. Paul Rudolph's entrance in the Arts and Architecture Building at Yale is at the scale of the city; most people use the little door at the side in the stair tower.

Much of the function of ornament is rhetorical—like the use of Baroque pilasters for rhythm, and Vanbrugh's disengaged pilasters at the entrance to the kitchen court at Blenheim (59) which are an architectural fanfare. The rhetorical element which is also structural is rare in Modern architecture, although Mies has used the rhetorical I-beam with an assurance that would make Bernini envious.

58

59

6.   *Accommodation and the Limitations of Order:*

The Conventional Element

In short, that contradictions must be accepted.*

A valid order accommodates the circumstantial contradictions of a complex reality. It accommodates as well as imposes. It thereby admits "control *and* spontaneity," "correctness *and* ease"—improvisation within the whole. It tolerates qualifications and compromise. There are no fixed laws in architecture, but not everything will work in a building or a city. The architect must decide, and these subtle evaluations are among his principal functions. He must determine what must be made to work and what it is possible to compromise with, what will give in, and where and how. He does not ignore or exclude inconsistencies of program and structure within the order.

I have emphasized that aspect of complexity and contradiction which grows out of the medium more than the program of the building. Now I shall emphasize the complexity and contradiction that develops from the program and reflects the inherent complexities and contradictions of living. It is obvious that in actual practice the two must be interrelated. Contradictions can represent the exceptional inconsistency that modifies the otherwise consistent order, or they can represent inconsistencies throughout the order as a whole. In the first case, the relationship between inconsistency and order accommodates circumstantial exceptions to the order, or it juxtaposes particular with general elements of order. Here you build an order up and then break it down, but break it from strength rather than from weakness. I have described this relationship as "contradiction accommodated." The relationship of inconsistency within the whole I consider a manifestation of "the difficult whole," which is discussed in the last chapter.

Mies refers to a need to "create order out of the desperate confusion of our time." But Kahn has said "by order I do not mean orderliness." Should we not resist bemoaning confusion? Should we not look for meaning in the complexities and contradictions of our times and ac-

*David Jones, *Epoch and Artist*, Chilmark Press, New York, 1959.

46

knowledge the limitations of systems? These, I think, are the two justifications for breaking order: the recognition of variety and confusion inside and outside, in program and environment, indeed, at all levels of experience; and the ultimate limitation of all orders composed by man. When circumstances defy order, order should bend or break: anomalies and uncertainties give validity to architecture.

Meaning can be enhanced by breaking the order; the exception points up the rule. A building with no "imperfect" part can have no perfect part, because contrast supports meaning. An artful discord gives vitality to architecture. You can allow for contingencies all over, but they cannot prevail all over. If order without expediency breeds formalism, expediency without order, of course, means chaos. Order must exist before it can be broken. No artist can belittle the role of order as a way of seeing a whole relevant to its own characteristics and context. "There is no work of art without a system" is Le Corbusier's dictum.

60

Indeed a propensity to break the order can justify exaggerating it. A valid formalism, or a kind of paper architecture in this context, compensates for distortions, expediencies, and exceptions in the circumstantial parts of the composition, or for violent superimpositions in juxtaposed contradictions. In recent architecture Le Corbusier in the Villa Savoye, for example, accommodates the exceptional circumstantial inconsistencies in an otherwise rigid, dominant order. But Aalto, in contrast to Le Corbusier, seems almost to create the order out of the inconsistencies, as can be seen in the Cultural Center at Wolfsburg. An historical example will perhaps help to illustrate this relation of order and exception. The appliqué of arches and pilasters on the Palazzo Tarugi (60) maintains itself against the sudden impositions of "whimsical" windows and asymmetrical voids. The exaggerated order, and therefore exaggerated unity, along with certain characteristics of scale, are what make the monumentality in the Italian palazzo and some of the work of Le Corbusier. The circumstantial oppositions in their compositions, however, are the secret of their kind of monumentality—that which is neither dry nor pompous. Although Aalto's order is not quite so easily grasped at first glance, it involves similar relationships of order and the circumstantial.

In engineering it is the bridge (61) that vividly expresses the play of exaggeratedly pure order against circumstantial inconsistencies. The direct, geometric order of the upper structure, derived from the sole, simple function of conveying vehicles on an even span, strongly contrasts with the exceptional accommodation of the structural order below, which through distortion—the expedient device of elongated or shortened piers—accommodates the bridge to the uneven terrain of the ravine.

A play of order and compromise also supports the idea of renovation in building, and of evolution in city planning. Indeed, change in the program of existing buildings is a valid phenomenon and a major source of the contradiction I am endorsing. Many compositions that acknowledge circumstantial exceptions, like the Palazzo Tarugi, result from renovations that maintain an expresssion of the whole. Much of the richness of the Italian urban scene at eye level results from the tradition of modifying or modernizing every several generations the commercial ground floor interiors, for example, the frankly stylish contemporary bars, located in the frames of old palazzi. But the building's original order must be strong. A good deal of clutter has not managed to destroy the space of Grand Central Station but the introduction of one foreign element casts into doubt the entire effect of some modern buildings. Our buildings must survive the cigarette machine.

I have been referring to one level of order in architecture—that individual order that is related to the specific building it is part of. But there is convention in architecture, and convention can be another manifestation of an exaggeratedly strong order more general in scope. An architect should use convention and make it vivid. I mean he should use convention unconventionally. By convention I mean both the elements and methods of building. Conventional elements are those which are common in their manufacture, form, and use. I do not refer to the sophisticated products of industrial design, which are usually beautiful, but to the vast accumulation of standard, anonymously designed products connected with architecture and construction, and also to commercial display elements which are positively banal or vulgar in themselves and are seldom associated with architecture.

The main justification for honky-tonk elements in architectural order is their very existence. They are what we have. Architects can bemoan or try to ignore them or even try to abolish them, but they will not go away. Or they will not go away for a long time, because architects do not have the power to replace them (nor do they know what to replace them with), and because these commonplace elements accommodate existing needs for variety and communication. The old clichés involving both banality and mess will still be the context of our new architecture, and our new architecture significantly will be the context for them. I am taking the limited view, I admit, but the limited view, which architects have tended to belittle, is as important as the visionary view, which they have tended to glorify but have not brought about. The short-term plan, which expediently combines the old and the new, must accompany the long-term plan. Architecture is evolutionary as well as revolutionary. As an art it will acknowledge what is and what ought to be, the immediate and the speculative.

Historians have shown how architects in the mid-nineteenth century tended to ignore or reject developments in technology when related to structure and methods as unconnected with architecture and unworthy of it; they substituted in turn Gothic Revivalism, Academic revivalism or the Handicraft Movement. Are we today proclaiming advanced technology, while excluding the immediate, vital if vulgar elements which are common to our architecture and landscape? The architect should accept the methods and the elements he already has. He often fails when he attempts per se the search for form hopefully new, and the research for techniques hopefully advanced. Technical innovations require investments in time and skills and money beyond the architect's reach, at least in our kind of society. The trouble with nineteenth century architects was not so much that they left innovation to the engineers as that they ignored the technical revolution developed by others. Present-day architects, in their visionary compulsion to invent new techniques, have neglected their obligation to be experts in existing conventions. The architect, of course, is responsible for the how as well as the what in his building, but his innovating role is primarily in the what; his experimentation is limited more to his organization of the whole than to technique in the parts. The architect selects as much as creates.

These are pragmatic reasons for using convention in architecture, but there are expressive justifications as well. The architect's main work is the organization of a unique whole through conventional parts and the judicious introduction of new parts when the old won't do. Gestalt psychology maintains that context contributes meaning to a part and change in context causes change in meaning. The architect thereby, through the organization of parts, creates meaningful contexts for them within the whole. Through unconventional organization of conventional parts he is able to create new meanings within the whole. If he uses convention unconventionally, if he organizes familiar things in an unfamiliar way, he is changing their contexts, and he can use even the cliché to gain a fresh effect. Familiar things seen in an unfamiliar context become perceptually new as well as old.

Modern architects have exploited the conventional element only in limited ways. If they have not totally rejected it as obsolete or banal, they have embraced it as symbolic of progressive industrial order. But they have seldom used the common element with a unique context in an uncommon way. Wright, for instance, almost always employed unique elements and unique forms, which represented his personal and innovating approach to architecture. Minor elements, like hardware by Schlage or plumbing fixtures by Kohler of Kohler, which even Wright was unable to avoid using, read as unfortunate compromises within the particular order of his buildings, which is otherwise consistent.

Gropius in his early work, however, employed forms and elements based on a consistent industrial vocabulary. He thus recognized standardization and promoted his machine aesthetic. The inspiration for windows and stairways, for instance, came from current factory architecture, and these buildings look like factories. Latter-day Mies employs the structural elements of vernacular American industrial architecture and also those of Albert Kahn with unconscious irony: the elegant frame members are derived from standard steel manufacturers' catalogues; they are expressed as exposed structure but they are ornament on a fire-resistant frame; and they make up complex, closed spaces rather than the simple industrial spaces they were originally designed for.

It was Le Corbusier who juxtaposed objets trouvés and commonplace elements, such as the Thonet chair, the officer's chair, cast iron radiators, and other industrial objects, and the sophisticated forms of his architecture with any sense of irony. The nineteenth century statue of the Virgin within the window of the east wall of the Chapel at Ronchamp is a vestige from the former church which stood on the spot. Besides its symbolic value, it represents a banal object of sculpture vividly enhanced by its new setting. Bernard Maybeck is the unique architect in recent times to employ contradictory combinations of vernacular industrial elements and eclectic stylistic elements (for example, industrial sash and Gothic tracery) in the same building. Using convention unconventionally is otherwise almost unknown in our recent architecture.

Poets, according to Eliot, employ "that perpetual slight alteration of language, words perpetually juxtaposed in new and sudden combinations." [29] Wordsworth writes in his preface to the *Lyrical Ballads* of choosing "incidents and situations from common life [so that] ordinary things should be presented to the mind in an unusual aspect." [30] And Kenneth Burke has referred to "perspective by incongruity." [31] This technique, which seems basic to the medium of poetry, has been used today in another medium. The Pop painter gives uncommon meaning to common elements by changing their context or increasing their scale. Through "involvement in the relativity of perception and the relativity of meaning," [32] old clichés in new settings achieve rich meanings which are ambiguously both old and new, banal and vivid.

The value of such contradictory meanings has been acknowledged in both evolutionary and revolutionary architecture—from the collages of fragments of post-Roman architecture, the so-called Spolium architecture in which column capitals are used as bases, for instance, to the Renaissance style itself, where the old Classical Roman vocabulary was employed in new combinations. And James Ackerman has described Michelangelo as "rarely adopting a motif [in his architecture] without giving it a new form or a new meaning. Yet he invariably retained essential features from ancient models in order to force the observer to recollect the source while enjoying the innovations." [33]

Ironic convention is relevant both for the individual building and the townscape. It recognizes the real condition of our architecture and its status in our culture. Industry promotes expensive industrial and electronic research but not architectural experiments, and the Federal government diverts subsidies toward air transportation, communication, and the vast enterprises of war or, as they call it, national security, rather than toward the forces for the direct enhancement of life. The practicing architect must admit this. In simple terms, the budgets, techniques, and programs for his buildings must relate more to 1866 than 1966. Architects should accept their modest role rather than disguise it and risk what might be called an electronic expressionism, which might parallel the industrial expressionism of early Modern architecture. The architect who would accept his role as combiner of significant old clichés—valid banalities —in new contexts as his condition within a society that directs its best efforts, its big money, and its elegant technologies elsewhere, can ironically express in this indirect way a true concern for society's inverted scale of values.

I have alluded to the reasons why honky-tonk elements in our architecture and townscape are here to stay, especially in the important short-term view, and why such a fate should be acceptable. Pop Art has demonstrated that these commonplace elements are often the main source of the occasional variety and vitality of our cities, and that it is not their banality or vulgarity as elements which make for the banality or vulgarity of the whole scene, but rather their contextual relationships of space and scale.

Another significant implication from Pop Art involves method in city planning. Architects and planners who peevishly denounce the conventional townscape for its vulgarity or banality promote elaborate methods for abolishing or disguising honky-tonk elements in the existing landscape, or, for excluding them from the vocabulary of their new townscapes. But they largely fail either to enhance or to provide a substitute for the existing scene because they attempt the impossible. By attempting too much they flaunt their impotence and risk their continuing influence as supposed experts. Cannot the architect and planner, by slight adjustments to the conventional elements of the townscape, existing or proposed, promote significant effects? By modifying or adding conventional elements to still other conventional elements they can, by a twist of context, gain a maximum of effect through a minimum of means. They can make us see the same things in a different way.

Finally, standardization, like convention, can be another manifestation of the strong order. But unlike convention it has been accepted in Modern architecture as an enriching product of our technology, yet dreaded for its potential domination and brutality. But is it not standardization that is without circumstantial accommodation and without a creative use of context that is to be feared more than standardization itself? The ideas of order and circumstance, convention and context—of employing standardization in an unstandard way—apply to our continuing problem of standardization versus variety. Giedion has written of Aalto's unique "combination of standardization with irrationality so that standardization is no longer master but servant."[34] I prefer to think of Aalto's art as contradictory rather than irrational—an artful recognition of the circumstantial and the contextual and of the inevitable limits of the order of standardization.

61

7.   *Contradiction Adapted*

The façades of two eighteenth century Neapolitan villas express two kinds, or two manifestations, of contradiction. In the Villa Pignatelli (62) the mouldings, which dip, become string courses and window heads at once. In the Villa Palomba (63) the windows, which disregard the bay system and puncture the exterior panels, are positioned by interior needs. The mouldings in the first villa adapt easily to their contradictory functions. The windows of the second villa clash violently with the panel configurations and pilaster rhythm: the inside order and the outside order are in an uncompromisingly contradictory relation.

In the first façade contradiction is adapted by accommodating and compromising its elements; in the second façade contradiction is juxtaposed by using contrasting superimposed or adjacent elements. Contradiction adapted is tolerant and pliable. It admits improvisation. It involves the disintegration of a prototype—and it ends in approxima-

62

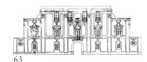

63

tion and qualification. On the other hand, contradiction juxtaposed is unbending. It contains violent contrasts and uncompromising oppositions. Contradiction adapted ends in a whole which is perhaps impure. Contradiction juxtaposed ends in a whole which is perhaps unresolved.

These types of contradiction occur in the work of Le Corbusier. Contrasts in the plans of the Villa Savoye (5) and the Assembly Building in Chandigarh (64) correspond to those in the elevations of the Villa Pignatelli and the Villa Palomba. In the Villa Savoye the positions of some of the columns in the rectangular bay system adjust slightly to accommodate to particular spatial needs—one column is moved and another removed. In the Assembly Building although the grid of columns also adjusts to the exceptional plastic form of the assembly hall, in the juxtaposition of the hall itself and the grid, they do not adapt—the juxtaposition is violent and uncompromising not only in plan but also in sections, where it appears to have been thrust violently into the grid (65).

Kahn has said: "It is the role of design to adjust to the circumstantial." The interior rectangles of Palladio's palace plans are frequently distorted into nonrectangular configurations in order to adjust to the Vicenza street patterns. The resultant tensions give a vitality to the buildings not apparent in their ideal counterparts illustrated in the *Quattro Libri*. In the Palazzo Massimo (66) a curving rather than an angular distortion accommodated the façade to the street, which also curved before it was changed in the nineteenth century. In the typical gambrel roof the need to accommodate living space within a roof angle essentially determined by drainage and structural functions results in an eloquent distortion of the original gable. These examples are distinguishable from the expressionistic distortions of Rococo or of German Expressionism where the distorted is not contrasted with the undistorted.

Besides circumstantial distortion, there are other techniques of adaptation. The expedient device is an element in all anonymous architecture that is dependent on a strong conventional order. It is used to adjust the order to circumstances which are contradictory to it: such circumstances are often topographical. The bracket on the house at Domegge (67) is a device that expedites the tense transition from symmetrical façade to symmetrical gable and at the same time accommodates the asymmetrical overhang on the right side. A vivid play of order and the circumstantial is,

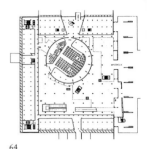

64

65

66

67

68

in fact, a characteristic of all Italian architecture, with its bold contradictions of monumentality and expediency. The ornamented post in the center of the inner portal at Vézelay (68), which is a shore for the lunette, interrupts the axis to the altar. It is an expedient device made eventful. Kahn's uniquely deep beams over the great span of the gymnasium in the project for the Trenton Community Center are exceptional devices to maintain the consistency of the domes of the roof. They are made manifest in plan by the filled-in-columns that support them (69). Lutyens' work abounds in devices: the split at the side of the house called The Salutation in Sandwich (70), is an expedient device which is spatial. By introducing natural illumination at the central stair landing, it breaks the order and promotes surprise in the classical prism of the house. (In some of Jasper Johns' painting the device is similarly made explicit by arrows and notation.)

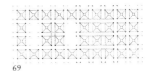

69

70

Le Corbusier today is a master of the eventful exception, another technique of accommodation. He breaks the order of the bays in the ground floor of the Villa Savoye (5) by moving one column and removing another, as I have shown, to accommodate exceptional circumstances involving space and circulation. In this eloquent compromise Le Corbusier makes the dominant regularity of the composition more vivid.

71

The exceptional location of windows, like the eventful exception in columns, usually produces an altered symmetry. For example, the windows at Mount Vernon (71) do not follow an exact symmetrical pattern. Instead, the window pattern is the result of earlier renovations, and it breaks the dominant order of the central pediment and symmetrical wings. In McKim, Mead and White's Low House (72) the blatantly exceptional window positions in the north façade contradicted the consistent symmetrical order of the outside shape to admit the circumstantial complexities of its domestic program. The very subtly distorted relationships of the windows in H. H. Richardson's house for Henry Adams in Washington (73) reflected the particular circumstances of the private functions inside, yet they maintained the regularity and symmetry demanded by the public function of a monumental building on Lafayette Square. Here the subtle compromise between order and circumstance, outside and inside, and private and public functions, produced ambiguous rhythms and vibrant tensions in the façade.

72

The varied openings in the Palazzo Tarugi (60), exceptional in form and position, break the dominant pilaster order of the outside in typical Italian fashion. Lewis Mumford, in a seminar at the University of Pennsylvania in 1963, compared the exceptional window positions in the south façade of the Doges' Palace with Eero Saarinen's windowed façade of the American Embassy in London. The dominant consistent rhythms in the Embassy building tend to deny the circumstantial complexities within its modern program and to express the dry purity of a civic bureaucracy. The chapel wing at Versailles is an eventful exception beyond the scale of columns or windows. Through its position, form, and height it contributes a vitality and validity to the dominant symmetrical order of the whole, a vitality conspicuously lacking at Caserta, for example, where the exterior order of the enormous and complex palace is entirely consistent.

73

In Modern architecture we have operated too long under the restrictions of unbending rectangular forms supposed to have grown out of the technical requirements of the frame and the mass-produced curtain wall. In contrasting Mies' and Johnson's Seagram Building (74) with Kahn's project for an office tower in Philadelphia (75) it can be seen that Mies and Johnson reject all contradictions of diagonal wind-bracing in favor of an expression of a rectilinear frame. Kahn once said that the Seagram Building was like a beautiful lady with hidden corsets. Kahn, in contrast, expresses the wind-bracing—but at the expense of such vertical elements as the elevator and, indeed of the spaces for people.

74

In many works of Le Corbusier and Aalto, however, a balance, or perhaps a tension, is achieved between the rectilinearity of standard techniques, and the diagonal which expresses exceptional conditions. In his apartments at Bremen (76), Aalto has taken the rectangular order of Le Corbusier's basic dwelling unit, which makes up his high-rise apartment slabs (77), and distorted it into diagonals in order to orient the dwelling unit toward the south for light and for the view. The north-facing stairs and circulation areas remain strictly rectilinear in plan. Even in the most extreme units an essential rectilinearity and regularity of space is maintained. And in Aalto's Wolfsburg Cultural Center (78) the rectangular configuration of the whole composition is barely maintained as he organizes the necessarily diagonal shapes of the auditoriums.

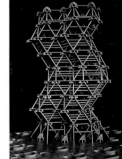

75

56

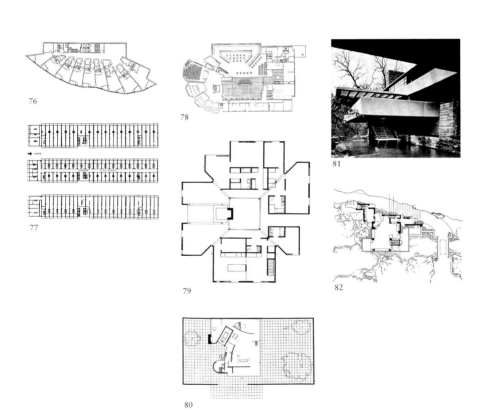

76

77

78

79

80

81

82

This is different from Kahn's Goldenberg House project (79) where the exceptional diagonal is in part an element of the structural pattern and partially spatial, to make a series of spaces that go around the corners of the building continuously, rather than one side overlapping the other.

Mies allows nothing to get in the way of the consistency of his order, of the point, line, and plane of his always complete pavilions. If Wright camouflages his circumstantial exceptions, Mies excludes them: less is more. Since 1940 Mies has not used a circumstantial diagonal, and in his series of courthouse projects of the 1930's (80) the diagonal is a function of the free plan rather than a condition of the circumstantial. Because the diagonal is dominant rather than exceptional and loosely contained in its rectangular frame, there is little tension between the diagonals and the rectangles. The diagonal chords of the trusses in Mies' large-span buildings are, of course, not circumstantial exceptions.

83

In the Villa Savoye, again, the exceptional diagonal of the ramp is clearly expedient in section and elevation (12) and allows Le Corbusier to create a strong opposition to the regular order of column bays and envelope. This attitude contrasts greatly with that of Wright, whose insistence on horizontal continuity at the expense of all else is well known. Even in the unusually exposed stair at Fallingwater (81) Wright suppresses all diagonals: there are no strings or railings, but only the horizontal planes of the treads and the vertical lines of the rods from which the stair is hung. Similarly, in the interior (82) Wright hides the stairs between walls (as he does in virtually all his houses), while Le Corbusier glories in the expressed diagonals of the ramp and the continuous diagonal of the spiral stair (5, 83). We have already seen how Le Corbusier accommodates architecture intimately to the exceptional needs of the automobile in the Villa Savoye (84). But Wright's order allows no inconsistencies: the bridge is perpendicular and analogous to the order of the house and the curving path of the automobile is not recognized. The driveway is like a path in the woods begrudgingly dotted in plan (82, 85). That the car can turn is almost fortuitous.

84

85

The diagonal, when suggested by circumstances inside or out, is seldom discordant. It hides within the order or else it dominates the composition as a motif. In the Vigo Schmidt House project the diagonal becomes part of the overall triangular module. In the David Wright House the

whole building becomes a diagonal ramp. In the Guggenheim Museum, where the diagonal spiral is the dominant
motival order in a more complex program, the rectangular
perpendicular form does express exceptional circumstances.
Inside, the vertical order of the structure, and particularly of
the shaft containing toilets is expressed in order to provide
stable measure for the converging spiral ramp.

Aalto, then, adapts the order to the circumstantial
exception symbolized by the diagonal. So does Kahn in the
examples given, although in the early schemes for the
capitol at Dacca an extreme rigidity predominates, despite
the huge size and complexity of the project. Le Corbusier
juxtaposes the exceptional diagonal. Mies excludes it.
Wright hides it or surrenders his whole order to it: the exception becomes the rule.

86

These ideas are applicable to the design and perception of cities, which have more extensive and complex
programs, of course, than individual buildings. The consistent spatial order of the Piazza S. Marco, for example (86),
is not without its violent contradictions in scale, rhythm,
and textures, not to mention the varying heights and styles
of the surrounding buildings. Is there not a similar validity
to the vitality of Times Square (87) in which the jarring
inconsistencies of buildings and billboards are contained
within the consistent order of the space itself? It is when
honky-tonk spills out beyond spatial boundaries to the no-
man's land of roadtown, that it becomes chaos and blight.
(If in *God's Own Junkyard* Peter Blake had chosen examples of roadside landscape for his book which were less
extremely "bad," his point, at least involving the banality of
roadside architecture, would ironically have been stronger.)
It seems our fate now to be faced with either the endless
inconsistencies of roadtown (88), which is chaos, or the
infinite consistency of Levittown (or the ubiquitous Levit-
town-like scene illustrated in figure 89), which is boredom. In roadtown we have a false complexity; in Levittown
a false simplicity. One thing is clear—from such false
consistency real cities will never grow. Cities, like architecture, are complex and contradictory.

87

88

89

The party moved on, but deviated a little from the straight way, in order to glance at the ponderous remains of the temple of Mars Ultor, within which a convent of nuns is now established,—a dove-cote, in the war-god's mansion. At only a little distance, they passed the portico of a Temple of Minerva, most rich and beautiful in architecture, but woefully gnawed by time and shattered by violence, besides being buried midway in the accumulation of soil, that rises over dead Rome like a floodtide. Within this edifice of an antique sanctity, a baker's shop was now established, with an entrance on one side; for, everywhere, the remnants of old grandeur and divinity have been made available for the meanest necessities of our day.*

If "contradiction adapted" corresponds to the kid glove treatment, "contradiction juxtaposed" involves the shock treatment. The Villa Pignatelli (62) *adapts varia-tions,* but the Villa Palomba (63) *juxtaposes contrasts:* its contradictory relationships become manifest in discordant rhythms, directions, adjacencies, and especially in what I shall call superadjacencies—the superimpositions of various elements.

90

Le Corbusier supplies a rare modern example of juxta-posed contradictions in the Millowners' Building in Ahmed-abad (90). From the important approach from the south, the repetitive pattern of the brise-soleil invokes rhythms which are violently broken by the entrance void, the ramp, and the stairs. These latter elements, consisting of varying diagonals, create violent adjacencies from the side and violent superadjacencies from the front, in relation to the rectangular static floor divisions within the boxlike form. The juxtapositions of diagonals and perpendiculars also create contradictory directions: the meeting of the ramp and stairs is only slightly softened by the exceptionally large void and by the modified rhythm of the elements at that part of the façade. But these contradictions in the visual experience are even richer when you move closer and penetrate the building. The adjacencies and superadjacen-cies of contrasting scales, directions, and functions can

* Nathaniel Hawthorne, *The Marble Faun,* Dell Publishing Co., Inc., New York, 1961.

make it seem like a miniature example of Kahn's viaduct architecture. In Le Corbusier's Palace of the Two Assemblies at Chandigarh (65) the conical assembly hall jammed into the rectangular grid represents a more three-dimensional superadjacency of a very violent kind.

The city street façade can provide a type of juxtaposed contradiction that is essentially two-dimensional. Frank Furness' Clearing House (91), now demolished like many of his best works in Philadelphia, contained an array of violent pressures within a rigid frame. The half-segmental arch, blocked by the submerged tower which, in turn, bisects the façade into a near duality, and the violent adjacencies of rectangles, squares, lunettes, and diagonals of contrasting sizes, compose a building seemingly held up by the buildings next door: it is an almost insane short story of a castle on a city street. All these relationships of structure and pattern contradict the severe limitations associated with a façade, a street line, and contiguous row houses.

91

The rectangular face of the Palazzo del Popolo in Ascoli Piceno (92) illustrates juxtaposed contradiction that comes from repeated renovation rather than from the instantaneous stroke of a single architect. This façade teems with the violent adjacencies and superadjacencies of open and closed arcades, continuous and interrupted string courses, big and little windows, "porte" and "portone," and clocks, cartouches, balconies, and store fronts. All of these produce broken rhythms and reflect the contradictory dualities of public and private, ordered and circumstantial scales. The unflinching wings and striped patterns of Butterfield's All Saints Church, Margaret Street, London (93), clash when they come together. The relative independence of the form of the parts, despite their closeness, is a most significant example of contradiction juxtaposed as distinct from contradiction adapted.

92

It is the texture of Mannerist rustication which clashes in the same way when it abuts the precise detail of the classical orders in a Renaissance façade. But Michelangelo's loggia in the center of the upper floor of the rear façade of the Palazzo Farnese in relation to the walls adjacent to it reflects a more ambiguous kind of contradiction (94). Giacomo della Porta's exceptional central elements on the floor below—pilasters, arches and architrave—vary only slightly in rhythm and not at all in scale, and the transition from the typical window bays on each side to the middle bays is consistent in detail and scale. The openings of

93

Michelangelo's loggia above are violently contrasting in scale and rhythm with the typical elements to the sides as well as in the higher floor elevation which they imply. The pilasters also, because of their elevation and height, violently break the frieze below the cornice; and the cornice itself recedes rather than advances to match the projections and boldness of the elements below it. The scale of this cornice is smaller because of the increased rhythm of the modillions, yet the modillions themselves (lions' heads) are identical to those on the other cornice and the mouldings are continuous throughout. Similarly ambiguous combinations of contradictions both juxtaposed and adapted, occur in the intermediate bays within the niche.

In Michelangelo's Medici Chapel in San Lorenzo (95) the almost furniture-like scale of ornament of the marble elements within the bays abuts the very big scale of the giant order of pilasters. Classical orders make for another kind of contrasting adjacency when the giant order is juxtaposed on the minor order and the proportion is constant regardless of size. Jefferson's combinations of column sizes at the University of Virginia (96) contradict the maxim that every magnitude requires its own structure. But the juxtapositions of elements contrasting in size yet proportional in shape, like the pyramids of Gizeh, characterize a primary technique of monumentality. In the cathedral façades at Granada (97) and Foligno (98) the adjacencies of varying-sized circles, semicircles, and triangles in the openings and pediments, and at Eastbury (99) Vanbrugh's giant arched openings, proportioned similarly to the arched windows upon which they are superimposed, create a strange tension not unlike that exploited in Jasper Johns' paintings of superimposed flags (100). The guest house which stood behind the Low House by McKim, Mead and White was a miniature imitation of that house in its distinctive overall form.

Besides these violent adajcencies there are contrasts of direction within the whole. The Church of the Holy Sepulchre in Jerusalem (101), much renovated, and Aalto's Cultural Center at Wolfsburg (78), pre-renovated, so to speak, contain walls and series of columns with contradictory directions of almost equal intensity. The wings and projections of the Shingle Style house called Kragsyde in Manchester-by-the-Sea (102), are less contained within a dominant perimeter, but nevertheless include a multiplicity of directions, especially in elevation.

94

95

97

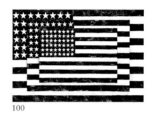

100

101

96

98

102

99

Juxtaposed directions create rhythmic complexities and contradictions. Figure (103) illustrates a chair at Caserta that contains violently contrasting curvilinear and rectangular rhythms. At another scale, the interior of Adler and Sullivan's Auditorium (104) has juxtapositions of swooping curves and diverse repetitions. In some anonymous Italian architecture (105) adjacent contrasting arcades contain contrapuntal rhythms.

Superadjacency is inclusive rather than exclusive. It can relate contrasting and otherwise irreconcilable elements; it can contain opposites within a whole; it can accommodate the valid non sequitur; and it can allow a multiplicity of levels of meaning, since it involves changing contexts—seeing familiar things in an unfamiliar way and from unexpected points of view. Superadjacency can be considered a variation of the idea of simultaneity expressed in Cubism and in certain orthodox Modern architecture, which employed transparency. But it is in contrast to the perpendicular interpenetration of space and form characteristic of the work of Wright. Superadjacency can result in a real richness as opposed to the surface richness of the screen which is typical of "serene" architecture. Its manifestations, as we shall see, are as diverse as Bramante's layered walls in the Belvedere Courtyard in the Vatican Palace (106) and Kahn's "ruins . . . wrapped around buildings" in his Salk Institute for Biological Studies (107).

103

104

105

Superadjacency can exist between distant elements, such as the propylon before a Greek temple, which frames the composition and ties the foreground to the background. Such superimpositions change as one moves in space. Superadjacency can also occur where the superimposed elements actually touch instead of being related only visually. This is the method in Gothic and Renaissance architecture. The nave walls of Gothic cathedrals contain arcades of varying orders and scales. The shafts and ribs, band courses, and arches which make up these arcades penetrate and are superimposed upon each other. At Gloucester Cathedral (108) the superadjacency is contradictory in scale and direction: the enormous diagonal buttress crosses the plane of the delicate order of arcades in the transept's wall. All Mannerist and Baroque façades involve superadjacencies and interpenetrations on the same plane. Giant orders in relation to minor orders express contradictions in scale in the same building, and the series of superimposed pilasters in Baroque architecture implies spatial depth in a flat wall.

106

Vignola's sculptural superimposition of portal and portico in his pavilion at Bomarzo (17) and the amputated pilasters of the entrance façade of the Belén church in Cuzco are perhaps intriguing solecisms, but the complex superadjacencies in the cloister façades at Tomar (109) compose a wall validly containing spaces within itself. The multiple layers of columns—engaged and disengaged, large and small, directly and indirectly superimposed—and the profusion of superimposed openings, architraves, and horizontal and diagonal balustrades create contrasts and contradictions in scale, direction, size, and shape. They make a wall containing spaces inside itself. I shall return to this kind of valid redundancy in the next chapter concerning the difference between the inside and the outside.

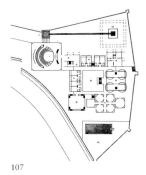

107

The diverse structural elements that surround the great door in the Porta Pia (110, 111) are superimposed for ornament as well as structure. It abounds in redundant and rhetorical superadjacencies of a kind of ornament that is "about" structure. The vulnerable edges of the opening are protected by rusticated trim at the sides. Superimposed on the trim are pilasters that further define the sides of the door and support, together with the scrolled brackets above, the heavy complex of the pediment. This important opening is made eventful in the bearing wall by additional juxtapositions. The diagonal pediment protects the rectangular inscription block and the inverse segment of the sculptural garland which, in turn, plays against the curve of the semicircular relieving arch. The arch is at the head of a series of redundant structural spanning elements, including the horizontal lintel, which in turn relieves the flat arch, which is a continuation of the rusticated trim. Brackets or corbeling, which decrease the span, are suggested by the diagonals of the top corners of the opening. The exaggerated keystone is superimposed on the flat-arch, the lintel, and the tympanum of the arch.

108

In their complex relationships these elements are in varying degrees both structural and ornamental, frequently redundant, and sometimes vestigial. In the almost equal combination of horizontal, vertical, diagonal, and curve they correspond to Sullivan's violently superimposed frames around the bull's-eye window of the boxlike Merchants' National Bank in Grinnell, Iowa (112).

109

In Lutyens' project for Liverpool Cathedral (113) the scattered minute windows seen as black dots impose themselves in an independent pattern on the symmetrical, monumental forms of the whole building. The pliable pattern of little windows accommodates service areas required for up-keep of the building and creates human scale that contrasts with the rigid monumentality. In Philadelphia the gridiron street pattern of the local scale of circulation is superimposed upon the resultant diagonal avenues which correspond to the regional scale of circulation in the city because they originally connected the center with the outlying towns. These juxtapositions create unique, residual, triangular blocks containing unusually shaped buildings, which give the city visual variety and quality. The "squares" in Manhattan formed by the unique diagonal intersections of Broadway—for instance, Madison, Union, Herald, and Times Squares—became events each with its individual character, which added vitality and tension to the overall gridiron of that city. The almost inevitable contradictory diagonal of the railroad tracks in the typical American gridiron town of the plains also vividly implies the contrasting scale of the whole region. The nineteeenth century American "elevated" which was juxtaposed above the street anticipated the multi-level city like Sigmond's 1958 plan for Berlin (114) which proposed a multi-level city with large-scale circulation elevated above the local traffic. In this kind of superimposition the degree of separation lies between the changing, almost incidental superimpositions of forms that are very separate in space and the interpenetration of superimpositions on the same plane. Superadjacencies at this intermediate degree are closely related but not touching, like the configuration of a separated lining. They are also rare in Modern architecture.

The Romanesque arcades on the cathedral at Lucca (115), the Gothic traceries of the cathedral at Strasbourg (116), or the interior of the choir at Notre Dame, Paris (117), the Renaissance galleries at Chambord (118), or the outside second floor colonnettes of Gaudí's Casa Battló (119), or the columns in the gallery inside his Casa Güell (120), are all disengaged and superimposed on contrasting window patterns. The big public-scale and the rigid order outside contrast vividly with the small private-scale patterns required within. This play of layers of openings is sometimes discordant in rhythm and scale: Vanbrugh's giant arched opening at Eastbury (99) and Armando Brazini's in the Forestry Building at the E.U.R. site in Rome (121) illustrated the same kind of superadjacency on the inner and outer walls, but Brazini's was rhythmically discordant.

110

111

112

113

66

114

118

115

116

119

117

120

121

123

126

122

127

124

125

128

On Vanbrugh's entrance façade to the kitchen court at Blenheim (59), disengaged columns, which frame the grand opening, are discordantly superimposed upon the windows that make up part of the regular rhythmic pattern behind. The same thing happens at Seaton Delaval (122), where the disengaged columns block some of the windows. The façade of St. Maclou, Rouen (123), is made up of layers of diagonal elements—traceried pediments, roofs, and buttresses—differing in function though analogous in form. These juxtapositions are relatively separated in comparison with the façade of Il Redentore (51), whose ambiguously superimposed diagonals are broken pediments and exposed buttresses at the same time.

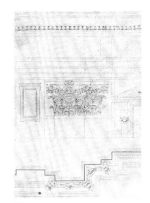

129

Other buildings contain similar degrees of spatial superadjacencies on the inside taking the form of extremely articulated or separated linings. In the choir of the Wieskirche (124) the colonnade, which runs closely parallel to the walls, makes changing rhythmic juxtapositions against the pilasters and window openings of the walls. Soane's interior arch in the Insolvent Debtors' Court, London (125), makes a more contradictory superadjacency against the windows of the wall almost immediately beyond.

130

In Modern architecture contradictory juxtapositions of scale involving immediately adjacent elements are even rarer than superadjacencies. Such a manipulation of scale is seen in the accidental collage of the colossal head of Constantine and the louvered shutters in the courtyard of the Capitoline Museum (126). Significantly, it is usually in non-architectural configurations (127) that such contrasts in scale occur today. In another context I have referred to the adjacencies of giant and minor orders in Mannerist and Baroque architecture. In the rear façade of St. Peter's (128, 129) Michelangelo makes an even more contradictory contrast in scale: a blank window is juxtaposed with a capital bigger than the window itself. In the cathedral façade at Cremona (130) there is a violent adjacency of little arcades and an enormous rose window high up. This reflects within the building both the scale of the building itself and the scale of the town it dominates so that the building accommodates the close view and yet commands from a distance. In the cathedral at Cefalu (131) the symbolically important mosaic figure of Christ is correspondingly big in relation to the other ornament. The enormous central door, which is equal to the giant scale of the columns of the portico of the Temple of Apollo at Didyma (132), con-

131

trasts with the little side doors of the same façade. Like Lutyens at Middleton Park (133), Le Corbusier in the Villa Stein (134) contrasts the scale of the entrance and service doors. This contrast is intensely vivid, not because they are adjacent, but because the doors have equivalent positions in an essentially symmetrical façade. In the Casa Güell (135) Gaudí superimposes the large door for vehicles and the little door for pedestrians. A vivid tension evolves from all these juxtaposed contradictions. Sometimes close changes of scale are encountered in our cities, but these usually occur more through accidents than design, like the vestigial Trinity Church on Wall Street or some juxtapositions of expressways and existing buildings (136), which are perversions of the hyperproximities of little houses and grand cathedrals or city walls in medieval cities. Some city planners, however, are now more prone to question the glibness of orthodox zoning and to allow violent proximities in their planning, at least in theory, than are architects within their buildings.

132

133

134

135

136

The external configuration is usually rather simple, but there is packed into the interior of an organism an amazing complexity of structures which have long been the delight of anatomists.

The specific form of a plant or animal is determined not only by the genes in the organism and the cytoplasmic activities that these direct but by the interaction between genetic constitution and environment. A given gene does not control a specific trait, but a specific reaction to a specific environment.*

Contrast between the inside and the outside can be a major manifestation of contradiction in architecture. However, one of the powerful twentieth century orthodoxies has been the necessity for continuity between them: the inside should be expressed on the outside. But this is not really new—only our means have been new. The Renaissance church interior, for instance (137), has a continuity with its exterior; the interior vocabulary of pilasters, cornices, and drip mouldings is almost identical in scale and sometimes in material with its exterior vocabulary. The result is subtle modification but little contrast and no surprise.

Perhaps the boldest contribution of orthodox Modern architecture was its so-called flowing space, which was used to achieve the continuity of inside and outside. The idea has been emphasized by historians ranging from Vincent Scully's discovery of its early evolution in Shingle Style interiors to its flowering in the Prairie House and its culmination in De Stijl and the Barcelona Pavilion. Flowing space produced an architecture of related horizontal and vertical planes. The visual independence of these uninterrupted planes was scored by connecting areas of plate glass: windows as holes in the wall disappeared and became, instead, interruptions of wall to be discounted by the eye as a positive element of the building. Such cornerless architecture implied an ultimate continuity of space. Its emphasis on the oneness of interior and exterior space was permitted

137

* Edmund W. Sinnott, *The Problem of Organic Form*, Yale University Press, New Haven, 1963.

by new mechanical equipment which for the first time made the inside thermally independent of the outside.

But the old tradition of enclosed and contrasted inside space, which I want to analyze here, has been recognized by some Modern masters, even if it has not been much emphasized by the historians. Although Wright did in fact "destroy the box" in the Prairie House, the rounded corners and solid walls of the Johnson Wax Administration Building are analogous to the diagonal and rounded corners of Borromini's interiors and those of his eighteenth century followers—and for the same purpose: to exaggerate a sense of horizontal enclosure and to promote the separateness and unity of the interior space by the continuity of the four walls. But Wright, unlike Borromini, did not puncture his continuous walls with windows. That would have weakened the bold contrast of horizontal enclosure and vertical openness. And it also would have been too traditional and structurally ambiguous for him.

The essential purpose of the interiors of buildings is to enclose rather than direct space, and to separate the inside from the outside. Kahn has said: "A building is a harboring thing." The function of the house to protect and provide privacy, psychological as well as physical, is an ancient one. The Johnson Wax Building fosters a further tradition: the expressive differentiation of the inside and outside spaces. Besides enclosing the inside with walls, Wright differentiated the interior light, an idea with a rich evolution from Byzantine, Gothic, and Baroque architecture to that of Le Corbusier and Kahn today. The inside *is* different from the outside.

But there are other valid means of differentiating and relating inside and outside space which are foreign to our recent architecture. Eliel Saarinen said that just as a building is the "organization of space in space. So is the community. So is the city."[35] I think this series could start with the idea of a room as a space in space. And I should like to apply Saarinen's definition of relationships not only to the spatial relationships of building and site, but to those of interior spaces within interior spaces. What I am talking about is the baldacchino above the altar and within the sanctuary. Another classic building of Modern architecture, again admittedly not typical, illustrates my point. The Villa Savoye (12) with its wall openings which are, significantly, holes rather than interruptions, restricts any flowing space rigidly to the vertical direction. But there is a spatial impli-

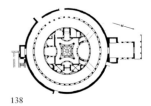

138

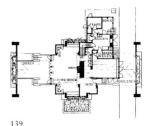

139

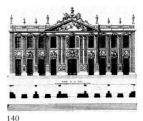

140

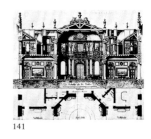

141

cation beyond that of enclosure which contrasts it with the Johnson Wax Building. Its severe, almost square exterior surrounds an intricate interior configuration glimpsed through openings and from protrusions above. In this context the tense image of the Villa Savoye from within and without displays a contrapuntal resolution of severe envelope partly broken and intricate interior partly revealed. Its inside order accommodates the multiple functions of a house, domestic scale, and partial mystery inherent in a sense of privacy. Its outside order expresses the unity of the idea of house at an easy scale appropriate to the green field it dominated and possibly to the city it will one day be part of.

A building can include things within things as well as spaces within spaces. And its interior configurations can contrast with its container in other ways besides those of the Villa Savoye's. The circular perimeters of bearing wall and colonnade in Hadrian's Maritime Theatre at Tivoli (138) produce another version of the same spatial idea. Even Wright, although only be suggestion, contains the interior intricacy of his Evans House (139) with a rectangular envelope implied by the sculptural corner posts. At the other extreme, the intricacies within the plan of the typical Tudor manor, Barrington Court (13), for example, are hidden, maybe excessively and expressed only incidentally, if at all, on its rigid, symmetrical façades. In another symmetrical Tudor plan the kitchen balances the chapel. The intricacies revealed in section in the château at Marly (140, 141) are a concession to light and convenience inside. Because they are not expressed on the outside, the interior light is surprising. Fuga's walls wrap around S. Maria Maggiore (142), and Soane's walls enclose the distorted intricacies of courtyards and wings of the Bank of England (143) in the same way and for similar reasons: they unify outside, in relation to the scale of the city, the contradictory spatial intricacies of chapels or banking rooms which evolved in time. Crowded intricacies can be excluded as well as contained. The colonnades at St. Peter's (144) and at the Piazza del Plebiscito in Naples (145), respectively exclude the intricacies of the Vatican Palace complex and the city complex, in order to achieve unity for their piazzas.

Sometimes the contradiction is not between the inside and the outside but between the top and the bottom of the building. The curving dome and drum on pendentives in Baroque churches protrude beyond the parapets of their

142

143

144

149

145

146

150

147

152

148

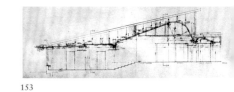

153

151

rectangular bases. I have already mentioned in the P.S.F.S. skyscraper the curved base, rectangular shaft, and angled top as manifestations of multiple functions contained within the building (41). In the Castel Sant' Angelo (146) the rectangular elements evolve from a circular base. The Romantic roof-scapes of Richardson's Watts-Sherman House (147) and the multidomed trulli of Puglia (148) contrast with the severe exterior perimeters of their lower walls. From the outside, the space within a space can become the thing behind a thing. The enormous clerestory of Wollaton Hall (149) reads as a big-scale thing behind a smaller-scale thing. In S. Maria della Pace (150) the super-imposition of enclosing elements, which are successively convex, perpendicular, and then concave, become contrasting things behind things to work transitions between the outside and the inside.

Essentially, Le Corbusier's plan of the Villa Savoye exemplifies crowded intricacies within a rigid frame. Some of the plans of his other houses of the '20's suggest starting with the frame and then working inward. Similar things happen in elevation in his High Court Building at Chandigarh (151). Like the rear of McKim, Mead and White's Low House (72), but at another scale, it contains intricacies within a rigid façade. The severe roof and wall envelope of the house contain complex spaces and floor levels which are expressed by varying window positions. Similarly, the single, sheltering gable of the Emmental-type house in Switzerland (152), and the constant shed of Aalto's Maison Carrée (153), contradict the interior spaces below. And similar tensions in the rear façade of Mt. Vernon (71) result from the contrast of the severe pedimented envelope and the irregular window positions. In the side façade of Hawksmoor's Easton Neston (154), the windows are positioned by particular interior requirements in defiance of its horizontal order. Crowded intricacy within a rigid frame has been a pervasive idea. It exists in such diverse examples as a fantasy of Piranesi (155) and the composition of a Michelangelo niche (156). More purely expressive examples are the façades of the parish church in Lampa, Peru (157), and the chapel entrance in Fontaine-bleau (158), which contain enormous pressures within their borders like a Mannerist painting.

154

155

Containment and intricacy have been characteristic of the city as well. Fortified walls for military protection and the greenbelt for civic protection are examples of this phenomenon. Contained intricacy might be one of the viable methods for dealing with urban chaos and the end-lessness of roadtown; through the creative use of zoning and positive architectural features it is possible to concen-trate the intricacies of roadtowns and junkyards, actual and figurative. And like the sculpture which consists of com-pressed automobiles by John Chamberlain and the photo-graphs through telescopic lens in Blake's *God's Own Junk-yard*, they achieve an ironically compelling kind of unity.

Contradiction between the inside and the outside may manifest itself in an unattached lining which produces an additional space between the lining and the exterior wall. Plan diagrams (159) illustrate that such layers between the inside space and the outside space can be more or less contrasting in shape, position, pattern, and size. Diagram (159a) illustrates the simplest kind which is analogous and attached. A different material inside, wainscoting in this case, provides the contrast. The Byzantine mosaics inside the chapel of Galla Placidia represent a lining attached but contrasting in richness of texture, pattern, and color with the drab brickwork of the exterior. The pilasters, archi-traves, and arches of Renaissance walls, such as Bramante's façade in the Belvedere Court in the Vatican, can imply layers while the colonnade of the loggia of the south façade of the Louvre makes spatial layers. The colonnettes in the interior of the cathedral at Rouen (160) or the disengaged pilasters in the anteroom of Syon House (161) represent more detached kinds of layers also, but their subtle contrast to the outside depends more on scale than on form and texture. The lining becomes semidetached in Percier and Fontaine's curtained bedroom at Malmaison, which is derived from a Roman military tent. The graduated series of symbolic doors at Karnak (162) are multiple linings in relief similar in two dimensions to the generic idea of nests of toy eggs or wooden dolls. These doors within doors, like the multi-framed doors in Gothic porches, differ from mul-ti-pedimented Baroque openings, which juxtapose triangular and segmental shapes.

The graduated series of things in things or enclosures within enclosures which characterize the Egyptian temple carry out in space the motif of the multi-framed doors at Karnak. The series of walls at Edfu (163, 164) are de-tached linings. The outer linings enhance the enclosed inner spaces by making them seem protected and mysteri-ous. They resemble the layers of fortifications in medieval

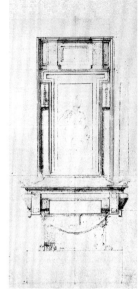

156

157

158

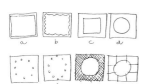

159

160

161

162

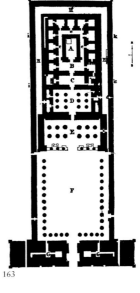

163

164

castles, or the spatial nest in which Bernini contained his little Pantheon, S. Maria dell' Assunzione at Arricia (165). The same tensions occur between the hovering layers of the enclosing sanctuary screens and the outer walls of the cathedral at Albi (166) and other cathedrals in Catalonia and the Languedoc. The multiple domes of the Baroque represent, in section, layers which are analogous but detached. Through their central oculi one can see spaces beyond spaces. In the project by the Asam Brothers (167), for instance, the inner dome with its oculus masks high windows, thus producing surprising effects of light and a more complex space. On the exterior the upper dome increases the effect of scale and height. In their Abbey church at Weltenburg (168) the clouds of the frescoed upper dome, which are viewed through the oculus of the lower dome, increase the sense of space. In S. Maria in Canepanova in Pavia (169) the effect of the layered dome is seen on the outside rather than the inside.

The multiple domes of the S. Cecilia Chapel in S. Carlo ai Catinari in Rome (170) are detached and contrasting in shape. Beyond the oval oculus of the lower dome is seen a rectangular space flooded with light, containing a sculptural quartet of musical angels. Beyond this zone, in turn, floats an even more brilliant oval lantern. Soane uses interior domes in square spaces even in small areas like the breakfast room at Lincoln Fields Inn (171). His fantastic juxtapositions of domes and lanterns, squinches and pendentives, and a variety of other ornamental and structural shapes elsewhere (35) work to enrich the sense of enclosure and light. These layered structural-ornamental elements are sometimes vestigial (almost in a two dimensional pattern), but they give the complex effect of actually detached spatial layers. Armando Brazini's neo-Baroque church of the Cuore Immaculata di Maria Santissima in Rome (172, 173) has a quasi-circular plan containing a Greek cross plan. The Greek cross plan is reflected on the outside in four pedimented porches marking the ends of the cross. These porches, in turn, are made convex to accommodate to the circular plan. In Modern architecture Johnson has been almost unique in emphasizing multiple enclosure in plan and section. The canopy inside his guest house in New Canaan (174) and the Soanian canopy within the synagogue in Port Chester (175) are both inner layers. Kahn employs detached layers on the outside: he "wraps ruins around buildings." In the project for the

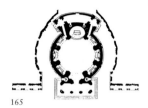

165

166

167

171

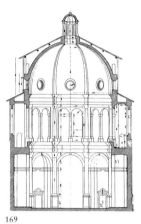

169

172

173

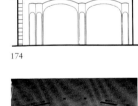

174

170

175

176

179

181

177

180

182

178

184

Meeting House for the Salk Institute for Biological Studies (107) he juxtaposes in plan circles within squares, and squares within circles. According to Kahn, inside glare will be counteracted by the juxtaposition of apertures, contrasting in size and shape, in the double-layered walls. Kahn has talked of the modification of light more than the spatial expression of enclosure as his reason for the contrasting layers. Lutyens' motif of the circle in the square appears in his stairs with round wells within square rooms.

183

In the vestibule of S. Croce in Gerusalemme (176) and in the interiors of SS. Sergius and Bacchus (177) and of St. Stephen Walbrook (34) it is the series of columns which define the inner, detached and contrasting layer of enclosure. These supports, along with the domes above them, make the intraspatial relationships of the interior. St. Stephen Walbrook is a square space containing an octagonal space at the lower level (178). Its squinch-like arches, at the intermediate level between the columns and the dome, make a transition to the dome above. Similarly, in Vierzhenheiligen (31) the piers along with the domes define curving spaces within the rectangular and hexagonal walls of the perimeter. But the inner layers are less independent than those in St. Stephen. In plan as well as section, the curve sometimes touches the outer wall and becomes common with it (179). Both the plan and section of Neresheim in Southern Germany (180) show that the complex curves of the inner circle sinuously inflect as they near the outer oval. These intraspatial relationships are at once more complex and more ambiguous than those of St. Stephen Walbrook's.

Layers are implied in Michelangelo's Sforza Chapel in S. Maria Maggiore (181, 182) in the violent penetrations of rectangular space and curved space in plan and of barrel vaults, domes and niche-vaulting in section. The ambiguous juxtapositions of these two kinds of shapes as well as the implied intense compression and enormous scale of the flatly curved spaces (which by implication extend beyond the actual enclosure) give this interior its peculiar power and tension (183).

Detached linings leave spaces in between. But the architectural recognition of the in-between varies. Edfu is almost all layers. The residual spaces are closed and dominate the small space at the center. St. Basel's (184) is like a series of churches within a church. The intricate maze of residual spaces inside results from the proximity of the chapels to each other toward the center, and the closeness of the wrapping wall toward the outside. In Charles V's palace at Granada (185), the Villa Farnese at Caprarola (186), and the Villa Giulia (187), the courtyards dominate because they are large and their shapes contrast with the shape of the perimeters. They make the primary space; the rooms of the palaces are leftover space. As in the preliminary scheme of Kahn's Unitarian Church in Rochester (188), the residual spaces are closed. In contrast, the linings of columns and piers in SS. Sergius and Bacchus, St. Stephen Walbrook, Vierzhenheiligen, and Neresheim define residual spaces which open on the dominant spaces, although they are separate from them in varying degrees. In the Stupinigi Palace (189) because the dominant space is so open, the distinction between dominant and residual spaces in the main hall is ambiguous. In fact, the inner lining is so open that there remains only a vestige of a central inner space, indicated by four piers and the very complex vaulting patterns of the ceiling. The complex oculus and other openings of the inner dome in S. Chiara, Brà (190, 191), define residual space, which is open in order to elaborate space and manipulate light. The detachment of the inner and outer window openings in Aalto's Imatra Church (192) similarly modifies light and space. The use of this method is unique in recent architecture.

The wooden vaulting of seventeenth century Polish synagogues (193), which imitates masonry, makes closed linings in the upper section. In contrast to the previous examples their residual space is closed. Closed poché determined primarily by exterior spatial forces rather than the inherent structure of the form is almost unknown in Modern architecture except for Aalto's unique Concert Podium (194) composed of a wood skin-frame structure, which directs sound as well as space. Residual space in between dominant spaces with varying degrees of openness can occur at the scale of the city and is a characteristic of the fora and other complexes of late Roman urban planning. Residual spaces are not unknown in our cities. I am thinking of the open spaces under our highways and the buffer spaces around them. Instead of acknowledging and exploiting these characteristic kinds of space we make them into parking lots or feeble patches of grass—no-man's lands between the scale of the region and the locality.

Residual space that is open might be called "open poché." Kahn's "servant space," which sometimes harbors

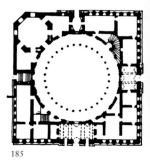

185

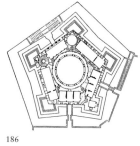

186

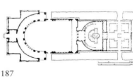

187

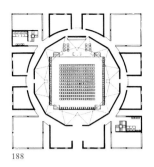

188

191

189

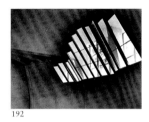

192

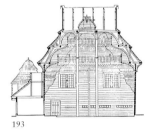

193

194

190

mechanical equipment, and the poché in the walls of Roman and Baroque architecture are alternative means of accommodating an inside different from the outside. Aldo van Eyck has said: "Architecture should be conceived of as a configuration of intermediary places clearly defined. This does not imply continual transition or endless postponement with respect to place and occasion. On the contrary, it implies a break away from the contemporary concept (call it sickness) of spatial continuity and the tendency to erase every articulation between spaces, i.e., between outside and inside, between one space and another (between one reality and another). Instead the transition must be articulated by means of defined in-between places which induce simultaneous awareness of what is significant on either side. An in-between space in this sense provides the common ground where conflicting polarities can again become twin phenomena." [36]

Residual space is sometimes awkward. Like structural poché it is seldom economic. It is always leftover, inflected toward something more important beyond itself. The qualifications, contrasts, and tensions inherent in these spaces are perhaps cogent to Kahn's statement that "a building should have bad spaces as well as good spaces."

Redundant enclosure, like crowded intricacies, is rare in our architecture. With some significant exceptions in the work of Le Corbusier and Kahn, Modern architecture has tended to ignore such complex spatial ideas. The "utility core" of Mies or early Johnson is not relevant because it becomes a passive accent in a dominant open space, rather than an active parallel to another perimeter. Contradictory interior space does not admit Modern architecture's requirement of a unity and continuity of all spaces. Nor do layers in depth, especially with contrapuntal juxtapositions, satisfy its requirements of economic and unequivocal relationships of forms and materials. And crowded intricacy within a rigid boundary (which is not a transparent framework) contradicts the modern tenet which says that a building grows from the inside out.

What are the justifications for multiple enclosure and for the inside's being different from the outside? When Wright expressed his dictum: "an organic form grows its structure out of conditions as a plant grows out of the soil, both unfold similarly from within," [37] he had a long precedent behind him. Other Americans had advocated what was at the moment a healthy thing—a needed battle cry:

Greenough: Instead of forcing the functions of every sort of building into one general form, adopting an outward shape for the sake of the eyes or association, without references to the inner distribution, let us begin from the heart as a nucleus and work outward.[38]

Thoreau: What of architectural beauty I now see, I know has grown gradually from within outward, out of the necessities and character of the indweller.[39]

Sullivan: [The architect] must cause a building to grow naturally, logically, and poetically out of its condition.[40] . . . Outward appearances resemble inner purposes.[41]

Even Le Corbusier has written: "The plan proceeds from within to without; the exterior is the result of an interior."[42]

But Wright's biological analogy is self-limiting, because the development of a plant is influenced into particular distortions by the particular forces of its environment as well as by its genetic order of growth. D'Arcy Wentworth Thompson saw form as a record of development in environment. The inherently rectangular order of structure and space of Aalto's apartment house in Bremen (76, 195) yields to the inner needs for light and space toward the south, like the growth of a flower toward the sun. But generally speaking, for Wright the exterior and interior space of his invariably isolated buildings was continuous, and as he was an urbanophobe, the suburban environment of his buildings, when specifically regional, was not so particularly limiting spatially as an urban context. (The flowing plan of the Robie House, however, adapts to the constriction of the back sides of its corner lot.) Wright however, I believe, refused to recognize the setting that was not sympathetic to the direct expression of the interior. The Guggenheim Museum is an anomaly on Fifth Avenue. But the Johnson Wax Building perhaps makes a negative gesture toward its indifferent urban environment by dominating and excluding it.

Contrast and even conflict between exterior and interior forces exist outside architecture as well. Kepes has said: "Every phenomenon—a physical object, an organic form, a feeling, a thought, our group life—owes its shape and character to the duel between opposing tendencies; a physical configuration is a product of the duel between native constitution and outside environment."[43] This interplay has always been vivid in the concentrations of the

195

urban environment. Wright's Morris Store (196, 197) is another one of the exceptions he was confident enough to make. Its strong contradictions between the inside and the outside—between the particular, private and the general, public functions, make it a traditional urban building rare in Modern architecture. As Aldo van Eyck says: "Planning on whatever scale level should provide a framework—to set the stage as it were—for the twin-phenomenon of the individual and the collective without resorting to arbitrary accentuation of either one at the expense of the other." [44] Contradiction, or at least a contrast, between the inside and the outside is an essential characteristic of urban architecture, but it is not only an urban phenomenon. Besides the Villa Savoye and obvious examples like the domestic Greek temples of the Greek Revival which were crammed expediently with series of cells, the Renaissance villa such as Hawksmoor's Easton Neston or Westover in Virginia (198) juxtaposed symmetrical façades on asymmetrical plans.

196

Contradictory interplays between inside and outside spatial needs can be seen in the following examples in which the front and the back contrast. The diagram (199) illustrates six general cases. The concave façade in the Baroque church accommodates spatial needs that are specifically different on the inside and the outside. The concave exterior, at odds with the church's essential concave spatial function inside, acknowledges a contrasting exterior need for a spatial pause in the street. At the front of the building outside space is more important. Behind the façade the church was designed from the inside out, but in front it was designed from the outside in. The space left over by this contradiction was taken care of with poché. The plans of the two pavilions by Fischer von Erlach (200) illustrate through the concave curves in one the inside-dominant space and through the convex curves in the second the outside-dominant space. The concave façade of Lutyens' Grey Walls (56) accommodates an entrance court whose curve is determined by the turning radius of a car, and which concludes the vista of the approach. Grey Walls is a rural Piazza S. Ignazio (201). The concave exterior of Aalto's studio at Munkkiniemi (202) shapes an outdoor amphitheatre. These examples produce residual spaces inside.

Fischer von Erlach's Karlskirche (42), mentioned earlier, combines a small oval church with a large rectangular façade that accommodates to its particular urban setting by

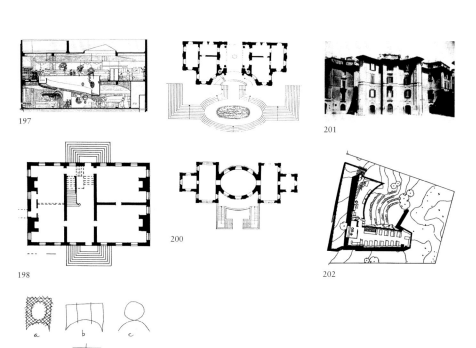

197

198

199

200

201

202

means of a false façade rather than by poché. The concave façade of the garden pavilion of the Arcadian Academy in Rome (203) is in even more contradictory contrast to the villa behind it. The façade has been given its particular size and shape in order to terminate the terraced garden. In the Sanctuary of Saronno (204) there is contradiction in style as well as in scale between the façade and the rest of the building.

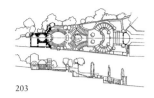

203

204

In the Baroque church the inside is different from the outside, but the back is also different from the front. American architecture, and especially Modern architecture with its antipathy to the "false front," has emphasized the free-standing, independent building even in the city—the building which is an isolated pavilion rather than one which reinforces the street line has become the norm. Johnson has called this the American tradition of "plop architecture." Aalto's dormitory at M.I.T. (205) is exceptional. The curving front along the river and its fenestration and materials contrast with the rectangularity and other characteristics of the rear: exterior as well as interior forces of use and space and structure vary back and front. And the P.S.F.S. building, which is a tower, has four different sides because it recognizes its specific urban setting: party walls, street façades—backs, fronts and corner. Here the freestanding building becomes a fragment of a greater exterior spatial whole, but the typical freestanding building of Modern architecture, except for some surface treatment and screens, which act to de-emphasize the spatial enclosure or to recognize orientation differences, seldom changes front and back for exterior spatial reasons. To the eighteenth century, also, this was a conventional idea. The ingenious double axis hotel in Paris (206), even in its originally more open setting, accommodated outside spaces differently at the front and back. With similar justification, Hawksmoor's Easton Neston (154) yields a tense disunity between front and side. The discontinuous elevation on the intimate garden side away from the long axis, accommodates varieties of spaces and levels inside and necessities of scale outside. The side elevation of the Strozzi Palace (207) anticipates its hidden position on a side alley.

205

Designing from the outside in, as well as the inside out, creates necessary tensions, which help make architecture. Since the inside is different from the outside, the wall —the point of change—becomes an architectural event. Architecture occurs at the meeting of interior and exterior forces of use and space. These interior and environmental forces are both general and particular, generic and circumstantial. Architecture as the wall between the inside and the outside becomes the spatial record of this resolution and its drama. And by recognizing the difference between the inside and the outside, architecture opens the door once again to an urbanistic point of view.

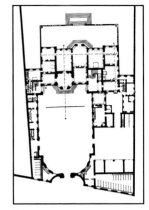

206

10.   The Obligation Toward the Difficult Whole

. . . Toledo [Ohio] was very beautiful.*

207

An architecture of complexity and accommodation does not forsake the whole. In fact, I have referred to a special obligation toward the whole because the whole is difficult to achieve. And I have emphasized the goal of unity rather than of simplification in an art "whose . . . truth [is] in its totality."[45] It is the difficult unity through inclusion rather than the easy unity through exclusion. Gestalt psychology considers a perceptual whole the result of, and yet more than, the sum of its parts. The whole is dependent on the position, number, and inherent characteristics of the parts. A complex system in Herbert A. Simon's definition includes "a large number of parts that interact in a non-simple way."[46] The difficult whole in an architecture of complexity and contradiction includes multiplicity and diversity of elements in relationships that are inconsistent or among the weaker kinds perceptually.

* Gertrude Stein, *Gertrude Stein's America*, Gilbert A. Harrison, ed., Robert B. Luce Inc., Washington, D. C., 1965.

89

Concerning the positions of the parts, for instance, such an architecture encourages complex and contrapuntal rhythms over simple and single ones. The "difficult whole" can include a diversity of directions as well. Concerning the number of parts in a whole, the two extremes—a single part and a multiplicity of parts—read as wholes most easily: the single part is itself a unity; and extreme multiplicity reads like a unity through a tendency of the parts to change scale, and to be perceived as an overall pattern or texture. The next easiest whole is the trinity: three is the commonest number of compositional parts making a monumental unity in architecture.

208

But an architecture of complexity and contradiction also embraces the "difficult" numbers of parts—the duality, and the medium degrees of multiplicity. If the program or structure dictates a combination of two elements within any of the varying scales of a building, this is an architecture which exploits the duality, and more or less resolves dualities into a whole. Our recent architecture has suppressed dualities. The loose composition of the whole used in the "binuclear plan" employed by some architects right after the Second World War, was only a partial exception to this rule. But our tendency to distort the program and to subvert the composition in order to disguise the duality is refuted by a tradition of accepted dualities, more or less resolved, at all scales of building and planning—from Gothic portals and Renaissance windows to the Mannerist façades of the sixteenth century and Wren's complex of pavilions at Greenwich Hospital. In painting, duality has had a continuous tradition—for example, in compositions of the Madonna and Child and of the Annunciation; in enigmatic Mannerist compositions such as Piero della Francesca's *Flagellation* (208); and in the recent work of Ellsworth Kelly (209), Morris Louis (210), and others.

209

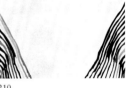

210

Sullivan's Farmers' and Merchants' Union Bank in Columbus, Wisconsin (211), is exceptional in our recent architecture. The difficult duality is prominent. The plan reflects the bisected inside space which accommodates the public and the clerks on different sides of the counter running perpendicular to the façade. On the outside the door and the window at grade reflect this duality: they are themselves bisected by the shafts above. But the shafts, in turn, divide the lintel into a unity of three with a dominant central panel. The arch above the lintel tends to reinforce duality because it springs from the center of a panel below,

211

yet by its oneness and its dominant size it also resolves the duality made by the window and the door. The façade is composed of the play of diverse numbers of parts—single elements as well as those divided into two or three are almost equally prominent—but the façade as a whole makes a unity.

Gestalt psychology also shows that the nature of the parts, as well as their number and position, influences a perceptual whole and it also has made a further distinction: the degree of wholeness can vary. Parts can be more or less whole in themselves, or, to put it in another way, in greater or lesser degree they can be fragments of a greater whole. Properties of the part can be more or less articulated; properties of the whole can be more or less accented. In the complex compositions, a special obligation toward the whole encourages the fragmentary part or, as Trystan Edwards calls it, the term, "inflection."[47]

Inflection in architecture is the way in which the whole is implied by exploiting the nature of the individual parts, rather than their position or number. By inflecting toward something outside themselves, the parts contain their own linkage: inflected parts are more integral with the whole than are *un*inflected parts. Inflection is a means of distinguishing diverse parts while implying continuity. It involves the art of the fragment. The valid fragment is economical because it implies richness and meaning beyond itself. Inflection can also be used to achieve suspense, an element possible in large sequential complexes. The inflected element can be called a partial-functioning element in contrast to the double-functioning element. In terms of perception it is dependent on something outside itself, and in whose direction it inflects. It is a directional form corresponding to directional space.

The interior of the church of the Madonna del Calcinaio in Cortona (137) is composed of a limited number of elements which are uninflected. Its windows and niches (212), pilasters and pediments, and the articulated elements of its altar, are independent wholes, simple in themselves and symmetrical in form and position. They add up to a greater whole. The interior of the pilgrimage church at Birnau in Bavaria (213), however, contains a diversity of inflections directed toward the altar. The complex curves of the vaults and arches, even the distortions of the pilaster capitals, inflect toward this center. The statues and the multitude of fragmental elements of the side altars (214)

212

213

214

218

219

215

216

220

217

are inflected parts, asymmetrical in form yet symmetrical in position, which integrate into a symmetrical whole. This subordination of parts corresponds to Wölfflin's "unified unity" of the Baroque—which he contrasts with the "multiple unity" of the Renaissance.

A comparison of the entrance fronts of Blenheim Palace (215) and Holkham Hall (216) illustrates the use of inflection on the exterior. Holkham Hall achieves an extensive whole through the addition of similar wholes which are always independent: most of its bays are pedimented pavilions which could stand alone as single buildings—Holkham Hall could almost be three buildings in a row. Blenheim achieves a complex whole through fragmental parts, separate but inflected. The last two bays of the central block, when taken alone, are dualities incomplete in themselves. But in relation to the whole they become inflected terminations to the central pavilion, and a confirmation of the pedimented center of the whole composition. The piers at the corners of the porch and the broken pediments above them are also terminal inflections, similarly reinforcing the center. The bays at the far extremities of this enormous façade form pavilions which are not inflected. They are perhaps expressive of the relative independence of the kitchen and stable wings. Vanbrugh's method of creating a strong whole in such a large and diverse if symmetrical façade follows the traditional Jacobean method of the century before: at Aston Hall (217) the wings of the forecourt façade and the towers, parapeted pediments, and windows inflect in position and/or shape toward its center.

The varying configurations of the wings and windows, roofs and ornaments of the orphanage of the Buon Pastore near Rome (218, 219, 220) are an orgy of inflections of enormous scope similar to the scale of Blenheim. This neo-Baroque complex by Armando Brazini, (bizarre in 1940 and admittedly questionable for an asylum for little girls) astonishingly composes a multitude of diverse parts into a difficult whole. At all levels of scale it is an example of inflections within inflections successively directed toward different centers—toward the short façade in the front, or the anticlimactically small dome near the center of the complex, with its unusually big cupola. When you stand close enough to see a smaller element of inflection, you sometimes need to turn almost 180 degrees to see its counterpart at a great distance. An element of suspense is introduced when you move around the enormous building. You are aware of elements related by inflection to elements already seen or not yet seen, like the unraveling of a symphony. As a fragment in plan and elevation, the asymmetrical composition of each wing is wrought with tensions and implications concerning the symmetrical whole.

At the scale of the town, inflection can come from the position of elements which are in themselves uninflected. In the Piazza del Popolo (221) the domes of the twin churches confirm each building as a separate whole, but their single towers, symmetrical themselves, become inflective because of their asymmetrical positions on each church. In the context of the piazza each building is a fragment of a greater whole and a part of a gateway to the Corso. At the smaller scale of Palladio's Villa Zeno (222) the asymmetrical positions of the symmetrical arched openings cause the end pavilions to inflect toward the center, thus enforcing the symmetry of the whole composition. This kind of inflection of asymmetrical ornament within a symmetrical whole is a dominant motif in Rococo architecture. For example, on the side altars at Birnau (214), and on the characteristic pairs of sconces (223), or andirons, doors, or other elements, the inflection of the rocaille is part of an asymmetry within a larger symmetry that exaggerates the unity yet creates a tension in the whole.

Direction is a means of inflection in the Villa Aldobrandini (224). Its front is articulated into additive parts or bays, but the unique diagonals of the fragmentary pediments on the end bays tend to direct the ends toward the center, and unify that dominating façade. In the plan of Monticello (225) the enclosing diagonal walls inflect the extremities toward the center focus. In Siena the distortion of its façade inflects the Palazzo Publico (226) toward its dominating piazza. Here distortion is a method of confirming the whole rather than of breaking it, as in the case of contradiction accommodated. Baroque details, such as coupled pilasters in the end bays of a series of pilastered bays, become devices of inflection because they create variations in rhythm to terminate a sequence. Such methods of inflection are largely used to confirm the whole—and since monumentality involves a strong expression of the whole, as well as a certain kind of scale, inflection becomes a device of monumentality as well.

Inflection accommodates the difficult whole of a duality as well as the easier complex whole. It is a way of

221

222

223

224

resolving a duality. The inflecting towers on the twin churches on the Piazza del Popolo resolve the duality by implying that the center of the whole composition is located in the space of the bisecting Corso. In Wren's Royal Hospital at Greenwich (227) the inflection of the domes by their asymmetrical position similarly resolves the duality of the enormous masses flanking the Queen's House. Their inflection further enhances the centrality and importance of this diminutive building. The unresolved dualities of the end pavilions facing the river, on the other hand, reinforce the unifying quality of the central axis by their own contrasting disunity.

225

The French chevet contrasts with the blunt termination of the English Gothic choir, because it inflects to terminate and enhance the whole. In the church of the Jacobins in Toulouse (228) the inflection of the chevet tends to resolve the duality of the nave, which is bisected by the row of columns. The apse in Furness' library at the University of Pennsylvania similarly resolves the duality formed by the arched interior wall opposite. One column bisects the nave at the end of the Late Gothic parish church at Dingolfing (229), a hall-type church, but the juxtaposition of the central bay and window behind, which evolve from the complex vaulting above, resolve the original duality. The directional inflecting of the side walls of the nave of the parish church in Rimella (230) counteracts the disunifying effect of the two bays of the nave. Their inflection toward the center increases enclosure and strengthens the whole. A minor intermediate bay also binds the major bays together.

226

Lutyens' work abounds in dualities. The duality of the entrance façade of the castle at Lambay (231), for instance, is resolved by the inflecting shape of the opening in the juxtaposed garden wall. In contemporary architecture rare examples of inflection are found in the vestigial broken pediments of Moretti's apartment house on the Via Parioli (10). They partially resolve the duality of the pair of wings which distinguish sets of apartments. The subtly balanced duality of Wright's Unity Temple (232) is devoid of inflections unless the directional entrance pedestal is one.

227

Modern architecture tends to reject inflection at all levels of scale. In the Tugendhat House no inflecting capital compromises the purity of the column's form, although the sheer forces in the supported roof plane must thus be

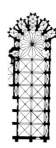

228

ignored. Walls are inflected neither by bases nor cornices nor by structural reinforcements, such as quoins, at corners. Mies' pavilions are as independent as Greek temples; Wright's wings are interdependent but interlocked rather than independent and inflected. However, Wright, in accommodating his rural buildings to their particular sites, has recognized inflection at the scale of the whole building. For example, Fallingwater is incomplete without its context—it is a fragment of its natural setting which forms the greater whole. Away from its setting it would have no meaning.

229

If inflection can occur at many scales—from a detail of a building to a whole building—it can contain varying degrees of intensity as well. Moderate degrees of inflection have a kind of implied continuity that affirms the whole. Extreme inflection literally becomes continuity. Today we emphasize our opportunities to express the literal continuities of structure and materials—such as the welded joint, skin structures, and reinforced concrete. Except for the flush joint of early Modern architecture, implied continuity is rare. The shadow joint of Mies' vocabulary tends to exaggerate separation. And Wright, especially, articulates a joint by a change in profile when there is a change in material—an expressive manifestation of the nature of materials in Organic architecture. But a contrast between expressive continuity and real discontinuity of structure and materials is a characteristic of the façade of Saarinen's dormitory at the University of Pennsylvania. In section its continuous curves defy the changes in materials, structure, and use. In the precise walls of Machu Picchu (233) the same profile continues between the built-up jointed masonry and the rock in situ. The arched shape of the opening of Ledoux's entrance at Bourneville (58) spans two kinds of structure (corbeled and arched) and two kinds of material (rusticated masonry at the top and smooth masonry at the bottom). Similar contradictions occur in Rococo furniture. Cabriole legs (234) disguise the joint and express continuity in their shape and ornament. The continuous grooves common to the leg and the seat-frame imply a continuity beyond inflection which is somewhat contradictory to the material and the structural relationship of these separate frame elements. The ubiquitous rocaille is another ornamental device for expressive continuity common to the architecture and furniture of the Rococo.

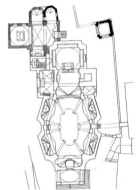

230

231

Some of Wright's early interiors (235) parallel in the

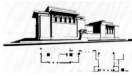

232

motif of the wood strip the rocaille-filled interiors of the Rococo (236). In Unity Temple and the Evans House (235) these strips are used on the furniture, walls, ceilings, light fixtures, and window mullions, and the pattern is repeated on the rugs. As in the Rococo, a continuous motif is used to achieve a strong whole expressive of what Wright called plasticity. He employed a method of implied continuity for valid expressive reasons, and in ironic contradiction to his dogma of the nature of materials and his expressed hatred of the Rococo.

233

On the other hand, an architecture of complexity and contradiction can acknowledge an expressive *dis*continuity, which belies a certain structural continuity. In the choir screen in the cathedral at Modena (237), where one uninflected element precariously supports another in its visual expression, or in the abrupt abutments of the uninflected wings of All Saints Church, Margaret Street (93), a formal discontinuity is implied where there is a structural continuity. Soane's Gate at Langley Park (238) is made up of three architectural elements totally uninflected and independent; besides the dominance of the middle element, it is the sculptural elements which are inflected and which give unity to the three parts.

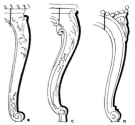

234

The Doric order (239) works a complex balance among extremes of both expressive and structural continuities and discontinuities. The architrave, the capital, and the shaft are noncontinuous structurally but only partially noncontinuous expressively. That the architrave sits on the capital is expressed by the uninflected abacus. But the echinus in relation to the shaft expresses structural continuity consistent with expressive continuity. The horizontal and vertical elements of Saarinen's T.W.A. Terminal and Frederick Kiesler's Endless House are without structural contradiction: they are continuous everywhere. However, precast concrete that is assembled offers ambiguous combinations of continuity and discontinuity, both structural and expressive. The surfaces of the Police Administration Building in Philadelphia include patterns of shadow joints separating precast elements whose curving inflections, however, evolve continuous profiles—a paradoxical play of continuity and discontinuity inherent in the expression and the structure of the architecture.

235

A kind of implied continuity or inflection is inherent in Maki's "group form." This, the third category in the designation of complex architecture he calls "collective

236

form," includes "generative" parts with their own "link-age," and wholes in which the system and unit are integral. He has referred to other characteristics of group form which indicate some of the implications of inflection in architecture. A consistency of the basic parts and their sequential relationship permit a growth in time, a consistency of human scale, and a sensitivity to the particular topography of the complex.

237

The "group form" contrasts with Maki's other basic category, the "mega-form." The whole, which is dominated by hierarchical relationships of parts rather than by the inherent inflective nature of the parts, can also be a characteristic of complex architecture. Hierarchy is implicit in an architecture of many levels of meaning. It involves configurations of configurations—the interrelationships of several orders of varying strengths to achieve a complex whole. In the plan of Christ Church, Spitalfields (240), it is the sequence of orders of supports—higher, lower, and middle; large, small, and medium—that make the hierarchical whole. Or in a palace façade of Palladio (48), it is the juxtapositions and adjacencies of parts (pilasters, windows, and mouldings) and the contrasts of large, small, and relatively important that conduct the eye to the image of the whole.

238

The dominant binder is another manifestation of the hierarchical relationships of parts. It manifests itself in the consistent pattern (the thematic kind of order) as well as by being the dominant element. This is not a difficult whole to achieve. In the context of an architecture of contradiction it can be a doubtful panacea, like the fallen snow which unifies a chaotic landscape. At a scale of the town in the Medieval period it is the wall or castle which is the dominant element. In the Baroque it is the axis of the street against which minor diversities play. (In Paris the rigid axis is confirmed by cornice heights, while in Rome the axis tends to zigzag and is punctuated by connecting piazzas with obelisks.) The axial binder in Baroque planning sometimes reflects a program devised by an autocracy, which could easily exclude elements that today must be considered. Arterial circulation can be a dominant device in contemporary urban planning. In fact, in the program the consistent binder is most often represented by circulation, and in construction the consistent binder is usually the major order of structure. It is an important device of Kahn's viaduct architecture and Tange's collective forms

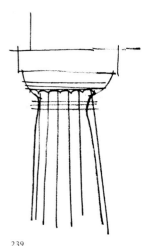

239

for Tokyo. The dominant binder is an expediency in renovations. James Ackerman has referred to Michelangelo's predilection for "symmetrical juxtaposition of diagonal accents in plan and elevation" in his design for St. Peter's, which was essentially a renovation of earlier construction. "By using diagonal wall-masses to fuse together the arms of the cross, Michelangelo was able to give St. Peter's a unity that earlier designs lacked." [48]

The dominant binder, as a third element connecting a duality, is a less difficult way of resolving a duality than inflection. For example, the big arch unambiguously resolves the duality of the double window of the Florentine Renaissance palazzo. The façade of the double church of S. Antonio and S. Brigidá by Fuga (241) is resolved by inflected broken pediments—but also by a third ornamental element, which dominates the middle. Similarly, the façade of S. Maria della Spina, Pisa (242) is dominated by a third pediment. In plan the domed bays of Guarini's church of the Immaculate Conception in Turin (14) are inflected in shape, but they are also resolved by a minor intermediate bay. The ornamental pediment at the center of the elevation of Charleval (243) is also a dominant third element, as are the gable and the stair at the front of the farmer's house near Chieti (244)—similar, in this context, to the function of the stair to the entrance of Stratford Hall, Virginia (245). There is no inflection in the composition of the Villa Lante (246), but an axis between the two equal pavilions, which focuses on a sculpture placed at a cross-axis, dominates the twin pavilions as a third element, thus emphasizing a whole.

But a more ambiguously hierarchical relationship of uninflected parts creates a more difficult perceptual whole. Such a whole is composed of equal combinations of parts. While the idea of equal combinations is related to the phenomenon both-and, and many examples apply to both ideas, both-and refers more specifically to contradiction in architecture, while equal combinations refer more to unity. With equal combinations the whole does not depend on inflection, or the easier relationships of the dominant binder, or motival consistency. For example, in the Porta Pia (110, 111) the number of each kind of element in the composition of the door and the wall is almost equal—no one element dominates. The varieties of shapes (rectangular, square, triangular, segmental, and round) being almost equal, the predominance of any one shape is also precluded,

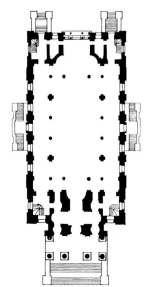

240

241

242

and the equal varieties of directions (vertical, horizontal, diagonal, and curving) have the same effect. There is similarly an equal diversity in the size of the elements. The equal combinations of parts achieve a whole through superimposition and symmetry rather than through dominance and hierarchy.

243

The window above Sullivan's portal in the Merchants' National Bank in Grinnell, Iowa (112), is almost identical to the Porta Pia in its juxtaposition of an equal number of round, square and diamond-shaped frames of equal size. The diverse combinations of number analyzed in his Columbia Bank façade (groups of elements involving one, two, and three parts) have almost equal value in the composition. However, there the unity is based upon the relation of horizontal layers rather than on superimposition. The Auditorium (104) exploits the complexity of directions and rhythms that such a program can yield. The simple semicircles of the wall ornament, structure, and segmental ceiling coves counteract, in plan and section, the complex curves of the proscenium arches, rows of seats, balcony slopes, boxes, and column brackets. These, in turn, play against the rectangular relationships of ceilings, walls, and columns.

244

This sense of the equivocal in much of Sullivan's work (at least where the program is more complex than that of a skyscraper) points up another contrast between him and Wright. Wright would seldom express the contradiction inherent in equal combinations. Instead, he resolved all sizes and shapes into a motival order—a single predominant order of circles or rectangles or diagonals. The Vigo Schmidt House project is a consistent pattern of triangles, the Ralph Jester House of circles, and the Paul Hanna House of hexagons.

245

Equal combinations are used to achieve a whole in Aalto's complex Cultural Center at Wolfsburg (78). He does not disperse the parts nor make them similar as Mies does at I.I.T. As I have pointed out before, he achieves a whole by combining an almost equal number of diagonal and rectangular elements. S. Maria delle Grazie in Milan (247) works equal combinations into an extreme form by contrasting opposite shapes in its exterior composition. The dominant triangle-rectangle composition in the front combines with the dominant circle-square composition in the back. Michelucci's church of the Autostrada (4), like the Church of the Holy Sepulchre in Jerusalem (plan only

246

illustrated in 110), consists of almost equal combinations of contrasting directions and rhythms in columns, piers, walls, and roofs. A similar composition is that of the Berlin Philharmonic Hall (248). The plastic forms of indigenous Mediterranean architecture (249) are simple in texture, but rectangles, diagonals, and segments are blatantly combined. Gaudí's dressing table in the Casa Güell (250) represents an orgy of contrasting dualities of form: extreme inflection and continuity are combined with violent adjacencies and discontinuities, complex and simple curves, rectangles and diagonals, contrasting materials, symmetry and asymmetry, in order to accommodate a multiplicity of functions in one whole. At the scale of furniture, the prevalent sense of the equivocal is expressed in the chair illustrated in (103). Its back configuration is curving and its front is rectangular. It is not dissimilar in its difficult composition to Aalto's bentwood chair illustrated in (251).

247

Inherent in an architecture of opposites is the inclusive whole. The unity of the interior of the Imatra church or the complex at Wolfsburg is achieved not through suppression or exclusion but through the dramatic inclusion of contradictory or circumstantial parts. Aalto's architecture acknowledges the difficult and subtle conditions of program, while "serene" architecture, on the other hand, works simplifications.

However, the obligation toward the whole in an architecture of complexity and contradiction does not preclude the building which is unresolved. Poets and playwrights acknowledge dilemmas without solutions. The validity of the questions and vividness of the meaning are what make their works art more than philosophy. A goal of poetry can be unity of expression over resolution of content. Contemporary sculpture is often fragmentary, and today we appreciate Michelangelo's unfinished Pietàs more than his early work, because their content is suggested, their expression more immediate, and their forms are completed beyond themselves. A building can also be more or less incomplete in the expression of its program and its form.

248

The Gothic cathedral, like Beauvais, for instance, of which only the enormous choir was built, is frequently unfinished in relation to its program, yet it is complete in the effect of its form because of the motival consistency of its many parts. The complex program which is a process, continually changing and growing in time yet at each stage at some level related to a whole, should be recognized as

249

essential at the scale of city planning. The incomplete program is valid for a complex single building as well.

Each of the fragmental twin churches on the Piazza del Popolo, however, is complete at the level of program but incomplete in the expression of form. The uniquely asymmetrically placed tower, as we have seen, inflects each building toward a greater whole outside itself. The very complex building, which in its open form is incomplete, in itself relates to Maki's "group form;" it is the antithesis of the "perfect single building"[49] or the closed pavilion. As a fragment of a greater whole in a greater context this kind of building relates again to the scope of city planning as a means of increasing the unity of the complex whole. An architecture that can simultaneously recognize contradictory levels should be able to admit the paradox of the whole fragment: the building which is a whole at one level and a fragment of a greater whole at another level.

250

In *God's Own Junkyard* Peter Blake has compared the chaos of commercial Main Street with the orderliness of the University of Virginia (252, 253). Besides the irrelevancy of the comparison, is not Main Street almost all right? Indeed, is not the commercial strip of a Route 66 almost all right? As I have said, our question is: what slight twist of context will make them all right? Perhaps more signs more contained. Illustrations in *God's Own Junkyard* of Times Square and roadtown are compared with illustrations of New England villages and arcadian countrysides. But the pictures in this book that are supposed to be bad are often good. The seemingly chaotic juxtapositions of honky-tonk elements express an intriguing kind of vitality and validity, and they produce an unexpected approach to unity as well.

251

It is true that an ironic interpretation such as this results partly from the change in scale of the subject matter in photographic form and the change in context within the frames of the photographs. But in some of these compositions there is an inherent sense of unity not far from the surface. It is not the obvious or easy unity derived from the dominant binder or the motival order of simpler, less contradictory compositions, but that derived from a complex and illusive order of the difficult whole. It is the taut composition which contains contrapuntal relationships, equal combinations, inflected fragments, and acknowledged dualities. It is the unity which "maintains, but only just maintains, a control over the clashing elements which compose it. Chaos is very near; its nearness, but its avoidance, gives . . . force."[50] In the validly complex building or cityscape, the eye does not want to be too easily or too quickly satisfied in its search for unity within a whole.

Some of the vivid lessons of Pop Art, involving contradictions of scale and context, should have awakened architects from prim dreams of pure order, which, unfortunately, are imposed in the easy Gestalt unities of the urban renewal projects of establishment Modern architecture and yet, fortunately are really impossible to achieve at any great scope. And it is perhaps from the everyday landscape, vulgar and disdained, that we can draw the complex and contradictory order that is valid and vital for our architecture as an urbanistic whole.

252

253

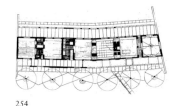

254

1. Project, Pearson House, Chestnut Hill, Pa., Robert Venturi, 1957. (254–259)

This project for a house was designed in 1957. It is a rare manifestation of the idea of multiple enclosure in my work because layers of enclosure require programs of a scale which I have not yet had the opportunity to exploit. It involves things in things and things behind things. It exploits the idea of contrasting spatial layers between the inside and the outside in the series of parallel walls in plan and in the open inner domes supported on diagonal frames in section; the idea of contrapuntal, rhythmic juxtaposition in the relation of the pier openings of the porch, and of the lower and upper windows and of the cupolas above the inner domes; and the idea of a series of spaces en suite which are general in shape and unspecific in function, separated by servant spaces specific in shape and function.

255

256

2. Renovations of the James B. Duke House, The Institute of Fine Arts, New York University, Robert Venturi, Cope and Lippincott, Associated Architects, 1959. (260–264)

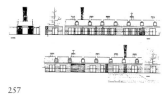

257

This mansion on upper Fifth Avenue was donated to the Institute of Fine Arts for use as a graduate school of the History of Art. It was designed by Horace Trumbauer in 1912; its interiors are by Alavoine. It is a copy of the Hôtel Labottière in Bordeaux on the outside, but it is blown up in scale and expanded in size—a Louis XIV scale in a Louis XVI building. Its Edwardian-Louis XVI details are exceptionally fine inside and out.

Our approach was to touch the inside as little as possible and to create harmony between the old and the new through contrasting juxtapositions: to separate the joint between the old and the new layers, to create change by adding to rather than modifying existing interior elements, to consider the new elements furniture rather than architecture and to use furniture and equipment which is commonplace and standard but enhanced by its uncommon

258

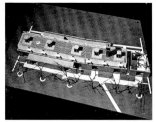

259

260

261

262

263

264

setting. These elements are the bentwood chairs, and steel library shelving by Remington Rand whose rectangular geometry was superimposed on that of the wall panels, but separated from them by specially designed brass brackets with a sliding detail to avoid the mouldings and—from the floor—by specially designed feet for the posts.

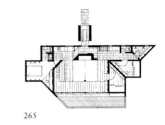

265

3. A Project for a Beach House, Robert Venturi, 1959. (265–271)

This weekend cottage, set among dunes on a beach, is to face the view of the ocean. It contains the simplest living accommodations, since the inhabitants are expected to spend most of the day on the beach. There is a small terrace on the ocean front and an open belvedere on the roof accessible by ladder and trap near the chimney.

The walls are balloon frame. The roof is wood-plank, toenailed so that the whole structure is a skin and a quasi-frame at the same time. An exception occurs at the inverse clerestory and at the front opening, where the span is exceptionally long, and where there are some expedient frame members: one post and some beams. This exception at the center makes the overall skin structure more apparent. (The floor is raised on wood piles and beams.)

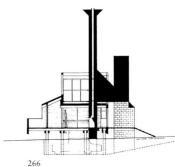

266

Expressively, the house has only two elevations: the front, oriented toward the sea, and the back for entering. It has no sides, so to speak; and the front is different from the back to express its directional inflection toward the ocean view. The fireplace-chimney at the rear center is a focus for the diagonal walls, which radiate, at first symmetrically, to form the inner spaces. Because of these complex configurations in elevation and plan, the roof is hipped and gabled at the same time, and its original symmetrical form is distorted at the extremities of the building by varying interior demands, and by exterior forces of orientation and view. At the pointed end, the exterior spatial-expressive demands of a house "without sides," directed toward the view, dominate the secondary spatial needs of a shower inside.

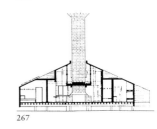

267

The whole outside surface is natural cedar shingles. Barge boards at the juncture of the roof and wall are minimized to make roof and wall look more continuous. The overlapping scales of the walls end in a skirt over the piles. Windows and porch openings punch varying holes in

268

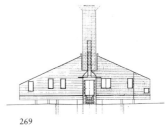

269

the continuous skin. The interior surfaces, which you see beyond the windows and within the porch, are contrastingly painted board surfaces, like the inside lining of a cape. The soffits of the openings, where the skin is cut, are painted a contrasting color. The shingles never touch the block chimney and its buttress, which divides near its base, and forms an open vestibule as well.

270

4. Headquarters Building, North Penn Visiting Nurse Association, Venturi and Short, 1960. (272–277)

Economy dictated a small building with conventional construction. The setting suggested a bold scale and a simple form to compensate for the large buildings around. The program dictated a complex inside, however, with varieties of spaces and special storage accommodations. Level parking for five staff cars on the steeply sloping site necessitated a retaining-walled auto court up front. And a pedestrian entrance with a minimum of outside steps similarly dictated a building immediately on the street.

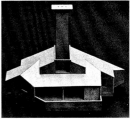

271

The resultant building is a distorted box both simple and complex. Because they are adjacent and similar in area, the court and the building set up a duality. The prow of the building acts as an inflection toward the court to resolve the duality, yet this distortion of the boxlike building simultaneously enforces the duality by complementing the curved wall at the opposite side of the parking court and by making the court more symmetrical and, therefore, independent of the building. The building at this point is more sculptural than architectural. Outside spatial forces dominate the interior forces, and it is designed from the outside in. The "awkward" interior created here is a subordinate space—merely the dentist's dark room.

Distortion works in the open side of the duality too: the slight curve of the retaining wall of the essentially rectangular court acknowledges and resists the pressure of the earth behind. The building box is distorted further by the east wall being parallel to the property line on this half-urban site. The surface of this originally plain box is also distorted. The windows on the front eat into it to provide integral overhangs toward the south. They also work integrally with the interior storage cabinets along that wall parallel to the roof framing.

272

273

The window indentations become large and few, sometimes coupled as well as set back, and they increase the scale of the small building. On the outside the scale of the lower windows is increased by the device of an extended frame—in this case, an applied wood moulding which accommodates the contradiction between the inside and outside scales. The complex positioning of the windows and openings of this façade also counteracts the simplicity of the box. They are not random but rather an originally regular rhythmic series distorted by interior complexities and circumstances.

274

The entrance on the court side at an intermediate landing is similarly complex in composition and bold in scale. It is made up almost equally of rectangular, diagonal, and segmental elements juxtaposed in a manner similar to some Renaissance doors. The rectangularity of the overall opening results from the block and plank structure of the building. In contrast the arch derives not from the nature of the materials and structure of its wood frame but from its symbolism as an entrance. Furthermore, and more important, as a circumstantial exception to the general order of the composition, it becomes a focus. The diagonal posts are expediencies similarly eventful: they shore up the center beam which supports the exceptional span of the roof planks at this opening, and they contrast with the post, which is vertical in the large window opening in the front, and more analogous in its position to the rectangular composition of the building. The big opening of the arch, appropriate in scale for a civic building, is juxtaposed upon the man-scaled doors, which are sheltered. There is a juxtaposition here of scales as well as shapes.

275

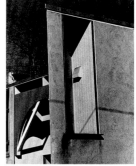

276

As for the program complexities of the interior, a hint of the storage intricacies is confirmed in the alternating recessions of windows and closets in the front. Another manifestation is the diagonal wall in the plan of the hall—another expedient distortion to accommodate the program complexities, which are squeezed inside their rigid enclosure.

The inconsistent floor and roof structure is similarly accommodating to the bearing walls of the rigid perimeter. The first floor front is a two-way slab accommodating the irregular interior bearing walls. Steel and wood joists for the floors and roof otherwise run variously parallel with the walls containing window storage combinations. Here, as in the entrance opening, the span is wood planks, which permit openings and windows to reach the thin cornice line

277

and make the box look more abstract. I have already mentioned the expedient post, vertical or diagonal, used when these surface spans become exceptionally long.

To emphasize thinness of surface and contradict the plasticity of the form of the box, the stucco surface is detailed with a minimum of corner-turnings by means of the wood-surfaced window reveals. I have "destroyed the box," not through spatial continuities but by circumstantial distortions.

5. F.D.R. Memorial Competition, Robert Venturi, John Rauch, George Patton, and Nicholas Gianopulos, 1960. (278–283)

This is a directional earth form that contrasts and thereby enhances the white sculptural forms of the three major Washington memorials already existing in the neighborhood. It is not a fourth sculptural form next to a parking lot. It is several things at once: an open, white marble promenade along the Potomac, which recognizes and utilizes the river's edge for pedestrians; an integral street, which accommodates the visitors' parking and is enclosed by canyon-like walls contrasting with the open avenues around; and, on the other side, it is a green grass mound which is a background for the cherry trees on the basin. The complex curve of the vertical section on the riverside accommodates a multiplicity of ramps, stairs, and passages, and a surface in bas-relief, which is interesting close-up—yet by its extreme continuity, suggested and actual, this curve contributes a scale appropriately monumental and visible from a distance. On the other side the continuous curve in section accommodates varying materials—grass, ground cover, vine, and concrete cap, in sequence and in relation to the varying degrees of the slope. A variety of spaces is afforded by the sequence of open park: tight vehicular canyon, close pedestrian passage, and open directional promenade, in turn relieved by details like trees and benches, and at the middle, on axis with the Washington obelisk, by a vision-slit spanned by a little vehicular bridge.

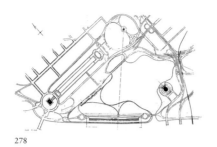

278

279

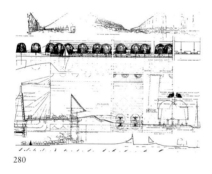

280

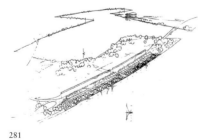

281

282

283

6. Renovation of Restaurant in West Philadelphia, Venturi and Short, 1962. (284–288)

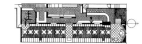

284

The design of this restaurant involved the renovation of two adjacent dilapidated row houses whose first floor fronts had been previously converted into shops. The restaurant was to be a modest neighborhood place that catered to students. The owners stipulated that it was to retain the simple atmosphere of the former establishment a block away, which had been known as "Mom's," where students "would feel comfortable in their T-shirts." The budget was to (and finally did) match the modest character of the place.

285

In the interior as well as on the façade, we acknowledged rather than disguised the duality of the existing layout with its bearing party-wall down the middle. Another design determinant was a second, parallel bearing-wall, which came to divide the small serving area from the kitchen. The west side accommodates the dining room with booths and tables; the east side the kitchen, serving areas, toilets, counter, and entry. Beyond the vestibule at the entry there are interior steps, which make the transition to the higher level of the first floor of the former houses. On the extreme east side is the foyer to the future apartments above.

286

We decided to exploit rather than disguise the modest budget, and in keeping with the modest character of the place in which catsup bottles dot every table, we tended to use conventional means and elements throughout but in such a way as to make the common things take on a new meaning in their new context. This was also a reaction to the typically over-designed "modern" fixtures available today. For the main lighting fixtures we used large-size white porcelain R.L.M.'s—an old-fashioned industrial fixture that is solid but cheap and, in the context we gave it, elegant. The chairs were Thonet bentwood, which are also almost anonymously designed objects, although now perhaps becoming chi-chi. The booths were designed not as the exaggeratedly low, pseudo-luxuriously upholstered types that expose the sitter but as the more traditional, high kind with comfortable but modest padding and with an appropriate sense of privacy. The air conditioning ducts were exposed for economy and to create the same kind of incidental functional ornament that developed from the exposed mechanical ceiling fans of the past. The ceiling is acoustic tile, the floors tinted concrete and resilient tile.

The wall ornamentation consists of surprisingly cheap painted patterns on the plaster above the wainscoting of the booths. The patterns of the letters spelling the proprietor's name, which extend almost the whole length of the room, have the character of conventional stencils. On the facing wall a direct reflection is juxtaposed against the "windows" to the open kitchen. These illogicalities emphasize the more ornamental function of the typography. The enormous letters create a scale and unity appropriate to a public place and make a contrast to the inevitable individual scale of the multiple tables and booths. Besides the letters, stripes make old-fashioned borders, which both distinguish and camouflage the junction of wall and ceiling. The color scheme admits a light value on the ceiling and a medium value on the floor. The walls continue the duality by being medium in value at the bottom half (the 5 foot wainscoting) and light in value above. The colors are secondary and cheerful but masculine in character. The colors on the sign outside are unrelated to those inside because the outside is different from the inside. They are primary and more vivid.

287

288

Since this restaurant is composed of two houses, its new façade is a juxtaposition of one and two elements— again a play in dualities. The old row houses, which have an almost continuous cornice, are identical in the upper stories. Duality is minimized by painting these stories an allover dark, neutral gray. A duality is necessarily emphasized on the ground floor by the central structural pier between large openings. The face of the wall is left undisturbed except for the applied dark gray. Within the frames of the two openings a contrastingly new and varied wall treatment—concave on the entrance side, convex on the other—occurs. These differences further emphasize the dual-ity on the ground floor of the façade.

But it is the porcelain-enameled sign at the level of the second floor that boldly concludes the simultaneous play of duality and unity, derived from the existing composition of the building. In its extension across the whole front the sign encourages unity; yet in its division of colors—blue on the right and yellow on the left—it points up the duality of the original building. In the continuity of the punched letters on white plastic, continuity across is reestablished.

The cup similarly attracts the eye by being unifying and disrupting at once. With it the sign evolves from two

112

dimensions to three, so that it can be seen by pedestrians as they approach parallel to the façade, in contrast to the flat part of the sign which can be seen at a distance. The cup's leaves, as the central transition between the blue and yellow sides, are alternately blue and yellow and change visually as you move past them. At night the letters become translucent white light, and the cup was to have been outlined in neon before the sign was modified by the owners. The bold scale of the letters is appropriate to their advertising function. And the division of the word plays up the duality and catches the eye reluctant to read advertisements.

In the end we were one-upped by the owners whose changes made a parody of our parody.

7. Meiss House Projects, Princeton, N. J., Venturi and Short, 1962. (289–295)

The site for this house in Princeton was a very large corner lot, flat and facing south toward the back with a view onto an old stable and a field of the Institute for Advanced Studies. It contained some patches of young trees and a row of old apple trees. The program called for a large study for the professor, easily accessible from the front door and from his small bedroom; plenty of particularized storage space, and an indoor swimming pool, in addition to the usual rooms in a medium-sized house. The clients liked privacy and plenty of sun inside.

The composition of Scheme One is a duality. From the front it superimposes a long gable-roofed element on the back of a shed-roofed one. Essentially, the front zone contains entrances, circulation, storage, services, and swimming pool, and it shields the back element, which contains the rooms for living. Upstairs in the front are two guest rooms, one of which the wife would also use as an office. The violent meeting of these independent roof forms seen from the front allows various clerestory windows for the shed-roofed back zone.

The duality is resolved by the perimeter, especially severe at the sides, which contains the two elements and contributes unity to the composition at this level. Also, in plan the back wall looking onto the long terrace is particularly complex in window indentations—which modify the sunlight or affect the interior space—in contrast with the

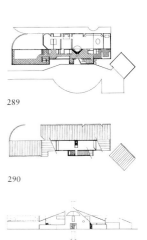

289

290

291

292

113

severe front wall. The front wall's irregular window openings balance the otherwise over-symmetrical pediment façade. The wall in front, a third superimposed element, and the garage, slanted in plan to suggest an auto court, imply enclosure.

The clients did not like Scheme One because they thought a linear plan precluded privacy outside in the back. Therefore the essentially L-shaped plan evolved into a similarly sunny and particularly complex character in the back walls, which contrasted with the severe, closed character of the front walls of the L. However, the complex roofs here meld into each other rather than abut violently. The upstairs bedrooms, windows, and balcony are carved within these roofs so as not to break their continuity with the dormers. But the shed-roof, entrance-front space does abut the other roofs, and the resultant clerestory window hints from the front at the complexity in the back. The fenced service yard, pointed at the end, emphasizes the wall-like protective function on the front or outside perimeter of the L. The clients didn't like this scheme either.

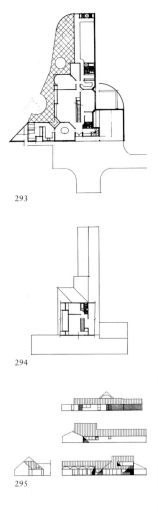

293

294

8. Guild House, Friends Housing for the Elderly, Philadelphia, Venturi and Rauch, Cope and Lippincott, Associated Architects, 1960–1963. (296–304)

The program required 91 apartments of varying types with a common recreation room, to house elderly people who want to remain in their old neighborhood. Local zoning limited the building height to six stories.

The small urban site faces south on Spring Garden Street. The interior program suggested a maximum of apartments facing south, southeast, and southwest for light and for the interesting activity of the street—yet the urban character of the street suggested a building that would not be an independent pavilion, but instead would recognize the spatial demands of the street in front. This results in a building inflected in shape, whose front is different from its back. The front façade is separated from the back at its top ends where the common room terraces occur in order to emphasize the vestigial role of the street façade. The contrastingly intricate side façades, more sensitive to interior than exterior spatial demands in their exact configurations, accommodate the need for maximum southeast and south-

295

114

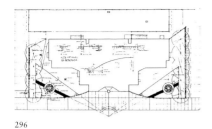

296

297

298

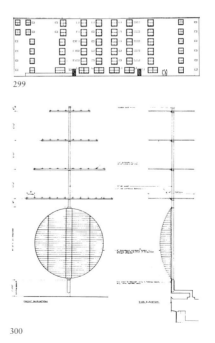

299

300

west light, views, and garden space below.

The interior spaces are defined by intricate mazes of walls, which accommodate the very complex and varied program of an apartment house (as opposed to an office building, for example), and the irregular framing allowed by flat plate construction. There is a maximum of interior volume and a minimum of corridor space. The corridor is an irregular and varied residual space rather than a tunnel.

Economy dictated not "advanced" architectural elements, but "conventional" ones. We did not resist this. The dark brown brick walls with double-hung windows recall traditional Philadelphia row houses or even the tenement-like backs of Edwardian apartment houses. Their effect is uncommon, however, because they are subtly proportioned and unusually big. The change in scale of these almost banal elements contributes an expression of tension and a quality to these façades, which now read as both conventional and unconventional forms at the same time.

The big round exposed column at the center of the street façade is polished black granite. It accommodates and emphasizes the exceptional entrance opening on the ground floor, and it contrasts with the white, glazed brick area, which extends to the middle of the second floor on this small section of the street façade. The balcony railings on this floor, like those on the other floors, are perforated steel plate, but here they are painted white rather than black to create a continuity of surface in this area despite the change in material. The central window on the top floor reflects the special spatial configuration of the common room inside and relates to the entrance below, increasing the scale of the building on the street and at the entrance. Its arched shape also permits a very big opening to penetrate the wall and yet remain a hole in a wall rather than a void in a frame. The television antenna atop this axis and beyond the otherwise constant height line of the building strengthens this axis of scale-change in the zone of the central façade, and expresses a kind of monumentality similar to that at the entrance at Anet. The antenna, with its anodized gold surface, can be interpreted two ways: abstractly, as sculpture in the manner of Lippold, and as a symbol of the aged, who spend so much time looking at T.V.

The ornamental line created by a row of white bricks contradictorily intersects the row of upper windows, but it terminates the otherwise plain façade. With the area of white glazed bricks on the front below, it also sets

301

302

303

304

up a new and larger scale of three stories, juxtaposed on the other smaller scale of six stories demarked by the layers of windows.

9. Residence in Chestnut Hill, Pa., Venturi and Rauch, 1962. (305–316)

This building recognizes complexities and contradictions: it is both complex and simple, open and closed, big and little; some of its elements are good on one level and bad on another; its order accommodates the generic elements of the house in general, and the circumstantial elements of a house in particular. It achieves the difficult unity of a medium number of diverse parts rather than the easy unity of few or many motival parts.

The inside spaces, as represented in plan and section, are complex and distorted in their shapes and interrelationships. They correspond to the complexities inherent in the domestic program as well as to some whimsies not inappropriate to an individual house. On the other hand, the outside form—as represented by the parapeted wall and the gable roof which enclose these complexities and distortions —is simple and consistent: it represents this house's public scale. The front, in its conventional combinations of door, windows, chimney and gable, creates an almost symbolic image of a house.

The contradiction between inside and outside, however, is not total: inside, the plan as a whole reflects the symmetrical consistency of the outside; outside, the perforations in the elevations reflect the circumstantial distortions within. Concerning the inside, the plan is originally symmetrical with a central vertical core from which radiate two almost symmetrical diagonal walls that separate two end spaces in front from a major central space in back. This almost Palladian rigidity and symmetry is distorted, however, to accommodate to the particular needs of the spaces: the kitchen on the right, for instance, varies from the bedroom on the left.

A more violent kind of accommodation occurs within the central core itself. Two vertical elements—the fireplace-chimney and the stair—compete, as it were, for central position. And each of these elements, one essentially solid, the other essentially void, compromises in its shape and

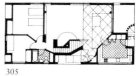
305

306

307

308

309

310

311

312

313

314

315

position—that is, inflects toward the other to make a unity of the duality of the central core they constitute. On one side the fireplace distorts in shape and moves over a little, as does its chimney; on the other side the stair suddenly constricts its width and distorts its path because of the chimney.

This core dominates as the center of the composition at this level; but at the level of its base, it is a residual element dominated itself by the spaces around it. On the living room side its shape is rectangular, and parallel to the important rectangular order of the important space there. Toward the front it is shaped by a diagonal wall accommodating to the also important and unique directional needs of the entrance space in its transition from big outer opening to inner entrance doors. The entrance space also competes for center position here. The stair, considered as an element alone in its awkward residual space, is bad; in relation to its position in a hierarchy of uses and spaces, however, it is a fragment appropriately accommodating to a complex and contradictory whole and as such it is good. From still another point of view its shape is not awkward: at the bottom the stair is a place to sit, as well as ascend, and put objects later to be taken upstairs. And this stair, like those in Shingle Style houses, also wants to be bigger at its base to accommodate to the bigger scale of the first floor. The little "nowhere stair" from the second floor similarly accommodates awkwardly to its residual core space: on one level, it goes nowhere and is whimsical; at another level, it is like a ladder against a wall from which to wash the high window and paint the clerestory. The change in scale of the stair on this floor further contrasts with that change of scale in the other direction at the bottom.

316

The architectural complexities and distortions inside are reflected on the outside. The varying locations and sizes and shapes of the windows and perforations on the outside walls, as well as the off-center location of the chimney, contradict the overall symmetry of the outside form: the windows are balanced on each side of the dominating entrance opening and chimney-clerestory element in the front, and the lunette window in the back, but they are asymmetrical. The protrusions above and beyond the rigid outside walls also reflect the complexity inside. The walls in front and back are parapeted to emphasize their role as screens behind which these inner intricacies can protrude. Indentations of the windows and porch on the sides at all but one of the corners, increase the screenlike quality of the front and back walls in the same way as the parapets do at their tops.

When I called this house both open and closed as well as simple and complex, I was referring to these contradictory characteristics of the outside walls. First, their parapets along with the wall of the upper terrace in the back, emphasize horizontal enclosure yet permit an expression of openness behind them at the upper terrace, and above them at the chimney-clerestory protrusion. Second, the consistent shape of the walls in plan emphasizes rigid enclosure, yet the big openings, often precariously close to the corners contradict the expression of enclosure. This method of walls—layered for enclosure, yet punctured for openness—occurs vividly at the front center, where the outside wall is superimposed upon the two other walls housing the stair. Each of these three layers juxtaposes openings of differing size and position. Here is layered space rather than inter-penetrated space.

The house is big as well as little, by which I mean that it is a little house with big scale. Inside the elements are big: the fireplace is "too big" and the mantel "too high" for the size of the room; doors are wide, the chair rail high. Another manifestation of big scale inside is a minimum of subdivisions of space—also for the sake of economy, the plan minimizes purely circulation space. Outside the manifestations of big scale are the main elements, which are big and few in number and central or symmetrical in position, as well as the simplicity and consistency of the form and silhouette of the whole, which I have already described. In back the lunette window is big and dominating in its shape and position. In front the entrance loggia is wide, high, and central. Its big scale is emphasized by its contrast with the other doors, smaller in size yet similar in shape; by its shallowness for its size; and by the expedient position of the inner entrance behind it. The applied wood moulding over the door increases its scale, too. The dado increases the scale of the building all around because it is higher than you expect it to be. These mouldings affect the scale in another way also: they make the stucco walls even more abstract, and the scale, usually implied by the nature of materials, more ambiguous or noncommital.

The main reason for the large scale is to counterbalance the complexity. Complexity in combination with small scale in small buildings means busyness. Like the other organized complexities here, the big scale in the small building achieves tension rather than nervousness—a tension appropriate for this kind of architecture.

The setting of the house is a flat, open, interior site, enclosed at its boundaries by trees and fences. The house sits near the middle, like a pavilion, with no planting at all near it. The driveway axis perpendicular to the middle of the house is distorted in its position by the circumstantial location of a sewer main at the curb of the street.

The abstract composition of this building almost equally combines rectangular, diagonal, and curving elements. The rectangles relate to the just dominant order of the spaces in plan and section. The diagonals relate to directional space at the entrance, to particular relationships of the directional and nondirectional spaces within the rigid enclosure on the first floor, and to the enclosing and water-shedding function of the roof. The curves relate to the directional-spatial needs at the entry and outside stair; to spatial-expressive needs in section in the dining room ceiling, which is contradictory to the outside slope of the roof; and to the symbolism of the entrance and its big scale, which is produced by the moulding on the front elevation. The exceptional point in the plan refers to the expedient column support, which contrasts with the otherwise wall-bearing structure of the whole. These complex combinations do not achieve the easy harmony of a few motival parts based on exclusion—based, that is, on "less is more." Instead they achieve the difficult unity of a medium number of diverse parts based on inclusion and on acknowledgement of the diversity of experience.

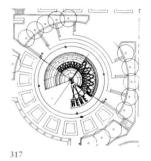
317

10. Fountain Competition, Philadelphia Fairmount Park Art Commission, Venturi and Rauch, Denise Scott Brown, 1964. (317–322)

This fountain was to be located within the open city block that terminates the Benjamin Franklin Parkway in front of City Hall. The block is common to the gridiron plan of the center of the city and is surrounded by streets with plenty of local traffic. Beyond it, except along the through-axis to the Parkway, looms a jumble of high office buildings. The interior of the almost square block contains an existing round pavilion called the Information Center.

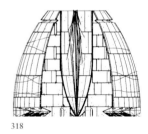
318

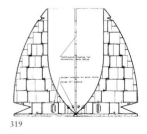
319

The landscaping and paving layout, including the 90 foot diameter basin for the fountain itself, were elements established by the competition program. The Benjamin Franklin Parkway is a boulevard whose axis is about a mile in length, and diagonal to and intersecting with the normal gridiron plan of the city. It connects City Hall with the Art Museum and Fairmount Park beyond.

320

In the other direction it can also be considered an extension of the park into the center of the city because its green trees make a continuity with the park itself, and it is also under legal jurisdiction of the Fairmount Park Commission. The Parkway acts as an important arterial approach to the center of the city and focuses on the dominant form of City Hall—the field against which the fountain is to be viewed. City Hall is light in color, large in size and scale, and ornate in pattern and silhouette. These characteristics of space, form, scale, and circulation, which make up the context of the fountain, largely determine its form.

321

The form is big and bold so that it will read against its background of big buildings and amorphous space, and also from the relatively long distance up the Parkway. Its plastic shape, curving silhouette, and plain surface also contrast boldly with the intricate rectangular patterns of the buildings around, although they are analogous to some of the mansard roof shapes on City Hall. This was not meant to be an intricate Baroque fountain to be read only close-up, or from a car stalled in traffic.

322

But the action of the water itself, as well as the context of the surroundings, determines the particularities of the sculpture's form. The scale of the water's action matches that of the sculpture: the central jet is 60 feet high and relates to the scale as well as to the axis of the Parkway. Its constant stream is shielded from the prevailing wind by the concave, inner surface of the sculptural form. It is exposed only toward the Parkway, and it is set off by the dark background of the enclosure. From most parts of the plaza only the reverberations of the great jet within the misty and mossy artificial grotto are evident. The large aluminum shield corresponds to little glass shields that protect the flame from drafts in some kinds of old-fashioned candelabra.

If the inner surface of the sculpture is concave to accommodate to the large-scale water action there, the outer

122

surface is convex to accommodate to the small-scale water action outside. This consists of a constant sheet of water issuing from a weir near the top of the surface and continuously dripping from its lower edge into the pool. The legend HERE BEGINS FAIRMOUNT PARK is glimpsed through a screen of droplets. This waterfall, with the polished, elongated letters on the sloping surface of the base behind, relates to the scale of the individual walking around the immediate plaza and is designed to engage his interest.

Lettering is traditional on monuments. The legend designates the dramatic penetration of the biggest urban park in the world into the heart of the city. When the legend is read from the front elevation it appears to say PARK HERE, not inappropriately for a monument over an underground parking lot.

The central jet is spotlighted by quartz lamps recessed in the base. In the winter, when the jet is inactive, incandescent lamps with amber lenses flood the angular maze of the in-between core structure with yellow light. The central space is then dark. The angled base is floodlighted by amber-lensed incandescent lamps. This continuous band contrasts with the looming dark body above, and at close range it illuminates the legend.

The material is aluminum to lighten the weight on the spans of the garage below. Its surface is sandblasted to promote a dark, mat, warm gray finish. The sheets are welded, but the joints are not ground smooth. The structure is a skin structure with stacked, bent-plates inside (themselves bent into "Z" sections), which act both as spacers between the contradictory inside and outside silhouettes and as integral bracing, like the inner corrugations of laminated cardboard box sections. The geometry of the inner plates is angular, and it contacts the curvilinear surfaces of the outer plates at welded points. This airy poché is exposed at the openings of the enclosure, back and front. A series of vertical manholes for maintenance are located in the lower plates. These contribute a scale that contrasts with the monumental scale of the whole.

This fountain is big and little in scale, sculptural and architectural in structure, analogous and contrasting in its context, directional and nondirectional, curvilinear and angular in its form, it was designed from the inside out and from the outside in.

11. Three Buildings for a Town in Ohio, Venturi and
    Rauch, 1965. (323–347)

323

The three buildings for a town in Ohio are a town
hall, a Y.M.C.A., and a public library, or rather an extensive
addition to one. These buildings relate to each other urban-
istically and to the center of the town they are a part of.
They are a part of the beginning stage as well, of a larger
plan for the renewal of the center of the town which is the
design responsibility of planning consultants whom we are
working under.

The town hall: the town hall is like a Roman temple
in its general proportions, and also because it is free-standing, but—in contrast with a Greek temple—a directional
building whose front is more important than its back.
What corresponds to the base, the giant columns and the
pediment of the porch of the temple is, in this city hall, the
partially disengaged wall in front with its giant arched
opening superimposed on the three-storied wall beyond. I
like Louis Sullivan's use of the giant arch to give image,
unity, and monumental scale to some of his late banks which
are important but small buildings on the main streets of mid-
Western towns. The change in size and scale in the front of
the town hall is analogous also to the false fronts of western
towns, and for the same reason: to acknowledge the urban
spatial demands of the street. But this building has two
settings at once. Besides its position as an important if
smallish, building along Main Street, it also sits at the end
of the central plaza across Main Street where it terminates
the longitudinal axis of the plaza. Also, to the observer on
Main Street the building rests right on the ground with its
first floor always visible as an integral base; from within the
plaza which is lower than Main Street, however, the first
floor is obscured in perspective by the elevation and depth
of the street immediately in front of it and by the ramped
steps leading up which form another kind of base for the
building. In this context the arch of the façade appears to
spring directly from a different and greater-scaled base. The
same building in different contexts is read in different
ways.

The contradiction in scale and character between the
front and back of this building derives from the particular
program inside as well as the urban setting outside. The
dichotomy in the program of a town hall between the
monumental spaces for the mayor and the council on one

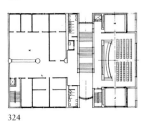

324

325

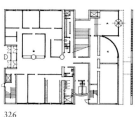

326

hand, and the routine offices for the administrative departments on the other hand are often explicitly articulated into a pavilion for the former connected with an office slab for the latter, a composition based on the Pavillon Suisse or perhaps the Armée du Salut. (Another approach perhaps is to base the town hall on another composition of Le Corbusier's, La Tourette, where the composition looks incomplete but is essentially closed.) But this scheme for a small town hall accommodates these two kinds of spaces within a relatively simple enclosure for the sake of scale and economy. (The mayor said he wanted "a sensible, square, masonry building.") The monumental and more ceremonial rooms up front are unique and static—with the growth of the town only a few more council members will ever be added and there will never be more than one mayor—while the small scale, but relatively extensive and flexible office spaces behind are expansible: you can add on to the back. This is an open-ended building in the back because bureaucracy is always growing. Between the front and the back is a common zone for vertical circulation and services. The first floor contains police facilities in the back and the main entrance in the front. It is assumed that the public will frequent less and less a town hall so that the bill-paying and information areas are not on the ground floor. The small repetitive windows toward the back and the greater height of the buttressed front façade from the side reflect further these interior variations of function. The structure is concrete bearing wall forming parallel or perpendicular zones spanned by concrete joists. In the back zone there is an interior column in the center to facilitate flexibility within the bearing walls. The wide corridor or gallery which is anticipated here is appropriate for an office area with wider public use. Since the bearing walls are concrete, the openings can be very big. The surface material is dark brick similar to but not matching the existing big factory in the center of the town. The front screen wall, however, is faced with very thin white marble slabs to reemphasize the contrast between the front and the back. On the front also, the juxtaposition of the big arched opening on the smaller windows of the wall behind changes to the same plane at the council chamber on the third floor. The window here matches the big scale of the front screen: it consists of one piece of glass about 28 by 30 feet. The enormous flag is perpendicular to the street so that it reads from up the street like a commercial sign.

327

328

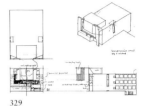

329

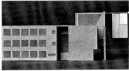

330

331

The Y.M.C.A.: this building follows closely the conventional, rather explicit, and complex recommendations for the interior program of a Y.M.C.A. of this size. Our variations might include the zoning of the athletic spaces behind, the social spaces up front, the elevation above the basement level of the extensive locker rooms, and some characteristics which come from the sloping site along the length of the building and the need for entrances in the back from the parking and from the anticipated shopping area behind, as well as in the front from the plaza. But the position of the building along the side of the plaza and opposite the existing, dominating factory had the greatest effect on the outside expression of the building.

This building had to be big in scale to complement and not be overpowered by the factory opposite. This was accomplished by the size, number, and relationship of the elements of the front façade. The openings in the wall were few and big to increase the scale. The relationship of the openings which are the dominant elements of the façade make up a relatively constant rhythm without focus in the center or emphasis at the terminations. This characteristic also gives greater unity and scale to the building. In its overall composition it does not create a beginning, middle, and end which make up three things; it is just one continuous thing resulting from the constant, even boring, rhythm. In this way it can compete with the factory opposite which is bigger as a whole but smaller in its individual parts. And it is appropriately secondary to the smaller city hall on another side of the plaza. The front façade, like that of the city hall, is "false"—a free-standing wall—contradictory in relation to the interior space. The almost constant rhythm of grid-opening is played against the smaller and more irregular rhythms of the two-story building-proper behind. A contrapuntal juxtaposition contrasts the "boredom" of the false façade with the "chaos" of the back façade which reflects the interior circumstantial complexities. The front wall contains a buffer zone between building and plaza for skaters in the winter on the left side, and an outdoor niche with fireplace for them on the right where it becomes a retaining wall, and also a great ramp on axis with the existing church on Main Street. The structure is concrete bearing wall, which allows big openings close together—it is indeed, a quasi-frame construction. The dark face brick relates to the existing factory and increases the unity of the plaza and the center of the town.

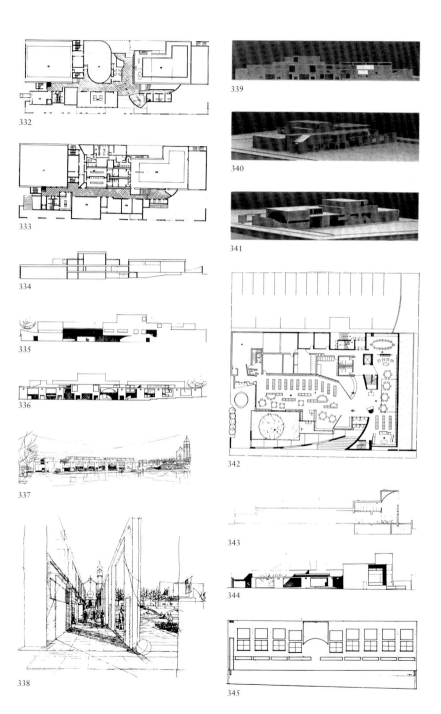

332

333

334

335

336

337

338

339

340

341

342

343

344

345

The library addition: the interior program is almost entirely conventional. Our approach was to wrap around rather than add to, the existing buff brick building with new interior spaces on the back and the north side and with a new detached wall in front which contains a court in its residual space. The old building is covered over but modified as little as possible for economy. The wraparound wall, in its big scale and dark brick material increases the unity of Main Street. Through the big, grilled openings in the front outer wall is glimpsed the older, lighter, small-scale building so that its architecture is respected. From close-up the new is juxtaposed upon the old.

346

347

12. Copley Square Competition, Venturi and Rauch, Gerod Clark and Arthur Jones, 1966. (348–350)

For a large open space in an American city Copley Square in Boston is quite contained—on the south by the hotel, on the west by the Public Library, at the northwest corner by the new Old South Church and by the row of commercial buildings on the north. But the open corner toward the southwest where the diagonal Huntington Avenue is to be terminated, and the leaking corner toward the southeast between Trinity Church and Copley Plaza tend to weaken the sense of enclosure. And toward the east the space is enclosed ambiguously by Trinity Church itself which tends to sit in the square rather than along it. The varying heights, rhythms and scales of these buildings as well as the streets which separate them from the center of the space, further diminish the spatial unity of the existing square.

The rules of the competition confined the area to be designed within the block defined by the interior sidewalks of the three streets and the diagonal sidewalk along the northwest side of Trinity Church; of course, we could not change nor anticipate change in any of the disparate buildings around the space.

So we made a non-piazza; we filled up the space to define the space.

We filled it with non-dense matter, a consistent but rich grid of trees. These trees are too far apart to make a traditional bosquet, yet too dense to be read as discreet elements. When you walk among them they are far enough

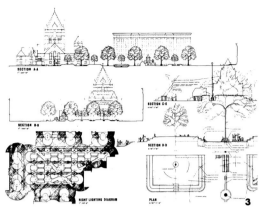

348

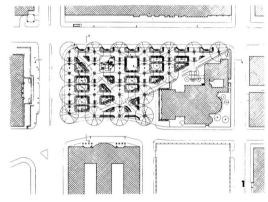

349

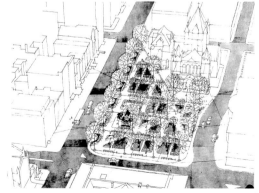

350

apart to filter light with variety and to veil the church tantalizingly (you have to struggle to see the great façade) but from without, along the streets, they are a rigid form which defines the space and identifies the place. Their form as a whole, however (unlike our fountain project for Philadelphia in a different kind of context), is not a sculptural form sitting *in* a space because that would compete with Trinity Church. It is an overall, three-dimensional repetitive pattern without a climax, separated from the surroundings by the border of streets, and in contrast with Trinity Church which at one level of focus is accent enough in the whole composition. In the context of the "boring" consistent grid inside the square the chaotic buildings to the north become "interesting" and vital elements of the composition.

Besides the mosaic of trees and tall lampposts, there is at a lower level, a grid-order made up of stepped mounds about four feet high between walkways. This grid reflects in miniature the gridiron pattern of the part of Boston surrounding Copley Square. It imitates the hierarchy of streets, big, little and medium found in the real city. Like the real gridiron city, it contains diagonal "avenues" which facilitate circulation and whose juxtaposition creates exceptional, residual blocks.

Within the blocks of the lower grid is another pattern of benches, trash cans and drains in phase with the grid of trees and lampposts. This furniture, like the lampposts, is composed of conventional elements given new value by their new context. These "vulgar" elements are not specially designed; they are only thoughtfully chosen. (Compare these aluminum lampposts with the tastefully exotic bronze-like, anodized aluminum ones around the green in New Haven.) Materials are similarly plain except for the precious brick areas under the benches which make more vivid the banality of the blacktop walkways and the precast concrete of the stepped block sections, gutters and drains. There is grass only on top of the blocks where it will receive a minimum of wear. Rows of flowers atop the blocks border the avenues to extend the width of the avenues visually. Where the blocks are cut through, the cheek walls have very bold inscriptions of nursery rhymes, etc., cast into the concrete to interest children who cannot see over the blocks.

The grid of trees, lampposts and street furniture and that of the hierarchy of streets are out of phase with each other along the north-south axes. These slight irregularities of rhythms contrast with the violent irregularities which come from the juxtapositions of the diagonal avenues upon the gridiron pattern of the streets which are manifest as I have said, in the residual, fragmentary blocks, triangular and polygonal in shape. Indeed, because of these contrapuntal juxtapositions of diagonals and the truncations at the borders almost no typical or pure blocks remain. And of these, two are made exceptional. One block is reversed in section: that is, depressed exactly in the manner that the typical ones are elevated in order to make a little piazza to sit in in contrast with the typical walks you sit along; the other is level to contain a miniature replica of Trinity Church. The fragmentary blocks along the north side, gouged out with niches to sit in, are further exceptions.

This play of exceptions to the order, slight or violent, creates tensions within the grid that contradict the boringness of the pattern. But there is a play of scale too which creates within the pattern a kind of monumentality as well as ambiguity and tension. It involves a particular relationship of size and proportion. The juxtapositions of streets of different size on the grid results in blocks of different size but similar proportion, and a combination of trees, one big and two little, within the grid pattern, makes for a similar relationship of elements of different size but same proportion. (This idea is anathema to orthodox Modern architects who hold that change in size means change in proportion to reflect exclusively a structural basis for form and proportion. On the other hand Jasper Johns in his paintings juxtaposes conventionally proportioned flags which are big, little and medium in size.) The species of trees was chosen with this in mind: the form of the mature Plane tree, about 60 feet in height, has a similar proportion to that of the mature Scholar tree, about 25 feet high. The element which most vividly exemplifies this idea is the replica in cast concrete of Trinity Church in front of Trinity Church.

There is a reason for this little replica and that of the gridiron "streets" too—a reason other than those reasons already mentioned effecting ambiguity, tension, scale and monumentality: the miniature imitation is a means for explaining to a person the whole which he is in but cannot see all of. To reassure the individual by making the whole comprehensible in this way within a part is to contribute a sense of unity to a complex urban whole. This kind of imitation in miniature involves as well an imitation of one aspect of life. To condense experience and make it more vivid, to pretend, that is, is a characteristic of play: children play house. Adults play Monopoly. In this square it is a simulation of urban circulation and space. The little church is play sculpture for children too.

Another characteristic of play which is lacking in Modern, architect-designed urban spaces is the opportunity for choice and improvisation: that is, for people to use the same spaces in many different ways including ways the spaces are not explicitly designed for. The grid, whether in the form and scale of the town plan or countryside of the American mid-west or the columned interiors of a mosque in Cairo or Cordova, allows for improvisation and variety of use. In a Victorian mansion there are probably more ways of using the eventful stairway than of walking through and sitting in a typical modern square. When form follows function explicitly, the opportunities for implicit functions decrease. There are probably more ways to use this square which is "just a grid" than there are to use those which are interesting, sensitive and human. And more important, there are more ways to *see* it. It is like the intricate pattern of a plaid fabric. From a distance it is an overall repetitive pattern—from a great distance, indeed, it is a plain blur—but close up it is intricate, varied and rich in pattern, texture, scale and color. (In this spatial plaid there is the added dimension I have mentioned, of slight and violent exceptions.) It is a question of focus: as one moves around and through the composition, he can focus on different things and relationships in different ways. There are opportunities to see the same thing in different ways, the old thing in new ways. As there is not a single, constant accent—a fountain, reflecting pool nor the great church itself, for instance, neither is there a single static focus when you move within and around the square. There is the opportunity for a variety of focuses, or rather for changing focus. The main paradox of this design is that the boring pattern is interesting.

Violent juxtapositions of blurred and sharp focuses come from levels of relationships which relate more or less to the whole, or in complex compositions, to wholes within wholes. These changing relationships within complex wholes make for complex kinds of unity some of whose immediate interior relationships involve distinct disunity. Not all the relationships are always all right. I think "relating" buildings is an eighth crutch of Modern architecture which Philip Johnson might have included. Buildings like Trinity Church and the Boston Public Library don't have to be "related" in easy and obvious ways. And they shouldn't be because their relationships cannot be just immediate to the interior setting of the square, but to greater wholes outside themselves and their immediate setting. Our little grid from a distance (like the plaid pattern) is a big blur because of its consistency at this level of focus: it does not always relate close-up and in detail therefore to the fine buildings around it. Richardson and McKim, Mead and White don't need that kind of explicit homage.

Another crutch of Modern architecture is the piazza compulsion derived from our justifiable love of Italian towns. But the open piazza is seldom appropriate for an American city today except as a convenience for pedestrians for diagonal short-cuts. The piazza, in fact, is "un-American." Americans feel uncomfortable sitting in a square: they should be working at the office or home with the family looking at television. Chores around the house or the weekend drive have replaced the passeggiata. The traditional piazza is for collective use as well as individual use, and public ceremonies involving crowds are even harder to imagine in Copley Square than passeggiate. Our square therefore is not an open space to accommodate non-existing crowds (empty piazzas are intriguing only in early de Chiricos), but to accommodate the individual who comfortably walks through the maze and sits along the "streets" rather than in a "piazza." We are in the habit of thinking that open space is precious in the city. It is not. Except in Manhattan perhaps, our cities have too much open space in the ubiquitous parking lots, in the not-so-temporary deserts created by Urban Renewal and in the amorphous suburbs around.

Notes

1   T. S. Eliot: *Selected Essays, 1917–1932,* Harcourt, Brace and Co., New York, 1932; p. 18.
2   *Ibid.;* pp. 3–4.
3   Aldo van Eyck: in *Architectural Design 12,* vol. XXXII, December 1962; p. 560.
4   Henry-Russell Hitchcock: in *Perspecta 6, The Yale Architectural Journal,* New Haven, 1960; p. 2.
5   *Ibid.;* p. 3.
6   Robert L. Geddes: in *The Philadelphia Evening Bulletin.* February 2, 1965; p. 40.
7   Sir John Summerson: *Heavenly Mansions,* W. W. Norton and Co., Inc., New York, 1963; p. 197.
8   *Ibid.;* p. 200.
9   David Jones: *Epoch and Artist,* Chilmark Press, Inc., New York, 1959; p. 12.
10 Kenzo Tange: in *Documents of Modern Architecture,* Jurgen Joedicke, ed., Universe Books, Inc., New York, 1961; p. 170.
11 Frank Lloyd Wright: in *An American Architecture,* Edgar Kaufmann, ed., Horizon Press, New York, 1955; p. 207.
12 Le Corbusier: *Towards a New Architecture,* The Architectural Press, London, 1927; p. 31.
13 Christopher Alexander: *Notes on the Synthesis of Form,* Harvard University Press, Cambridge, 1964; p. 4.
14 August Heckscher: *The Public Happiness,* Atheneum Publishers, New York, 1962; p. 102.
15 Paul Rudolph: in *Perspecta 7, The Yale Architectural Journal,* New Haven, 1961; p. 51.
16 Kenneth Burke: *Permanence and Change,* Hermes Publications, Los Altos, 1954; p. 107.
17 Eliot, *op. cit.;* p. 96.
18 T. S. Eliot: *Use of Poetry and Use of Criticism,* Harvard University Press, Cambridge, 1933; p. 146.
19 Eliot: *Selected Essays, 1917–1932, op. cit.;* p. 243.
20 *Ibid.;* p. 98.
21 Cleanth Brooks: *The Well Wrought Urn,* Harcourt, Brace and World, Inc., New York, 1947; pp. 212–214.
22 Stanley Edgar Hyman: *The Armed Vision,* Vintage Books, Inc., New York, 1955; p. 237.
23 *Ibid.;* p. 240.

24 William Empson: *Seven Types of Ambiguity*, Meridian Books, Inc., New York, 1955; p. 174.

25 Hyman, *op. cit.*; p. 238.

26 Brooks, *op. cit.*; p. 81.

27 Wylie Sypher: *Four Stages of Renaissance Style*, Doubleday and Co., Inc., Garden City, 1955; p. 124.

28 Frank Lloyd Wright: *An Autobiography*, Duell, Sloan and Pearce, New York, 1943; p. 148.

29 Eliot: *Selected Essays, 1917–1932, op. cit.*; p. 185.

30 Brooks, *op. cit.*; p. 7.

31 Burke, *op. cit.*; p. 69.

32 Alan R. Solomon: *Jasper Johns*, The Jewish Museum, New York, 1964; p. 5.

33 James S. Ackerman: *The Architecture of Michelangelo*, A. Zwemmer, Ltd., London, 1961; p. 139.

34 Siegfried Giedion: *Space, Time and Architecture*, Harvard University Press, Cambridge, 1963; p. 565.

35 Eliel Saarinen: *Search for Form*, Reinhold Publishing Corp., New York, 1948; p. 254.

36 Van Eyck, *op. cit.*; p. 602.

37 Frank Lloyd Wright: *Modern Architecture*, Princeton University Press, Princeton, 1931. (front end paper)

38 Horatio Greenough: in *Roots of Contemporary American Architecture*, Lewis Mumford, ed., Grove Press, Inc., New York, 1959; p. 37.

39 Henry David Thoreau: *Walden and Other Writings*, The Modern Library, Random House, New York, 1940; p. 42.

40 Louis H. Sullivan: *Kindergarten Chats*, Wittenborn, Schultz, Inc., New York, 1947; p. 140.

41 *Ibid.*; p. 43.

42 Le Corbusier, *op. cit.*; p. 11.

43 Gorgy Kepes: *The New Landscape*, P. Theobald, Chicago, 1956; p. 326.

44 Van Eyck, *op. cit.*; p. 600.

45 Heckscher, *op. cit.*; p. 287.

46 Herbert A. Simon: in *Proceedings of the American Philosophical Society*, vol. 106, no. 6, December 12, 1962; p. 468.

47 Arthur Trystan Edwards: *Architectural Style*, Faber and Gwyer, London, 1926; ch. III.

48 Ackerman, *op. cit.*; p. 138.

49 Fumihiko Maki: *Investigations in Collective Form*, Special Publication No. 2, Washington University, St. Louis, 1964; p. 5.

50 Heckscher, *op. cit.*; p. 289.

Photograph Credits

1. © Ezra Stoller Associates.
2. Alexandre Georges.
3. Heikki Havas, Helsinki.
4. Ugo Mulas, Milan.
5. The Museum of Modern Art.
6. © Country Life.
7. Reproduced by permission of Roberto Pane from his book, *Bernini Architetto*, Neri Pozza Editore, Venice 1953.
8. From Walter F. Friedländer, "Das Casino Pius des Vierten," *Kunstgeschichtliche Forschwangen*, Band III, Leipzig 1912.
9. © Country Life.
10. A. Cartoni, Rome.
11. Harry Holtzman.
12. The Museum of Modern Art.
13. Reproduced by permission of Penguin Books Ltd., Harmondsworth-Middlesex, from John Summerson, *Architecture in Britain, 1530–1830*, Baltimore 1958.
14. Reproduced by permission of Henry A. Millon from his book, *Baroque and Rococo Architecture*, George Braziller, New York 1965.
15. Reproduced by permission of Country Life Ltd., London, from A.S.G. Butler, *The Architecture of Sir Edwin Lutyens*, vol. I, 1935. © Country Life.
16. © Country Life.
17. From Leonardo Benevolo, "Saggio d'Interpretazione Storica del Sacro Bosco," *Quaderni dell'Istituto di Storia dell'Architettura*, NN. 7–9, Rome 1955.
18. © Kerry Downes.
19. Reproduced by permission of Penguin Books Ltd., Harmondsworth-Middlesex, from Nikolaus Pevsner, *An Outline of European Architecture*, Baltimore 1960. Photo: Alinari-Anderson.
20. George C. Alikakos.
21. Reproduced by permission of Giulio Einaudi Editore, Turin, from Paolo Portoghesi and Bruno Zevi (editors), *Michelangiolo Architetto*, 1964.
22. A. F. Kersting, London.
23. Cabinet des Estampes, Bibliothèque Nationale, Paris.
24. Reproduced by permission of Penguin Books Ltd., Harmondsworth-Middlesex, from Rudolf Wittkower, *Art and Architecture in Italy, 1600–1750*, Baltimore 1958.
25. Reproduced by permission of Electa Editrice, Milan, from Maria Venturi Perotti, *Borromini*, 1951. Photo: Vescovo.
26. Reproduced by permission of Professor Eberhard Hempel from Rudolf Wittkower, *Art and Architecture in Italy, 1600–1750*, Penguin Books, Inc., Baltimore 1958.
27. Alinari.
28. Hirmer Fotoarchiv, Munich.
29. A. F. Kersting, London.
30. Reproduced by permission of A. Zwemmer Ltd., London, from Kerry Downes, *Hawksmoor*, 1959.
31. From Nikolaus Pevsner, *An Outline of European Architecture*, Penguin Books Inc., Baltimore 1960.
32. Soprintendenza ai Monumenti, Turin. Photo: Nevi Benito.
33. Reproduced by permission of Arnoldo Mondadori Editore, Milan, from Giulio Carlo Argan (editor), *Borromini*, 1952.

34. Reproduced by permission of Penguin Books Ltd., Harmondsworth-Middlesex, from John Summerson, *Architecture in Britain, 1530–1830,* Baltimore 1958.

35. © Trustees of Sir John Soane's Museum.

36. © Trustees of Sir John Soane's Museum.

37. A. F. Kersting, London.

38. © Warburg Institute. Photo: Helmut Gernsheim.

39. © Warburg Institute. Photo: Helmut Gernsheim.

40. © A.C.L., Brussels.

41. Courtesy Philadelphia Saving Fund Society.

42. Reproduced by permission of Herold Druck- und Verlagsgesellschaft M.B.H., Vienna, from Hans Sedlmayr, *Johann Bernhard Fischer von Erlach,* 1956.

43. Courtesy Leo Castelli Gallery.

44. Tatsuzo Sato, Tokyo.

45. Alinari-Anderson.

46. Reproduced by permission of Penguin Books Ltd., Harmondsworth-Middlesex, from Anthony Blunt, *Art and Architecture in France, 1500–1700,* Baltimore 1957.

47. Marshall Meyers.

48. From *Andrea Palladio,* Der Zirkel, Architektur - Verlag G.m.b.H., Berlin 1920.

49. The Metropolitan Museum of Art, Dick Fund, 1936.

50. MAS, Barcelona.

51. Bildarchiv Foto Marburg, Marburg/Lahn.

52. Courtesy Courtauld Institute of Art.

53. Alinari.

54. From James S. Ackerman, *The Architecture of Michelangelo,* A. Zwemmer Ltd., London 1961.

55. Reproduced by permission of Electa Editrice, Milan, from Maria Venturi Perotti, *Borromini,* 1951.

56. Reproduced by permission of Country Life Ltd., London, from Laurence Weaver, *Houses and Gardens by Sir Edwin Lutyens,* New York 1925. © Country Life.

57. © Country Life.

58. From Yvan Christ, *Projets et Divagations de Claude-Nicolas Ledoux, Architecte du Roi,* Editions du Minotaure, Paris 1961. Photo: Bibliothèque Nationale.

59. A. F. Kersting, London.

60. Alinari.

61. Foto Locchi, Florence.

62. Reproduced by permission of Roberto Pane from his book, *Ville Vesuviane del Settecento,* Edizioni Scientifiche Italiane, Naples 1959.

63. Reproduced by permission of Roberto Pane from his book, *Ville Vesuviane del Settecento,* Edizioni Scientifiche Italiane, Naples 1959.

64. From *Architectural Forum,* September 1962.

65. Reproduced by permission of Verlag Gerd Hatje, Stuttgart-Bad Cannstatt, from Le Corbusier, *Creation is a Patient Search,* Frederick A. Praeger, Inc., New York 1960.

66. Alinari.

67. Reproduced by permission of Carlo Bestetti-Edizioni d'Arte, Rome, from Giuseppe Mazzotti, *Venetian Villas,* 1957.

68. Jean Roubier, Paris.

69. Courtesy Louis I. Kahn.

70. © Country Life.

71. Courtesy Mt. Vernon Ladies' Association.

72. William H. Short.

73. Reproduced by permission of The Macmillan Company,

New York, from Elizabeth Stevenson, *Henry Adams*. © 1955 Elizabeth Stevenson.

74. © Ezra Stoller Associates.
75. Robert Damora.
76. Courtesy Alvar Aalto.
77. Reproduced by permission of Editions Girsberger, Zurich, from *Le Corbusier, Oeuvre complète 1946–1952*, 1955. © 1953.
78. Reproduced by permission of George Wittenborn, Inc., New York, from Karl Fleig (editor), *Alvar Aalto*, 1963.
79. Courtesy Louis I. Kahn.
80. The Museum of Modern Art.
81. Hedrich-Blessing.
82. The Museum of Modern Art.
83. The Museum of Modern Art.
84. The Museum of Modern Art.
85. © Ezra Stoller Associates.
86. Charles Brickbauer.
87. Courtesy Peter Blake.
88. Courtesy Peter Blake.
89. Courtesy Peter Blake.
90. © Lucien Hervé, Paris.
91. James L. Dillon & Co., Inc., Philadelphia.
92. Touring Club Italiano, Milan.
93. A. F. Kersting, London.
94. Reproduced by permission of Giulio Einaudi Editore, Turin, from Paolo Portoghesi and Bruno Zevi (editors), *Michelangiolo Architetto*, 1964.
95. Reproduced by permission of Giulio Einaudi Editore, Turin, from Paolo Portoghesi and Bruno Zevi (editors), *Michelangiolo Architetto*, 1964.
96. University News Service, University of Virginia.
97. MAS, Barcelona.
98. Touring Club Italiano, Milan.
99. From Colen Campbell, *Vitruvius Britannicus*, vol. II, London 1717.
100. Collection: Mr. & Mrs. Burton Tremaine, Meriden, Conn.

101. Reproduced by permission of Penguin Books Ltd., Harmondsworth-Middlesex, from Kenneth John Conant, *Carolingian and Romanesque Architecture, 800–1200*, Baltimore 1959.
102. From George William Sheldon, *Artistic Country-Seats; Types of Recent American Villa and Cottage Architecture, with Instances of Country Clubhouses*, D. Appleton and Company, New York 1886.
103. Photo by Georgina Masson, author of *Italian Villas and Palaces*, Thames and Hudson, London 1959.
104. Photo by John Szarkowski, author of *The Idea of Louis Sullivan*, The University of Minnesota Press, Minneapolis. © 1956 The University of Minnesota.
105. Pix Inc.
106. Archivo Fotografico, Monumenti Musei e Gallerie Pontificie, Vatican City.
107. Reproduced by permission, from *Progressive Architecture*, April 1961.
108. Photo by Martin Hürlimann, author of *Englische Kathedralen*, Atlantis Verlag, Zurich 1956.
109. Courtesy Casa de Portugal. Photo: SNI-YAN.
110. Alinari.
111. Reproduced by permission of Giulio Einaudi Editore, Turin, from Paolo Portoghesi and Bruno Zevi (editors), *Michelangiolo Architetto*, 1964.
112. Chicago Architectural Photo Co.
113. Reproduced by permission of Country Life Ltd., London, from A.S.G. Butler, *The Architecture of Sir Edwin Lutyens*, vol. Ill, New York 1950. © Country Life.

114. Reproduced by permission, from *Architectural Design*, December 1962.
115. Photo by Martin Hürlimann, author of *Italien*, Atlantis Verlag, Zurich 1959.
116. Bildarchiv Foto Marburg, Marburg/Lahn.
117. Jean Roubier, Paris.
118. Bildarchiv Foto Marburg, Marburg/Lahn.
119. MAS, Barcelona.
120. MAS, Barcelona.
121. Robert Venturi.
122. From Colin Campbell *Vitruvius Britannicus*, vol. III, London 1725.
123. Jean Roubier, Paris.
124. Gebrüder Metz, Tübingen.
125. © Trustees of Sir John Soane's Museum.
126. Alinari.
127. Cunard Line.
128. Alinari.
129. Reproduced by permission of Giulio Einaudi Editore, Turin, from Paolo Portoghesi and Bruno Zevi (editors), *Michelangiolo Architetto*, 1964.
130. Photo by Martin Hürlimann, author of *Italien*, Atlantis Verlag, Zurich 1959.
131. Courtesy of Anton Schroll and Co., Vienna, publisher of Heinrich Decker, *Romanesque Art in Italy*, 1958.
132. Reproduced by permission of Verlag Gebr. Mann, Berlin, from H. Knackfuss, *Didyma*, part I, vol. III, 1940.
133. Reproduced by permission of Country Life Ltd., London, from A.S.G. Butler, *The Architecture of Sir Edwin Lutyens*, vol. I, 1935. © Country Life.
134. The Museum of Modern Art.
135. MAS, Barcelona.
136. California Division of Highways.
137. Alinari.
138. Reproduced by permission of Harry N. Abrams, Inc., New York, from Henry A. Millon and Alfred Frazer, *Key Monuments of the History of Architecture*, 1964.
139. Reproduced by permission of Henry-Russell Hitchcock from his book *In the Nature of Materials*, Duell, Sloan & Pearce, New York 1942.
140. Archives Nationales, Paris.
141. Archives Nationales, Paris.
142. Touring Club Italiano, Milan.
143. © Trustees of Sir John Soane's Museum.
144. Reproduced by permission of Architectural Book Publishing Co., Inc., New York, from W. Hegemann and E. Peets, *The American Vitruvius*. © 1922 Paul Wenzel and Maurice Krakow.
145. Reproduced by permission of Architectural Book Publishing Co., Inc., New York, from W. Hegemann and E. Peets, *The American Vitruvius*. © 1922 Paul Wenzel and Maurice Krakow.
146. J. B. Piranesi, *Vedute di Roma*, vol. 13. New York Public Library Art Room.
147. Reproduced by permission of Yale University Press, New Haven, from Vincent Scully, *The Shingle Style*, 1955.
148. Reproduced by permission of Architectural Book Publishing Co., Inc., New York, from Katharine Hooker and Myron Hunt, *Farmhouses and Small Provincial Buildings in Southern Italy*, 1925.
149. A. F. Kersting, London.
150. Alinari.
151. The Museum of Modern Art.
152. Theo Frey, Weiningen.
153. Reproduced by permission of

George Wittenborn, Inc., New York, from Karl Fleig (editor), *Alvar Aalto*, 1963.

154. Reproduced by permission of Country Life Ltd., London, from H. Avray Tipping and Christopher Hussey, *English Homes, Period IV–Vol. II, The Work of Sir John Vanbrugh and His School, 1699–1736*, 1928. © Country Life.

155. Reproduced by permission of Propyläen Verlag, Berlin, from Gustav Pauli, *Die Kunst des Klassizismus und der Romantik*, 1925.

156. Alinari.

157. Abraham Guillén, Lima.

158. Archives Photographiques, Caisse Nationale des Monuments Historiques, Paris.

159. Robert Venturi.

160. Bildarchiv Foto Marburg, Marburg/Lahn.

161. © Country Life.

162. Robert Venturi.

163. From Russell Sturgis, *A History of Architecture*, vol. I, The Baker & Taylor Company, New York 1906.

164. Reproduced by permission of Propyläen Verlag, Berlin, from Heinrich Schafer and Walter Andrae, *Die Kunst des Alten Orients*, 1925.

165. Reproduced by permission of Penguin Books Ltd., Harmondsworth-Middlesex, from Rudolf Wittkower, *Art and Architecture in Italy, 1600–1750*, Baltimore 1958.

166. Pierre Devinoy, Paris.

167. Staatlichen Graphischen Sammlung, Munich.

168. Hirmer Verlag, Munich.

169. Reproduced by permission, from *L'Architettura*, June 1964.

170. Alinari.

171. © Trustees of Sir John Soane's Museum.

172. Robert Venturi.

173. Robert Venturi.

174. The Museum of Modern Art.

175. © Ezra Stoller Associates.

176. Ernest Nash, Fototeca Unione, Rome.

177. Reproduced by permission of Penguin Books Ltd., Harmondsworth-Middlesex, from Nikolaus Pevsner, *An Outline of European Architecture*, Baltimore 1960.

178. Reproduced by permission of Penguin Books Ltd., Harmondsworth-Middlesex, from Nikolaus Pevsner, *An Outline of European Architecture*, Baltimore 1960.

179. Friedrich Hewicker, Kaltenkirchen.

180. Courtesy Prestel Verlag, Munich. Photo: Erich Müller.

181. Reproduced by permission of Giulio Einaudi Editore, Turin, from Paolo Portoghesi and Bruno Zevi (editors), *Michelangiolo Architetto*, 1964.

182. Reproduced by permission of Giulio Einaudi Editore, Turin, from Paolo Portoghesi and Bruno Zevi (editors), *Michelangiolo Architetto*, 1964.

183. Alinari-Anderson.

184. Reproduced by permission of Penguin Books Ltd., Harmondsworth-Middlesex, from G. H. Hamilton, *The Art and Architecture of Russia*, Baltimore 1954.

185. Reproduced by permission of Penguin Books Ltd., Harmondsworth-Middlesex, from George Kubler and Martin Soria, *Art and Architecture in Spain and Portugal and Their American Dominions, 1500–1800*, Baltimore 1959.

186. Reproduced by permission of Touring Club Italiano, Milan, from L. V. Bertanelli (editor),

Guida d'Italia, Lazio, 1935.

187. Reproduced by permission of Alec Tiranti Ltd., London, from J. C. Shepherd and G. A. Jellicoe, *Italian Gardens of the Renaissance*, 1953.

188. Courtesy Louis I. Kahn.

189. Alinari.

190. Reproduced by permission of Rudolf Wittkower, from his book, *Art and Architecture in Italy, 1600–1750*, Penguin Books, Inc., Baltimore 1958.

191. Riccardo Moncalvo, Turin.

192. Heikki Havas, Helsinki.

193. Reproduced by permission of Arkady, Warsaw, from Maria and Kazimierz Piechotka, *Wooden Synagogues*, 1959.

194. Reproduced by permission of George Wittenborn, Inc., New York, from Karl Fleig (editor), *Alvar Aalto*, 1963.

195. G. Kleine-Tebbe, Bremen.

196. From *Architectural Forum*, February 1950.

197. From *Architectural Forum*, February 1950.

198. Reproduced by permission of The University of North Carolina Press, Chapel Hill, from Thomas Tileston Waterman, *The Mansions of Virginia, 1706–1776*, 1946. © 1945.

199. Robert Venturi.

200. Reproduced by permission of Herold Druck- und Verlagsgesellschaft M.B.H., Vienna, from Hans Sedlmayr, *Johann Bernhard Fischer von Erlach*, 1956.

201. Alinari.

202. From *Casabella*, no. 217, 1957.

203. Reproduced by permission of Alec Tiranti Ltd., London, from J. C. Shepherd and G. A. Jellicoe, *Italian Gardens of the Renaissance*, 1953.

204. Touring Club Italiano, Milan.

205. The Museum of Modern Art.

206. Reproduced by permission of Penguin Books Ltd., Harmondsworth-Middlesex, from Nikolaus Pevsner, *An Outline of European Architecture*, Baltimore 1960.

207. Soprintendenza alle Gallerie, Florence.

208. Istituto Centrale del Restauro, Rome.

209. Collection: The Whitney Museum of American Art.

210. Courtesy André Emmerich Gallery.

211. Photo by John Szarkowski, author of *The Idea of Louis Sullivan*, The University of Minnesota Press, Minneapolis. © 1956 The University of Minnesota.

212. Soprintendenza alle Gallerie, Florence.

213. Hirmer Fotoarchiv, Munich.

214. Hirmer Fotoarchiv, Munich.

215. From Colen Campbell, *Vitruvius Britannicus*, vol. I, London 1715.

216. From John Woolfe and James Gandon, *Vitruvius Britannicus*, vol. V, London 1771.

217. Courtesy City Museum and Art Gallery, Birmingham.

218. Robert Venturi.

219. Robert Venturi.

220. Robert Venturi.

221. Robert Venturi.

222. Reproduced by permission of Electa Editrice, Milan, from *Palladio*, 1951.

223. H. Roger-Viollet, Paris.

224. Slide Collection, University of Pennsylvania.

225. From I. T. Frary, *Thomas Jefferson, Architect and Builder*, Garrett and Massie, Inc., Richmond 1939.

226. Robert Venturi.

227. From Colen Campbell *Vitruvius Britannicus*, vols. I and III, London 1715 and 1725.

228. Reproduced by permission of Penguin Books Ltd., Harmondsworth-Middlesex, from Nikolaus Pevsner, *An Outline of European Architecture*, Baltimore 1960.

229. Bildarchiv Foto Marburg, Marburg/Lahn.

230. From Leonardo Benevolo, "Le Chiese Barocche Valsesiane," *Quaderni dell'Istituto di Storia dell'Architettura*, NN. 22–24, Rome 1957.

231. © Country Life.

232. The Museum of Modern Art.

233. Sheila Hicks.

234. Reproduced by permission of Connaissance des Arts, Paris, from Stephanie Faniel, *French Art of the 18th Century*, 1957.

235. Chicago Architectural Photo Co.

236. Bayerische Verwaltung der staatlichen Schlösser, Gärten und Seen, Munich.

237. Courtesy of Anton Schroll and Co., Vienna, from Heinrich Decker, *Romanesque Art in Italy*, 1958.

238. © National Buildings Record, London.

239. Robert Venturi.

240. Reproduced by permission of A. Zwemmer Ltd., London, from Kerry Downes, *Hawksmoor*, 1959.

241. Reproduced by permission of Roberto Pane from his book *Ferdinando Fuga*, Edizioni Scientifiche Italiane, Naples 1961.

242. Italian State Tourist Office.

243. Reproduced by permission of Penguin Books Ltd., Harmondsworth-Middlesex, from Anthony Blunt, *Art and Architecture in France, 1500–1700*, Baltimore 1957.

244. Reproduced by permission of Architectural Book Publishing Co., Inc., New York, from Katharine Hooker and Myron Hunt, *Farmhouses and Small Provincial Buildings in Southern Italy*, 1925.

245. Wayne Andrews.

246. From "Bagnaia," *Quaderni dell'Istituto di Storia dell'Architettura*, N. 17, Rome 1956.

247. Alinari.

248. Reproduced by permission, from *Architectural Design*, December 1962.

249. Reproduced by permission of Architectural Book Publishing Co., Inc., New York, from Katharine Hooker and Myron Hunt, *Farmhouses and Small Provincial Buildings in Southern Italy*, 1925.

250. From Archivo Amigos de Gaudí, Barcelona. Photo: Aleu.

251. Reproduced by permission of George Wittenborn, Inc., New York, from Karl Fleig (editor), *Alvar Aalto*, 1963.

252. Wallace Litwin.

253. George Cserna.

254. Office of Venturi and Rauch.

255. Office of Venturi and Rauch.

256. Office of Venturi and Rauch.

257. Office of Venturi and Rauch.

258. Office of Venturi and Rauch.

259. Office of Venturi and Rauch.

260. Leni Iselin.

261. Leni Iselin.

262. Leni Iselin.

263. Leni Iselin.

264. Edmund B. Gilchrist.

265. Office of Venturi and Rauch.

266. Office of Venturi and Rauch.

267. Office of Venturi and Rauch.

268. Office of Venturi and Rauch.

269. Office of Venturi and Rauch.

270. George Pohl.

271. George Pohl.

272. Office of Venturi and Rauch.

273. George Pohl.

274. George Pohl.

275. George Pohl.

276. George Pohl.
277. Rollin R. La France.
278. Office of Venturi and Rauch.
279. Office of Venturi and Rauch.
280. Office of Venturi and Rauch.
281. Office of Venturi and Rauch.
282. Office of Venturi and Rauch.
283. Office of Venturi and Rauch.
284. Office of Venturi and Rauch.
285. Lawrence S. Williams, Inc.
286. Lawrence S. Williams, Inc.
287. Lawrence S. Williams, Inc.
288. George Pohl.
289. Office of Venturi and Rauch.
290. Office of Venturi and Rauch.
291. Office of Venturi and Rauch.
292. Office of Venturi and Rauch.
293. Office of Venturi and Rauch.
294. George Pohl.
295. Office of Venturi and Rauch.
296. Office of Venturi and Rauch.
297. Office of Venturi and Rauch.
298. Office of Venturi and Rauch.
299. Office of Venturi and Rauch.
300. Office of Venturi and Rauch.
301. William Watkins.
302. William Watkins.
303. William Watkins.
304. William Watkins.
305. Office of Venturi and Rauch.
306. Office of Venturi and Rauch.
307. Office of Venturi and Rauch.
308. Office of Venturi and Rauch.
309. George Pohl.
310. Rollin R. La France.
311. George Pohl.
312. George Pohl.
313. Rollin R. La France.
314. Rollin R. La France.
315. Rollin R. La France.
316. Rollin R. La France.
317. Office of Venturi and Rauch.
318. Office of Venturi and Rauch.
319. Office of Venturi and Rauch.
320. Office of Venturi and Rauch.
321. Rollin R. La France.
322. Rollin R. La France.
323. Office of Venturi and Rauch.
324. Office of Venturi and Rauch.
325. Office of Venturi and Rauch.
326. Office of Venturi and Rauch.
327. Office of Venturi and Rauch.
328. Office of Venturi and Rauch.
329. Office of Venturi and Rauch.
330. George Pohl.
331. George Pohl.
332. Office of Venturi and Rauch.
333. Office of Venturi and Rauch.
334. Office of Venturi and Rauch.
335. Office of Venturi and Rauch.
336. Office of Venturi and Rauch.
337. Office of Venturi and Rauch.
338. Office of Venturi and Rauch.
339. George Pohl.
340. George Pohl.
341. George Pohl.
342. Office of Venturi and Rauch.
343. Office of Venturi and Rauch.
344. Office of Venturi and Rauch.
345. Office of Venturi and Rauch.
346. George Pohl.
347. George Pohl.
348. Office of Venturi and Rauch.
349. Office of Venturi and Rauch.
350. Office of Venturi and Rauch.

This volume is dedicated to Robert Venturi (1925–2018)

2

Complexity and Contradiction at Fifty

On Robert Venturi's "Gentle Manifesto"

Martino Stierli
David B. Brownlee

The Museum of Modern Art, New York

Contents

Interpretation

Introduction

Anniversaries generally seem to occur at arbitrary times, but the fiftieth anniversary of Robert Venturi's *Complexity and Contradiction in Architecture*, written in the decade of the March on Washington, a rising tide of protests against the Vietnam War, and the Stonewall Riots, coincided with another moment of cultural turmoil. When the conference "*Complexity and Contradiction in Architecture* at Fifty" took place November 10 through 12, 2016,[1] the divisive American presidential election that brought Donald Trump to power had just occurred and the streets around The Museum of Modern Art were crowded with people protesting the outcome of the vote. No one could miss the point that books are written—and conferences are held—in the context of their times.

The Museum of Modern Art and the University of Pennsylvania cosponsored the anniversary conference and this volume, which grows from it. This partnership is fitting. Venturi's book was based in large part on materials that he assembled for a lecture course that he taught at the University of Pennsylvania from 1961 to 1965, and his papers are now housed at the Architectural Archives at Penn. The book was selected by Arthur Drexler, then the architecture curator at the Museum, to inaugurate an intended series of texts on modern architectural theory.

•

Complexity and Contradiction was famously characterized by Vincent Scully, in his introduction to the book, as "probably the most important writing on the making of architecture since Le Corbusier's *Vers une architecture*, of 1923."[2] While described by Venturi himself as a "gentle manifesto," it is generally agreed that *Complexity and Contradiction* has lived up to the loftier assessment made by Scully.

The book is conventionally identified as a potent and early expression of postmodernism. Its title became shorthand for the postmodern condition, and the book has many recognizably postmodern features: it expands the architectural canon, embraces the vernacular, and adopts linguistic modes for the interpretation of art. But focusing on those things, true as they are, is a projection onto the book of characteristics of what came later. This volume embodies a broader approach, including both a historical framing of the text and a critical consideration of its impact. It comprises a selection of essays by historians and architects who spoke at the conference, as well as a few additional contributions.

In the first section, "Context" Martino Stierli writes the institutional history of the book project, explaining how an alliance between the Graham Foundation and The Museum of Modern Art produced a work that seemed to challenge the Museum's long commitment to modernism. A detailed account of the teaching that Venturi did at Penn is provided by Lee Ann Custer, who draws parallels between the methods and content of his course and the book that he was writing at the same time. Mary McLeod discovers and disentangles the important roles played in the making of the book by Venturi's several collaborators, including Denise Scott Brown. The concept of complexity is explored by Joan Ockman, mapping the larger intellectual terrain and the theories of knowledge that were being restructured by ideas about ambiguity and contradiction in the mid-twentieth century. The modern appreciation of mannerism, the object of Venturi's sustained interest, is the focus of an essay by Andrew Leach. To conclude this section, Jean-Louis Cohen discusses one of Venturi's earliest executed architectural works as context for his writing: the tactful renovation of the James B. Duke House for use by New York University's Institute of Fine Arts.

In the second section, "Interpretation" Dianne Harris examines the dissonance between the book's measured, largely formalist argument and the social tumult of its day, thus calling attention to the continuing detachment of the architectural profession from social concerns. Venturi's interest in literary theory serves as the invitation for Peter Fröhlicher's consideration of the structure and rhetoric of the architect's writing. Emmanuel Petit investigates the position assigned to Venturi in the history of modern architecture by Colin Rowe and Vincent Scully, in particular through the lens of his relationship to Le Corbusier. Finally, the engagement of modern artists with seeing and perception is the central theme of Stanislaus von Moos's essay, which positions Venturi's text in relation to "the twentieth century's preoccupation with pure visibility."

Punctuating the longer essays are reflections by some of today's most distinguished practitioners and teachers of architecture from several generations: Deborah Berke, Sam Jacob, Stephen Kieran and James Timberlake, Rem Koolhaas (in conversation with Martino Stierli), Michael Meredith, Pier Paolo Tamburelli, and Stanley Tigerman (in conversation with David B. Brownlee).

●

Many large debts were incurred in the making of this book and the anniversary conference. Special acknowledgment is made of Denise Scott Brown, whose work continues to inspire and challenge, and whose conversation with William Whitaker was the grand finale of the conference.

Beyond those whose writing is featured here, we are grateful to all the conference panelists and moderators, who also included David G. De Long, Deborah Fausch, Alice T. Friedman, Kersten Geers, Christine Gorby, Kathryn Hiesinger, Momoyo Kajima, and Enrique Walker. William Whitaker, the curator and collections manager of the Architectural Archives of the University of Pennsylvania, gave crucial support to all the authors and, together with Lee Ann Custer, organized the anniversary exhibition at the Architectural Archives' Harvey & Irwin Kroiz Gallery: *Back Matter: The Making of Robert Venturi's "Complexity and Contradiction in Architecture."* The Philadelphia Museum of Art hosted the Saturday morning panel. The Vanna Venturi House ("Mother's House") and Louis I. Kahn's Margaret Esherick House were opened to conference participants by their generous owners: David Lockard, and Paul Savidge and Dan Macey, respectively. Darlene Jackson, Yessica Manan, Bret Taboada, and Jocelyn Wong provided unstinting organizational support.

This book has benefited greatly from the editorial guidance of Alexander Scrimgeour, who sharpened both the prose and the arguments put forward in these essays, and from Amanda Washburn's elegant design, which honors the spirit of the first edition of Venturi's manifesto, with which it is coupled here in facsimile. We thank Matthew Pimm, Production Manager, for expertly shepherding both books to print. Jocelyn Wong, together with Erin Wrightson, must also be thanked for her efforts in securing the numerous images that grace this volume. In addition, our gratitude is due to Cerise Fontaine for her guidance at the onset of the project. Lastly, we are profoundly grateful to Christopher Hudson and Don McMahon, MoMA's Publisher and Editorial Director, respectively, for their unstinting nurturance of this project.

The conference was made possible through the generosity of Elise Jaffe and Jeffrey Brown, to whom we owe our sincere thanks. Further support was provided by the Keith L. and Katherine Sachs Program in Contemporary Art at the University of Pennsylvania, as well as Penn's School of Arts and Sciences (Office of the Dean), School of Design (Office of the Dean), the Mellon Humanities+Urbanism+Design Initiative, and the University Research Foundation. For their major support of this publication we thank, again, Elise Jaffe and Jeffrey Brown, as well as the Graham Foundation for Advanced Studies in the Fine Arts and The Dale S. and Norman Mills Leff Publication Fund.

David B. Brownlee
Frances Shapiro-Weitzenhoffer Professor
of the History of Art,
University of Pennsylvania

Martino Stierli
The Philip Johnson Chief Curator
of Architecture and Design,
The Museum of Modern Art, New York

Notes

1. The conference took the publication date of *Complexity and Contradiction* to be 1966, as in its colophon, but in fact it was released in early 1967; see Martino Stierli and Mary McLeod in this volume, pp. 19 and 67n9. To avoid unduly complicating matters, however, the date 1966 likewise goes unchallenged in the following essays, except where the chronology of its publication is explicitly addressed.

2. Vincent Scully, introduction to *Complexity and Contradiction in Architecture*, by Robert Venturi, The Museum of Modern Art Papers on Architecture 1 (New York: The Museum of Modern Art in association with the Graham Foundation for Advanced Studies in the Fine Arts, Chicago, 1966), 11.

Robert Venturi and MoMA:
Institutionalist and Outsider

Martino Stierli

It has always seemed paradoxical that Robert Venturi's "gentle manifesto" was published by The Museum of Modern Art. In his treatise, Venturi was not exactly "gentle" with the likes of Philip Johnson or Mies van der Rohe, whose minimalist, abstract architectural aesthetic the Museum had championed for decades, but which Venturi famously deemed "a bore." In hindsight, MoMA's embrace of Venturi's polemics can best be understood in the larger context of the crisis of architectural discourse and late modernist architecture in the 1960s, in which, under the directorship of Arthur Drexler, the Museum's Department of Architecture and Design played a pivotal role. It is impossible not to see the publication of *Complexity and Contradiction in Architecture* in 1966 in direct relationship with the epochal and highly controversial *Architecture of the École des Beaux-Arts* exhibition Drexler organized at the Museum in 1975. While both that revisionist exhibition of nineteenth-century French academic architecture and Venturi's manifesto are now regarded as landmarks in the genesis of postmodernism—albeit in both cases somewhat against the intentions of the respective authors—Drexler's show proved that, within a decade of

Fig. 1. Installation view of the exhibition *Le Corbusier: Buildings in Europe and India*. The Museum of Modern Art, New York, January 29–April 15, 1963. Photographic Archive. The Museum of Modern Art Archives, New York

the publication of Venturi's book, The Museum of Modern Art itself had become an active agent in the formulation and dissemination of postmodernist thinking, rather than simply providing a platform for others to promote it.

What seems to make perfect sense in retrospect, however, was not self-evident in the climate of the mid-1960s: Why would an institution such as MoMA have an interest in publishing a piece of writing by a relatively young and little-known architect that appeared to launch a frontal attack against its aesthetic values and beliefs? Why give a platform to a Young Turk from Philadelphia who sought to undermine the ideological foundations on which this institution had been erected? The history of Venturi's relationship to The Museum of Modern Art is, of course, more complex and contradictory than these questions suggest. In order to answer some of them, it will be necessary to unpack the complex networks of actors and institutional agency surrounding the publication of *Complexity and Contradiction* as well as to locate its publication in the larger historical context of emergent architectural postmodernism and the disillusionment with the dominant narratives of teleological modernism and its aesthetic and political idealism.

Drexler, Entenza, and the MoMA–Graham Foundation Entente

The publication of *Complexity and Contradiction* as the first volume of The Museum of Modern Art Papers on Architecture was the result of an initiative started several years earlier by Drexler together with John D. Entenza, the director of the Graham Foundation for Advanced Studies in the Fine Arts, Chicago. In a letter sent to Entenza on November 11, 1963, Drexler indicates his wish to put in writing a publication project that the two of them had discussed earlier, presumably during an encounter Drexler mentions they had at Yale University.[1] As a model for a possible future collaboration, which the Graham Foundation would fund and cosponsor, Drexler noted the successful partnership between the two institutions for the exhibition *Le Corbusier: Buildings in Europe and India* at the Museum in 1963 (fig. 1). Drexler also clarified, however, that he was "not yet ready to present [this proposal] formally" and that his description must therefore be "understood as . . . unofficial and tentative." He went on to identify two areas of architectural publishing that he felt were currently underserved, namely teaching aids for college and junior college levels, on the one hand, and theoretical studies and serious criticism on the other.

As far as the former were concerned, Drexler suggested that the Museum should begin publishing "detailed monographs on key buildings in the history of modern architecture" that comprised inexpensive portfolios of sample photographs accompanied by printed information sheets. Conversely, the theoretical studies should contribute to the scholarly discourse. Drexler lamented that "at the present time there is no university or other institution publishing historical and theoretical material on modern architecture." The envisaged series of publications, which he proposed be named "The Museum of Modern Art Papers on Architecture, published for the Graham Foundation, etc.," could fill this gap. Drexler explicitly referenced a manuscript by Venturi on the subject of complexity in architecture, which he found "quite interesting," adding: "after it has been edited it most certainly should be published." Indeed, Drexler had been in direct contact with Venturi regarding his nascent manuscript since September 1963.[2]

In order to allow for wide dissemination as well as a regular publication rhythm of roughly three volumes per year, the series should, he wrote, be "printed as inexpensively as possible and it should be paperbound."[3] (These initial plans would prove to be too ambitious, and the series saw only two volumes, the second of which, Joseph Rykwert's historical study *On Adam's House in Paradise*, was not published until 1972 [fig. 2]).[4] As a possible model, Drexler explicitly mentioned Emil Kaufmann's *Three Revolutionary Architects: Boulleé, Ledoux, and Leqeu*, which was published by the American Philosophical Society in Philadelphia in 1952. This study was a somewhat odd reference for Drexler to invoke. Whereas Kaufmann's earlier studies of the French revolutionary architects—notably his seminal *Von Ledoux bis Le Corbusier: Ursprung und Entwicklung der autonomen Architektur* (From Ledoux to Le Corbusier: Origin and Development of Autonomous Architecture, 1933)—had used late eighteenth-century architecture to historically legitimize Le Corbusier's modernism, his 1952 revisitation of the subject refrained from making any explicit links to the present. Moreover, Venturi wrote from the perspective of a practicing architect rather than as a historian, and he made quite explicitly "operative" use of specific aspects of architectural history, in particular Italian and English Baroque and Mannerist architecture. It is thus questionable how familiar Drexler actually was with Venturi's treatise at this stage—which might also help explain his critical reaction to the submitted manuscript later.

Fig. 2. Cover of Joseph Rykwert's *On Adam's House in Paradise: The Idea of the Primitive Hut in Architectural History*. The Museum of Modern Art Papers on Architecture 2. New York: The Museum of Modern Art in association with the Graham Foundation for Advanced Studies in the Fine Arts, Chicago, 1972

Venturi had originally written to the Graham Foundation to request financial support for his book project at the suggestion of his mentor and former employer Louis I. Kahn on February 15, 1962.[5] His letter included a folder of illustrations as well as a twenty-page outline of the book, indicating that he had already been working on his subject for some time.[6] On April 18, 1962, Entenza had informed the young architect by telegram that he had been selected for a fellowship and would be awarded $7,500.[7]

As part of the terms of the Graham Foundation grant, Venturi was to submit three progress reports over a one-year period,[8] which he did, albeit with considerable delay. Upon payment of the third and final installment of the grant, at the end of December, Entenza requested graphic material from Venturi that would be used for the annual presentation of funded projects, which would occur at the Graham Foundation the following spring.[9] While it is unclear whether this presentation actually took place, the official conclusion of the grant project was the book itself when it was eventually published several years later.

The young Philadelphia architect was by no means an unknown figure to MoMA's curatorial staff when Drexler launched the idea of a publication series. As early as November 1961, some two years before Drexler's letter to Entenza, research assistant Ellen Marsh had reached out to Venturi on behalf of the Department of Architecture and Design asking him to send photographs of "several examples of [his] most outstanding work, including residential," for the department's photo study and reference collection.[10]

Venturi complied with the request a few weeks later,[11] and the Museum still holds in its collection a substantial body of work by Venturi and his collaborators from the years up to and including 1961.[12] Even if he did not have much executed work to show at this early stage in his career, MoMA's request indicates that he was already considered among the important voices of his generation. Notably, he had completed the renovation of the James B. Duke House, the new home of the Institute of Fine Arts (IFA) of New York University, two years earlier. That project had its origins in Venturi's stay at the American Academy in Rome and in the acquaintance and friendship that he developed there with the art historian Richard Krautheimer, a faculty member at the IFA.[13] Venturi had also completed the small but ambitious headquarters of the North Penn Visiting Nurse Association, with its distorted forms and play with symmetry, scale, and historical reference.

This was perhaps his first built realization of a contemporary "complex and contradictory" architecture.

The manuscript for *Complexity and Contradiction* was so far advanced in early 1963 that Venturi was already actively searching for a suitable publisher before Drexler and The Museum of Modern Art became involved. In June of that year, he received a handwritten note from his former teacher and mentor at Princeton University, Jean Labatut, informing him that he had started to read his "very—VERY—interesting manuscript," adding that he had "not yet digested the title."[14] The project was evidently considered ready to be presented to external readers. Indeed, in a letter to Harvard University Press in early August 1963, Venturi explained how he intended to modify his text, possibly reacting to comments from Labatut or another reader.[15] In the same letter, Venturi mentioned that *Perspecta*, the Yale architecture journal, had committed to publishing a chapter of the book the following spring. A substantial section of the manuscript was indeed published by *Perspecta*, but not until 1965, in the double issue famously edited by Robert A. M. Stern (fig. 3). As will be seen, Venturi's prior commitment to the journal would prove a source of contention between Venturi and MoMA once the latter agreed to publish the book.

Harvard University Press did not pursue this publication project. For MoMA and for Drexler, however, whom Venturi contacted immediately afterward, Venturi's manuscript came at the right time and in the right place. In March 1964, only four months after Drexler had floated his book series idea to Entenza, the Museum agreed to publish the book.[16] On April 14, Entenza informed Drexler that the Graham Foundation had committed another $7,000 to underwrite the first publication of the series.[17] Venturi finished up his revisions and submitted the manuscript to Drexler just over a week later, on April 22, 1964.[18]

Once the Museum had begun to review the manuscript, however, several concerns regarding both the fact that excerpts would be published in *Perspecta* and the linguistic and writerly quality of the manuscript surfaced, considerably slowing down the publication process. (Conversely, Venturi's critical stance on late modernist architecture seems never to have troubled either Drexler or the editors involved.) The author's mounting frustration about this delay is evident in his exchange with the architectural historian Esther McCoy, who became something of a confidant to Venturi in this period. She first met Venturi that summer, while working on a Ford Foundation grant that enabled

Fig. 3. Cover of *Perspecta: The Yale Architectural Journal* 10/11. 1965. Edited by Robert A. M. Stern

her to travel around the United States to study the work of young architects, and supported her publication of a volume of essays on the topic. In a letter following their initial contact, Venturi asked McCoy for advice on how to balance his book contract with his commitment to publish an excerpt in *Perspecta*. McCoy, for her part, had also solicited a section of Venturi's manuscript for the influential Los Angeles–based *Arts & Architecture*, which had been published and edited by Entenza between 1938 and 1962. In his letter to McCoy, Venturi wrote that "he [Drexler] became angry; that is too much to appear before publication in his opinion and might hinder the sale of the book. It is true that I had told him it was only a chapter and failed to mention the preliminary material which *Perspecta* later . . . requested and I acceded to. I might have mentioned this wouldn't have happened if he had been more available and interested in helping me during that period."[19]

In her response, McCoy reminded Venturi that his "first obligation was to the [book] publisher," that *Arts & Architecture* could delay publishing excerpts, and that *Perspecta* should be willing to do the same.[20] Even though Venturi subsequently persuaded Stern to agree to remove some of the material originally intended for publication in the journal, this proved impossible because, Stern maintained, the magazine had already been typeset, preventing any changes.[21] The parts of the book featured in *Perspecta* were in fact substantial: the "gentle manifesto," which would constitute chapter 1, as well as chapter 2 ("Complexity and Contradiction vs. Simplification or Picturesqueness"), and the rather lengthy chapter 9 ("The Inside and the Outside"). Moreover, the journal also presented a selection of Venturi's built works and projects, which would feature in the closing chapter of the book.

While Venturi was becoming increasingly frustrated with MoMA's timeline, Drexler seems to have had continuing reservations about the quality of the manuscript. In a letter to McCoy on December 26, 1964, Venturi referred to a recent phone call with her in which he had mentioned rumors that Drexler no longer liked his manuscript and was trying to delay and "find excuses not to publish it."[22] Indeed, Helen M. Franc, former editorial assistant in the Museum's Department of Publications, later recalled that Drexler "didn't like the whole idea of the book," suggesting that this was the reason for the "teensy-weensy format with those postage-stamp illustrations."[23] The first freelance editor whom Drexler had asked to read it had found the manuscript, according to Franc, "unpublishable." Franc herself recognized the manuscript had "great ideas" but suggested an external editor with knowledge of the subject matter should take on the task.[24] That Drexler nonetheless pursued the publication of the manuscript would seem to contradict Franc's implication that he objected to Venturi's argument. Indeed, Venturi also reported to McCoy that Vincent Scully had spoken to Drexler, who had "emphatically" denied that he was unfavorably disposed to it. Actually, Venturi continued, "he considers this work 'the finest architectural aesthetic in twenty years' or something like that. I must learn to beware of rumors."[25]

Scully would, of course, go on to have an outsize role in the dissemination of Venturi's ideas, not least in his enthusiastic introduction to *Complexity and Contradiction*. As Scully recounts in his 1989 essay "Robert Venturi's Gentle Architecture," it was Stern who had first encouraged him to look at Venturi's work, prompting him to visit Guild House and the Vanna Venturi House in Philadelphia.[26] Scully then chose Venturi as one of six young architects for the annual "New Talent USA" issue of *Art in America* in 1961.[27] In Venturi's project for a Beach House of 1959, moreover, Scully found an echo of his own interests in *The Shingle Style* (1955) (fig. 4). In the end, Scully not only—as architecture critic Paul Goldberger notes—"effectively launched the career[s] of Louis Kahn and . . . Robert Venturi,"[28] but he can be seen as a seminal force in the emergence of postmodernism, not least through his explicit role in articulating MoMA's (that is, Drexler's) critical reevaluation of modernism.[29]

Drexler had used the summer of 1964 to solicit reviews from external and internal readers.[30] In her report, Franc had written that she found the manuscript "interesting though *very* tough going." She remarked: "The section in which Venturi discussed his architectural concepts I found far superior to those in which he went off on the 'new criticism' kick. Though I applaud his efforts to bring thinking about architecture into line with current thought about other cultural disciplines, some of his citations seemed simultaneously pretentious and naïve. . . . Can *some* of the beatification of Kahn be toned down? He comes out an even *lieberer Meister* than Sullivan to the young Wright; it becomes almost embarrassing!"[31] The efforts put into transforming Venturi's unruly manuscript into a publishable (if still idiosyncratic) book indicate that, at least formally, Venturi's thinking first had to be made to fit institutional expectations.

Drexler eventually hired Marian Wohl, Scully's personal editor and soon-to-be wife, to edit the manuscript.[32] Upon her

Fig. 4. Robert Venturi (American, 1925–2018). Project for a Beach House. 1959. The Architectural Archives of the University of Pennsylvania, Philadelphia. Gift of Robert Venturi and Denise Scott Brown

suggestion, Venturi agreed to revise portions of the text, which she characterized (to Drexler) as "a strange combination of sensitivity, intelligence, and disorganization, awkwardness and diffidence."[33] The editing was intensive and continued well into 1966, when Venturi started losing his patience. In a letter to Drexler from March of that year, he wrote: "I have continuously requested from you a meeting with the Museum publications department in order to work out a schedule. You have ignored my requests. It has been three years since this manuscript was finished; won't you please establish a firm schedule leading to the earliest possible publication date."[34]

Little acceleration of the project resulted, and despite being announced in MoMA's fall 1966 new books preview,[35] and although the book's colophon states 1966, *Complexity and Contradiction* was further delayed by distribution problems and only became available in bookstores in March 1967.[36] But Venturi seems to have quickly forgotten the delays. "The book is beautiful," he wrote to Drexler on March 14, adding: "the care which you and Ellen and the Publications Department lavished on it really shows."[37] Thus came to successful conclusion a project that had started several years earlier and which had undergone a considerable metamorphosis, reflecting a lengthy and thorough editing process as well as the changing interests of its author.

The consistent support of The Museum of Modern Art and the Graham Foundation as well as the responsible individuals at those two powerful institutions not only made possible the publication of *Complexity and Contradiction* but also laid the groundwork for its subsequent international visibility. Venturi's treatise could probably have found a different publisher, but at the time it was a good match for the vision, shared by Drexler and Entenza, of a joint platform for the dissemination of architectural theory. Beyond that, Venturi's argument crystallized a particular sensibility that can—for MoMA, for Drexler, and in the bigger picture—be understood as a sign of the fundamental crisis of late modernist architecture.

Questioning Modernism from Within

This brings us back to the question of how the publication of *Complexity and Contradiction* relates to the Museum's role as gatekeeper of (high) modernist architecture. As stated above, Venturi's first book-length publication could be read—and was indeed taken—as a frontal attack on latter-day modernism. Drexler noted in his foreword: "Venturi's book opposes what many would consider Establishment, or at least established, opinions. He speaks with uncommon candor."[38] What Venturi opposed most vehemently was what he called "simplification or picturesqueness," and it could not go unnoticed that the very first example of such architecture that Venturi referenced was Wiley House (fig. 5), designed in 1953 by Philip Johnson, the founder and long-term director of the Department of Architecture at MoMA. Venturi writes: "In the Wiley House . . . in contrast to his glass house, Philip Johnson attempted to go beyond the simplicities of the elegant pavilion. He explicitly separated and articulated the enclosed 'private functions' of living on a ground floor pedestal, thus separating them from the open social functions in the modular pavilion above. But even here the building becomes a diagram of an oversimplified program for living—an abstract theory of either-or. Where simplicity cannot work, simpleness results. Blatant simplification means bland architecture. Less is a bore."[39]

To be sure, Venturi's assessment of Johnson's work would qualify as "uncommon candor." That said, he presented an informed and nuanced argument that did not, as has often been asserted, simply condemn modernism *tout court*. Rather, *Complexity and Contradiction* opened up a way to reconsider the tenets of modern architecture by presenting a series of alternate and original readings of some of its finest achievements. Venturi repeatedly returns to Le Corbusier to illustrate complex and contradictory architecture, and on several occasions favorably references the architecture of postwar Italy. In fact, and perhaps somewhat surprisingly, both Drexler and Johnson apparently appreciated Venturi's book as essentially a reaffirmation of the

Fig. 5. Philip Johnson (American, 1906–2005). Robert C. Wiley House. New Canaan, Conn. 1953. Fig. 1 of Robert Venturi, *Complexity and Contradiction in Architecture*

modern project that suggested a course correction away from a path that had become too rigid and narrow. A note from Johnson to Venturi in April 1967 leaves no doubt of the older architect's support: "Dear Bob: People tell me there are horrible things about me in your book, but I haven't found them. I have been plowing gently, but I must say your argument is very 'dense.'"[40] It should also not be forgotten that Johnson continued to be an avid supporter of Venturi's intellectual endeavors, and when Venturi and Denise Scott Brown were proposing their seminal Learning from Las Vegas research studio at Yale, they approached Johnson for financial support.[41]

If Venturi's argument did not have an altogether clear and direct impact on Johnson's and Drexler's thinking, it certainly articulated the increasing concern about the fate of modernist architecture that was shared by all three. After his high-modernist beginnings, Johnson would come to embrace postmodernism fully —a move that was, however, not exactly condoned by Venturi and Scott Brown, as evidenced, following the completion of Johnson's iconic AT&T building, by Scott Brown's 1979 article in *The Saturday Review*, "High Boy: The Making of an Eclectic" (fig. 6).[42] There, Scott Brown observes that "the problem with Johnson the artist seems to be that he is not centered." She goes on to say that the building "is self-indulgent and lacks anguish. It does not demonstrate why its symbolic allusions to 'periods from Rome to the 1920s' are right for AT&T, or us, today. It should give the sense of pushing against the bounds and constraints of the commonplace to claim a little more for our bedraggled society, it should give this feeling even if it is built in gold." Citing the violent social upheaval of American society in the 1960s, she concludes: "Today's architects should expend their passionate grappling architecturally with its consequences. . . . The current flurries in architectural thought—radical eclecticism, postmodernism, the new rationalism, Beaux-Arts revivalism—serve to distract us from the more difficult task."[43]

Fig. 6. Cover of *Time* magazine. January 8, 1979. Featuring Philip Johnson carrying a model of his AT&T Building

Drexler, meanwhile, also showed signs of increasing doubt about the gospel of high modernism. In his 1957 exhibition *Buildings for Business and Government*, he had still fully embraced its abstract aesthetic and its application to all the institutions of the postwar American military-industrial-bureaucratic complex (fig. 7). Over the course of the 1960s, however, his attitude became more and more ambiguous. In the schism between the "Whites" and "Grays,"[44] which occurred at the fault line between neomodernism and postmodernism, Drexler positioned himself as a mediator between the two

7.

8.

camps. Already in his introduction to the catalogue of the 1964 exhibition *Twentieth Century Engineering* he emphasized the aesthetic qualities of the exhibited masterpieces of modern bridge and dam construction over their constructive principles, declaring: "The objectivity of engineering is a myth."[45] This suggests that he had started to question high-modernist doctrine by the mid-1960s and was thus particularly open at the time to the arguments in Venturi's treatise. The aforementioned 1975 exhibition *The Architecture of the École des Beaux-Arts*—which Scott Brown would a few years later critically reference in turn—still more clearly marked his rejection of a narrowly defined high modernism, which he now explicitly criticized for embracing the "reductionist imperative of the engineering style" (fig. 8).[46]

Four years after the Beaux-Arts exhibition, Drexler had developed an openly critical and pessimistic reading of the modernist project. His 1979 exhibition *Transformations in Modern Architecture* presented the history of postwar architecture as a narrative of decline (fig. 9).[47] In an accompanying lecture, he invoked the trauma of the Vietnam War and the assassinations of JFK as well as Martin Luther King in order to define the cultural situation of the present, a time when the belief in the modern project and the benevolent nature of the state and the corporate world on which it was built had been fundamentally shattered: "We are at the moment struggling with the consequences of our previous beliefs and actions. But the struggle has not yet revealed any new beliefs or actions."[48] Modernism had

Fig. 7. Installation view of the exhibition *Buildings for Business and Government*. The Museum of Modern Art, New York, February 27– April 28, 1957. Photographic Archive. The Museum of Modern Art Archives, New York

Fig. 8. Installation view of the exhibition *The Architecture of the École des Beaux-Arts*. The Museum of Modern Art, New York, October 29, 1975–January 4, 1976. Photographic Archive. The Museum of Modern Art Archives, New York

9.

lost its credibility as a progressive force, Drexler argued, and was increasingly complicit with reactionary forces and global capitalism. Nowhere did Venturi offer such a political assessment of modernism. But it is difficult not to see Drexler's increasing alienation from modernist doctrine as in tune with Venturi's initial, albeit mainly formalist critique.[49]

Indeed, *Complexity and Contradiction* turned out to become a true game changer for the discipline of architecture—to a degree and in a direction that Venturi may not have envisioned, given that he saw it as primarily concerned with questions of architectural form. As much as he would in subsequent years cast himself as an outsider in the architectural world and as a veritable enfant terrible of the profession, it is notable that the book was launched as a provocation from within the very establishment that Venturi set out to criticize. The dissemination of his iconoclastic ideas profited enormously from the institutional apparatus whose ideological foundations he challenged, while, conversely, his treatise had a lasting impact on The Museum of Modern Art's outlook on the trajectory of late modernist architecture. Its consequences are still with us today.

Fig. 9. Installation view of the exhibition *Transformations in Modern Architecture*. The Museum of Modern Art, New York, February 21–April 24, 1979. Photographic Archive. The Museum of Modern Art Archives, New York

I would like to thank Mechthild Ebert, Jake Gagne, and Phoebe Springstubb, who assisted me with research in various archives. At the Architectural Archives of the University of Pennsylvania, I am particularly indebted to William Whitaker for his guidance.

Notes

1. Drexler to Entenza, November 11, 1963, RM box 6611, "Venturi's Book," The Museum of Modern Art Archives, New York.
2. Venturi to Drexler, September 18, 1963, 225.XI.57, "'MSS: Early Original of C&C + Correspondence,'" drafts, correspondence and other documents, circa 1956–1966," VSB Collection, AAUP, Philadelphia (hereafter cited as VSB Collection, AAUP).
3. Drexler to Entenza, November 11, 1963. In another letter to Entenza, Drexler mentions a project by Charles Hamilton Burnette as another candidate for the proposed series. Burnette's research in the 1960s connected architecture with information technology, in sync with early explorations of systems theory by architects such as Nicholas Negroponte and Christopher Alexander. (See Charles Hamilton Burnette and Luis H. Summers, "An Organization of Information for Computer-Aided Communication in Architecture," *Review of Research in Visual and Environmental Education* 1, no. 1 [spring 1973]: 20–30.) Drexler to Entenza, November 20, 1963, RM box 6611, "Venturi's Book," The Museum of Modern Art Archives, New York.
4. Joseph Rykwert, *On Adam's House in Paradise: The Idea of the Primitive Hut in Architectural History*, The Museum of Modern Art Papers on Architecture 2 (New York: The Museum of Modern Art in association with the Graham Foundation for Advanced Studies in the Fine Arts, Chicago, 1972).
5. Venturi to Entenza, February 15, 1962, 225.XI.54, "Graham Foundation grant application (project description and résumé) with telegram announcing selection, 1962," VSB Collection, AAUP.
6. As I have argued elsewhere, *Complexity and Contradiction* can be considered a late result of Venturi's tenure at the American Academy in Rome from 1954 to 1956, during which time many of his intellectual preoccupations took shape. See Martino Stierli, "In the Academy's Garden: Robert Venturi, the Grand Tour and the Revision of Modern Architecture," *AA Files*, no. 56 (2007): 42–55.
7. Entenza to Venturi, April 18, 1962, 225.XI.54, "Graham Foundation grant application (project description and résumé) with telegram announcing selection, 1962," VSB Collection, AAUP.
8. Entenza to Venturi, "Terms of Grant," April 16, 1962, 225. XI.56, "Graham Foundation correspondence, especially with John Entenza, 1962–1963," VSB Collection, AAUP.
9. Entenza to Venturi, December 28, 1962, 225.XI.56, "Graham Foundation correspondence, especially with John Entenza, 1962–1963," VSB Collection, AAUP.
10. Ellen Marsh to Venturi, November 27, 1961, 225.VI.D.8, "Correspondence, 1962," VSB Collection, AAUP.

11. Venturi to Ellen Marsh, January 9, 1962, 225.VI.D.8, "Correspondence, 1962," VSB Collection, AAUP.
12. These are mainly photographs of plans and drawings as well as model photographs for a number of projects, including that for new artists' studios in the garden of the American Academy in Rome (1956), the residence for Forrest Pearson in Philadelphia (1958), the Vanna Venturi House in Philadelphia's Chestnut Hill (in several iterations), the Beach House project (1959), a project for a Community for the Aged in Gwynedd, Pennsylvania (1960), and the FDR Memorial competition in Washington, D.C. (1960). With the exception of the studios for the American Academy in Rome and the Community for the Aged, all of these projects were featured in the final section of *Complexity and Contradiction*.
13. See Jean-Louis Cohen's contribution to this volume, pp. 114–27. Upon publication of Venturi's treatise, Richard Krautheimer sent a note of congratulations to the author. Krautheimer to Venturi, April 2, 1967, 225.XI.58, "Correspondence, mostly congratulatory letters, 1956–1967," VSB Collection, AAUP.
14. Labatut to Venturi, June 12, 1963, 225.XI.57, "'MSS: Early Original of C&C + Correspondence,' drafts, correspondence and other documents, circa 1956–1966," VSB Collection, AAUP.
15. Venturi to Harvard University Press, August 8, 1963, 225.XI.57, "'MSS: Early Original of C&C + Correspondence,' drafts, correspondence and other documents, circa 1956–1966," VSB Collection, AAUP.
16. In a letter to Labatut on March 23, 1964, Venturi mentions that The Museum of Modern Art had agreed to move forward with the publication the preceding week. Venturi to Labatut, March 23, 1964, 225.XI.61, "List of individuals who received copies, and thank-you letters, 1967, undated," VSB Collection, AAUP.
17. Entenza to Drexler, April 14, 1964, RM box 6611, "Venturi's Book," The Museum of Modern Art Archives, New York.
18. Venturi to Drexler, April 22, 1964, RM box 6611, "Venturi's Book," The Museum of Modern Art Archives, New York.
19. Venturi to Esther McCoy, July 21, 1964, 225.VI.D.23, "Esther McCoy; correspondence, 1964, 1966, undated," VSB Collection, AAUP.
20. Esther McCoy to Venturi, August 22, 1964, 225.VI.D.23, "Esther McCoy; correspondence, 1964, 1966, undated," VSB Collection, AAUP.
21. Ibid. See also Robert Venturi, "Complexity and Contradiction in Architecture: Selections from a Forthcoming Book," *Perspecta* 9/10 (1965): 17–56.
22. Venturi to Esther McCoy, December 26, 1964, 225.VI.D.17, "Correspondence, 1964" (folder 1 of 4), VSB Collection, AAUP.
23. Helen M. Franc, interview with Sharon Zane, section dating from May 28, 1991, Oral History Program, pp. 114–15, The Museum of Modern Art Archives, New York.
24. For a detailed account of the editorial history, see Mary McLeod's contribution to this volume, pp. 50–75, esp. 69n29.

25. See note 22.
26. Vincent Scully, "Robert Venturi's Gentle Architecture," in *Modern Architecture and Other Essays*, ed. Neil Levine (Princeton, N.J.: Princeton University Press, 2003), 260–64.
27. See Vincent Scully, "New Talent USA: Architecture," *Art in America* 49, no. 1 (1961): 63.
28. Paul Goldberger, "Paul Goldberger Reflects on Vincent Scully's Legacy," *Architectural Record*, December 1, 2017, https://www.architecturalrecord.com/articles/13149-paul-goldberger-reflects-on-vincent-scullys-legacy.
29. This is most evident in the essay Scully published on the occasion of the inaugural Venice Architecture Biennale, *The Presence of the Past*, directed by Paolo Portoghesi in 1980. Taking Drexler's 1979 exhibition *Transformations in Modern Architecture* as a starting point, Scully argued that the contemporary work of Venturi in the United States and Aldo Rossi in Italy would form the basis for a renewal of the discipline. See Scully, "Where Is Modern Architecture Going?," in *Modern Architecture and Other Essays*, 158–69.
30. Drexler to Monroe Wheeler, July 30, 1964, RM box 6611, "Venturi's Book," The Museum of Modern Art Archives, New York. The letter names, besides the addressee, Mike Gladstone as a further reader.
31. Helen M. Franc to Drexler, September 4, 1964, RM box 6611, "Venturi's Book," The Museum of Modern Art Archives, New York.
32. Wohl to Drexler, December 13, 1964; Drexler to Wohl, December 15, 1964; Drexler to Entenza, December 16, 1964; Entenza to Drexler, December 18, 1964, RM box 6611, "Venturi's Book," The Museum of Modern Art Archives, New York. On Marian Wohl, see Mary McLeod in this volume, p. 69n28.
33. Wohl to Drexler, December 13, 1964, RM box 6611, "Venturi's Book," The Museum of Modern Art Archives, New York.
34. Venturi to Drexler, March 8, 1966, 225.XI.57, "'MSS: Early Original of C&C + Correspondence,' drafts, correspondence and other documents, circa 1956–1966," VSB Collection, AAUP. The progress of the publication seems to have been additionally delayed by an unexpected serious illness of Drexler's. Associate Curator Ludwig Glaeser responded on Drexler's behalf, confirming that the typescript was being finished and that the book was to be published in October 1966. See Ellen Marsh to Venturi, March 18, 1966, and Ludwig Glaeser to Venturi, March 24, 1966, both RM box 6611, "Venturi's Book," The Museum of Modern Art Archives, New York.
35. Announcement, "Fall 1966 Books, published by The Museum of Modern Art," 225.II E.10, "MoMA C&C," VSB Collection, AAUP.
36. Edward E. Fitzgerald (Doubleday & Company) to Venturi, November 21, 1967, 225.II E.10 "MoMA C&C," VSB Collection, AAUP.
37. Venturi to Drexler, March 14, 1967, 225.XI.61, "List of individuals who received copies, and thank-you letters, 1967, undated," VSB Collection, AAUP.

38. Arthur Drexler, foreword to *Complexity and Contradiction in Architecture*, by Robert Venturi, The Museum of Modern Art Papers on Architecture 1 (New York: The Museum of Modern Art in association with the Graham Foundation for Advanced Studies in the Fine Arts, Chicago, 1966), 9.

39. Venturi, *Complexity and Contradiction*, 25.

40. Johnson to Venturi, April 12, 1967, 225.XI.58, "Correspondence, mostly congratulatory letters, 1956–1967," VSB Collection, AAUP.

41. Venturi to Johnson, April 11 and April 17, 1968, 225.VI.A.6905. 39, "Correspondence," VSB Collection, AAUP.

42. Denise Scott Brown, "High Boy: The Making of an Eclectic," *Saturday Review*, March 17, 1979, 54–58, reprinted in Denise Scott Brown, *Having Words*, AA Words 4 (London: Architectural Association, 2009).

43. Scott Brown, *Having Words*, 96.

44. For a detailed discussion of the trajectory of Drexler's position vis-à-vis the emergence of postmodernism in architecture, see Felicity D. Scott, "When Systems Fail: Arthur Drexler and the Postmodern Turn," *Perspecta* 35 (2004): 134–53.

45. Arthur Drexler, introduction to *Twentieth Century Engineering* (New York: The Museum of Modern Art, 1964), n.p.

46. Arthur Drexler, "Engineer's Architecture: Truth and its Consequences," in *The Architecture of the École des Beaux-Arts*, ed. Arthur Drexler (New York: The Museum of Modern Art, 1977), 15. I am indebted to Matthew Worsnick, whose unpublished seminar paper "Engineering Fictions: The Polemics of Twentieth Century Engineering and Drexler's Drift toward the Beaux-Arts" was helpful in shaping my argument.

47. Arthur Drexler, *Transformations in Modern Architecture* (New York: The Museum of Modern Art, 1979).

48. Arthur Drexler, sound recording of lecture, "Transformations in Modern Architecture," Titus Auditorium, The Museum of Modern Art, New York, April 10, 1979, box 79.29, The Museum of Modern Art Archives, New York.

49. For the apparent lack of a political stance in *Complexity and Contradiction*, see Dianne Harris's contribution to this volume, pp. 130–41.

Stephen Kieran and James Timberlake

Manifestos do not abound in architecture, and when they do arrive, it is at moments of great cultural, economic, or technological inflection. Often utopian visions in search of an alternative future, they are generally of two sorts. Some manifestos seek to recover a paradise lost—think of Leon Battista Alberti's and Andrea Palladio's respective versions of Vitruvius's *Ten Books on Architecture*, which both bring the past forward, resurrecting the Roman author's original for a new age of humanist renewal. Other manifestos reach for an unseen paradise, apparent in Le Corbusier's invocation of "eyes that do not see" in *Towards a New Architecture* (1923) or Filippo Tommaso Marinetti's 1909 *Manifesto of Futurism*, each of which was imbued with the excitement and speed of the machine age and encouraged a break with the humanist past in favor of an industrialized tomorrow.

Robert Venturi's *Complexity and Contradiction in Architecture* is neither of these sorts of texts. It does not call for some historical ideal, nor for a nascent, unrealized future. Instead, it is (in the words of its author) a "gentle manifesto" that finds an uneasy place in the present, negotiating the past within the future and the future within the past while itself uncomfortably poised between them. Still, in the same way that the *Ten Books on Architecture* and *Towards a New Architecture* arose in moments of enormous cultural and technological change, so too is *Complexity and Contradiction* a product of its time. It was born amid the cultural unrest that permeated the United States in the 1960s—marked by the civil rights movement, the second-wave feminism of the women's movement, the sexual revolution, the anti–Vietnam War protests. The text reflects the ideas behind this period of unrest: the distrust of authority and the rejection of sweeping uniformity in favor of interventions within the world as it is, not as we want it to be.

Though its measured views, so focused on the present, make *Complexity and Contradiction* iconic, they can confuse our interpretation of the text. Manifestos are easier to grasp when they look forcefully back to the rule, measure, and composition of the past, or forward to the exciting image and technology of the future. But *Complexity and Contradiction* builds a different kind of framework, a distinctly nonutopian path sketched out through a study of the present, a path that accepts it in its unedited glory and welcomes the simultaneity of history, reveling equally in preservation and change. It guides the architect by casting away rule and image and prioritizing principles above all else. These principles (ambiguity, both-and, double-functioning elements, conventional elements, contradiction) are the subjects of individual chapters in the book, each of which functions as a primer that illuminates by example. For its authority, the writing draws upon the literary criticism of the early modernist T. S. Eliot and the New Critic Cleanth Brooks.

As students coming of age in the 1970s, what did *Complexity and Contradiction* mean to us? Above all, it established essential ethical limits for architecture that resonated with our deeply alienated generation, shining a light toward a future that neither obliterated nor lionized the past. Because the text is not simply black or white, but decidedly difficult and gray, it celebrates situational judgment over dogmatic principle. In recognizing context as the first act of design, it legitimized and engrained a research ethic that remains with us. For us, Le Corbusier's "eyes that do not see" were refracted through the prism of *Complexity and Contradiction* to become eyes that *do* see—eyes that look, record, and refine in ways that ultimately lead to ethical response and action.

Teaching Complexity and Contradiction at the University of Pennsylvania, 1961–65

Lee Ann Custer

Every spring semester from 1961 to 1965, Robert Venturi taught Theories of Architecture at the University of Pennsylvania in Philadelphia.[1] His surviving lecture notes reveal close connections between the course and the manuscript for *Complexity and Contradiction in Architecture*, which Venturi developed for four years from 1962 until shortly before its publication.[2] Despite the course's different format, it was a crucial testing ground for many of the ideas that would be taken up more polemically in the book, such as sensitivity to site, the embrace of ambiguity, and careful attention to the relationship of the part to the whole. In conjunction with an exploration of Venturi's own academic background, an examination of the course within the intellectual context of Penn in the 1960s, including the influential involvement of Denise Scott Brown, demonstrates that Theories of Architecture was a critical step in the making of *Complexity and Contradiction*. As he recalled in 1991, "the book came out of the course. I would not have dreamt of doing it [otherwise]."[3]

Approximately sixty first-year graduate students of architecture and the occasional advanced undergraduate attended Venturi's weekly two-hour classes in the large lecture room

Fig. 1. Robert Venturi working in the slide room at the University of Pennsylvania, Philadelphia. February 1961. George Pohl Collection. The Architectural Archives of the University of Pennsylvania, Philadelphia

in Hayden Hall.[4] The lectures focused on what Venturi classified as the "elements" of architectural design:[5] site and context, use and program, structure and form, materials and texture, mechanical equipment, ideas about space, sequences of spaces, light, scale, composition with an emphasis on unity and proportion, composition with an emphasis on balance and rhythm, ornament, and technology in architecture.[6] Although they were rearranged slightly over the five iterations of the course, each such element was the core subject for a single lecture. Venturi explicitly grounded the discussion of his own elements in the Vitruvian trilogy of commodity, firmness, and delight, considering each of his topics as complementary to Vitruvius's broader themes.[7] In an introductory and concluding lecture, Venturi laid out his aims: to illustrate the variety with which his elements had been handled throughout history, to convey the multiplicity of valid approaches to making architecture, and to emphasize the instructive comparisons, analogies, and examples that history provided (fig. 1).[8]

•

Venturi arrived at Penn's School of Fine Arts as a teaching assistant for Louis I. Kahn in 1954,[9] at a time when the curriculum was being overhauled. The instigator of these changes was G. Holmes Perkins, who came to Penn as dean in 1951 and shifted the school's Beaux-Arts approach to Bauhaus-oriented modernism.[10] He emphasized graduate education, added departments of landscape architecture and city planning, and hired new faculty, among them Venturi, Kahn, and Scott Brown along with Romaldo Giurgola, Robert Geddes, and George Qualls.[11] These prominent designers, as well as a few others, would come to be known as the Philadelphia School.[12]

Venturi's lecture course was part of Perkins's new architectural curriculum. As the dean shifted the school toward graduate-only education in 1959 and 1960, he launched four new theory courses.[13] Perkins and Giurgola taught the two upper-level classes on civic design and architecture, respectively,[14] while Venturi and Scott Brown taught the pair of introductory courses. Each fall from 1961 to 1963, Scott Brown presented Theories of Architecture, City Planning, and Landscape Architecture. As well as convening guest lectures on design philosophy as part of the course, she ran a weekly seminar that bridged these lectures and students' studio work—a hallmark of her teaching methodology in city planning (fig. 2).[15] In 1964 Scott Brown joined Venturi's Theories of Architecture course to lead

weekly seminars, continuing to emphasize the integration of
lecture room and studio.[16] This was the first time that Venturi
and Scott Brown taught together, anticipating their partnership
and the combination of research and design that they would
implement in their later studios on the New York City subway,
Las Vegas, and Levittown.[17] In her seminars for Theories of
Architecture, Scott Brown asked students to explore various
topics linked to the lectures, among them "components and
their coordination," "structure and light," and "scale."[18] In the
1964 and 1965 course bibliographies for Theories of Architecture, Venturi introduced reading materials from Scott Brown's
city planning and theory classes—a further sign of their collaborative and integrated thinking.[19]

As in *Complexity and Contradiction*, the driving force
of Venturi's lectures was vivid comparative visual analysis.
While emphasizing the Western European tradition and the
architecture of the United States, he chose examples from a
broad swath of architectural history to accompany his lectures, as well as a selection of contemporary projects by the
likes of Oscar Niemeyer and Kenzō Tange.[20] Frequently referenced buildings included San Carlo alle Quattro Fontane,
the Villa Savoye, and the works of Frank Furness. Venturi's
lecture on structure and form illustrated the relationship
between tectonics and aesthetics with a dazzling variety of
domes: Hagia Sophia, St. Peter's, Santa Maria della Salute,
Pier Luigi Nervi's Palazzetto dello Sport, and Thomas Ustick
Walter's dome for the United States Capitol (figs. 3a–g).[21] The
lecture on materials and texture presented an equally broad

Fig. 2. Denise Scott Brown at Rice
University, Houston, where she
taught with Robert Venturi in
January and February 1969. The
Architectural Archives of the Univer-
sity of Pennsylvania, Philadelphia

Figs. 3a–g. Robert Venturi. Slide
images from lecture IV, dated
February 4, 1964. The Architectural
Archives of the University of Pennsylvania, Philadelphia. Gift of Robert
Venturi and Denise Scott Brown
3a. and b. Hagia Sophia
3c. St. Peter's Basilica
3d. Santa Maria della Salute
3e. Pier Luigi Nervi (Italian, 1891–
1979) and Annibale Vitellozzi (Italian,
1902–1990). Palazzetto dello Sport,
Rome. 1956–57
3f. Thomas Ustick Walter (American,
1804–1887). Dome and extension
of the United States Capitol,
Washington, D.C. Elevation of dome.
c. 1859
3g. Thomas Ustick Walter (American,
1804–1887). Dome and extension
of the United States Capitol,
Washington, D.C. Section of dome.
c. 1859

3a.

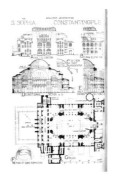

3b.

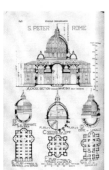

3c.

3d.

3e.

3f.

3g.

4a.   4b.   4c.

4d.   4e.

sampling: Louis Sullivan's Carson, Pirie, Scott and Company Building in Chicago as well as his National Farmers' Bank of Owatonna in Minnesota, Henry Hobson Richardson's Ames Gate Lodge, the seventeenth century–style Shofuso Japanese house in Philadelphia's Fairmount Park, and Mount Vernon (figs. 4a–e).[22]

In spite of the vast historical range of these examples, however, Venturi did not consider Theories of Architecture a history course.[23] Rather than being presented in a traditional chronological arrangement, the images were first and foremost tools for visual analysis and criticism.[24] Students recalled that they were often unable to recognize all of Venturi's examples[25] and reported that the visual juxtapositions were among the most memorable and impactful parts of the class.[26] Readers of *Complexity and Contradiction* were later given a similarly challenging transhistorical array,[27] demonstrating how Venturi was interested in learning from what others had built.[28]

Figs. **4a–e.** Robert Venturi. Slide images from lecture V, dated February 11, 1964. The Architectural Archives of the University of Pennsylvania, Philadelphia. Gift of Robert Venturi and Denise Scott Brown
4a. Louis Sullivan (American, 1856–1924). Carson, Pirie, Scott Building, Chicago. 1899. Detail of facade
4b. Louis Sullivan (American, 1856–1924). National Farmers' Bank of Owatonna, Minnesota. 1908. Detail of facade
4c. H. H. Richardson (American, 1838–1886). Ames Gate Lodge, North Easton, Mass. 1880–81
4d. Junzō Yoshimura (Japanese, 1908–1997). Shofuso, Philadelphia. 1953/1958
4e. Mount Vernon

In this approach, Venturi drew upon his undergraduate and graduate education at Princeton. There, the architectural historian Donald Drew Egbert had instilled in him the kind of historical sensibility that was being de-emphasized at other prominent architecture programs, notably at Harvard.[29] A copy of Egbert's Modern Architecture syllabus was tucked into Venturi's own lecture notes for Theories of Architecture—a testament to his influence.[30] Another professor of Venturi's, Jean Labatut, likely inspired Venturi's comparative method. To teach the relationship of buildings to their surroundings, for instance, Labatut compared houses in ancient Rome, medieval Europe, nineteenth-century New England, and twentieth-century garden cities.[31] Venturi adopted a similar methodology and centered his lectures on many of the same topics Labatut had, including unity, proportion, scale, rhythm, and light.[32]

Not only did Venturi utilize the comparative visual methodology of his Penn course in *Complexity and Contradiction*, but many of the book's foundational concepts were already evident in the lectures. In both the introductory class and the book's preface, Venturi quoted the same passages from T. S. Eliot and architectural historian Henry-Russell Hitchcock on the value of tradition and history. In the poet's case he turned to the 1919 essay "Tradition and the Individual Talent," where Eliot lamented, "In English writing . . . we seldom speak of tradition," and then explained why: "Tradition . . . cannot be inherited, and if you want it you must obtain it by great labour."[33] In both places, Venturi would maintain that a tradition laboriously assembled in this way was of crucial importance for architecture. He also approvingly quoted from Hitchcock's call (made in 1960) for a new, modern engagement with history: "Once, of course, almost all investigation of the architecture of the past was in aid of its nominal reconstruction. . . . Today, it is with no idea of repeating forms, but rather in the expectation of feeding more amply new sensibilities that are wholly the product of the present."[34] This conception of the usefulness of the past for the present was a fundamental premise in both Venturi's lectures and his book.

Another key idea that moved from the lectures to the book was that of the hierarchic "nesting" of larger and smaller architectural spaces. In lecture II of the course, devoted to site and context, and again in chapter 9 of *Complexity and Contradiction*, "The Inside and the Outside," Venturi quoted Eliel Saarinen's description of this phenomenon: "a building is the 'organization of space in space. So is the community. So is the city.'"[35] In the

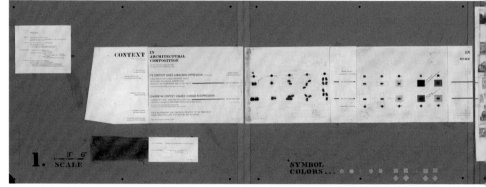

5a.

book, he added: "I think this series [of nested spaces] could start with the idea of a room as a space in space."[36]

Venturi also tested early drafts of the book on his students. On one occasion, his lecture notes directed him to "*read from something I've written* concerning degrees of continuity: and a particular attitude towards it. . . . Quote at length."[37] Cut and taped excerpts of an early manuscript of *Complexity and Contradiction* follow, in which he quotes Horatio Greenough, Henry David Thoreau, Sullivan, and Le Corbusier—architects and thinkers who advocated that buildings should seem to grow "from the inside out."[38] These were eloquent "antagonists," as Venturi called them, to whom he argued back that "the inside *is* different from the outside."[39] His notes show that he then turned to two examples that demonstrated his preferred distinction between interior and exterior: Alvar Aalto's Bremen apartment building and Frank Lloyd Wright's V. C. Morris Gift Shop.[40]

Venturi's embrace of "context," based loosely on Gestalt psychology, was another important theme that passed from the lectures to the book—one that can be traced back to his Princeton days, and specifically to his MFA thesis of 1950 (figs. 5a–c).[41] For that project, he designed a chapel for his high school alma mater, the Episcopal Academy in Merion, Pennsylvania, which was designed to link two older buildings. To justify a design that explicitly embraced its historical context, he assembled a large portfolio of examples where the surrounding buildings were also of paramount importance, among them the Trevi Fountain and the Campidoglio.[42] His appreciation of architectural contexts, Venturi avowed, had been shaped by his first trip to Europe in 1948.[43] His further experience of Rome from 1954 to 1956—when he was, thanks to a Rome Prize Fellowship, a guest of the American

Figs. 5a–c. Robert Venturi. "Context in Architectural Composition." MFA thesis, Princeton University. February 1950. The Architectural Archives of the University of Pennsylvania, Philadelphia. Gift of Robert Venturi and Denise Scott Brown
5b. Trevi Fountain. Detail of 5a.
5c. Piazza del Campidoglio. Detail of 5a.

5b.

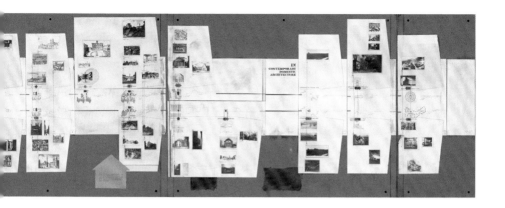

Academy—expanded his encyclopedia of architectural ideas and his appreciation of the city's multiepochal architectural ensemble.[44]

In addition to these clear commonalities between the major theoretical underpinnings of Theories of Architecture and *Complexity and Contradiction*, Venturi's distinctive specialized terminology is apparent in both endeavors. In lecture III ("Use"), for instance, Venturi celebrated "double-functioning" elements, such as piers that defined space as well as provided support, which Venturi claimed had been "discouraged in modern architecture."[45] The idea reappears in chapter 5 of the book, "Contradictory Levels Continued: The Double-Functioning Element," where Venturi hewed closely to his own lecture notes: "The double-functioning element has been used infrequently in Modern architecture."[46] In lecturing on compositional unity, Venturi coined the phrase "the difficult whole," explaining that "the degree of multiplicity has much to do with effecting the sense of the whole."[47] Chapter 10 of the book ("The Obligation Toward the Difficult Whole") reiterates: "An architecture of complexity and contradiction also embraces the 'difficult' numbers of parts—the duality, and the medium degrees of multiplicity."[48] Occasionally the same diagram illustrates the same idea in a lecture and the book. Venturi's lecture notes, for instance, contain thumbnail sketches of what he called "linings"—the layers between inside and outside space; the same images recur as figure 159 of *Complexity and Contradiction* (figs. 6a–b).[49]

Venturi's lecture notes are a complex palimpsest of the five iterations of the course—bearing the evidence of annual reuse and modification (fig. 7). The surviving notes likely correspond most closely to the final 1965 version of the course,

5c.

6a.

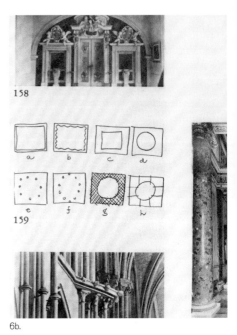
158

159

6b.

Figs. 6a–b.
6a. Robert Venturi. Handwritten notes, lecture VII. c. 1965. The Architectural Archives of the University of Pennsylvania, Philadelphia. Gift of Robert Venturi and Denise Scott Brown
6b. Detail of p. 77 of Robert Venturi, *Complexity and Contradiction in Architecture*

but these successive edits are undated and the notes by themselves do not make it possible to determine precisely when an idea appeared or whether its appearance preceded or coincided with its use in the evolving book manuscript. Indeed, in some cases, the book may have shaped the class, especially in the later years when the manuscript was nearing completion.

In addition to the lecture notes, however, the Venturi archive contains the dated outlines that he handed out to students at each lecture, and these show conclusively that a large number of his most important ideas were presented in the earliest versions of the lectures, predating his work on the book. For instance, the idea of the "relation between exterior and interior space" is already mentioned in a 1961 lecture outline, along with his distinctive references to Sullivan, Wright, Le Corbusier, and Thoreau.[50] The phrase "the double functioning of elements" appeared in 1962, and was anticipated by the phrase "the generic and the specific function" in a 1961 outline.[51] The "difficult whole" did not appear on a lecture outline until 1964, but the related idea of "unity through multiplicity of parts" was used in 1961.[52] We can thus see that, while each fed into the other, Theories of Architecture was a potent incubator for the central tenets of *Complexity and Contradiction*.

But if much of the book's content was anticipated in the lectures, not all the lecture content was moved into the book, which largely omitted the practical side—the tools that Venturi's students could apply directly to their studio work. Absent from the written project was, for instance, the discussion of daylight, which was illustrated with slides of Monet's famous Rouen Cathedral series.[53] He also spoke to students about where heating and cooking equipment could best be located in modern American homes and had instructive advice about chimneys and kitchens.[54] Nor does the book reissue the warning that Venturi made to his students about the "dangers" of focusing on composition at the cost of other elements of design. With his own slant apparent, he warned against "a tendency to ignore context[,] to discount materials and methods, to discount changing effects of light and color," and so on.[55]

In other words, the book both lacked the practical content of the lectures and adopted a far more polemical tone. Indeed, Venturi seems to have shied away from taking strong positions in the classroom, noting, for example, in a humorous and telling aside in his lecture on ornament, that ornament "is still a dangerous subject and a dirty word. Probably you should not spread it around that we are devoting a whole lecture to it in this course . . . although I make up for it partly by devoting half a lecture to technology next week."[56] Although the exact criteria for the inclusion or exclusion of material in the book or the course are not explicit from the archival records, Venturi appears to have wanted to explore subjects that ran counter to the faculty establishment at Penn and to some extent curtailed such ideas in his lectures for fear of what he called "corrupting the morals of architectural minors," as well as potential pushback from Perkins.[57] Some of his more notorious bon mots therefore appear for the first time in the book, including "less is a bore" and "is not Main Street almost all right?"[58] Nor did he discuss his own work extensively in class, whereas the substantial last section of the book is dedicated to his own designs.[59]

In general, the first five lectures (the introduction, and those on site, use, structure and form, and materials and texture) were related more closely to the book than those of the second half of the class, which were devoted to mechanical equipment, ideas of space, sequences of spaces, light, scale, balance and rhythm, and ornament.[60] Broadly speaking, over the years, Venturi also made far more extensive revisions to the first, more theoretical lectures than to the later lectures. Especially in 1962, 1964, and

1965, he expanded explanations, added new examples, and refined his terminology. This work was mirrored in the evolving book manuscript.[61] It was during this phase that some of the most idiosyncratic passages in *Complexity and Contradiction*, such as the references to Pop art and the idea of a corresponding Pop architecture, as well as the actual words "complexity and contradiction," were introduced, appearing at the same time in both Venturi's teaching and writing.[62]

A number of influential figures shaped these later revisions,[63] among whom Scott Brown exerted a unique impact—particularly, but not exclusively, through her collaboration on the 1964 version of the course. Her influence is clearly seen in the 1964 and 1965 lectures, to which Venturi added an aerial view of Levittown, a discussion of Kevin Lynch's idea of spatial sequences, and an increased emphasis on the city or regional scale of building.[64] Scott Brown had taught about Levittown with David Crane as early as 1960, and she assigned readings from Lynch in her city planning courses in 1961.[65] But her ideas can also be identified in Venturi's earlier teaching. In 1963, he added the "Team 10 Primer" (published the year prior) to his course bibliography, following the path blazed by Scott Brown who had been assigning the writings of its authors, Alison and Peter Smithson, since 1961.[66] Moreover, a mention of Scott Brown was added to the 1965 outline for lecture III, in connection with the idea of "function as the beginning in the design process," seemingly relying on her expertise for ideas that Venturi had been addressing in this lecture since 1962.[67] As confirmed by her own account, Scott Brown's specialization in city and regional planning began to permeate the course even before her direct involvement in 1964.[68] And her influence is detectable, of course, in the final version of *Complexity and Contradiction*, with its enlarged attention to examples reflecting her interests, such as billboard architecture, Times Square, and city planning in general.[69]

Fig. 7. Robert Venturi. Handwritten notes, lecture X. c. 1965. The Architectural Archives of the University of Pennsylvania, Philadelphia. Gift of Robert Venturi and Denise Scott Brown

●

The relationship between the course and the book was complex: the two endeavors were indelibly linked but did not collapse into one another. Their differences reflected their divergent objectives—one was a training tool for future architects, and the other was what Venturi called a "gentle manifesto" directed to a wider audience and posterity.[70] This sensitivity to

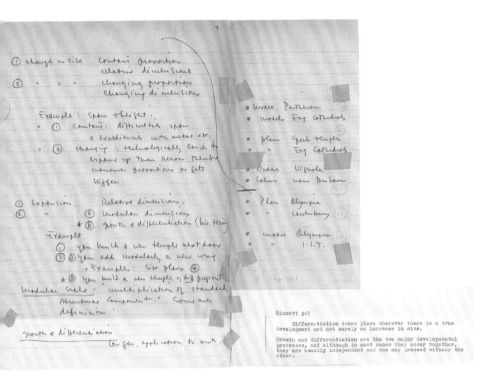

context—or even to the site-specificity of the two projects—
could be likened to that of the buildings Venturi admired. At
the beginning of his lecture on "Site and Context," he compared the relationship between architecture and setting exemplified by Fallingwater and the Villa Rotunda. In his notes,
we read: "Frank Lloyd Wright said to a friend of mine concerning Falling Water, 'give me a good site, and I'll give you
a good building.' Palladio would never have said that."[71] For
Venturi's course, such a site was offered by the dynamic academic setting of Penn in the first half of the 1960s; for the book
it was the launch of a planned series of publications on architecture by The Museum of Modern Art—and the public who
were to read them.[72] In this sense, the course and the book were
thus both unmistakably the same and undoubtedly different,
even contradictory, in a way that perhaps only Venturi could
accomplish.

Notes

1. This study is based on extensive research at the Architectural Archives of the University of Pennsylvania, Philadelphia (hereafter cited as AAUP). It owes much to the support of David B. Brownlee, Martino Stierli, William Whitaker, and Heather Isbell Schumacher. For documentation of course dates, see: syllabi and lecture outlines, Architecture 410, spring 1961; Architecture 412, spring 1962 and 1963; Architecture 512, spring 1964 and 1965; 225.XI.1–53, AAUP by the gift of Robert Venturi and Denise Scott Brown (hereafter cited as VSB Collection, AAUP). See also Penn's Graduate School of Fine Arts course bulletins for academic years 1960–61 through 1964–65, copies on file, 277.44–47, University of Pennsylvania Bulletin Collection, AAUP. In spring 1965 Venturi taught the course at both Penn and Yale. Lecture outlines, Architecture 11, spring 1965, 225.XI.26–38, VSB Collection, AAUP.

2. Robert Venturi, *Complexity and Contradiction in Architecture*, The Museum of Modern Art Papers on Architecture 1 (New York: The Museum of Modern Art in association with the Graham Foundation for Advanced Studies in the Fine Arts, Chicago, 1966). Venturi's proposal to the Graham Foundation for Advanced Studies in the Fine Arts, dated February 15, 1962, marks the beginning of the written project that would grow into *Complexity and Contradiction*, 030.II.A.61.2, Louis I. Kahn Collection, University of Pennsylvania and the Pennsylvania Historical and Museum Collection. Housed in the AAUP's Harvey and Irwin Kroiz Gallery, the resources of the Kahn Collection are used with the permission of AAUP (hereafter cited as Kahn Collection, AAUP).

3. Venturi in an oral history interview by Peter Reed, June 1–July 20, 1991. Archives of American Art, Smithsonian Institution, Washington, D.C.

4. Course syllabi for 1964 and 1965 indicate that Venturi delivered lectures in "F. A.," Room 107, from 9 to 11 am. "F. A." was the Graduate School of Fine Arts, housed in Hayden Hall. Course syllabi, Architecture 512, spring 1964, 225.XI.7 and spring 1965, 225. XI.24, VSB Collection, AAUP. Surviving class rosters list an enrollment of sixty-six students in 1963 and fifty-seven students in 1964. See student lists, spring 1963, 225.XI.53, and Scott Brown Teaching Records, Arch. 512, spring 1964, VSB Collection, AAUP. Regarding the advanced undergraduate curriculum, see interview transcript, G. Holmes Perkins, c. 1987, box 3, folder 39, Department of Multimedia and Educational Technology Services Records, UPB 1.9MM, University Archives and Records Center, University of Pennsylvania, Philadelphia (hereafter cited as interview transcript, Perkins, UARC). Additional information: Richard Bartholomew interview with the author, October 17, 2016; Denise Scott Brown interview with the author, October 29, 2016.

5. Venturi explains "elements" as "a single part of a complex thing" in his handwritten notes for lecture I, c. 1965, 225.XI.26, VSB Collection, AAUP.

6. Course outline, Architecture 412, spring 1962, 054.288, G. Holmes Perkins Collection, AAUP.

7. Venturi, handwritten notes for lecture I, c. 1965, 225.XI.24–26, VSB Collection, AAUP. Another source for Venturi's "elements" was Julien Guadet, *Éléments et Théorie de l'Architecture* (Paris: Librarie de la Construction Moderne, 1905). See letter from Venturi to Mr. Woodruff, dated May 21, 1964, in which Venturi notes that he will add in a series of spatial elements "the wall, the roof, the ceiling," etc., "in the manner of Gaudet [*sic*]," to the spring 1965 version of the course, 225.XI.51, VSB Collection, AAUP.

8. Venturi, handwritten notes for lecture I, c. 1965, 225.XI.24–26; lecture XIII, c. 1965, 225.XI.38; and lecture XIV, c. 1965, 225.XI.39, VSB Collection, AAUP.

9. David B. Brownlee, David G. De Long, and Kathryn B. Hiesinger, *Out of the Ordinary: Robert Venturi, Denise Scott Brown and Associates; Architecture, Urbanism, Design* (Philadelphia: Philadelphia Museum of Art in association with Yale University Press, 2001), 7.

10. Joanna Patricia Scott, "Origins in Excellence: The Practical Ethos of G. Holmes Perkins and the Philadelphia School" (PhD diss., University of Pennsylvania, 2004), 25–28. See also interview transcript, Perkins, UARC. Note that although Venturi's pedagogical approach is markedly pluralistic in Theories of Architecture, there are indications that some of his thinking was in tension with Perkins's agenda. For instance, Venturi wrote that ornament was a "dangerous subject . . . certainly when I have discussed this @ Penn[,] still a Bauhaus-oriented place—Perkins and faculty establishment." (The hyphenated word after "Bauhaus" is hard to decipher; "oriented" is a conjecture.) Venturi, handwritten notes for lecture XIII, c. 1965, 225.XI.38, VSB Collection, AAUP.

11. Scott, "Origins," 34–35; interview transcript, Perkins, UARC.

12. Jan C. Rowan, "Wanting To Be . . . The Philadelphia School," *Progressive Architecture*, April 1961, 130–63.

13. Interview transcript, Perkins, UARC; Scott Brown interview with the author, October 29, 2016.

14. Graduate School of Fine Arts course bulletin for academic year 1959–60, dated January 1959, copy on file 277.43, University of Pennsylvania Bulletin Collection, AAUP.

15. Scott Brown interview with the author, October 29, 2016; Scott Brown Teaching Records, Arch 411, fall 1961; Arch 411 fall 1962; Arch 411 fall 1963, VSB Collection, AAUP.

16. Course syllabus for 1964, 225.XI.7, VSB Collection, AAUP. Scott Brown had also audited the course twice prior. Scott Brown interview with the author, October 29, 2016.

17. Scott Brown interview with the author, October 29, 2016. See also Brownlee, De Long, and Hiesinger, *Out of the Ordinary*, 46–47; and Nicholas Korody, "Learning from *Learning from Las Vegas* with Denise Scott Brown, Part 2: Pedagogy," *Archinect*, October 5, 2016, https://archinect.com/features/article/149971833/learning-from-learning-from-las-vegas-with-denise-scott-brown-part-2-pedagogy.

18. Exercise 1, Components & Their Coordination, dated January 14, 1964, 225.XI.7; Exercise 3, Structure & Light, dated February 4, 1964, 225.XI.51; Exercise 4, Scale, dated February 11, 1964, 225. XI.7, VSB Collection, AAUP.

19. Course syllabus, spring 1964, 225.XI.7; course syllabus, spring 1965, 225.XI.24, VSB Collection, AAUP.

20. Course slide lists, c. 1962–65, 225.XI.3, 225.XI.6, 225.XI.8, VSB Collection, AAUP. To reassemble Venturi's lecture images, slide call numbers were matched to images in Penn's Fine Arts Library Image Collection with the generous help of Christal Springer and Elizabeth Beck. Findings were presented in the exhibition *Back Matter: The Making of Robert Venturi's "Complexity and Contradiction,"* November 12, 2016–March 3, 2017, AAUP, organized by William Whitaker and Lee Ann Custer.

21. Slide list, lecture IV, dated February 4, 1964, 225.XI.8, VSB Collection, AAUP.

22. Slide list, lecture V dated February 11, 1964, 225.XI.8, VSB Collection, AAUP.

23. In notes for feedback on students' term papers, Venturi wrote that this was "not a damn hist. course" and that "description and history" were "incidental" to it. Venturi, handwritten notes for lecture XIV, c. 1965, 225.XI.39, VSB Collection, AAUP. See also Venturi, handwritten notes for lecture I, c. 1965, 225.XI.24–26, VSB Collection, AAUP.

24. Richard Bartholomew interview with the author, October 17, 2016. See also handwritten notes for lecture I, c. 1965, 225.XI.24–26, VSB Collection, AAUP.

25. Richard Bartholomew interview with the author, October 17, 2016. See also student comments, Scott Brown teaching records, Arch 512, spring 1964, VSB Collection, AAUP.

26. Richard Bartholomew, Steven Goldberg, John Lobell, Terry and David Vaughan interviews with the author, October and November 2016.

27. For instance, to describe the adaptation of a building to its environment, Venturi compared Le Corbusier's Assembly Building in Chandigarh, Palladio's Palazzo Massimo, a house at Domegge, a portal at Vézelay Abbey, Kahn's Trenton Bath House, Edwin Lutyens's The Salutation in Sandwich, Mount Vernon, and McKim, Mead, and White's Low House—one of many such diverse panoplies in the book. Venturi, *Complexity and Contradiction*, 54–55.

28. Although this usage of the past could be interpreted as the beginnings of what has come to be called "postmodernism," it is important to note that Venturi still felt an obligation to be as objective and as "complete" as he was subjective in the course—a sentiment that he did not necessarily face with the book. Therefore, while some of Venturi's notes indicate an opposition to what he referred to as "modern architecture," he took care to explain a variety of different approaches to an architectural problem. Often he even differentiated between different periods in the careers of well-known protagonists of modern architecture such as Walter Gropius, Ludwig

Mies van der Rohe, and Le Corbusier. See Venturi's handwritten notes for lecture I and lecture XIII, c. 1965, 225.XI.24–26 and 225. XI.38, respectively, VSB Collection, AAUP. For more on the origins of postmodernism, see Andrew Leach, "Continuity in Rupture: Postmodern Architecture before Architectural Postmodernism," and Martino Stierli, "Taking on Mies: Mimicry and Parody of Modernism in the Architecture of Alison and Peter Smithson and Venturi/Scott Brown," in *Neo-Avant-Garde and Postmodern Postwar Architecture in Britain and Beyond*, ed. Mark Crinson and Claire Zimmerman (New Haven, Conn.: Yale University Press, 2010), 127–49 and 151–74, respectively.

29. See Robert Venturi, "Donald Drew Egbert: A Tribute, " in *Iconography and Electronics upon a Generic Architecture: A View from the Drafting Room* (Cambridge, Mass.: MIT Press, 1996), 43–45.

30. Donald Drew Egbert's syllabus, Art 314, Modern Architecture, Princeton University, filed in Venturi teaching materials, 225. XI.25, VSB Collection, AAUP. Venturi also mentioned Egbert in his handwritten notes for lecture III, c. 1965, 225.RV.28, VSB Collection, AAUP.

31. Jean Labatut, Architectural Expression 409, Problem IV, Space Relationships of Buildings to Surroundings, Jean Labatut Papers, C0709, box 50, folder 4, Princeton University Archives (hereafter PUA).

32. Labatut, 410 Architectural Expression, course overview, Second Term 1941–42, Jean Labatut Papers, C0709, box 50, folder 4, PUA. Venturi discusses his academic work with Labatut in "Statement for Michael Wurmfeld," dated December 22, 1976, 225. VI.D.3593, VSB Collection, AAUP.

33. Venturi, handwritten notes for lecture I, c. 1965, 225.XI.26, VSB Collection, AAUP. The same passage is quoted in Venturi, *Complexity and Contradiction*, p. 19; it is from T. S. Eliot, "Tradition and the Individual Talent," *Selected Essays, 1917–32* (New York: Harcourt, Brace and Co., 1934), 3–4.

34. Venturi, *Complexity and Contradiction*, 20; Venturi, handwritten notes for lecture I, c. 1965, 225.XI.26, VSB Collection, AAUP. The quoted passage is from Henry-Russell Hitchcock, "Food for Changing Sensibility," *Perspecta* 6 (1960): 2–3.

35. Venturi, handwritten notes for lecture II, c. 1965, 225.XI.27, VSB Collection, AAUP; cf. Venturi, *Complexity and Contradiction*, 72.

36. Venturi, *Complexity and Contradiction*, 72.

37. Venturi, handwritten notes for lecture II, c. 1965, 225.XI.27, VSB Collection, AAUP. Emphasis the author's.

38. Venturi, *Complexity and Contradiction*, 84–85.

39. Ibid., 72; Venturi, handwritten notes for lecture II, c. 1965, 225. XI.27, VSB Collection, AAUP.

40. Venturi's handwritten notes for lecture II (see preceding note) mention these buildings on a separate piece of paper taped to the side of his notes. In *Complexity and Contradiction* they are discussed on pp. 85 and 86.

41. Robert Venturi, "Context in Architectural Composition: M.F.A. Thesis," in *Iconography and Electronics*, 333–74.

42. The selected reproductions in Venturi, *Iconography and Electronics*, are more complete and more legible in the original version: Robert Venturi, "Context in Architectural Composition" (MFA thesis, Princeton University, 1950), VSB Collection, AAUP.

43. Venturi, *Iconography and Electronics*, 336.

44. See Martino Stierli, "In the Academy's Garden: Robert Venturi, the Grand Tour and the Revision of Modern Architecture," *AA Files*, no. 56 (2007): 42–55; Denise Costanzo, "'I Will Try My Best to Make It Worth It': Robert Venturi's Road to Rome," *Journal of Architectural Education* 72, no. 2 (2016): 269–83.

45. Venturi, handwritten notes for lecture III, c. 1965, 225.XI.28, VSB Collection, AAUP.

46. Venturi, *Complexity and Contradiction*, 40.

47. Venturi, handwritten notes for lecture XI, c. 1965, 225.XI.36, VSB Collection, AAUP.

48. Venturi, *Complexity and Contradiction*, 90.

49. Venturi, handwritten notes for lecture VII, c. 1965, 225.XI.32, VSB Collection, AAUP; Venturi, *Complexity and Contradiction*, 77.

50. Venturi, lecture II outline spring 1961, 225.XI.1, VSB Collection, AAUP.

51. Venturi, lecture III outline spring 1961, 225.XI.1 and spring 1962, 225.XI.2, VSB Collection, AAUP; and folder 054.288, G. Holmes Perkins Collection, AAUP.

52. Venturi, lecture XI outline, dated April 18, 1961, 225.XI.1, and Lecture XI outline, dated April 7, 1964, 225.XI.7, VSB Collection, AAUP.

53. Venturi, handwritten notes for lecture IX, c. 1965, 225.XI.34, VSB Collection, AAUP.

54. Venturi, handwritten notes for lecture VI, c. 1965, 225.XI.31, VSB Collection, AAUP.

55. Venturi, handwritten notes for lecture XI, c. 1965, 225.XI.36, VSB Collection, AAUP.

56. Venturi, handwritten notes for lecture XIII, c. 1965, 225.XI.38, VSB Collection, AAUP.

57. Ibid. See also note 10.

58. Venturi, *Complexity and Contradiction*, 25 and 102, respectively.

59. One exception is his Beach House, included on one slide list. Venturi, lecture XII slide list, dated April 14, 1964, 225.XI.8, VSB Collection, AAUP. There is also a page of undated notes filed in a folder labeled "Lecture XV, Penn, 1965," where Venturi writes "in this last lecture, should we discuss technology or my own work and of course in fairness to you, I decided on my own work." This indicates there was a desire among students to hear about Venturi's work from him, and also that he likely devoted a little time to it at the end of the course. See Venturi's undated handwritten notes, c. 1965, 225. XI.40, VSB Collection, AAUP.

60. The lecture on unity falls somewhere in between, being partly picked up in the book.

61. This characterization is based on careful study of course outlines. It is possible that changes could have also resulted from Venturi

including an increasing amount of information on the outlines, but handwritten edits suggest that the lectures did evolve in accordance with dated outlines. See Venturi, course outlines, spring 1961, 225.XI.1; spring 1962, 225.XI.2; spring 1963, 225.XI.5; spring 1964, 225.XI.7, spring 1965, 225.XI.23; lecture materials c. 1964, 225.XI.9–22; lecture materials c. 1965, 225.XI.24–40, VSB Collection, AAUP. Major milestones in the evolution of the book project preceding its publication by The Museum of Modern Art include Venturi's 1962 proposal to the Graham Foundation, 030.II.A.61.2, Kahn Collection, AAUP; Venturi's 1963 manuscript submission to Graham Foundation, 225.XI.95, VSB Collection, AAUP; and Venturi's 1965 article version, "Complexity and Contradiction in Architecture: Selections from a Forthcoming Book," *Perspecta* 9/10 (1965): 17–56.

62. For Pop art, see 1965 lecture I, II, III outlines, 225.XI.24, 225.XI.27, 225.XI.28; for "complexity and contradiction," see 1963 lecture XIV, 225.XI.5, and 1964 lecture XIV outline in 225.XI.7, VSB Collection, AAUP.

63. See Mary McLeod's contribution to this volume, pp. 50–75.

64. For Levittown, see lecture II slide list, dated January 21, 1964, 225.XI.8; for Lynch, see lecture VII outline, dated March 3, 1964, 225.XI.7 for city planning, see lecture VIII outline, dated March 6, 1962, 225.XI.2, VSB Collection, AAUP.

65. Scott Brown teaching records, Exercise #20, dated October 17, 1960, City Planning 501, fall 1960 and List of Required Reading, Arch 411, fall 1961, VSB Collection, AAUP.

66. Venturi course bibliography, spring 1963, 225.XI.5, and Scott Brown teaching records, List of Required Reading, Arch 411, fall 1961, VSB Collection, AAUP.

67. Venturi, lecture III outline, dated February 2, 1965, 225.XI.28, VSB Collection, AAUP; and lecture III outline, 1962, 054.288. G. Holmes Perkins Collection, AAUP. See also Venturi's lecture notes: "Design begins with function . . . D. Scott Brown here." Venturi, handwritten notes for lecture III, c. 1965, 225.XI.28, VSB Collection, AAUP.

68. Scott Brown interview with the author, October 29, 2016.

69. On the published version of *Complexity and Contradiction*, as compared to previous manuscript iterations, see note 61. Note also Venturi's addition of the Fairmount Park Fountain competition of 1964 in the book's final section, in which the urban setting is imperative. He completed the design with Scott Brown and John Rauch.

70. Venturi, *Complexity and Contradiction*, 22.

71. Venturi, handwritten notes for lecture II, c. 1965, 225.XI.27, VSB Collection, AAUP.

72. As it turned out, however, only two publications were published in the series, the second being Joseph Rykwert, *On Adam's House in Paradise: The Idea of the Primitive Hut in Architectural History*, The Museum of Modern Art Papers on Architecture 2 (New York: The Museum of Modern Art in association with the Graham Foundation for Advanced Studies in the Fine Arts, Chicago, 1972).

Pier Paolo Tamburelli

There are 350 images in *Complexity and Contradiction*. It is a surprising quantity for a book of the 1960s—even for a book on architecture. Most architecture books of the period, even lavishly illustrated ones, had far more text and far fewer images. The images in Venturi's book flow parallel to the text, producing a narration of their own. This is the consequence of the way Venturi assembled *Complexity and Contradiction*, which grew out of the sequences of slides he used for his lectures at the University of Pennsylvania. In the manuscript that Venturi submitted to the Graham Foundation in 1963, the text and the atlas of images were still entirely separated. In the book's final version, too, the images and the text remain somehow distant. Their relationship is very different from the illustrated manifestos of Le Corbusier: there, the images and texts reinforce one another, producing a sort of obsessive mantra, but in Venturi's book, images and text do not perfectly coincide. A gap remains, an in-between. This gap creates an inner tension that was already at the time of its publication the most fascinating aspect of the book.

Fifty years later, what is surprising is actually the text. Confronted with the contemporary proliferation of collections of exquisite architectural images (simply put together without a sense of needing the slightest justification), Venturi's exercise seems incredibly humble and astonishingly honest. Venturi felt obliged to explain his series of images. He did not escape the trouble of delivering a text.

Venturi is not a great writer (the good writer is Denise!). He does not achieve the unsettling tautological poetry of Rossi, and he does not master the dry wit of Koolhaas. Somehow Venturi is *too gentle* to be a good writer. And nevertheless there is plenty of text in *Complexity and Contradiction*. Venturi probably knew the writing was not the best part of the book, but he felt that images alone would not be enough. In this project, words were necessary to challenge the images.

In *Complexity and Contradiction* images are combined with incredible skill. Venturi puts together Roman Baroque architecture with Pop art, Thomas Jefferson and Jasper Johns, Alvar Aalto and Vignola. The combinations are so visually convincing that it seems pointless to question them. And then, exactly at this point—as if he were the only one not entirely satisfied with his visual alchemy, as if he feared being fooled by his own bravura—Venturi inserts his text. And he inserts it as an element of disturbance, to slow down the pace at which one goes through the pages, to introduce a certain friction, to challenge the perfection of taste. Skill is necessary, and there is plenty of it in *Complexity and Contradiction*, and yet—if architecture is to be considered a form of thinking—skill is not enough.

Venturi's Acknowledgments:
The Complexities of Influence

Mary McLeod

*I feel the role of prima donna culture hero even in its modern
form as prima donna anticulture antihero is a late Romantic
theme as obsolete for the architect and for the complex inter-
dependencies of architectural practice today as is the "heroic
and original" building for architecture. An architect strong
on his own feet does not need this illusionary support at the
expense of other architects. As a firm, we look best when
we stand as we are, a group of strong individuals who share
enthusiasms and work well together, not as a pyramid with
the figurehead of an Architect at the top.*

—Robert Venturi

Robert Venturi included this statement in his "Note on Authorship and Attribution" in the first edition of *Learning from Las
Vegas* (1972). Although he intended it as a comment about
designing buildings, his rejection of the singular culture hero
applies, in many respects, to his writing as well.[1] Nevertheless,
few would question Venturi's authorship of *Complexity and
Contradiction in Architecture*—or challenge that it is *his* book
and *his* argument. Anyone who has spent time in the archives
at the University of Pennsylvania cannot help but be astonished
at the amount of time and energy that Venturi put into this
groundbreaking book. Like the design of his "Mother's House"
(the Vanna Venturi House, 1959–64), it went through numerous
revisions: from the early Graham Foundation report submitted
in April 1963 (which itself went through draft after draft) to
the manuscript published by The Museum of Modern Art some
three and a half years later.[2]

The four years that Venturi spent writing the book were a
period of intense productivity. He was like a sponge, constantly

reading books, seeking advice from those he trusted, and spending hours debating and discussing ideas with colleagues as he sought to strengthen and to refine his argument. One senses an immense intellectual hunger in this "young" designer and teacher (Venturi turned forty in 1965)—and that his reading was largely instrumental. He treated it primarily as a way to figure out and support positions.[3] An examination of his many manuscripts for the book also makes it clear that Venturi was not a natural writer: the early drafts are wordy and repetitive, often awkward, although some of his pithy phrases were there from the start. One also senses that the book would never have been written—at least not in the form that made it so transformative—without the support and assistance of several people around him.

This is true, of course, of many books, especially first books. What is not so typical of architects is his public acknowledgment of those who helped him. Most of the iconic publications by twentieth-century architects do not include acknowledgments— Le Corbusier's *Vers une architecture* (1923), Aldo Rossi's *L'architettura del citta* (1966), and Rem Koolhaas's *Delirious New York* (1978), to name just a few. Venturi devoted an entire page to thanking two institutions (the Graham Foundation and the American Academy in Rome) and seven people. Even more unusual for that time, four of those seven are women. In this regard, *Complexity and Contradiction* was not just a "gentle" manifesto (as the title of the first chapter has it) but also an unusually generous one. Such intellectual and personal generosity would continue to mark Venturi's writings—for example, his long list of thank-yous on receiving the Pritzker Prize in 1991 and his short essays paying homage to those who were important to him, such as Louis I. Kahn and his architecture history teacher at Princeton, Donald Drew Egbert.[4] Indeed, the words "learning from," so central to the writings of both Denise Scott Brown and Venturi, might be seen as part of this same sensibility. Whether these expressions of gratitude were due to honesty, humility, old-fashioned "gentlemanliness," or, as some might even claim, "feminism," they can be seen as challenging the whole ethos of the solitary male artistic genius.[5] This does not mean that Venturi was not part of the male-dominated architecture culture of his era and benefited from it in many ways—such as having the support of women in subservient positions—but simply that, unlike most of his male peers, he emphasized that architecture was a collaborative process.[6]

The first five people of the seven cited by Venturi in the acknowledgments for *Complexity and Contradiction* are Vincent

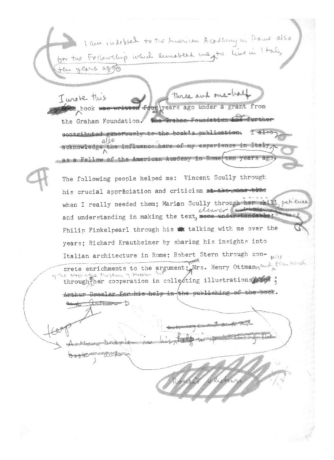

The manuscript draft contains typed and handwritten text. Visible typed content includes:

I wrote this book was written four years ago under a grant from
the Graham Foundation. The Graham Foundation has further
contributed generously to the book's publication. I also
acknowledge the influence here of my experience in Italy,
as a Fellow of the American Academy in Rome ten years ago.

The following people helped me: Vincent Scully through
his crucial appreciation and criticism at the same time
when I really needed them; Marion Scully through her skill
and understanding in making the text more understandable;
Philip Finkelpearl through his talking with me over the
years; Richard Krautheimer by sharing his insights into
Italian architecture in Rome; Robert Stern through concrete enrichments to the argument; Mrs. Henry Ottmann
through her cooperation in collecting illustrations;
Arthur Drexler for his help in the publishing of the book.

Fig. 1. Robert Venturi. Early draft of the acknowledgments to *Complexity and Contradiction in Architecture*. c. 1965. The Architectural Archives of the University of Pennsylvania, Philadelphia. Gift of Robert Venturi and Denise Scott Brown

Scully, Marion Scully, Philip Finkelpearl, Denise Scott Brown, and Robert Stern, all of whom had a substantial role in the development of the book. The last two, Mrs. Henry Ottmann and Miss Ellen Marsh, both worked at The Museum of Modern Art and helped collect photographs and obtain rights.[7] At that time it was rare, and perhaps it still is, to acknowledge those who assisted an author with such tasks, especially if they were young women—something that Harriet Bee, then an editorial assistant at MoMA, mentioned to me.[8] One should note, however, that Venturi altered the acknowledgments in the course of revisions that he made in 1965 or possibly as late as in 1966 (fig. 1). In one draft he thanked Arthur Drexler, then the director of the Department of Architecture and Design at MoMA, "for his help in publishing the book," but this line was mysteriously eliminated. An acknowledgment to art historian Richard Krautheimer also got cut at some point—probably very late—and replaced with that to Scott Brown.[9] It was not until the second edition in 1977 that Venturi, in a supplemental note, expressed his gratitude to Krautheimer, for sharing "his insights on Roman Baroque architecture."[10] Curiously, Venturi omitted any mention of Kahn, whose secretary typed his application to the Graham Foundation (which funded the writing of his first draft)—in fact, he explicitly denied Kahn's influence in a memorandum sent to Stanislaus von Moos.[11] Two other individuals who are not cited by name but were clearly influential, if in indirect ways, are his beloved professor Egbert (mentioned in the second edition) and Jean Labatut, his thesis adviser and studio teacher at Princeton.

On his acknowledgments page, Venturi starts by citing the American architectural historian Vincent Scully (1920–2017), who had been teaching in the art history department at Yale University for nearly two decades, and would continue to do so for many years (fig. 2). (Philip Johnson once called him "the most influential architectural teacher ever.")[12] Venturi refers to Scully's "crucial appreciation and criticism when I really needed them." This appreciation comes across vividly in Scully's extravagant (though still convincing) claim in his introduction to the book that *Complexity and Contradiction* "is probably the most important writing on the making of architecture since Le Corbusier's *Vers une architecture*, of 1923."[13] In that introduction, which has become almost as famous—and notorious—as the book itself, Scully compares the two architects in sweeping, rhetorical prose, arguing that they represent different moments and different styles (one "sculptural," "actively heroic," and "demand[ing] a noble purism"; the other "scenographic," "consistently anti-heroic," and "compulsively qualifying"). Both of them, he says, learned from the past, created "generous and varied forms," and embodied a "larger, more humane" vein of architecture.[14]

Scully's support, though, extended far beyond the introduction, which Venturi asked him to write in June 1965.[15] Earlier that year, he had campaigned vigorously for Venturi to follow Paul Rudolph as chair of Yale's architecture school.[16] Venturi appreciated Scully's unqualified endorsement at a moment when he felt as if his own career was at a standstill. He was deeply frustrated by his lack of commissions: again and again, his designs—for the FDR Memorial (1960), the Meiss House (1962), and the Fairmount Park Fountain (1964)—were not getting built.

Venturi's debt to Scully began years before they met, however. He first read Scully's *The Shingle Style* in the mid-1950s, when he was a fellow at the American Academy.[17] In 1987,

Fig. 2. Vincent Scully viewing slides at Yale University. 1960s. Manuscripts and Archives, Yale University, New Haven, Conn.

Venturi would describe that experience as "a thrilling and significant revelation, both focusing and freeing my vision."[18] Shortly after returning home, he received his "first commission," a shingled beach house. It wasn't built, but the project, Venturi explained, "sent me on my architectural way."[19] He includes it in the compendium of his designs at the end of *Complexity and Contradiction*, and earlier, in the chapter "Contradiction Adapted" there is a photo of the back facade of McKim, Mead & White's Low House.[20]

Scully and Venturi probably met for the first time in 1963 through Stern, then a very precocious young architecture student at Yale.[21] Stern admired Venturi's work and urged Scully to go to Philadelphia to see it. Scully did—and was immediately convinced by what he saw, especially by Guild House, which he praises in his introduction to *Complexity and Contradiction* not only for its direct realism but also for the composition of its fenestration, comparing it to "the sad and mighty discordances" of Michelangelo's apses at St. Peter's.[22]

For years, Scully had been a strong advocate of what he called "heroic" modern architecture. He believed that Kahn was the greatest of contemporary American practitioners, and in 1962 wrote a monograph on him. But Scully was deeply disillusioned with the blatant destruction of downtown New Haven and became increasingly critical of urban renewal and the heroic Brutalist architecture that he had originally championed, including Rudolph's A&A Building at Yale. As much as he admired Kahn, he realized that Venturi's work captured something essential about present-day society—namely, that the days of heroic form-makers were over and that architecture must somehow accept and express the complexities and compromises of current reality.

That didn't mean that the two men were always in sync, and Scully often pushed Venturi to extend his argument to urban issues.[23] In fact, Scully stresses this dimension in his introduction, alluding to "contradictions and complexities of urban experience at all scales" and the "shift of perspective from the Champs-Elysées to Main Street," and declaring that Venturi's proposals, "in their recognition of complexity and their respect for what exists, create the most necessary antidote to that cataclysmic purism of contemporary urban renewal."[24] (One might almost think he was writing about *Learning from Las Vegas*.) The emphasis on urbanism is all the more curious given that Venturi's discussion of urban issues in *Complexity and Contradiction* consists only of the surprising last two pages of his text and his comments on the 1966 Copley Square competition included in the compendium of his designs—a last-minute addition written after Scully had finished his introduction.[25] There, Venturi decries "ubiquitous parking lots" and the "not-so-temporary deserts created by Urban Renewal."[26] These brief criticisms of contemporary planning are, nevertheless, one of the major differences between the final version of the book and his earlier drafts.

Scully's support and championing of Venturi continued after the publication of *Complexity and Contradiction*; he even included images of Venturi's work on the covers of books in 1969 and 1974.[27] Not since Sigfried Giedion's support of Le Corbusier and Walter Gropius (and, later, of Alvar Aalto) or Bruno Zevi's of Frank Lloyd Wright had a historian been such a passionate advocate of a contemporary architect.

Fig. 3. Marion Scully with her daughters Ann Wohl (left) and Maika Wohl (right). 1962

The second name in the acknowledgments is Marion Scully (née Marian LaFollette, born 1927) (fig. 3).[28] Venturi thanks her for "her skill, patience and understanding in making the text clearer." Given her own public reticence and her withdrawal from the world of architecture after her divorce from Scully in 1978, her role in the book has received little attention; nor is the archival record completely clear. What is certain is that from January to June 1965 she edited the manuscript that Venturi had submitted to MoMA, not only making the usual corrections that any copy editor would but also sharpening and clarifying the text—eliminating redundant words, breaking up overly long sentences, and finding the precise phrase when needed—and asking Venturi for rewrites where the writing was awkward or unclear (fig. 4).

How did she become involved with the book? Drexler had struggled to find someone in New York to edit Venturi's text after the first freelance editor he sent it to complained that it was unpublishable, and he finally asked Scully for a suggestion, probably in November 1964.[29] He recommended Marion (then still Marion Wohl from a previous marriage), who had edited his book *The Earth, the Temple and the Gods: Greek Sacred Architecture* (1962).[30] Drexler agreed to hire her, and on January 4, 1965, he wrote to Venturi confirming that she would edit the text. She and Venturi had their first meeting later that month.[31] Venturi was teaching at Yale that semester, giving a version of his Penn lecture course on architecture theory, and the two of them would spend hours going over the manuscript. By all accounts, it was a most amicable working relationship, and Venturi seems to have thrived under her patient but pointed guidance.[32]

55

given interest. But this kind of segregating and excluding of elements is a _method_ in the analytical process of achieving a complex art. It should not be mistaken for a _goal_.

An architecture of complexity and contradiction, however, does not mean picturesqueness or subjective expressionism. A false complexity has recently countered the false simplicity of an earlier Modern architecture. It promotes an architecture of symmetrical picturesqueness, which Minoru Yamasaki calls "serene." But it represents a new formalism as unconnected with experience as the former cult of simplicity. Its intricate forms do not correspond to genuinely complex programs, and its intricate ornament, dependent on industrial techniques in execution, is dryly reminiscent of handicraft techniques. Gothic tracery or Rococco rocaille, besides their expressive validity in relation to the whole, came from a valid showing-off of hand skills and expressed a kind of tension which was derived from the immediacy and individuality of the method. This kind of complexity through exuberance, can not have a past in our architecture. It is tension rather than exuberance is characteristic of our art, tension, rather than serenity.

The best twentieth-century architects have usually rejected simplification (that is, simplicity through reduction) in order to promote complexity within the whole. The works of Alvar Aalto and Le Corbusier, who often disregards his polemical

---

Wohl's role in the book's evolution is evident from her carefully inscribed inserts and editing corrections (all of which Venturi seems to have accepted): the difference between the opening paragraph in the *Perspecta* excerpt published in 1965 and the same paragraph in the book speaks for itself.[33] She also helped Venturi with the academic apparatus in the book—insisting in one note to him that "no page references on footnotes is beginning to feel like no pants."[34]

Her role in Venturi's career, moreover, went beyond the book itself. She was close friends with Louise and David Trubek, who lived down the street in New Haven, and it was through their friendship that Venturi would become the architect of new summer houses on Nantucket for them and for Louise's sister, Alice Wislocki.[35]

The next individual whom Venturi mentions in his acknowledgments is Philip Finkelpearl (1925–2014), who was his closest male friend. Venturi thanks Finkelpearl for "talking with me

Fig. 4. Page from a draft manuscript of Robert Venturi's *Complexity and Contradiction in Architecture* with annotations by Marion Scully. c. 1965. The Architectural Archives of the University of Pennsylvania, Philadelphia. Gift of Robert Venturi and Denise Scott Brown

over the years" (fig. 5); their conversations would continue until Finkelpearl's death in 2014.[36] It was Finkelpearl who proposed the title *Complexity and Contradiction in Architecture* (which won out over numerous false starts: we can all be happy that it wasn't called "Complexity and Accommodation," or even worse, "Complexity and Intrusion"—maybe a joke?).[37] And when Venturi was once asked where he got all his literary references to the New Criticism—"Was it freshman English?"—he immediately responded, "Oh no, it was all from Philip Finkelpearl."[38]

Venturi and Finkelpearl first met at Princeton University in 1946–47, when they were both rooming at Witherspoon Hall.[39] The two of them were stranded at Princeton during spring break, with term papers to write, and they soon became close friends (fig. 6). They were not quite the typical Princeton students of those years—both were outsiders, if in different ways. Finkelpearl, the son of a pharmacist from Pittsburgh, was Jewish (a rarity at Princeton at the time); he had gone to public high school (also unusual at Princeton then), and decided to apply to the university simply because the brother of one of his close friends did. Venturi, despite his prep-school education, was the son of Italian immigrants who had not graduated from college—his mother, in fact, had to leave school at thirteen.[40] Finkelpearl's own education, unlike Venturi's, had been interrupted by the war.[41] His senior thesis at Princeton was on fin-de-siècle British literature and the New Criticism, but at Harvard he specialized on Elizabethan and Jacobean literature, writing his dissertation on the poet and playwright John Marston. Later, he would publish a highly regarded book on him, citing T. S. Eliot in his introduction.[42]

Fig. 5. Robert Venturi (left) and Philip J. Finkelpearl (right) at Alison Lurie's parents' house, White Plains, N.Y. 1953

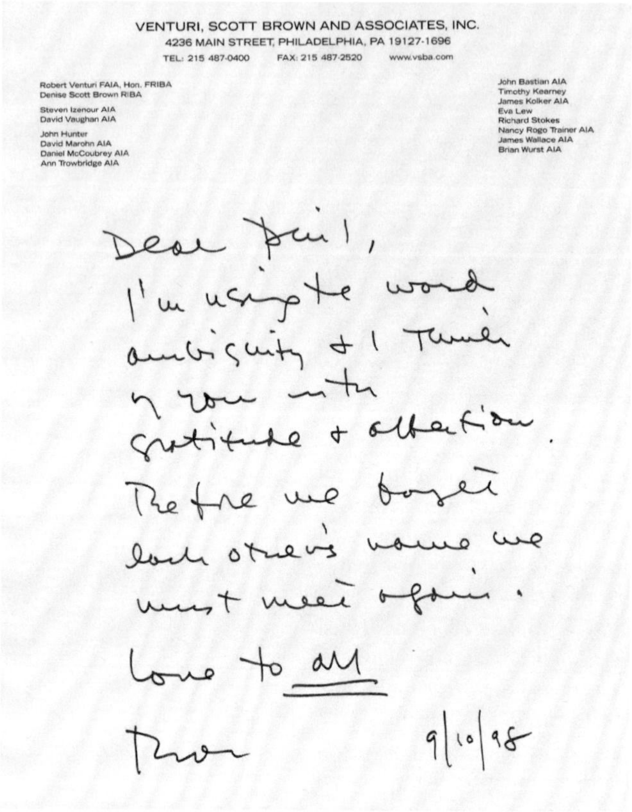

VENTURI, SCOTT BROWN AND ASSOCIATES, INC.
4236 MAIN STREET, PHILADELPHIA, PA 19127-1696
TEL: 215 487-0400   FAX: 215 487-2520   www.vsba.com

Robert Venturi FAIA, Hon. FRIBA
Denise Scott Brown RIBA
Steven Izenour AIA
David Vaughan AIA
John Hunter
David Marohn AIA
Daniel McCoubrey AIA
Ann Trowbridge AIA

John Bastian AIA
Timothy Kearney
James Kolker AIA
Eva Lew
Richard Stokes
Nancy Rogo Trainer AIA
James Wallace AIA
Brian Wurst AIA

Dear Phil,

I'm using the word ambiguity + I think of you with gratitude + affection.

The fire we forget each others name we must meet again.

Love to all

Bob

9/10/98

It was, in fact, Finkelpearl who introduced Venturi to Eliot's work. The two of them attended not one but two lectures by Eliot at Princeton,[43] and this was the beginning of Venturi's preoccupation with the poet, whom he quoted in his 1953 Rome Prize application—and then again many times after that, most notably in *Complexity and Contradiction*.[44] Finkelpearl also either lent or gave him a copy of William Empson's *Seven Types of Ambiguity*,[45] and was, most likely, responsible for introducing Venturi to the writings of all the other literary and cultural critics cited in *Complexity and Contradiction*, who include Cleanth Brooks, Kenneth Burke, Stanley Edgar Hyman, Wylie Sypher, and the Welsh poet and painter David Jones.[46] Ironically, however, as immersed as Finkelpearl had been in the New Criticism as an undergraduate, he had rejected it by the 1960s, focusing instead on the social and political context of theater, something the New Criticism had eschewed.[47]

Fig. 6. Letter from Robert Venturi to Philip J. Finkelpearl thanking him for having introduced him to the notion of "ambiguity." September 10, 1998

One important topic for both men was Mannerism. Venturi had, as he once explained, an "epiphany" during his last weeks in Rome,[48] when he realized it was Mannerist architecture, not Baroque architecture, that fascinated him.[49] In their conversations during the 1950s and early 1960s, Finkelpearl introduced Venturi to ideas of literary Mannerism and critics who had grappled with it. One of the sections in Venturi's Graham Foundation report was titled "Mannerism and Poetry," and after submitting his revised manuscript to MoMA in April 1964, he wrote to Drexler that he still hoped to improve this section after meeting with "a literary friend of mine"—that friend was Finkelpearl, who was then teaching English literature at Vassar College in Poughkeepsie, New York.[50]

Venturi's friendship with Finkelpearl also extended to his family. In 1947, Finkelpearl had married a painter, Katherine (Kitty) Dice, and in the following years Venturi would visit them in their small apartment in Cambridge, Massachusetts, in their home in Poughkeepsie, and in their Shaker house (originally the trustees' office) in Harvard, Massachusetts, for which Venturi would design a fireplace. The three of them would stay up long nights, with Venturi showing drawings of his latest projects and spending hours with Finkelpearl going over the pieces he had written.[51]

Venturi also loved the popular culture he encountered at the Finkelpearls': things like boxed cereal, which he had never eaten as a child, and their wonderfully flamboyant car, a used '57 Dodge Coronet with fins. Kitty, who was more interested in Abstract Expressionism than Pop art, explained that she and Phil had grown up with popular culture, so it was nothing special for them; for Venturi, however—so shielded from it by his very cultured, Fabian socialist, pacifist, health-conscious, vegetarian mother—their everyday, middle-class existence held a special fascination. One of Venturi's gifts to their son Tom (who is now New York City's Commissioner of Cultural Affairs) was a signed Lichtenstein print. Ellen, their daughter, received a Warhol.[52]

The fifth person to whom Venturi extends his appreciation (here I depart slightly from his order in the acknowledgments) is Robert Stern (born 1939) (fig. 7). Venturi thanks him for "concrete enrichments to the argument." And once more, it seems an apt description, summarizing Stern's role in the evolution of the book.

Venturi and Stern first met in 1962, while Stern was a graduate student in Yale's MArch program and editing a double issue of the student journal *Perspecta*. He was also taking

Fig. 7. Robert A. M. Stern presenting his MArch thesis to a jury including Philip Johnson, Paul Rudolph, Vincent Scully, and Robert Venturi in Yale's A&A building, New Haven, Conn., 1965

art history classes, and recounts that Helen Searing, a doctoral student in the department, proposed that he consider Venturi's work for inclusion in *Perspecta*.[53] Stern immediately went down to Philadelphia to meet him, and soon Venturi would become a mentor and friend, "critting" his studio projects and encouraging him to explore new, more unconventional design ideas. In a role reversal, Stern also became a kind of adviser and interlocutor for Venturi, especially when he was being considered for the chair of architecture at Yale in the fall and winter of 1964–65. Scully and Stern both describe spending hours with Venturi in a seminar room, coaching him before his public lecture and his interview with Yale president Kingman Brewster, Jr.[54]

By this point, Stern's editing of the *Perspecta* double issue featuring three sections of Venturi's book was complete.[55] Stern and Venturi had decided to publish the opening polemic, chapter 2 (then called simply "Complexity versus Picturesqueness"), and chapter 9 ("The Inside and the Outside"). As Stern recalls, editing these excerpts was primarily a matter of cleaning up the prose, not changing the argument. He did ask Venturi to omit his sharp comments about Paul Rudolph's architecture (Rudolph was then chair of Yale's architecture school), something Venturi couldn't quite manage to do.[56] Among the differences between the *Perspecta* version and the final book are that the excerpts include a greater number of quotations and more extensive photographic documentation, especially of Venturi's own work.[57] An additional difference is that there are no images of American suburbia, the commercial strip, or Main Street in the journal. That's not surprising, since Peter Blake's *God's Own Junkyard* (1964) had just come out and its impact was yet to be felt. As it turns out, this was one of the topics that Stern and Scully discussed with Venturi; they were both urging him to think more about cities.[58]

This points to the complexities of influence at work here. Several commentators, including Venturi himself, link his criticism of Blake—and especially that all-important question, "Is not Main Street almost all right?"—with Scott Brown.[59] But while his position certainly owed a lot to her, his newfound attention to urban issues may be a case of overdetermination: Scully, Stern, and Scott Brown were all pushing him to extend his argument beyond his Princeton/Rome formalism—that is, his fascination with architectural composition—and to consider "complexity and contradiction" in a broader social framework. The change came quickly: as late as December 1965, Venturi turned down an invitation from Stern to speak at a symposium at the Architectural League of New York, titled "The Shape of Cities of Our Time," explaining that as interested as he was in the subject, he was "not yet qualified" to speak on urban issues, although he would attend.[60] Just a year later, Venturi would make his all-important trip with Scott Brown to Las Vegas.

Denise Scott Brown (born 1931) was certainly not the least of the five protagonists in Venturi's acknowledgments, even though she was a late addition (fig. 8). He thanks her for

Fig. 8. Denise Scott Brown in her basement office at the University of Pennsylvania, Philadelphia. 1963

"sharing her insights into architecture and city planning."[61] That sharing may have begun as early as 1959, when Venturi participated in the final design review of her project in David Crane's planning studio, which examined strategies for accommodating migrant workers in Chandigarh, India. Then a student in the master's program in city planning, Scott Brown proposed smaller interventions rather than large-scale, tabula-rasa solutions. Venturi's discussions with her began in earnest in 1960 when they first talked about the restructuring of the theory sequence at Penn, with Venturi teaching one semester and Scott Brown the other, although she would not start until the next academic year.[62] They were good friends and colleagues—two outsiders (and not the Harvard types who made up the bulk of the new hires by the head of Penn's School of Fine Arts, G. Holmes Perkins).[63] They discussed ideas, visited buildings, and criticized each other's work. And they shared a sensibility for things a bit "off" (fig. 9): whether back facades, the vernacular, signs, pop culture (for her, Africa and the Independent Group; for him, contemporary American Pop art), or Mannerism, which Scott Brown knew from John Summerson's courses at the Architectural Association (AA) in London. Beyond that, he appreciated that she had spent time in Italy, and she spoke Italian.

Scott Brown also gave Venturi comments about a draft of his Graham Foundation report, which she had handwritten on a yellow legal pad, most likely in March or April 1963. Unfortunately, these notes seem to be missing from the archives, but that summer, when Venturi was revising the manuscript to submit to publishers, he wrote a to-do list reminding himself: "read Denise first."[64] The following year, Scott Brown collaborated

Fig. 9. Denise Scott Brown (American, born 1931). Photograph of a rural shop in KwaZulu-Natal, South Africa. 1957

with Venturi on an architectural project for the first time: the Fairmount Park Fountain competition for Philadelphia.

Just as Finkelpearl introduced Venturi to notions of complexity and ambiguity in literary criticism, Scott Brown brought to his attention notions of complexity in other fields, especially planning and social sciences, where phrases such as "organized complexity," "messy vitality," and "non-linear dynamics" were becoming increasingly common. As a student in urban planning, Scott Brown had taken courses with Walter Isard, a brilliant economist who emphasized "immeasurable variables" and spoke of "industrial complex analysis."[65] She also recalls mentioning Kurt Gödel to Venturi after reading an article in the *New Republic*—he is one of the names that appears in the first paragraph of *Complexity and Contradiction*.

Having attended Giancarlo De Carlo's summer school in Venice and knowing the Smithsons' work from her time at the AA, Scott Brown was very familiar with the ideas of Team 10 members, who were also exploring ideas of complexity as they challenged the strictures of modern movement urbanism. The reading lists for the courses she taught at Penn include essays by the Smithsons, John Voelker, Fumihiko Maki, and the 1962 *Architectural Design* version of the "Team 10 Primer," some of which would appear on Venturi's own reading list by 1964.[66] She remembers discussing Aldo van Eyck's ideas with him, especially his notions of "labyrinthian clarity" and "the in-between realm."[67] Venturi cites van Eyck twice in *Complexity and Contradiction*.

More surprising, while Venturi already knew Lutyens's public and commercial work, it was Scott Brown who first alerted Venturi to his domestic architecture. They had gone to Princeton one fall weekend in 1960 or 1961, apparently for postgame celebrations. Venturi always skipped the football, preferring to spend time in Marquand Library instead, and that was where Scott Brown pointed out A. S. G. Butler's three-volume memorial set. He promptly bought his own set on remainder (in fact, he bought two), and would spend hours poring over Lutyens's plans.[68] Hence the many images of Lutyens's houses in *Complexity and Contradiction*, and also perhaps the curious curved wall of the entrance hall in the Vanna Venturi House.

But undoubtedly Venturi's greatest debt to Scott Brown in *Complexity and Contradiction* was the realization that the American vernacular, Main Street, was "almost all right." (He himself makes this clear in his 1997 memorandum to

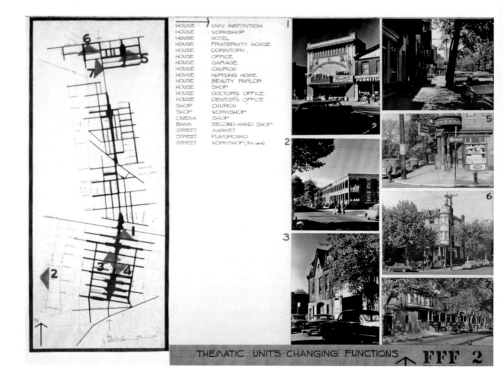

HOUSE	UNIV. INSTITUTION
HOUSE	WORKSHOP
HOUSE	HOTEL
HOUSE	FRATERNITY HOUSE
HOUSE	DORMITORY
HOUSE	OFFICE
HOUSE	GARAGE
HOUSE	CHURCH
HOUSE	NURSING HOME
HOUSE	BEAUTY PARLOR
HOUSE	SHOP
HOUSE	DOCTOR'S OFFICE
HOUSE	DENTIST'S OFFICE
SHOP	CHURCH
SHOP	WORKSHOP
CINEMA	SHOP
BANK	SECOND-HAND SHOP
STREET	MARKET
STREET	PLAYGROUND
STREET	WORKSHOP (for cars)

THEMATIC UNITS·CHANGING FUNCTIONS   FFF 2

von Moos.)[69] Unlike Scully, who valued traditional cities but had serious reservations about the commercial landscape, Scott Brown, like Venturi, saw the "bad" examples in *God's Own Junkyard* as having their own aesthetic power. In the fall of 1964, she devoted her Form, Force, Functions studio at Penn to examining Fortieth Street in West Philadelphia (fig. 10). It was the first of her commercial-strip projects. She proposed that Fortieth Street "was not all right but almost"—and that rather than razing large areas, only small interventions were required.[70] Although neither Scott Brown nor Venturi probably quite knew it, the ground had been laid for an even closer collaboration between them—and for their next endeavor. In November 1966, only three months before *Complexity and Contradiction* was published, after nearly two years of living on opposite coasts, they would be together in Las Vegas.

Fig. 10. Peter Batchelor. Student project showing changing building functions in West Philadelphia. Contribution to Denise Scott Brown's Form, Force, Functions studio at the University of Pennsylvania. 1964

Much of the material in this essay is drawn from interviews or conversations with people close to Venturi, most of whom are discussed in this paper: Denise Scott Brown, Philadelphia, June 18–19, 2016, and telephone conversations, June 26 and October 28, 2016; Marian LaFollette, Branford, Conn., August 24, 2016, and telephone conversations, November 3, 2016 and September 6, 2018; Vincent Scully, Lynchburg, Va., August 26, 2016; Robert A. M. Stern, New York, July 20, 2016; Katherine Finkelpearl, August 29, 2016, and telephone conversation, November 2, 2016; Harriet Bee, telephone conversation, August 4, 2016; and Louise Trubek, telephone conversation, November 1, 2016. Besides wishing to express my gratitude to these individuals, I would like to thank Lluís Alexandre Casanovas Blanco, Lee Ann Custer, Stephen R. Frankel, Christine Gorby, Catherine (Tappy) Lynn, Alexander Scrimgeour, Suzanne Stephens, James Venturi, and especially William Whitaker, curator of the Architectural Archives of the University of Pennsylvania. I am also grateful to Kurt Streich and Brendan Pettersen, my teaching assistants at Columbia University, for their help with images.

Notes

Epigraph
Robert Venturi, "Note on Authorship and Attribution," in *Learning from Las Vegas*, by Robert Venturi, Denise Scott Brown, and Steven Izenour (Cambridge, Mass.: MIT Press, 1972), xii. This note was omitted in the revised (second) edition of the book, published by The MIT Press in 1977.

1. *Complexity and Contradiction in Architecture* and to an even greater extent *Learning from Las Vegas* might both be seen as attempts to loosen the "sway of the Author," to borrow a phrase from Roland Barthes's essay "The Death of the Author" (1967, reprinted in Roland Barthes, *Image-Music-Text*, 1977). Even if Venturi would not have rejected the idea of a person or persons behind the text, his use of "I" in his opening sentence of *Complexity and Contradiction* might be seen as undermining the tyranny (and implicit universalism) of the authorial voice in the sweeping assertions of modern-movement polemics. He might also have agreed with Barthes's declaration that "text is a tissue of quotations drawn from the innumerable centers of culture." In fact, one of the challenges that Venturi and his editors faced in the course of editing *Complexity and Contradiction* was determining which of his numerous quotations should be cut. Perhaps, too, it is not completely coincidental that both texts were published in 1967 (see note 9).

2. Venturi's Graham Foundation report was dated March 1963, but he seems to have submitted it the following month. Venturi, Scott Brown Collection, The Architectural Archives of the University of Pennsylvania, Philadelphia (hereafter cited as VSB Collection, AAUP). Unfortunately, many of the papers in this collection, including most of the manuscripts of *Complexity and Contradiction in Architecture*, are not dated.

3. In a memorandum to Stanislaus von Moos and Denise Scott Brown, "Concerning the Writing of *C&C in Architecture* in the Early '60s" (October 23, 1997, 2 typed pages, Finkelpearl papers, Harvard, Mass.), Venturi writes: "Occasional references in the footnotes of the text do not represent influences but rather buttresses to the existing ideas in my mind." Von Moos believes that this memorandum was written in response to a draft of a chapter ("Scenes from Learning") for his book *Venturi, Scott Brown & Associates: Buildings and Projects, 1986–1998* (New York: Monacelli Press, 1999), which he gave Venturi to review and subsequently revised. Stanislaus von Moos, e-mail to the author, July 12, 2018. I am grateful to Katherine Finkelpearl for showing me this document and other papers related to Venturi that she and her husband saved over the years. Venturi often sent Philip Finkelpearl letters or essays he had written, including angry diatribes that he never mailed or published.

4. See, especially, Venturi's collection of essays *Iconography and Electronics upon a Generic Architecture: A View from the Drafting Room* (Cambridge, Mass.: MIT Press, 1996).

5. At a gala for the Beverly Willis Architectural Foundation on February 25, 2016, Julia Donoho, who had campaigned vigorously for Venturi and Scott Brown to receive the AIA Gold Medal, called Venturi a "feminist."

6. At the risk of sounding hagiographic, I know of no other twentieth-century male architect who publicly challenged the heroic status of the architect with the same passion as Venturi did, or who named—as he did in the compendium of the firm's work in the first edition of *Learning from Las Vegas*—all the major participants working on a design job.

7. Unfortunately, I have been unable to find much information about these two women, who worked as research assistants at The Museum of Modern Art, New York. A paid death notice in *The New York Times*, February 8, 2007, indicates that Ellen Marsh, later Schleicher (1932–2007), taught art at the Spence School in New York after working at MoMA. Correspondence with Venturi indicates that she was at the Museum from at least 1961 to 1967. I have located no biographical records of Mrs. Henry Ottmann (whose first name in MoMA's records is given as Henry), although there is considerable correspondence between her and Venturi concerning photographs for the book.

8. Harriet Bee, telephone conversation with the author, August 4, 2016. Bee helped Venturi with all the captions in the second edition of the book. She was pregnant at the time, often heroically climbing a library ladder to pull books from the shelves at the Italian Cultural Institute in New York. She later became Director of Publications at The Museum of Modern Art. One of the few architects to credit women in the 1960s was Bernard Rudofsky, who also generously thanked several women who assisted him, including Ellen Marsh, in his acknowledgments to *Architecture without Architects: A Short Introduction to Non-Pedigreed Architecture* (New York: The Museum of Modern Art, 1964).

9. Krautheimer had introduced Venturi to many of the buildings in Rome that appear in *Complexity and Contradiction*. It is likely that the book was already in galleys when Venturi changed the acknowledgments to include Scott Brown, since he appears to have attempted to keep the same line count. In fact, it might have been as late December 1966. Despite bearing a publication date of 1966, *Complexity and Contradiction* was not actually released until March 1967. MoMA sent Venturi an "advance copy" of the book on February, 28, 1967. Frances Keech (secretary to Gray Williams, Jr., the Museum's Director of Publications) to Venturi, February 28, 1967, VSB Collection, AAUP.

10. Robert Venturi, "Note to the Second Edition," in *Complexity and Contradiction in Architecture*, 2nd ed. (New York: The Museum of Modern Art in association with the Graham Foundation for Advanced Studies in the Fine Arts, Chicago, 1977), 14.

11. In his 1997 memorandum "Concerning the Writing of *C&C in Architecture*" (see note 3), under the heading "No Influence," Venturi states: "Via Louis Kahn who was going from geometrical structural grandeur à la Ann [*sic*] Tyng and Buckminster Fuller in the '50s to Corbusian béton brut à la heroic abstract form in the '60s. (Louis Kahn's eventual historical reference derived from Princeton via me.)" Kahn wrote letters of recommendation in support of Venturi's applications for the Rome Prize and the Graham Foundation grant, the latter of which enabled Venturi to write the first draft of the book. I am indebted to William Whitaker for this information.

     The relationship between Kahn and Venturi is complicated and would require an entire essay on that subject. In brief, one might say that they both suffered from an "anxiety of influence," to use Harold Bloom's phrase; in Venturi's case it might be seen in part as an example of what Bloom calls *kenosis*, a "movement towards discontinuity with the precursor," in which the "later poet . . . seems to humble himself," accepting "reduction from divine to human status" (Harold Bloom, *The Anxiety of Influence: A Theory of Poetry*, 2nd ed. [New York: Oxford University Press, 1997], 14–15). In the spring of 1950, Venturi had asked Kahn to serve as juror on his master's thesis review at Princeton and then worked for him briefly before going to Rome in 1954 and again for about nine months after his return, from the summer of 1956 to March 1957. In his short homage to Kahn in 1993 (*Iconography and Electronics*, 87), Venturi refers to himself as "a true student of Kahn," whom he calls a "great architect" and a "great teacher." However, Venturi also believed that Kahn was indebted to him both professionally and personally. Formally, this is perhaps most evident in Kahn's facade of the dining hall at the Phillips Exeter Academy in Exeter, N.H., which recalls the front facade of the Vanna Venturi House: note the overscaled gables and large central chimneys in both designs. The relationship between Venturi and Kahn was undoubtedly further complicated by Venturi's support of Kahn's romantic partners Anne Tyng and Harriet Pattison at difficult moments in their lives.

12. Richard Conniff, "The Patriarch," *Yale Alumni Magazine*, March/April 2008, http://archive.li/NXheM.

13. Vincent Scully, introduction to *Complexity and Contradiction in Architecture*, by Robert Venturi (New York: The Museum of Modern Art in association with the Graham Foundation for Advanced Studies in the Fine Arts, Chicago, 1966), 11. All subsequent citations of *Complexity and Contradiction* refer to this edition unless otherwise noted.

14. Ibid., 12–14.

15. Venturi to Scully, June 28, 1965, VSB Collection, AAUP. In this letter, Venturi asks Scully to write the introduction "for reasons of friendship and philosophy, although you've done so much for me already."

16. For an account of Scully's campaign to have Venturi appointed as the new chair of architecture, see Robert A. M. Stern and Jimmy Stamp, *Pedagogy and Place: 100 Years of Architectural Education at Yale* (New Haven, Conn.: Yale University Press, 2016), 238–40.

17. Vincent Scully, *The Shingle Style: Architectural Theory and Design from Richardson to the Origins of Wright* (New Haven, Conn.: Yale University Press, 1955).

18. Robert Venturi, "Homage to Vincent Scully and his *Shingle Style*, with Reminiscences and Some Outcomes" [1987], in *Iconography and Electronics*, 41–42.

19. Ibid.

20. See Venturi, *Complexity and Contradiction*, 106–107 (for the Beach House, 1959) and 55 (for the north facade of the Low House). In his homage to Scully, Venturi refers to the Beach House as his "first commission" but in *Complexity and Contradiction* Venturi gives earlier dates for two other projects.

21. Stern first met Venturi in 1962 and encouraged Scully to look at his work. Scully had already included a project of Venturi's in an essay, "New Talent USA: Architecture" (*Art in America* 49, no. 1 [1961]: 63), but had completely forgotten about it. See Stern and Stamp, *Pedagogy and Place*, 237–38, 602n228; Robert A. M. Stern, e-mail to the author, October 24, 2016.

22. Scully, introduction, 13, 16.

23. Vincent Scully, interview with the author, Lynchburg, Va., August 26, 2016.

24. Scully, introduction, 12, 16, 13.

25. Venturi, *Complexity and Contradiction*, 102–103 and 128–32.

26. Ibid., 133.

27. Scully selected an image of Venturi's 1962 Meiss House for the cover of his *American Architecture and Urbanism* (New York: Praeger, 1969), juxtaposing it with a prewar image of Main Street. For the paperback edition (New York: Henry Holt, 1988) he used a photo of the Vanna Venturi House for its 1988 paperback edition, and the cover of his 1974 book *The Shingle House Today* featured one of the Trubek and Wislocki houses. Venturi, in turn, deeply appreciated his support and would continue to do so: at the Pritzker Prize Ceremony in 1991, he explicitly acknowledged Scully's crucial support when "I was either out or outré." "Robert Venturi's

Response at the Pritzker Prize Award Ceremony at the Palacio de Iturbide, Mexico City, May 16, 1991," in Venturi, *Iconography and Electronics*, 100.

28. Marian LaFollette now uses her maiden name. While a student at Radcliffe College in the 1960s, she changed the spelling of her first name to "Marion," as it appears in the first edition of *Complexity and Contradiction*, later reverting to "Marian," as it appears in the second. Marian LaFollette, telephone conversation with the author, September 6, 2018.

29. After failing to get a contract from Harvard University Press, Venturi submitted his manuscript, a much-revised version of his 1963 Graham Foundation report, to The Museum of Modern Art in September 1963 (Venturi to Drexler, September 18, 1963). In February 1964, the museum received a grant from the Graham Foundation for its publication, and in April 1964, Venturi submitted yet another revised version of the manuscript (Venturi to Drexler, April 22, 1964). Drexler envisioned the book as the first in a new series of "papers" on architecture theory (hence the small format—the second book in the series was Joseph Rykwert's *On Adam's House in Paradise: The Idea of the Primitive Hut in Architectural History* [New York: The Museum of Modern Art in association with the Graham Foundation for Advanced Studies in the Fine Arts, Chicago, 1972]). According to Helen M. Franc, an editorial assistant in the Department of Publications at MoMA, Drexler, a committed modernist, "didn't like the whole idea of the book." Franc suggested that this was the reason for the postage stamp–size images. Initially, Drexler had given the manuscript to a freelance editor to review (someone doing work for the Department of Painting and Sculpture), but that person, according to Franc, found it "unpublishable." Drexler then passed it on for review to Franc herself, who said that it had "great ideas" but that it needed serious editing and no one at the Museum could do it. It required, she explained, someone familiar with Renaissance and Baroque architecture and knowledgeable enough to handle the citations and illustrations. She thought he should approach someone at Yale (Helen M. Franc, interview with Sharon Zane, section dating from May 28, 1991, Oral History Program, pp. 114–15, The Museum of Modern Art Archives, New York). However, a letter from Venturi to Esther McCoy, December 26, 1964, raises questions regarding Franc's conclusion about Drexler's assessment of the book. Venturi apologizes to McCoy for believing rumors that Drexler did not like the manuscript, and then writes, "Since then Vincent Scully has spoken to Drexler about this, and Drexler denied it emphatically: in fact, he considers this work 'the finest architectural aesthetic in twenty years' or something like that." The letters cited are all from the VSB Collection, AAUP. See also Martino Stierli's contribution to this volume, pp. 12–27.

30. After graduating from Radcliffe in 1950 as an art history major, Marian LaFollette had worked for two years at Random House, where she had edited a series of architecture books for *Progressive*

Architecture; after marrying her first husband, Hellmut Wohl, a junior professor in Yale's art history department, she moved to New Haven, Conn. (She and Vincent Scully married before the publication of *Complexity and Contradiction*, hence the use of her new married name in the acknowledgments.) A letter from Venturi to Scully, dated November 27, 1964 (VSB Collection, AAUP), suggests that Drexler may have already contacted Marion Wohl about editing the text by late November 1964. One anecdote is hard to resist. Before hiring her, Drexler invited her to discuss the job over a lunch she remembers distinctly. Drexler ordered two fried eggs, strawberry chiffon for dessert, and a Gibson. The luncheon was a success. Marian LaFollette, interview with the author, Branford, Conn., August 24, 2016. Vincent Scully told me the same story.

31. Drexler to Venturi, January 4, 1965; Venturi to Drexler, January 22, 1964, VSB Collection, AAUP.

32. LaFollette, interview. Scully and Stern also gave positive accounts. Scott Brown said to me that she imagined Wohl's role was similar to that which she herself later played for Venturi when she edited his writings. There is, of course, one crucial difference: Wohl, who majored in art history at Radcliffe, was not an architect and said she had no influence on the actual argument or content of *Complexity and Contradiction*. She was, first and foremost, a very good editor.

33. The text was edited once again by someone (and possibly two people) at The Museum of Modern Art, but this paragraph remained nearly the same as it was in the version that Marion Wohl edited and that Venturi submitted to MoMA in June 1965. I have not been able to acertain who subsequently edited the text at MoMA. Harriet Bee thought it might have been Helen M. Franc but in her oral history Franc mentions Bee (then Schoenholz) doing an excellent job editing the book; however, Bee said that she only proofed the final galleys of the first edition (Harriet Bee, telephone conversation with the author, August 8, 2016). Thomas Hines, author of *Architecture and Design at the Museum of Modern Art: The Arthur Drexler Years, 1951–1986* (Los Angeles: Getty Research Institute, 2019), thought that the handwriting and comments might be Drexler's (and certainly the sarcasm, confidence in judgment, and knowledge of architecture all suggest him), but the handwriting on the MoMA manuscript is quite different, in my view, from the sample of Drexler's handwriting that Hines kindly sent me. Harriet Bee, e-mail to the author, October 23, 2016; Thomas Hines, e-mails to the author, October 24 and 25, 2016.

34. Marion Wohl, "For Bob—general," large index card, n.d., c. June 1965, VSB Collection, AAUP.

35. Marion Scully (as she was at the time) already owned a house in Nantucket. Louise Trubek, telephone conversation with the author, November 1, 2016. I am also grateful to Louise and David Trubek and Alice Wislocki for spending a long afternoon with William Whitaker, David B. Brownlee, and me at the Trubeks' apartment in Brooklyn, New York, April 7, 2017.

36. William Whitaker, who lived in the basement apartment of Venturi and Scott Brown's house in West Mount Airy, Philadelphia, from

1998 to 2003, says that the two men would speak to each other weekly on the phone. Decades afterward, Katherine Finkelpearl still regularly called Venturi and Scott Brown.

37. On several occasions, Venturi has acknowledged Finkelpearl as the source of his title, including in his 1997 memorandum to von Moos and Scott Brown (see note 3). Venturi clearly had difficulty in deciding on a title. Venturi called his Graham Foundation report "Complexity and Contradiction in Architecture," but seemed to have doubts as he revised it for publication. Two manuscripts in the VSB Collection, AAUP, show the typed word "Contradiction" crossed out, one manuscript replacing it with the handwritten word "Accommodation" and the other with "Intrusion"; in this latter case also replacing a handwritten "Accommodation." One wonders, here, if Venturi meant to write "Inclusion" rather than "Intrusion," or if he was just amusing himself. Even in a later version of the manuscript (not dated, but after the spring of 1965), Venturi seems to have still been vacillating about the title, crossing out the typed word "Contradiction" and writing "Accommodation" by hand, and then crossing it out again.

38. Venturi, telephone conversation with the author, April 2012. I called Venturi when one of my students at Columbia University, Lluís Alexandre Casanovas Blanco, was writing a paper on Venturi's interest in the New Criticism. I am indebted to Blanco, who is now a doctoral student at Princeton, for first encouraging me to think further about the relationship between Philip Finkelpearl and Venturi.

39. Besides Katherine (Kitty) Finkelpearl, with whom I had a long conversation in August 2016, I am indebted to James Venturi for giving me access to his film footage of a conversation between Philip and Katherine Finkelpearl, Robert Venturi, and Denise Scott Brown at the Finkelpearls' home in Shaker Village, Harvard, Mass., in 2007. The clips are from the film that James Venturi is producing and directing, titled *Learning from Bob and Denise*.

40. Denise Scott Brown, e-mail to the author, July 17, 2017. The best biographical account of Venturi's parents is in Frederic Schwartz's introduction to *Mother's House: The Evolution of Vanna Venturi's House in Chestnut Hill*, by Robert Venturi, ed. Frederic Schwartz (New York: Rizzoli, 1992), 17.

41. Before joining the navy in 1944, Finkelpearl had been a chemistry major, but after returning to Princeton two years later, he decided to major in philosophy, then quickly switched to English. Christine Gorby mentioned to me that Philip Finkelpearl had told her that Venturi and he had taken the same aesthetics course in philosophy (a class recommended for all architecture majors) and that neither of them understood much of it.

42. Philip J. Finkelpearl, *John Marston of the Middle Temple* (Cambridge, Mass.: Harvard University Press, 1969), viii.

43. Christine Gorby said that Philip Finkelpearl told her this when she interviewed him. In a letter to Finkelpearl, dated December 3, 2003, Venturi seeks to reconstruct their contacts with Eliot and recollects that at Princeton they also saw the end of a movie about

Eliot and his first wife, presumably *Tom and Viv* (1995). VSB Collection, AAUP.

44. The quotation in the Rome Prize application is from Eliot's "Tradition and the Individual Talent" (1921); see also Venturi, *Complexity and Contradiction*, 18–19, 22, 28, 51.

45. Katherine Finkelpearl could not find her husband's copy of Empson when she recently looked for it, and wondered if he had given it to Venturi. In a handwritten note to Philip Finkelpearl, dated September 10, 1998, Venturi writes, "I'm using the word ambiguity and I think of you with affection and gratitude." Finkelpearl papers, Harvard, Mass.

46. In 2007, Venturi insisted that he was not all that "literary" in the conversation with Scott Brown and the Finkelpearls filmed by James Venturi (see note 39). Venturi may have also known of Wylie Sypher's books from art-history classes. Neither Katherine Finkelpearl nor Scott Brown remember discussions about David Jones, whose book *Epoch and Artist* (New York: Chilmark, 1959) Venturi quotes in *Complexity and Contradiction* (pp. 21 and 46). He ordered the book from the Princeton University store (August 31, 1964, VSB Collection, AAUP), alluding to a review in *The New Yorker*. Given the connections between Jones and Eliot, he may well have heard of Jones from Finkelpearl; Eliot had called Jones's book-length poem *In Parenthesis* (London: Faber & Faber, 1937) "a work of genius" and wrote the introduction to its second printing in 1961.

47. I asked Katherine Finkelpearl if Venturi and Philip Finkelpearl had ever discussed their parallel, though not contemporaneous, moves away from formalist analysis (so apparent, in Venturi's case, in *Learning from Las Vegas*), but she had no recollection of such discussions. (The two couples sometimes talked about politics, and the Finkelpearls gave Venturi and Scott Brown yearly subscriptions to *The Nation* and *The New York Review of Books*.) In his "Note to the Second Edition," Venturi openly admits that when he used the word "architecture" in the title of *Complexity and Contradiction*, he meant "architectural form," and that he now wishes that "the title had been *Complexity and Contradiction in Architectural Form*, as suggested by Donald Drew Egbert." He goes on to explain, "In the early '60s, however, form was king in architectural thought, and most architectural theory focused without question on aspects of form." Venturi, "Note to the Second Edition," in *Complexity and Contradiction*, 2nd ed., 14.

48. James Venturi, video footage, 2007. This "epiphany" apparently occurred at the very end of his stay in Rome. See Stuart Wrede, "*Complexity and Contradiction* Twenty-Five Years Later: An Interview with Robert Venturi," in *American Art of the 1960s*, ed. John Elderfield (New York: The Museum of Modern Art, 1991), 142–63.

49. I have often wondered, as has Scott Brown, how this "epiphany" occurred, and if Venturi might have read Colin Rowe's essay "Mannerism and Modern Architecture" (1950). Richard Krautheimer, who was at the American Academy in Rome while Venturi was

in residence, must have discussed Italian Mannerist architecture with him, and he might have referred Venturi to Nikolaus Pevsner's essay "The Architecture of Mannerism" (1946). See Colin Rowe, "Mannerism and Modern Architecture," *Architectural Review* 107 (May 1950): 289–99; Nikolaus Pevsner, "The Architecture of Mannerism," in *The Mint: A Miscellany of Literature, Art and Criticism*, ed. Geoffrey Grigson (London: Routledge, 1946), 116–38.

50. Venturi to Drexler, April 22, 1964, VSB Collection, AAUP.

51. In one letter to Drexler in September 1963, Venturi mentions that he "spent a valuable 14 hours with my friend in Poughkeepsie editing the part of the MS that I am sending to *Perspecta*." Venturi to Drexler, September 18, 1963, VSB Collection, AAUP.

52. Katherine Finkelpearl, telephone conversation with the author, November 5, 2016. The children's charming thank-you notes (undated but with materials related to *Complexity and Contradiction*) are in the VSB Collection, AAUP.

53. Searing, however, does not remember the story in quite the same way. She believes it was Stern who first introduced her to Venturi's work. Helen Searing, conversation with the author, New York, November 11, 2016.

54. Scully, interview, August 26, 2016; Stern, interview, July 20, 2016. The public lecture, which must have been a job talk of sorts, was given in November 1964, before Venturi began teaching his theory class at Yale. See Venturi to Scully, November 27, 1964, VSB Collection, AAUP. It also seems likely that Marion Wohl had begun reviewing Venturi's manuscript by this date.

55. The editing of Venturi's *Perspecta* text by Stern and his coeditors seems to have occurred between the fall of 1963 and spring of 1964, the same period in which Venturi was in negotiations with The Museum of Modern Art regarding publication of *Complexity and Contradiction*. He finally got an official "yes" from Drexler in February 1964.

56. In a letter to Stern, dated October 30, 1963 (VSB Collection, AAUP), Venturi writes, "I still can't seem to leave out the references to Mr. Rudolph, although the first one is toned down." The letter accompanied a revised version of "Simplicity and Picturesqueness," which was the title of that section of the manuscript at that time (in the published book it is "Complexity and Contradiction vs. Simplification or Picturesqueness"). The reference to Rudolph in question is on p. 19 in *Perspecta* and on p. 24 in the book.

57. Robert Venturi, "Complexity and Contradiction in Architecture," *Perspecta: The Yale Architectural Journal*, ed. Robert A. M. Stern, nos. 9/10 (1965): 17–56. Note, for example, the Cleanth Brooks quotation in the last paragraph of the opening section of the *Perspecta* excerpt (p. 18), which is not in the published version of *Complexity and Contradiction*. Some of the quotations in the manuscript submitted to MoMA were eliminated by Marion Wohl and Venturi in the spring of 1965, others by an editor at MoMA after June 1965 (see note 33 above). Needless to say, Venturi's projects of 1964 and

1965—the Fairmont Park Fountain competition (1964) and Three Buildings for a Town in Ohio (1965)—were not included in *Perspecta*.

58. Robert A. M. Stern, interview with the author, New York, July 20, 2016.

59. In his 1997 memorandum (see note 3), Venturi credits Scott Brown for introducing him "to urban ideas that paralleled and reinforced my architectural ideas and led to the last pages on urbanism, involving the validity of the ordinary and the conventional and the relevance of the commercial vernacular—of evolutionary, rather than revolutionary, urbanistic development[,] where Main Street is almost all right. . . ."

60. Venturi then adds, almost prophetically, "When I have had more experience at this most important scale of architecture, I shall be ready to make effective generalizations and criticisms." Venturi to Stern, December 6, 1965, VSB Collection, AAUP.

61. Venturi may have included Scott Brown in the acknowledgments after their trip to Las Vegas in November 1966, when he was probably reminded all over again of their many discussions about architecture and city planning at Penn (see also note 9).

62. In an e-mail to the author, November 6, 2016, Scott Brown summarized their collaboration on the two-semester sequence. "Our earnest discussions began when we met in Fall 1960, including about the theories course he had taught for the first time earlier that year. I audited this course in 1961 and again in 1962, while I was getting into running mine, and from 1961 he saw the materials I was using in that course and also in my City Planning urban design studios. . . . In 1962 and '63 we consulted each other and swapped information and that may be when Bob's reading notes began to include urban material and Brutalist and Team 10 writing. In spring '64 he gave the lectures for his course and I organized all the rest according to the patterns of my course and we shared the making of the reading lists and reading and grading the term papers and exams." Scott Brown taught the fall semester, Contemporary Theories of Architecture, City Planning and Landscape Architecture (Architecture 411, later renamed Architecture 511) in 1961, 1962, and 1963. For this class, she coordinated a series of lectures by Penn faculty (which included one from her), and wrote the syllabus, reading list, and assignments.

63. Denise Scott Brown, interview with the author, Philadelphia, June 18, 2016. Before coming to Penn's School of Fine Arts as dean, G. Holmes Perkins taught at Harvard's Graduate School of Design (GSD). Many of the people whom he hired at Penn had links to the GSD either as students or former faculty; these include David A. Crane, Robert Geddes, Blanche Lemco (van Ginkel), George W. Qualls, Mario Romañach, Anne Tyng, David A. Wallace, and William Wheaton. In his 1997 memorandum (see note 3), Venturi mentions having felt like an outsider at Penn. Under the heading "No Influence," he writes: "Via the Philadelphia and the University of Pennsylvania architectural community in the late '50s and early '60s—where as a junior faculty member I was an outcast as one who had not gone to Harvard and did not follow academic Gropiusian Modernism of the time."

64. This note, with an asterisk next to it, is underlined and in the largest handwriting on the sheet. Venturi's to-do list is undated but was probably written in the first week of August. It refers to "Harvard Press" and seems to be an outline of points to discuss in a cover letter that Finkelpearl had recommended he write (Finkelpearl to Venturi, July 31, 1963, VSB Collection, AAUP). The letter Venturi sent to Harvard University Press is dated August 8, 1963 (VSB Collection, AAUP).

65. Walter Isard, who became a friend of Scott Brown's, was the founder of what he called Regional Science, and coauthor of *Industrial Complex Analysis and Regional Analysis* (Cambridge, Mass.: MIT Press, 1959).

66. While Venturi gave the lectures in Architecture 512 in the spring of 1964, Scott Brown was responsible that semester for structuring the remaining portions of the class, including teaching the seminars, writing the assignments, and helping students with their drawings. The class had become a joint endeavor (see note 62). I am grateful to her for giving me copies of the syllabuses of Architecture 511 and 512, which she considers by 1963–64 to be conceived of as one course. These course materials are now also part of the VSB Collection, AAUP.

67. As William Whitaker pointed out to me, Venturi had most likely also heard about these ideas from Kahn, who came back from the 1959 CIAM meeting at Otterlo, The Netherlands, especially excited by van Eyck's presentation. At that meeting, van Eyck concluded his talk with a discussion of the "threshold" (though not yet using that word) and the necessity of establishing an "in-between" place in architecture. Van Eyck was in residence as a research fellow at the University of Pennsylvania (at the invitation of Ian McHarg) from 1960 to 1964, so undoubtedly both Scott Brown and Venturi became more familiar with his architecture and thinking during that period.

68. A. S. G. Butler, *The Architecture of Sir Edwin Lutyens*, 3 vols. (London: Country Life, 1950). Denise Scott Brown, interview with the author, June 18, 2016. I am indebted to William Whitaker for the detail about Venturi purchasing two sets of Butler's memorial volumes.

69. See note 3.

70. Scott Brown divided the design section studio into two groups, one proposing larger interventions, the other more modest ones. However, it is clear from the program that she was deeply critical of large-scale, tabula-rasa urban renewal.

Rem Koolhaas in conversation with Martino Stierli

MARTINO STIERLI: You have very openly spoken about the significance of *Learning from Las Vegas* for your own architectural thinking. Did you have a similar interest in *Complexity and Contradiction*?

REM KOOLHAAS: Strangely, not.

MS: It's quite a different book anyway.

RK: It's a totally different book. I guess it was the combination of Scott Brown and Venturi that first resonated with me. But of course, later I started looking at *Complexity and Contradiction* very carefully. The discovery of the aesthetic of mannerism was a very important breakthrough, also for me, to understand the appeal of the generic. It was an argument that you can be historically aware and yet participate in contemporary society. I think that aspect was really important. But because it was never openly said, it left an enormous space for misunderstanding.

MS: What would you say is the relevance of the book today?

RK: What is very important now is that it's a book. It has a smallish format, it's not fat, and it has content, it has an argument, and all three conditions are absent from current architectural discourse. We have enormous formats, very fat books, and no argument. (*Laughs.*) As a work of combining images and text from many different periods, as an assembly, I see it as a crafted object.

MS: . . . as an architecture of the book in a way.

RK: Yes, exactly. It has an enormous density.

MS: Why do you think it's not possible to write this kind of book now? There are not many architects who are capable of using the book in such a way to redirect architectural discourse.

RK: We've all become part of a mentality and ideology that says you cannot change, you are powerless. And, in a way, there's a total denial of what individual efforts might achieve. Because you are part of a system that is all-powerful. Moreover, when Venturi wrote *Complexity and Contradiction* he had the advantage of talking to a very small circle; there was not yet a global audience for that.

MS: It was published by MoMA, so in a way it was the complete hegemonic institutionalization of discourse.

RK: Yes, exactly. It was an elite book for a super-limited audience in one particular context. It barely reached Europe. But since that elitism has completely disappeared, when I start something now, I would almost, by definition, think this needs to be something that is relevant in Colombia and Singapore. And maybe that is immediately a complicated issue.

MS: So, in that sense, the book is of its time.

RK: Yes, it is of its time but also reveals a lot about certain privileges that are gone.

MS: Yes, absolutely. The book very heavily draws on literary theory. It's very interesting that Venturi does this trans-disciplinary crossover in order to formulate an architecture theory, and I think you have done similar things, perhaps not so much with literary theory but with cinematic propositions of how to conceive of space. Do you see a certain resonance there?

RK: Absolutely. Particularly when Venturi and Scott Brown collaborated, it was appealing that the range of influences was so wide, which made it very interesting to communicate with it. With Venturi, I always felt that the cultivation had taken place in the heart of the academy, and with Scott Brown that it had taken place in the outside world. And that made for a very powerful combination.

Robert Venturi and the Idea of Complexity in Architecture circa 1966

Joan Ockman

*What were ducks in the scientist's world before the
revolution are rabbits afterwards.*

—Thomas S. Kuhn

What, if anything, do Jane Jacobs's *Death and Life of Great
American Cities* (1961), Christopher Alexander's *Notes on the
Synthesis of Form* (1964), and Robert Venturi's *Complexity
and Contradiction in Architecture* (1966) have in common?[1]
On first glance, these three books, published within five years
of each other, appear very different. Jacobs was a journalist and
urban activist; her interest in architecture was above all social,
and it was her life experience in Manhattan's West Village that
led to the eyes-on-the-street empiricism that she passionately
advocates in her book as the way to approach the problems of
cities. Alexander, a Vienna-born mathematician and architect,
educated at Cambridge University and Harvard's Graduate
School of Design, pioneered the use of computer modeling and
diagrammatic visualization to analyze problems of architectural
design and urban systems. At the time of writing *Complexity
and Contradiction*, Venturi was a practicing architect primarily concerned with formal matters, and he wrote his book to
explain and defend his own taste preferences, which ran against
the grain of modernist orthodoxy.

Yet Alexander would laud Jacobs as "a very brilliant critic"
in his essay "A City Is Not a Tree," which appeared a year after
Notes on the Synthesis of Form;[2] and Venturi would commend
Alexander's book in *Complexity and Contradiction* for pursuing
a conception of architecture that was not based on simplification.[3] As Alexander wrote in *Notes on the Synthesis of Form*:
"Today more and more design problems are reaching insoluble

levels of complexity. This is true not only of moon bases, factories and radio receivers, whose complexity is internal, but even of cities and teakettles."[4] As Jacobs asked rhetorically: "Why have cities not, long since, been identified, understood and treated as problems of organized complexity? . . . The theorists of conventional modern city planning have consistently mistaken cities as problems of simplicity."[5] Venturi, most simply, *liked* complexity. But no less than Alexander and Jacobs, he believed that architects were among the last to recognize that complexity had supplanted simplicity in the wider world of ideas. As he states in the opening paragraph of *Complexity and Contradiction*:

> I like complexity and contradiction in architecture. I do not like the incoherence or arbitrariness of incompetent architecture nor the precious intricacies of picturesqueness or expressionism. Instead, I speak of a complex and contradictory architecture based on the richness and ambiguity of modern experience, including that experience which is inherent in art. Everywhere, except in architecture, complexity and contradiction have been acknowledged, from Gödel's proof of ultimate inconsistency in mathematics to T. S. Eliot's analysis of "difficult" poetry and Joseph [*sic*] Albers' definition of the paradoxical quality of painting.[6]

Indeed, Alexander, Jacobs, and Venturi were all of the opinion that a paradigm shift had occurred that architecture could ill afford to ignore. It is noteworthy that the concept of the paradigm shift was introduced at the same time that complexity theory was gaining widespread currency in the sciences. In *The Structure of Scientific Revolutions* (1962), Thomas S. Kuhn—who was teaching at the University of California, Berkeley, where Alexander would join the faculty the following year—described the historical conditions under which received ideas in science begin to break down under the pressure of both new intuitions and new experimental findings. This process, he argued, caused what initially appeared to be anomalies with respect to the reigning theory to engender first a crisis of belief and then, in a sort of viral progression, a revolution in thought.[7]

So complexity was a revolution in the 1960s, or so it was claimed. But in an almost textbook case of Kuhn's thesis, the revolution had in reality been percolating within diverse fields for some time. Venturi, as is widely known, derived his notion of complexity in part from ideas in literary criticism. Commentators have for the past half century devoted considerable attention to Venturi's allusions to Anglo-American New Criticism. Undoubtedly this movement—to which Venturi was introduced as an undergraduate and graduate student at Princeton in the 1940s not least through his classmate, the future literary critic Philip J. Finkelpearl—deeply influenced him. The New Criticism would remain dominant in English departments in American universities through the mid-1960s, when it was increasingly overtaken by other schools of interpretation, such as structuralism and poststructuralism. What seems especially to have resonated with Venturi was T. S. Eliot's defense of the difficulty of modern poetry. As early as 1921, Eliot had stated that modern poets should write difficult poetry precisely because the modern world was difficult:

> It is not a permanent necessity that poets should be interested in philosophy, or in any other subject. We can only say that it appears likely that poets in our civilization, as it exists at present, must be difficult. Our civilization comprehends great variety and complexity, and this variety and complexity, playing upon a refined sensibility, must produce various and complex results. The poet must become more and more comprehensive, more allusive, more indirect, in order to force, to dislocate if necessary, language into meaning.[8]

For Eliot modern poetry had to correlate with modern life, and it is not difficult to see how a zeitgeist argument such as this might transfer to architecture. Yet by the time Venturi seized on it four decades later, it was hardly a world-shattering idea; indeed, difficulty was a veritable hallmark of literary modernism (think not only of Eliot, Ezra Pound, and James Joyce, but, in the French context, of writers from Stéphane Mallarmé to Maurice Blanchot). On the other hand, modern architecture had, at least until the 1950s, eschewed allusiveness and ambiguity in favor of abstract rationalism and schematic clarity. So it had some catching up to do. It is, of course, not a little ironic that Eliot's apologia for obscurantism in modernist poetry— "variety and complexity, playing upon a refined sensibility"— should be repurposed by Venturi as an argument for a populist or Pop architecture. The irreconcilability of an elitist aesthetic with a democratic one remains among the true contradictions in Venturi's book.

The New Criticism was doubtless one inspiration for Venturi's idea of complexity, and there are about a dozen explicit references to its exponents in *Complexity and Contradiction*—besides Eliot, we come upon Kenneth Burke, Cleanth Brooks, Stanley Hyman, William Empson, Wylie Sypher, and David Jones, all in the first half of the book. Yet if the New Criticism was already a little old hat by the 1960s, Venturi also found support for his argument in other places and other branches of knowledge. These include perceptual psychology, specifically Gestalt theory; biology; and finally, if less explicitly, recently fledged fields like information theory and cybernetics. It has been said of Le Corbusier that he had a spongelike mind, absorbing ideas and images from varied sources. The same may be said of Venturi, especially early in his career. The infiltration of extra-disciplinary thought into *Complexity and Contradiction* was not just a matter of happenstance or intellectual eclecticism, though. Complexity was in the air, and efforts were being made in many areas—from the unity of science in philosophy to general systems theory in the social sciences—to relate knowledge across disciplinary boundaries and, in reaction against burgeoning overspecialization, to transcend the great divides between the hard and soft sciences and the humanities.[9] Digging deeper into the three books by Jacobs, Alexander, and Venturi, we encounter a striking substrate of shared references.

Like the New Criticism, Gestalt theory was also a little past its prime by the 1960s, having originated in the first decades of the twentieth century. An experimental study by Max Wertheimer on the perception of apparent motion, published in 1912, is usually taken as its formal inception. In the 1920s, Wertheimer carried out research with two younger colleagues at the Berlin Psychological Institute, Kurt Koffka and Wolfgang Köhler, into how human beings distill meaningful perceptions from their complex and at times chaotic world. Among the gestaltists' chief findings was that the human mind possesses organizational proclivities that cause it to configure disparate elements in its environment into a total picture. This picture, or *Gestalt*, ends up being more than—or, as Koffka preferred, "something else than"—the sum of its parts.[10] Gestalt theory was, in a word, about relationality.

By the mid-1930s, many of the leading adherents of Gestalt had been forced into exile by the rise of fascism and transplanted to the United States. With their appointment at various American universities and the translation of key texts, Gestalt theory reached an English-speaking audience.

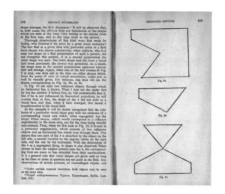

By midcentury—again, much like the New Criticism—it had attained wide currency, rivaling behaviorism as the dominant school in psychology (fig. 1). Besides its impact on studies of human behavior, cognition, problem-solving, and psychopathology, Gestalt ideas also had important implications for visual thinking. Among the artists and theorists who were strongly influenced by Gestalt were Josef Albers and György Kepes, both of whom had also emigrated to the USA in the 1930s. Albers had previously attended lectures on Gestalt at the Bauhaus in 1930–31.[11] Over the next several decades he would develop an influential pedagogy based on the interaction of color and other Gestalt-derived precepts, imparting them to students at Black Mountain College in North Carolina and at the Yale School of Art.

Venturi stumbled upon Gestalt theory in 1949 while working on his MFA thesis at Princeton, the design component of which was a new chapel on the campus of the Episcopal Academy, a private school outside Philadelphia. What interested him was how "context"—a concept he lays claim to coining in architecture—affects buildings, and, reciprocally, how new buildings change the meaning of the preexisting environment. "The intent of this thesis problem," he stated, "is to demonstrate the importance of and the effect of setting on a building. . . . Context is what gives a building its meaning."[12] In his 1996 book *Iconography and Electronics upon a Generic Architecture*, in which he published excerpts of his MFA thesis for the first time, he describes the "Eureka-like" moment when he came upon an article on Gestalt theory in a psychology journal in Princeton's library.[13]

About half a dozen references to Gestalt theory and cognate ideas appear in *Complexity and Contradiction*—in other words, about half as many as to the New Criticism, but not an

Fig. 1. Cover and spread from a mass-market paperback edition of Wolfgang Köhler, *Gestalt Psychology: An Introduction to New Concepts in Modern Psychology*. New York: Mentor, 1959. From Robert Venturi's library. The Architectural Archives of the University of Pennsylvania, Philadelphia

insignificant number. This includes two quotations from Albers. Besides the aforementioned one in the opening paragraph, another occurs in the chapter titled "Ambiguity." Venturi quotes a statement by Albers that had appeared in the catalogue for the traveling exhibition *Josef Albers: Homage to the Square*, organized in 1964 by The Museum of Modern Art's International Council: "The origin of art," Albers states, is "the discrepancy between physical fact and psychic fact" (fig. 2).[14] A year later, MoMA would mount *The Responsive Eye*, a major exhibition of over 120 paintings and constructions documenting the "new perceptual art" from post-painterly abstraction to Op art, in which Albers's work again featured centrally. Another work from that show, Ellsworth Kelly's painting *Green, Blue, Red* (1964), is reproduced in *Complexity and Contradiction*.

Apropos of Albers, and more directly in relation to architecture, we should recall that the first of Colin Rowe and Robert Slutzky's "Transparency" essays was published in 1963 in *Perspecta* 8.[15] This was the issue of Yale's architecture journal directly preceding the double one, number 9/10, that contained an extended preview of Venturi's forthcoming book.[16] Slutzky, a painter, had been Albers's student at the Yale School of Art, and had written his own MFA thesis in 1954 on the application of Gestalt theory to art education. Upon graduating from Yale, he was hired to teach design and color to architecture students at the University of Texas in Austin. There he met Rowe, with whom he collaborated in 1955 and 1956 on the two essays making up "Transparency." Their central concept is taken directly from Gestalt theory, and the authors begin with a long

Fig. 2. Josef Albers (American, born Germany, 1888–1976). *Movement in Gray*, 1939. Oil on masonite, 36 x 35 in. (91.4 x 88.9 cm). The Josef and Anni Albers Foundation, Bethany, Conn.

quotation from Kepes's *Language of Vision* (1944), in which the Hungarian-born theorist argues that space that possesses the properties of phenomenal transparency is characterized by contradictory visual cues and is equivocal in meaning. "By this definition," Rowe and Slutzky write, "the transparent ceases to be that which is perfectly clear and becomes instead that which is clearly ambiguous."[17]

The point to be made here is not so much that Venturi was influenced by Rowe and Slutzky's essay—it is not certain that he read it at the time, although its place and time of publication suggests this is likely—but rather to emphasize that Venturi's revindication of ambiguity in architecture in 1966 had more predecessors than William Empson. Interestingly, one of the early appraisals of Venturi's book was to come from Rowe, who reviewed it in *The New York Times Book Review* together with another book published in 1966, Reyner Banham's *The New Brutalism: Ethic or Aesthetic?* "Like some other architects—and many literary critics," Rowe argues, a little tongue-in-cheek, Venturi was preoccupied with "paradox, redundancy and ambiguity."[18] Overall, however, Rowe was appreciative of the fact that both Venturi and Banham, despite their diametric points of view—one formal, the other technological—were skeptical about modern architecture's utopian pretensions to be able to solve society's problems. A decade later, in a critique of Venturi's Yale Mathematics Building, Rowe offers a much harsher assessment of *Complexity and Contradiction*, faulting its author for cultivating "a taste for ambiguity in itself." Despite validating his aesthetic preferences with "the best authorities," Rowe now argues, Venturi's formal ambiguities have no inherent content. Compared to Le Corbusier's allusions, Venturi's are less profound; though clever and entertaining, their recherché connoisseurship is also, in his view, "a little pedantic."[19] "Just what *is* it that Venturi is trying to contradict?" Rowe asks. "The received myths of modern architecture? The doctrine of Walter Gropius? But then *who* is not trying to contradict *just* these?"[20]

Rowe's critique of ambiguity for its own sake raises a broader question. What is the relationship between formal complexity in architecture and other kinds of complexity? Can complex architectural forms serve *tout court* as metaphors—as "objective correlatives," to use T. S. Eliot's term—for social, urban, psychological, or scientific complexity? To what extent can architectural form intentionally reflect, or reflect upon, conditions of reality? This truly complex question, to which we shall return in our conclusion, has not lost its relevance today.

Like Rowe and Slutzky, Venturi invokes Kepes in *Complexity and Contradiction*, although the reference (in the chapter "The Inside and the Outside") is to Kepes's later book *The New Landscape in Art and Science* (1956). Underscoring one of Kepes's central arguments, Venturi affirms that "contrast and even conflict between exterior and interior forces" operate in all kinds of phenomena and at every scale, from living forms to cities.[21] In Kepes's words, "a physical configuration is a product of the duel between native constitution and outside environment."[22] Venturi notes that Frank Lloyd Wright, following his predecessors Louis Sullivan and Horatio Greenough, had made the case that a building should unfold "organically" like a plant, from inside to outside. For Venturi, this definition of organic architecture was "self-limiting."[23] The insights of twentieth-century biology, increasingly attuned to the way living forms were shaped not just by genetic predispositions but also by their surrounding environment, afforded a better model for contemporary architecture. The new research in the life sciences also offered architecture a way to move beyond the abstract space-time physics that had underwritten the aesthetic innovations of the earlier part of the century.

In this context, a book by the Scottish biologist D'Arcy Wentworth Thompson, *On Growth and Form*, originally published in 1917 but appearing in a revised edition in 1943 and then in an abridged version in 1961, was, much like Gestalt psychology, a touchstone for postwar architects and artists (fig. 3).[24] From the Independent Group exhibition *Growth and Form*, curated by Richard Hamilton at the Institute of Contemporary Arts in London in 1951 (and the essay collection *Aspects of Form: A Symposium on Form in Nature and Art*, which was prepared in conjunction with it)[25] to the writings of Kepes and others, Thompson's seminal treatise on the morphogenesis of plants and animals had a substantial reception. Venturi mentions Thompson in the paragraph preceding his citation of Kepes and also begins the chapter titled "The Inside and the Outside" with a quotation from Edmund W. Sinnott's *The Problem of Organic Form* (1963). Sinnott, a senior professor of botany at Yale (and author of a book on the architecture of New England meetinghouses and churches), pays homage to Thompson as "patron saint" in his book.[26] In the passage quoted by Venturi, Sinnott reiterates Thompson's fundamental concept that plant and animal forms always represent "a specific reaction to a specific environment" (fig. 4a).[27] Extrapolating this to architecture, Venturi argues that rather

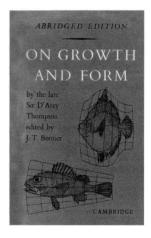

Fig. 3. Cover of D'Arcy Wentworth Thompson, *On Growth and Form*, abridged edition. Cambridge, U.K.: Cambridge University Press, 1961. From Robert Venturi's library. The Architectural Archives of the University of Pennsylvania, Philadelphia

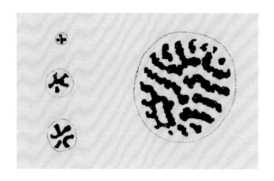

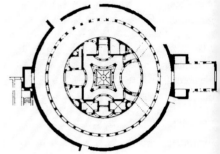

4a.   4b.

than reflexively striving for continuity between interior and exterior, architects should devise building envelopes that respond in a nuanced way to both internal content and external context (fig. 4b).

Finally—and to return to the three books with which we began and their web of interrelations—we find Venturi relying on an understanding of complex systems put forward by Herbert A. Simon (1916–2001) in an article titled "The Architecture of Complexity," published in 1962. Venturi cites Simon's article in the final chapter of *Complexity and Contradiction*, "The Obligation to the Difficult Whole." "By a complex system," Simon writes in the cited passage, "I mean one made up of a large number of parts that interact in a nonsimple way." A genuine polymath, Simon taught for many years at the Carnegie Institute of Technology and would win the Nobel Prize in Economics in 1978. In addition to his contributions to economics and statistics, he also did work in political science, mathematics, and biophysics, and he was a pioneering figure in the new fields of operations research, organizational theory, computer and information science, and artificial intelligence. Among his career ambitions was to bring the rigor of the hard sciences to problem-solving in the soft sciences. Although the word "architecture" is used in a generic sense in the title of his article, he begins by raising the possibility of applying a general definition of complexity to diverse kinds of systems, an objective that was also being pursued by his contemporaries Ludwig von Bertalanffy in general systems theory, Claude Shannon in information theory, and Norbert Wiener in cybernetics. Simon asks, Are metaphors and analogies carried across fields of knowledge helpful or misleading? The answer, he hypothesizes, depends on whether the similarities captured by the metaphoric usage are

Figs. 4a–b.
4a. Detail of an illustration by Frederick Orpen Bower showing "the effect of absolute size on structural complexity," from Edmund W. Sinnott, *The Problem of Organic Form.* New Haven, Conn.: Yale University Press, 1963
4b. Plan of Maritime Theater, Hadrian's Villa, Tivoli, Italy. Fig. 138 of Robert Venturi, *Complexity and Contradiction in Architecture*

significant or superficial. Calling himself a "pragmatic holist,"[30] he goes on to postulate that his definition of complex systems might well have applicability to problems not just in the natural and social sciences but also in the visual arts.

Among those whom Simon credits in "The Architecture of Complexity" as influencing his thinking is Warren Weaver (1894–1978). Like Simon, Weaver was a scientist, mathematician, and pioneer in computation and communications theory. He had published an article titled "Science and Complexity" in the journal *American Scientist* in 1948.[31] Upon his retirement as head of the Natural Sciences Division of the Rockefeller Foundation, a slightly revised version of this article was republished in the foundation's annual report.[32] It was there that Jacobs came upon it while writing *The Death and Life of Great American Cities* on a Rockefeller grant. In the concluding chapter of her book, "The Kind of Problem a City Is," she extensively paraphrases Weaver's argument concerning complexity.[33] Weaver identifies three different classes of problems in science: of simplicity, disorganized complexity, and organized complexity. It is the third class, involving a sizable but finite number of variables that are dynamically interrelated in an organic whole, that, according to Weaver, is most characteristic of the problems being confronted in modern-day genetics, bioresearch, and socioeconomics. Unlike the first class, which can be solved mathematically, or the second, whose solution can only be approximated statistically, problems of organized complexity require an entirely different mode of attack, namely the empirical methods of the laboratory, based on experimentation and the cumulative experience of trial and error.

Weaver's article was revelatory for Jacobs. It confirmed her own intuitions about the multifarious forces at play in cities and the "weird wisdom" associated with them.[34] "Cities," she writes in *Death and Life*, "happen to be problems of organized complexity."[35] As such, the statistical abstractions and tabula rasa mindset of modernist planners and policymakers were of little use. Instead, the city needed to be approached as a kind of petri dish, one in which specific environmental conditions elicited specific responses, and interacted with innate urban proclivities for self-organization and self-regeneration. "City processes . . . are always made up of interactions among unique combinations of particulars," she states, "and there is no substitute for knowing the particulars."[36] In subsequent writings Jacobs would increasingly incorporate insights from the evolving fields of complexity science and chaos theory.

This is most explicit in her late book *The Nature of Economies* (2000), where she draws a direct analogy between the behavior of urban and regional economies and that of ecosystems.

As for Alexander, despite the disarmingly conversational style of *Notes on the Synthesis of Form*, the notes at the back of the book (which was based on his doctoral dissertation at Harvard) reveal the breadth and depth of the intellectual background in which he was steeped, ranging from Gestalt psychology to theories of organic form (notably, once again, Thompson's), and from social anthropology to systems and information theory, including Simon's writings. His aforementioned essay "A City Is Not a Tree," written a year after leaving Harvard to teach at Berkeley, represents a further evolution in his understanding of complexity. Hired as a transportation planner to help program the stops on the new San Francisco Bay Area Rapid Transit (BART) system, he came to realize that the hierarchical logic of his earlier computer models was far too simple to account for the contingencies and nonlinearities of complex design problems such as those associated with the city. In "A City Is Not a Tree," he arrives at a new model of complexity, one predicated on overlaps, discontinuities, and accidents. To illustrate his argument, he reproduces a painting by Simon Nicholson (son of the artists Barbara Hepworth and Ben Nicholson) made up entirely of triangles (fig. 5), and comments: "The fascination of this painting lies in the fact that although constructed of rather few simple triangular elements, these elements unite in many different ways to form the larger units of the painting—in such a way, indeed, that if we make a complete inventory of the perceived units in the painting, we find that each triangle enters into four or five completely different kinds of unit, none contained in the others, yet all overlapping in that triangle."[37] This observation leads Alexander to arrive at a new diagram, the "semi-lattice," derived from set theory (fig. 6).

"A City Is Not a Tree" was an explicit critique of the tree, web, and stem diagrams favored at the time by contemporary architects—notably the members of the European group Team 10—to structure urban relationships. Not coincidentally, Alexander had in 1962 been a guest at Team 10's meeting in Royaumont, France, where the Dutch architect Aldo van Eyck presented a drawing suggesting that the part-to-whole relationship of leaves to trees was analogous to that of houses to cities (fig. 7). For Alexander such thinking was simplistic.[38]

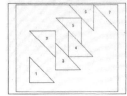

Fig. 5. Illustration from Christopher Alexander, "A City Is Not a Tree," pt. 2. *Architectural Forum* 122, no. 2. May 1965. Painting by Simon Nicholson above with Alexander's diagram of it below

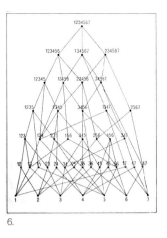

6.   7.

Alexander's semi-lattice would hardly be the final word on urban complexity, however. A couple of years later, Horst Rittel, his colleague in the College of Environmental Design at the University of California, Berkeley, would formulate the concept of "wicked problems." These were problems in planning that were so complex and refractory—especially in the context of a pluralistic society with conflicting interests—that they admitted no definitive, or even optimal, solution. At best, the planner might describe the various issues at stake.[39] Cities were examples of wicked problems par excellence. Alexander's diagram would also be challenged in turn by van Eyck, for whom no mathematical figure could ever adequately describe the city's "infinite reference."[40] Van Eyck instead likened the richness and ambiguity of urban experience to the poetic language of Shakespeare—a comment that brings us back full circle to Eliot and the New Critics.

Yet Alexander's diagram of overlapping sets, taken as "vital generator[s] of structure,"[41] is not a little reminiscent of Venturi's search for architectural forms that would bear out the argument of his book. Or vice versa: he sought a theory of complexity that could underwrite his preferred forms, which, in his early projects, coincidentally (or not) often featured angular shapes and oblique lines (as in his project for a Beach House; see fig. 4 on p. 18 of this volume). In further connecting the dots here, it is worth mentioning that van Eyck, whose ideas Venturi credits in *Complexity and Contradiction*, held a faculty appointment in the early 1960s at the University of Pennsylvania, Venturi's home base. At this time the Dutch architect was struggling toward his own conception of semantic complexity and ambiguity, which he elaborated in terms

Fig. 6. Christopher Alexander (American, born Austria, 1936). Diagram of a semi-lattice. From "A City Is Not a Tree," pt. 2. *Architectural Forum* 122, no. 2. May 1965

Fig. 7. Aldo van Eyck (Dutch, 1918–1999). "Tree is leaf and leaf is tree . . ." 1962. Illustration from Alison Smithson, ed., *Team 10 Primer*. Cambridge, Mass.: MIT Press, 1968

such as "twin-phenomena," "in-between-space," and the like.[42] It is also noteworthy that Denise Scott Brown was a guest teacher at Berkeley in 1965, where she got to know Alexander and the social planners there who were attempting to develop rigorous theories of urban complexity.

It is necessary, finally, to consider the relation of Venturi's theory to ideas coming from the English Townscape movement. Peter Laurence has laid particular emphasis on this connection,[43] although he has overlooked Venturi's equivocations about it in *Complexity and Contradiction*. Townscape was a self-described "radical visual philosophy" that originated in England in the late 1940s with the editorial group at the *Architectural Review*, led by Hubert de Cronin Hastings (under the nom de plume Ivor de Wolfe) and the journal's assistant editors Gordon Cullen and Ian Nairn. A reaction against the dogmatism and monotony of modernist town planning, it was directed to "achiev[ing] a new kind of organization through the cultivation of significant differences" in the urban environment.[44] Reaching back to eighteenth-century picturesque theory—to homegrown English landscaping principles of asymmetry, informality, and variety—the editors sought to validate what they called the "isness" of the built vernacular, inserting in each issue "casebooks" of exemplary (but also idiosyncratic) precedents. In May 1953 Venturi's first published essay, "The Campidoglio: A Case Study," had appeared in *Architectural Review* under the Townscape rubric.[45]

As an editor at *Architectural Forum* in the mid-1950s, Jacobs, too, became aware of the Townscape movement, and Cullen and Nairn were invited to provide a pictorial essay, possibly at her suggestion, to accompany her early article "Downtown Is for People," published in *Fortune* magazine in 1958.[46] Subsequently Jacobs and Nairn struck up a friendship, and she recommended him to the Rockefeller Foundation, which funded the research for his book *The American Landscape: A Critical View*.[47] Published in 1965, this was the fruit of a ten-thousand-mile road trip across the United States in 1959–60.[48] The Rockefeller grant was administered under the auspices of the University of Pennsylvania, and Nairn is listed on the faculty roster as a researcher associated with Penn's Landscape Architecture department in early 1962.[49]

A vivid and irreverent compendium of photography (mostly Nairn's own) and text, *The American Landscape* has been somewhat unjustly neglected (fig. 8). It constitutes a pendant to Peter Blake's *God's Own Junkyard*, which had appeared the year before and which Venturi would mischievously use as a foil in

Complexity and Contradiction to make his contrarian argument that the messiness of Main Street was "almost all right." Like Blake's diatribe, Nairn's is a no-holds-barred indictment of the ugliness of America. Unlike Blake, however, Nairn finds some redeeming features in the contemporary American landscape, and proposes to bring Townscape design methods of incremental modification and adjustment to bear on specific situations that were—also in his opinion—almost but not quite all right.

The affinities between the Townscape "philosophy" and Venturi's concepts of contextualism and complexity are evident. But by the time Venturi wrote his book he seems to have become wary—perhaps under Scott Brown's influence—of affiliating himself too closely with the English movement, which had already revealed its regressive side. He never mentions it explicitly, although there is an obvious allusion in his chapter "Accommodation and the Limitations of Order: The Conventional Element":

> Architects and planners who peevishly denounce the conventional townscape for its vulgarity or banality promote elaborate methods for abolishing or disguising honky-tonk elements in the existing landscape, or, for excluding them from the vocabulary of their new townscapes. But they largely fail either to enhance or to provide a substitute for the existing scene. . . . Cannot the architect and planner, by slight adjustments to the conventional elements of the townscape, existing or proposed, promote significant effects?[50]

Fig. 8. Spread from Ian Nairn, *The American Landscape: A Critical View.* New York: Random House, 1965

While Venturi here seems to be advocating something very similar to Nairn's prescriptions in *The American Landscape* for "sorting out the crap" and "unity-in-diversity"—"All the parts of present-day American life, from the Howard Johnsons to the plutonium plant," Nairn declares, "can get along together as long as they don't run into and blur one another"[51]—Venturi is also at pains to distance himself from an architecture of "precious intricacies" and "willful picturesqueness."[52] The vehemence of his distancing suggests that Townscape may have struck a little too close to home. His antipathy toward a picturesque and nostalgic aesthetic would resurface more emphatically a couple decades later, when he would feel compelled to put space between himself and the New Urbanism.[53]

In any case, Townscape, somewhat like the New Criticism, was becoming either outdated or irrelevant in the tumultuous 1960s. For Jacobs, it was too much a purely formal approach, little concerned with the real social and economic problems of American cities; for Venturi it was too much a product of old-world Englishness. In *Learning from Las Vegas*, coauthored six years after *Complexity and Contradiction* with Scott Brown and Steven Izenour, Venturi would move decisively beyond the well-mannered casebook of "significant effects."[54]

Meanwhile, as a new day of computer-driven research and "big data" began to dawn, the idea of complexity itself also took on a different complexion. Complexity theory has evolved far beyond where it was half a century ago, and is now part of the dominant discourse, bound up with an ideology of contemporaneity. Already in the 1980s, philosopher of science Isabelle Stengers expressed concerns that it was becoming a reflexive new zeitgeist theory, replacing the positivism of earlier twentieth-century science.[55] In architecture, complexity theory would become integral to parametric design, and a new aesthetic would emerge in its name. As one critic has argued recently, complexity in architecture is now a sine qua non of neo-avant-garde practice.[56]

In this context, it is not surprising that one of the leading popularizers of the concept of postmodernism in architecture, Charles Jencks, has undertaken a major revision of the definition that he initially put forward in 1977 in *The Language of Post-Modern Architecture*, a book strongly indebted to Venturi's *Complexity and Contradiction*. Switching his master trope from language to science some two decades later in *The Architecture of the Jumping Universe* (1995)—a book subtitled *A Polemic: How Complexity Science Is Changing Architecture and Culture*—Jencks calls complexity science "the heart of post-modernism."[57] In a characteristic Jencksian diagram (is it a semi-lattice?), he charts the rise of the complexity "revolution," which, according to his chronology, came to full fruition at the end of the twentieth century (fig. 9). Implicit in the mature logic of complexity is a new formal order, one that, instead of ironic and historically erudite juxtapositions, instead of overlapping forms, deploys smoother and more intricate geometries based on fractals and fluid connectivities, an iconography "of undulating movement, of surprising, billowing crystals, fractured planes, and spiralling growth, of wave-forms, twists and folds."[58]

From this standpoint it is worth revisiting Venturi's concept of "the difficult whole" in the last chapter of *Complexity and Contradiction*.[59] What, exactly, did Venturi mean in 1966 by calling the difficult whole an "obligation"? Was he enjoining his fellow architects to respect the forces of disjunction and fragmentation that, by the mid-1960s, were more rampant than ever in American cities? In acknowledging both the difficulty and the necessity of holding things together, was he suggesting that a dialectical tension between unity and disunity, similarity and difference, should exist in architecture; that architecture should embody the frictions inherent in a democratic society—that these frictions were precisely what made American society "almost all right"? To interpret Venturi's "gentle manifesto" this way is to overlay an ethical, even a protopolitical, reading on what is, to be sure, primarily

Fig. 9. Charles Jencks. "Post-Modern Sciences of Complexity." c. 1995. Illustration from Charles Jencks, *The Architecture of the Jumping Universe. A Polemic: How Complexity Science Is Changing Architecture and Culture*. Chichester, U.K.: Academy Editions, 1995

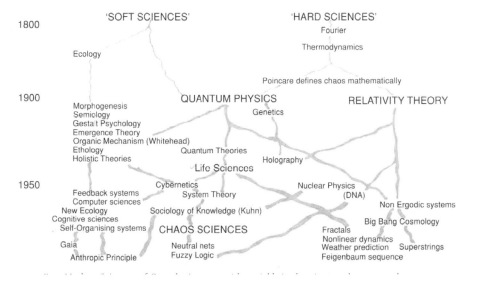

a formalist argument. Yet such a reading seems implicit in his argument, just as it more explicitly also permeates Jacobs's and Alexander's writings.

Given the smooth, seamless forms that characterize digital architecture in an age of uncritical neoliberalism, it may well turn out that *contradiction* is the more radical, or at least the more agonistic, of the two ideas that Venturi yokes together in his title. The fact that he leaves this second term almost entirely unanalyzed in the book remains provocative. To explore the meaning of contradiction in this context would take another paper. In any case, whatever postmodernism once was, and whatever it still signifies today, Venturi's book of 1966 stands at an inflection point between the humanist project of finding forms representative of a tolerant and pluralistic society and posthumanist concepts of complexity that have left behind modernism's social agenda.

Notes

Epigraph
Thomas S. Kuhn, *The Structure of Scientific Revolutions*, 2nd ed. (Chicago: University of Chicago Press, 1970), 111.

1. I wish to acknowledge a valuable essay by Peter Laurence, "Contradictions and Complexities: Jane Jacobs's and Robert Venturi's Complexity Theories," *Journal of Architectural Education* 59, no. 3 (February 2006): 49–60. Laurence's essay partly overlaps with the subject matter of the present paper, but as will become clear, my approach and conclusions differ from his.
2. Christopher Alexander, "A City Is Not a Tree," pt. 1, *Architectural Forum* 122, no. 1 (April 1965): 59.
3. Robert Venturi, *Complexity and Contradiction in Architecture*, The Museum of Modern Art Papers on Architecture 1 (New York: The Museum of Modern Art in association with the Graham Foundation for Advanced Studies in the Fine Arts, Chicago, 1966), 24.
4. Christopher Alexander, *Notes on the Synthesis of Form* (Cambridge, Mass.: Harvard University Press, 1964), 3.
5. Jane Jacobs, *The Death and Life of Great American Cities* (New York: Random House, 1961), 434–35.
6. Venturi, *Complexity and Contradiction*, 22.
7. Kuhn, *Structure of Scientific Revolutions*, 52–65.
8. T. S. Eliot, "The Metaphysical Poets," in *The Complete Prose of T. S. Eliot: The Critical Edition*, ed. Anthony Cuda and Ronald Schuchard, vol. 2, *The Perfect Critic, 1919–1926* (Baltimore, Md.: Johns Hopkins University Press, 2014), 381. Eliot's italics. Cf. Venturi, *Complexity and Contradiction*, 22.

9. A classic statement of this divide is C. P. Snow, *The Two Cultures and the Scientific Revolution* (New York: Cambridge University Press, 1959).

10. Kurt Koffka, *Principles of Gestalt Psychology* (New York: Harcourt, Brace, 1935), 176.

11. On Albers and Gestalt theory, see Roy R. Behrens, "Art, Design and Gestalt Theory," *Leonardo* 31, no. 4 (1998): 299–303; and Karen Koehler, "More Than Parallel Lines: Thoughts on Gestalt, Albers, and the Bauhaus," in *Intersecting Colors: Josef Albers and His Contemporaries*, ed. Vanja Molloy (Amherst, Mass.: Amherst College Press, 2015), 45–64.

12. Robert Venturi, "Context in Architectural Composition: M.F.A. Thesis," in *Iconography and Electronics upon a Generic Architecture: A View from the Drafting Room* (Cambridge, Mass.: MIT Press, 1996), 335.

13. Robert Venturi, "Introduction to My M.F.A. Thesis," ibid., 333.

14. *Josef Albers: Homage to the Square* (New York: The Museum of Modern Art, 1964), unpag. [15]. See Venturi, *Complexity and Contradiction*, 27.

15. Colin Rowe and Robert Slutzky, "Transparency: Literal and Phenomenal," *Perspecta* 8 (1963): 45–54.

16. Robert Venturi, "Complexity and Contradiction in Architecture: Selections from a Forthcoming Book," *Perspecta* 9/10 (1965): 17–56.

17. Rowe and Slutzky, "Transparency," 45.

18. Colin Rowe, "Waiting for Utopia," *New York Times Book Review*, September 10, 1967, 18 and 20.

19. Colin Rowe, "Robert Venturi and the Yale Mathematics Building," *Oppositions* 6 (Fall 1976): 13.

20. Ibid. Rowe's italics.

21. Venturi, *Complexity and Contradiction*, 85.

22. György Kepes, ed., *The New Landscape in Art and Science* (Chicago: Paul Theobald, 1956), 326; cited in Venturi, *Complexity and Contradiction*, 85.

23. Venturi, *Complexity and Contradiction*, 85.

24. D'Arcy Wentworth Thompson, *On Growth and Form*, abridged ed., ed. J. T. Bonner (Cambridge, U.K.: Cambridge University Press, 1961).

25. Lancelot Law Whyte, ed., *Aspects of Form: A Symposium on Form in Nature and Art* (Bloomington: Indiana University Press, 1961; orig. ed., London: Percy Lund Humphries, 1951).

26. Edmund W. Sinnott, preface to *The Problem of Organic Form* (New Haven, Conn.: Yale University Press, 1963), x.

27. Sinnott, *Problem of Organic Form*, 116; Venturi, *Complexity and Contradiction*, 71. The full passage quoted by Venturi is discontinuous; the first part appears in Sinnott on p. 44.

28. Herbert A. Simon, "The Architecture of Complexity," *Proceedings of the American Philosophical Society* 106, no. 6 (December 1962): 468; cited in Venturi, *Complexity and Contradiction*, 89.

29. Simon describes his career trajectory in his own words in "Herbert A. Simon—Biographical," 1978, http://www.nobelprize.org/nobel_

prizes/economic-sciences/laureates/1978/simon-bio.html, accessed July 17, 2018.

30. Simon, "Architecture," 468.

31. Warren Weaver, "Science and Complexity," *American Scientist* 36, no. 4 (October 1948): 536–44.

32. Warren Weaver, "Science and Complexity," *The Rockefeller Foundation Annual Report, 1958* (New York: Rockefeller Foundation, 1958), 7–15.

33. Jacobs, *Death and Life*, 429–33.

34. Jane Jacobs, "The Missing Link in City Redevelopment," *Architectural Forum* 104 (June 1956): 133.

35. Jacobs, *Death and Life*, 433.

36. Ibid., 441.

37. Christopher Alexander, "A City Is Not a Tree," pt. 2, *Architectural Forum* 122, no. 2 (May 1965): 61.

38. In a letter to Arthur Drexler, dated February 2, 1966, Venturi lauds "A City Is Not a Tree" as "excellent," commenting that Alexander's argument parallels that of his forthcoming book. I am grateful to Mary McLeod for sharing a copy of this document, conserved in the Venturi, Scott Brown Collection, Architectural Archives of the University of Pennsylvania.

39. Rittel formulated the concept of "wicked problems" at Berkeley around 1967. See C. West Churchman, "Wicked Problems," *Management Science* 14, no. 4 (December 1967): B–141; and Horst W. J. Rittel and Melvin M. Webber, "Dilemmas in a General Theory of Planning," *Policy Sciences* 4 (1973): 155–69.

40. On the interchange between Alexander and van Eyck, see van Eyck's remarks in *Team 10 Primer*, ed. Alison Smithson (Cambridge, Mass.: MIT Press, 1968), 98.

41. Alexander, "A City Is Not a Tree," pt. 2, 61.

42. See Venturi, *Complexity and Contradiction*, 19, 84, 86. Venturi's quotations of van Eyck come from the original publication of the "Team 10 Primer," which appeared as a special issue of *Architectural Design* in December 1962.

43. Laurence, "Contradictions and Complexities," 50–53.

44. Ivor de Wolfe, "Townscape: A Plea for an English Visual Philosophy Founded on the True Rock of Sir Uvedale Price," *Architectural Review* 106 (December 1949): 361.

45. Robert Venturi, "The Campidoglio: A Case Study," *Architectural Review* 113 (May 1953): 333–34; reprinted in Robert Venturi and Denise Scott Brown, *A View from the Campidoglio: Selected Essays, 1953–1984* (New York: Harper & Row, 1984), 12–13, with an accompanying note stating that the essay was extracted from Venturi's MFA thesis.

46. "Downtown Is for People," a dress rehearsal for the argument Jacobs would put forward in *The Death and Life of Great American Cities* three years later, was published in *Fortune* in April 1958 and anthologized the same year in *The Exploding Metropolis*, ed. William H. Whyte, Jr. (Garden City, N.Y.: Doubleday, 1958), 140–68.

47. See Peter Laurence, "The Death and Life of Urban Design: Jane Jacobs, The Rockefeller Foundation and the New Research in Urbanism," *Journal of Urban Design* 11, no. 2 (June 2006): 145–72; and Gillian Darley, "Ian Nairn and Jane Jacobs, the Lessons from Britain and America," *Journal of Architecture* 17, no. 5 (2012): 733–46.

48. Ian Nairn, *The American Landscape: A Critical View* (New York: Random House, 1965). Random House was also the publisher of Jacobs's *Death and Life of Great American Cities*.

49. The names of Aldo van Eyck and Gordon Cullen appear on the same faculty roster. See John Lobell and Mimi Lobell, "The Philadelphia School: 1955–1965. A Synergy of City, Profession, and Education," unpublished manuscript, c. 1980, http://creativity-discourse.com/wdp/wp-content/uploads/2012/06/PHILADELPHIA-SCHOOL.pdf, accessed July 17, 2018.

50. Venturi, *Complexity and Contradiction*, 52.

51. Nairn, *American Landscape*, 72, 146.

52. Venturi, *Complexity and Contradiction*, 22, 26.

53. See Stuart Wrede, "*Complexity and Contradiction* Twenty-Five Years Later: An Interview with Robert Venturi," *Studies in Modern Art*, vol. 1, *American Art of the 1960s*, ed. John Elderfield (New York: The Museum of Modern Art, 1991), 148, 153; and Robert Venturi, "À Bas Postmodernism, Of Course," *Architecture* 90, no. 5 (May 2001): 154–57.

54. In retrospect Venturi and Scott Brown would be even more emphatic in their disparagement of Townscape, calling it "cheesy" and "superficial." See Martino Stierli, *Las Vegas in the Rearview Mirror: The City in Theory, Photography, and Film* (Los Angeles: Getty Research Institute, 2010), 121, 143n37.

55. Isabelle Stengers, "Complexity: A Fad?" in *Power and Invention: Situating Science* (Minneapolis: University of Minnesota Press, 1997), 3. Cited by Douglas Spencer in *The Architecture of Neoliberalism: How Contemporary Architecture Became an Instrument of Control and Compliance* (London: Bloomsbury, 2016), 66.

56. Spencer, *Architecture of Neoliberalism*, esp. 62–67.

57. Charles Jencks, *The Architecture of the Jumping Universe. A Polemic: How Complexity Science Is Changing Architecture and Culture* (Chichester, U.K.: Academy Editions, 1995), 29.

58. Ibid., 13.

59. Venturi, *Complexity and Contradiction*, 89–103.

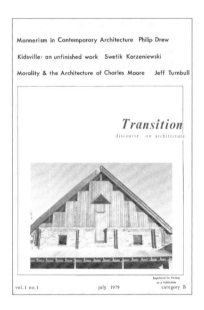

Mannerism in Contemporary Architecture   Philip Drew

Kidsville: an unfinished work   Swetik Korzeniewski

Morality & the Architecture of Charles Moore   Jeff Turnbull

Transition
discourse   on   architecture

vol. 1 no. 1   july 1979   category B

Dilemmas without Solutions

Andrew Leach

*You might say that mannerism is born whenever it is
discovered that the world has no fixed center, that I have
to find my way through the world inventing my own
points of reference.*

—Umberto Eco

The first issue of the Australian journal *Transition* (fig. 1),
launched in 1979, opened with a long essay by architect and critic
Philip Drew on "Mannerism in Contemporary Architecture."[1] His
article begins by recounting the formula, popularized by Arnold
Hauser,[2] of Mannerist art responding to a fifteenth-century
worldview thrown into crisis. He then moves on to cast as "mannerist" the phase of modern architecture's trajectory through
the twentieth century that followed its first, interwar, heroic
flourish. Regarded thus, mannerism abounds on the modern
stage: the work of Archigram and James Stirling and, later,
Arata Isozaki, the projects of Team 10 and the Architects'
Department of the London County Council; variations, that is,
on the humanist, brutalist, technological, and linguistic turns

Fig. 1. Cover of the inaugural issue of
Transition: Discourse on Architecture,
1979

of a postwar modernism presaging postmodernism. Drew's attention to Venturi is obvious in this context, given the latter's invocation of the Mannerist architecture of sixteenth-century Italy and seventeenth-century England and his citation of Elizabethan metaphysical poetry as read through the eyes of its modernist "New" critics. The modern mannerism Venturi would appear to embrace is, as Drew puts it, "the style of a cultivated international elite,"[3] drawing on popular culture but rendering it rarefied. His article is, admittedly, a blunt instrument, appearing in a review making its first tentative gestures toward a world of architectural debate with distinct nodes that had not (yet) reached the antipodes. The distance intrinsic to this reception echoes Venturi's distance from the architecture and literature that would start to be called mannerist from the 1920s and 1930s onward. Nonetheless, Drew's analysis chimes with an observation made widely before and since. He presciently observes that there "are a good many reasons for believing that the present era of mannerism will be a short one."[4] For a moment, however, that had even by the end of the 1970s run its course, Venturi had served "to legitimate the adoption of a mannerist aesthetic in contemporary architecture."[5]

This assertion is debatable, of course, but it serves as a key to a local, mediated reception of *Complexity and Contradiction in Architecture* that can be seen to encapsulate the first generational rejection, at the end of the 1970s, of the enthusiasm with which Venturi's early ideas were first greeted. Beyond Drew's article, the pages of *Transition* in its early years explore the question of Australia's relationship with the postmodern, where the question of modernism's legacy in Australia and its points of reference consistently becomes a matter of the postmodern, and where the task of defining postmodernism quickly leads authors and interlocutors to consider the shape and substance of a so-called Venturian postmodernism. This is the postmodernism that finds a springboard in the final polemical chapter of *Complexity and Contradiction* and which appeared, at least for a spell, to pose the question of Mannerism's contemporaneity. As a result, many of architecture's big names of the late 1970s and early 1980s who made it to Australia in those years found themselves quizzed by the young and hungry correspondents of *Transition* about their stance on postmodernism and, by extension, whether they considered themselves mannerist.[6]

It must be said that 1979 was late in the game for self-styled architectural theorists and critics to *start* getting excited about mannerism, and there is little value in trying to test

Venturi himself against an impression of what mannerism ought to contain, historically or contemporaneously. The now-beleaguered concept had enjoyed something of a renewal in the history of art and in the history of letters during the 1950s and 1960s, which left a trace in books that enjoyed an international circulation into the 1970s. Read ungenerously, Venturi himself was doing little more than scratching an itch that had formed in the minds of a good number of critics and historians anxious to understand, through history, the role of art in society in the wake of World War II and the role, in turn, of the individual artist (or architect) therein. Beyond the intellectual trajectory through Walter Friedlaender and Nikolaus Pevsner,[7] who together gave Mannerism both critical credence and regularity (first in the study of painting, then in architecture), the most widely read attempt to understand a revival of curiosity in Mannerism in midcentury architectural culture was an essay published nearly three decades before Drew's review, by the architectural historian Colin Rowe.[8]

Rowe's article appeared in *Architectural Review* in 1950, and in it he explored the varied ways in which twentieth-century architecture maintained a meaningful conversation with that of the sixteenth. He admits that Mannerism had not, to the end of the 1940s, enjoyed the popular profile of its historical progeny, the Baroque—a situation that had been entirely altered by the time Venturi put pen to paper—but that its "recurrence" in the "mainstream of modern architecture" raised the question of whether it had "some deeper significance."[9] Notably, he observes the demand implicit in the concept of mannerism for "an orthodoxy [be it classicism or functionalism] within whose framework" the mannerist work, whether historical or modern, "might be heretical."[10] Within this easy parallel lies scope for an analogous relationship between modern architecture and that of the Late Renaissance, which Rowe himself explores with great finesse. Within both ages he observes a capacity to pull into plain view the irreconcilable characteristics of what was taken to be a stable system. Le Corbusier's Villa Schwob (1912–16) at La Chaux-de-Fonds, Switzerland, and Palladio's Casa Cogollo in Vicenza, Italy (completed 1559), share "a formal ambiguity of the same order"—one responding to the tentative stability of the late nineteenth century, the other to the supposed perfection of the age of Bramante.[11] The present day, he notes memorably in concluding, "seems to be particularly susceptible to the uneasy violence of Mannerism, with marks both its own production and its historical admirations."[12]

Denise Costanzo has detailed the exchanges (and the echoes of the exchanges) between Rowe and Venturi on this theme, and Venturi's own notes show his attention to Rowe's treatment of ambiguity in the modern uptake of the cinquecento case.[13] But while Rowe's article was widely read among architects and critics, he was one of many scholars processing (directly or indirectly) this art-historical legacy for twentieth-century architectural culture. A session of the International Congress for the History of Art held in New York in 1961 laid out the state of the field as it had been revived since the war—an occasion that also documented the rearranged institutional landscape on both sides of the Atlantic created by the wave of intellectual migration from central Europe.[14] From this session came two major synthetic studies of the period, which were published by the end of the decade, by John Shearman and Craig Hugh Smyth.[15] James Ackerman likewise published his *Architecture of Michelangelo* and *Palladio* in these years.[16] It is stretching things to invoke a mannerist moment that enjoyed Venturi's participation, since much of this discussion was beyond his view and some of its documentation appeared after *Complexity and Contradiction* had been published. But it is just as difficult to sustain the idea of his interest in mannerism as a consequence solely of a private, direct encounter with its historical exemplars in Rome and their present-day advocates.

Indeed, his most direct systematic encounters with contemporary Italian architects and urbanists were mediated by the seminars organized for fellows of the American Academy in Rome by Bruno Zevi through the Istituto Nazionale di Urbanistica.[17] To describe these seminars as being shaped by Zevi's own assessment of the historical situation of the architectural and urban culture of Rome in the 1950s will hardly meet much resistance.[18] Likewise the observation that Zevi's view of history was replete with lessons and warnings. It follows that Zevi's own account of the parallels of historical Mannerism to the modern age are among the least nuanced we can encounter anywhere; his catalogue essay for the 1964 exhibition *Michelangiolo Architetto* positions the Holocaust as an echo, across time, of the Reformation, and the crisis of Reason as a recurrence of the crisis of Classicism.[19]

Venturi turns Rowe's celebration of Mannerism's ambiguity into an embrace of complexity, which as a projective principle, extending into his architectural practice, translated the gains that had been made across the 1940s and 1950s in studies of sixteenth- and seventeenth-century English literature.[20]

A paragonistic line ran through the postwar debates in numerous fields of arts and letters, looking for the parallels and relative positions among various practices and media within stylistic or chronological bounds. The *Journal of the History of Ideas* had published Paul Kristeller's essays on the "Modern System of the Arts" in 1951, and the *Journal of Aesthetics and Art Criticism* produced a special issue on "Baroque Style in Various Arts" in 1946—which included René Wellek's influential literary claim on the term—and returned to the theme in 1955.[21] That same year, Wylie Sypher picked up Panofsky's gauntlet (thrown down in the 1948 lecture *Gothic Architecture and Scholasticism*) to explore the "intrinsic analogies" that connect one department of culture to another within an epoch.[22] Sypher advanced a four-stage Renaissance while setting aside "the notion of parallels" in order to "have recourse to that more amenable, if less exact, term 'analogy.'"[23] He observed that the English metaphysical poetry of "tough wit" formed "the *mise en scène* for the drama of modern criticism."[24] This remains so for Sypher irrespective of the contemporary uncertainty with which scholars ranging from Jacob Burckhardt and Heinrich Wölfflin to T. S. Eliot and Mario Praz had framed and explained the Renaissance.[25] Much was at stake in the idea of a cultural apogee, including both its origins and its fate.

As for Sypher, so for Venturi, his sometime reader. In an early draft of *Complexity and Contradiction*, in a chapter then called "Mannerism and Poetry," Venturi himself writes, "I have been able to borrow terms constantly from literary criticism."[26] This is entirely consistent with the lines in his short essay "My Manifesto to Myself" (fig. 2) in which he expresses his admiration for Eliot's 1919 essay "Tradition and the Individual Talent," observing that "I consider it valid as well as convenient to my purposes to substitute architect for poet in this essay."[27] And in doing so, the term *mannerism* took on instrumental value for posing the question of the artist's place in the world and in history, invoking the linguistic analogy at a moment when the question of architecture was itself becoming a question of meaning. In the published version of *Complexity and Contradiction*, Venturi then wrote that "the obligation toward the whole in an architecture of complexity and contradiction does not preclude the building which is unresolved. Poets and playwrights acknowledge *dilemmas without solutions*. The validity of the questions and vividness of the meaning are what make their works art more than philosophy. A goal of poetry can be unity of expression over resolution

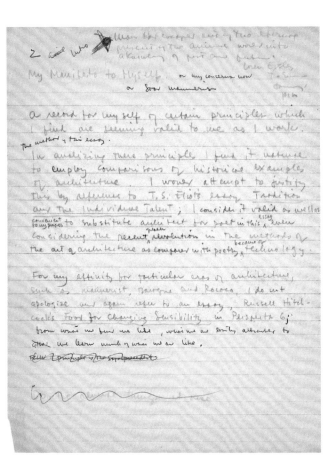

Fig. 2. Robert Venturi. "My Manifesto to Myself." c. 1961/1962. Manuscript. The Architectural Archives of the University of Pennsylvania, Philadelphia. Gift of Robert Venturi and Denise Scott Brown

of content. . . . A building can also be more or less incomplete in the expression of its program and its form" (italics added).[28] In the earlier draft "Mannerism and Poetry," this was less eloquent, but clearer: "An architecture of complexity and contradiction cannot be a mere reaction to the blandness or prettiness of current architecture," Venturi wrote. "Nor can it be perversity. If it is called Mannerism, it is not a mannerism. It represents an attitude common and justifiable in architecture throughout the past."[29]

It is a folly to attempt to define precisely Venturi's relationship to sources that he did not himself read systematically, and which foremost served to feed his thinking as an architect. His quotations function as dislocated fragments and not as parts of a difficult whole. The manuscript for "Mannerism

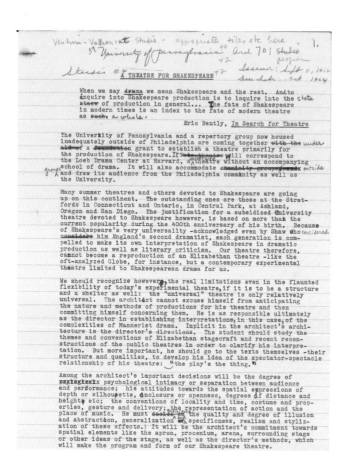

Fig. 3. Venturi-Vallhonrat Studio. "A Theatre for Shakespeare," draft design brief. c. 1961/1962. The Architectural Archives of the University of Pennsylvania, Philadelphia. Gift of Robert Venturi and Denise Scott Brown

and Poetry" lays this bare: long passages by canonical figures of modern literature are excerpted and joined together by ideas presented with an assumed but fragile authority—and thereby acquired as an authority, in history and in relation to it, for his own ideas and actions. In these first drafts, which he was writing in 1961 and 1962, Venturi speaks of the importance of considering the architecture and literature of Mannerism "mannerist" as such—a choice for ambiguity and paradox over "plain, discursive simplicity," to borrow the critic Cleanth Brooks's phrasing.[30] Art is—the arts are—a matter of the "unity of experience" rather than scientific detachment.

Across these same years, at the University of Pennsylvania, Venturi taught a studio involving the design of a Shakespearean theater, first with Robert Geddes and then with Carles Vallhonrat (fig. 3). The project brief explains the importance of "anticipating the nature and methods of productions for [the architect's] theatre and then committing himself concerning them." The "universal theater" is only relatively so. The architect, he writes, shares the director's responsibility "in establishing interpretations." Around 1962, this line is amended to add, "in this case, of the complexities of Mannerist drama. Implicit in the architect's architecture," he continues, are "the director's directions." The reading list is straightforward, in that it directly concerns the forms and needs of Elizabethan theater—the principles of which students need to grasp—rather than the critical literature of the 1940s and 1950s that recast early modern drama for the mid-century. A giveaway question mark lurks alongside Sypher's name in a draft of that list.[31] Mannerism in this sense offers a key to the architect's role as a creative figure of more intellectual substance than someone simply concerned with the masterful resolution of program into form, space, surface, and structure. In the studio brief, the reference is fleeting and seemingly incidental to the task at hand. Read alongside Venturi's other writing of the moment, however, the term takes on added significance as one of the vehicles through which he was placing himself into a tradition he was then in the process of defining—"Palladio, Borromini, van Brugh [*sic*], Hawksmoor, Soane, Le Doux, Butterfield, Furness, Sullivan, Lutyens, Corbusier, Aalto, Kahn, and others." The common thread among these figures, he writes, is constituted by "a conscious defying of dogmas and simplification."[32] Considered against the grain of his own claims, we also observe Venturi inserting himself into the canon.

Returning briefly to 1979: in his review of a series of publications on the office of what was then Venturi and Rauch, published in the *Journal of the Society of Architectural Historians* in 1979, the English literature scholar Philip J. Finkelpearl made specific note of Venturi's attention to the critical discourse on literature. In cautiously couched language he observes that "from one perspective CC may be viewed as an application of the methods of the so-called 'New Critics' of literature to architecture. . . . The resultant formal complexities he shows through painstaking analysis and extensive exemplification to be exciting and beautiful."[33] The architect's "similar concentration on 'difficult particulars'" is activated by what he describes as Venturi's "prodigious mastery of architectural history," in which works of architecture form the "spatial record" of "a dynamic struggle among opposing forces."[34] A longstanding friend of Venturi's, Finkelpearl is credited with introducing him to a passage from Brooks's *The Well Wrought Urn* (1946) that would inspire the title of his book, in which the critic refers to the legitimation of the poet's position above the fray of "the complexities and contradictions of experience."[35] There is something in this credo in Venturi's response to the invitation from Peter Eisenman, Michael Graves, and Thomas R. Vreeland to participate in a conference on the critical apparatus of architecture at Princeton in 1964. "Worrying about critical apparatuses is a luxury beyond my means," he wrote, "and going beyond my personal attitudes and interests doesn't interest me. Or rather, any contribution of mine . . . must derive from my authority as an accomplished architect."[36]

Venturi's appropriation of extradisciplinary knowledge for architecture was hardly new for the 1960s; his own "discovery" of Gestalt psychology while preparing his MFA dissertation is a commonplace of the time rather than an exceptional story of borrowing and adaptation by a figure whose thinking we have come to value. And yet there is also this insistence on the practice—on the work—of architecture. Ever king of the aphorism, he notes: "Our problem is too much apparatus and not enough architecture."[37]

Finkelpearl offers a study in contrasts. Mary McLeod's contribution to this volume (esp. pp. 56–59) explores his relationship with Venturi in greater detail, but it is enough, here, to note that they were both among a circle of students at Princeton who were invigorated by the world of letters. This group included, too, the preeminent translator William Weaver, who in a letter to Venturi (fig. 4) encouraged his "dilettantism." "I can't tell . . . if you are a genius," he wrote, "But any fool . . . can see that you have taste, intelligence, and talent, so you can make yourself a genius." A little later in the letter he implores him to come to Rome: it "cannot help but stimulate and educate anyone with two eyes and a head."[38] The New Criticism, at least as it appears in *Complexity and Contradiction*, ultimately helped Venturi to appreciate and explain the importance of those works and ideas that absorbed his attention, and it served less to connect him to contemporary literary thought than to keep in play the books that had been important to him during the years when he was a student.

Reading Finkelpearl's writings of the 1960s on the Jacobean poet John Marston, one encounters almost no commonality with the notion of complexity invoked by Venturi. For Finkelpearl, complexity is historiographic principle; for the architect, it is a matter of creation and artistic value. Finkelpearl's work on Marston, culminating in *John Marston of the Middle Temple* (1969), explores Marston's dramatic work as a product of the

July15

Dear Bob,

Excuse what may seem like bad typing in this note.
It isn't. I am using Mother's machine, which be-
haves worse than Judy Coplon and is as old as
Alger Hiss's Woodstock.

I wanted to answer your letter promptly, even if
my answer sounds brief. You seemed discouraged, and
I don't blame you. I know what a Princeton summer
is like, and I know what it is to postpone a trip
to Europe.

But don't let either of these things discourage you
about your work. Take the advice of a writer who
has been writing for seven years and has published
the impressive number of two (count them) 2 short
stories. Don't bother about other people, teachers,
time consumed, or anything else. I can't tell (am
not qualified, that is) if you are a genius. But
any fool (e.g. Shellman) can see that you have taste,
intelligence, and talent, so you can make yourself
a genius.

Another don't. Don't worry about being called a
dilettante. Anyone who tries to go his own way,
a new way, is sure to be called that, and worse.
Again take it from me. My whole family thinks I'm
a no good drifter who should have stuck to teaching,
but I simply can't be bothered about that.

Come to Rome when you can, dilettante or not. Life in
Rome cannot help but stimulate and educate anyone
with two eyes and a head. It is one of the few places
in the world where you can stop to look at something
beautiful without having to explain to people why
you stopped. It also has the advantage (more than
anyplace else) of being a city littered with beautiful things and people devoted to them.

What a letter this is. Excuse this preaching, but I
wanted you to know that discouragement is part of
the business and you mustn't let other people, taking
advantage of this discouragement, force you into something, some job or (worse still) some point of view
that will keep you from developing.

I will be in Princeton overnight probably, staying
at the Thorps. I will write you before then anyway
and wexxxxx will have at least a hasty meeting.

As ever, Bill

individual mind, responding to, if not shaped by, that mind's formation, and its difficult relationships to its many wider contexts—not least, institutions and their social, religious, and economic conditions.[39] His is a study seeking to recover and account for complexity in history, with no discernible regard for how writers might deploy his analysis in the present. Venturi's complexity may derive from historical examples

Fig. 4. Letter from William Weaver (attr.) to Robert Venturi. July 15, [1947]. The Architectural Archives of the University of Pennsylvania, Philadelphia. Gift of Robert Venturi and Denise Scott Brown

and be informed by the language of literary criticism, but it operates against historical complexity in favor of a formal complexity that insists upon the isolation of each example from history itself. Only by setting aside the historical context can the works of Italian Mannerism and English Palladianism to which he was drawn speak to each other across the centuries. Decontextualized as forms, and as compositions of architectural elements, they are treated, instead, as linguistic structures, stripped of their language. The way that Venturi took up the lessons of the New Criticism for architecture is thrown into relief by the scholarship of Finkelpearl, who had kept reading and moved on. There is an insistent architecturality to Venturi's writing that demands the subordination of his conceptual sources and historical cases to the question of how to design. As we recall from his response to Eisenman, Graves, and Vreeland, the proof in building was just that: a test of the legitimacy of ideas derived from observation and reflection.

In one sense, the article in *Transition* cited at the outset of this essay reflects one strain of Venturi's legacy: the difficulty of *Complexity and Contradiction* seemingly rendered simple by *Learning from Las Vegas*, thereafter locking the "Venturian" and "Venturian postmodernism" into place within the vocabulary of architecture's recent history. Another work from the same cultural setting as Drew's article offers an irreverent way beyond this sense of premature calcification. The Howard/Kronborg Clinic in Footscray—a suburb of Melbourne—was designed by the firm of Ashton Raggatt McDougall (ARM) in 1993 (Ian McDougall having been a founding editor of *Transition*) (fig. 5).[40] ARM has long positioned itself as working with the iterations of Venturi's ideas, its earlier projects using conscious, indeed self-conscious deformations to inform new work—sometimes confrontingly so. The facade of the Howard/Kronborg Clinic was generated by dragging the iconic photographic image of the Vanna Venturi House across a photocopier and working faithfully with the corrupted result.[41] Even Mrs. Venturi herself is rendered in black and white tiles as a kind of atomic shadow (fig. 6). The translation is direct and unceremonial; the results at once an homage and a provocation. In one sense it illustrates in architecture the apparently reductive reading of *Complexity and Contradiction* of which Venturi long complained. But it also holds a mirror to this book as a work that can be activated to new (complex) ends, as programmatically desacralized fragments are drawn

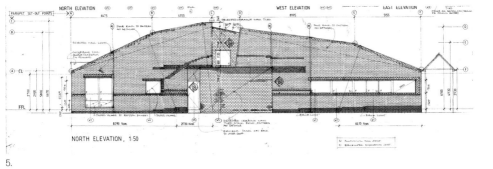

5.

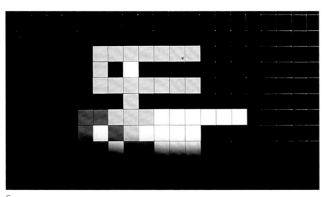

6.

Fig. 5. Ashton Raggatt McDougall.
Howard/Kronborg Clinic, Melbourne.
Completed 1993. Elevation. 1:50

Fig. 6. Ashton Raggatt McDougall.
Howard/Kronborg Clinic, Melbourne.
Completed 1993. Detail of facade with
profile of Vanna Venturi

from otherwise difficult wholes, and Venturi's long quotations are transformed into ARM's isolated citation of the facade at Chestnut Hill.

The Howard/Kronborg Clinic grapples with its own dilemmas, as Venturi had a generation earlier, suggesting an unanticipated extension of the intellectual and artistic tradition Venturi had begun to sketch out in "Mannerism and Poetry" at the start of the 1960s, with its conscious eschewal of dogma and simplicity, its invocation of an interwar sense of mannerism as deferent deformation, irony as commemoration, and anxiety masked as play. It offers no answers to the questions explored here, instead insisting, from the edges, upon the necessity of sacrilege. The sense of transgression, artfulness, and intellectualism that shaped the image of mannerism for modern architecture, and Venturi within it, remained, therefore, a valued tactic decades later, both true to the ideas that Venturi's distant readers encountered in *Complexity and Contradiction* and an apposite means to move beyond the postmodernism it seemed to have legislated.

Notes

Epigraph
Stefano Rosso, "A Correspondence with Umberto Eco: Genova-Bologna-Binghamton-Bloomington, August–September 1982, March–April 1983," trans. Carolyn Springer, *boundary 2* 12, no. 1 (autumn 1983): 3.

1. Philip Drew, "Mannerism in Contemporary Architecture," *Transition: Discourse on Architecture* 1 (1979): 4–10.
2. Arnold Hauser, *Der Manierismus: Die Krise der Renaissance und der Ursprung der modernen Kunst* (Munich: C. H. Beck, 1964). Translated by Eric Mosbacher in collaboration with the author as *Mannerism: The Crisis of the Renaissance and the Origin of Modern Art* (London: Routledge & Kegan Paul, 1965).
3. Drew, "Mannerism," 10.
4. Ibid.
5. Ibid., 8.
6. I take these observations further in "Transition to Discourse: Architectural Theory in Postmodern Australia," in *Exhibitions, Periodicals, and the Shaping of Postmodern Architecture: The Medium is the Message?* ed. Veronique Patteeuw & Léa-Catherine Szacka (London: Bloomsbury, 2018), 135–50.
7. Walter Friedlaender, *Mannerism and Anti-Mannerism in Italian Painting* [1930] (New York: Columbia University Press, 1957); Nikolaus Pevsner, "The Architecture of Mannerism," in *The Mint: A Miscellany of Literature, Art and Criticism*, ed. Geoffrey Grigson (London: Routledge, 1946), 116–38. The historiographical trajectory of this subject is neatly tracked in Manfredo Tafuri, *L'architettura del Manierismo nel Cinquecento europeo* (Rome: Officina, 1966), 17–38, on which see my *Crisis on Crisis, or Tafuri on Mannerism* (Basel: Standpunkte, 2017). See also Dirk De Meyer, "Mannerism, Modernity and the Modernist Architect, 1920–1950," *Journal of Architecture* 15, no. 3 (2010): 243–65.
8. Colin Rowe, "Mannerism and Modern Architecture," *Architectural Review* 107 (May 1950): 289–98.
9. Ibid., 292.
10. Ibid., 292.
11. Ibid., 291.
12. Ibid., 299.
13. Denise Costanzo, "Text, Lies and Architecture: Colin Rowe, Robert Venturi and Mannerism," *Journal of Architecture* 18, no. 4 (2013): 455–73. I refer to an unnumbered reference card in "Rome—Notes: Letters," 255.RV.113, Venturi, Scott Brown Collection, Architectural Archives of the University of Pennsylvania, Philadelphia (hereafter cited as VSB Collection, AAUP).
14. *The Renaissance and Mannerism*, vol. 2, *Studies in Western Art: Acts of the 20th International Congress of the History of Art* [1961] (Princeton, N.J.: Princeton University Press, 1963). Contributions include "Introduction: The Historiographical Background," by E. H. Gombrich (163–73); "Mannerism and *Maniera*," by Craig

Hugh Smyth (174–99); "*Maniera* as an Aesthetic Ideal," by John Shearman (200–21); "Power and the Individual in Mannerist Art," by Frederick Hartt (222–38); and "Mannerism in Architecture: Changing Aspects," by Wolfgang Lotz (239–46).

15. John Shearman, *Mannerism* (London: Penguin, 1967); Craig Hugh Smyth, *Mannerism and "Maniera"* (New York: Augustin, 1962).

16. James Ackerman, *The Architecture of Michelangelo*, 2 vols. (London: Zwemmer, 1961); James Ackerman, *Palladio* (London: Penguin, 1966).

17. Martino Stierli considers the exposure of architects and artists at the American Academy in Rome to contemporary Italian architecture, engineering and urbanism in *Venturis Grand Tour: Zur Genealogie der Postmoderne* (Basel: Standpunkte, 2011), 59–64.

18. Zevi's legacy has most recently been considered by Pippo Ciorra and Jean-Louis Cohen in *Zevi's Architects: History and Counter-History of Italian Architecture, 1944–2000* (Macerata, Italy: Quodlibet, 2018) and the exhibition of the same title at MAXXI, Rome, April 25–September 16, 2018.

19. Bruno Zevi, ed., "L'opera architettonica di Michelangiolo nel quarto centenario della morte. Modelli, fotografie e commenti degli studenti dell'Istituto di Architettura di Venezia," *Architettura. Cronache e storia* 9, no. 99 (1964): 654–712; and Bruno Zevi, "Introduzione. L'attualità di Michelangiolo architetto," in *Michelangiolo architetto*, ed. Bruno Zevi and Paolo Portoghesi (Turin: Einaudi, 1964). Venturi retained a number of letters from the INU dating to 1955, archives in "Rome—Notes: Letters," 255.RV.113, VSB Collection, AAUP.

20. On this theme, see Maarten Delbeke, "The Mannerism of Architecture and the City in *Complexity and Contradiction*," *Journal of the Society of Architectural Historians* 75, no. 4 (December 2016): 492–93; Maarten Delbeke, "Mannerism and Meaning in *Complexity and Contradiction in Architecture*," *Journal of Architecture* 15, no. 3 (2010): 267–82.

21. Paul Oskar Kristeller, "The Modern System of the Arts: A Study in the History of Aesthetics" (in two parts), *Journal of the History of Ideas* 12, no. 4 (October 1951): 496–527; 13, no. 1 (January 1952): 17–46; also René Wellek, "The Concept of Baroque in Literary Scholarship," in "Baroque Style in Various Arts," special issue, *Journal of Aesthetics and Art Criticism* 5, no. 2 (1946): 77–109.

22. Erwin Panosfky, *Gothic Architecture and Scholasticism* (Latrobe, Penn.: Archabbey Press, 1951); Wylie Sypher, *Four Stages of Renaissance Style: Transformations in Art and Literature, 1400–1700* (Garden City, N.Y.: Doubleday, 1955).

23. Sypher, *Four Stages*, 6.

24. Ibid., 5.

25. Ibid., 4–5.

26. Robert Venturi, "Mannerism and Poetry" (MS), c. 1961/1962, p. 2, 225.XI.75, "'Mannerism & Poetry,' typed and handwritten drafts [c. 1961–62]" VSB Collection, AAUP.

27. Robert Venturi, "My Manifesto to Myself" (MS), c. 1961/1962, currently untraceable (2018), VSB Collection, AAUP. Reference is made to T. S. Eliot, "Tradition and the Individual Talent," *Perspecta* 19 (1982): 36–42; originally published (in two parts) in *The Egoist* 6, no. 4 (September 1919): 54–55; 6, no. 5 (December 1919): 72–73.

28. Robert Venturi, *Complexity and Contradiction in Architecture*, The Museum of Modern Art Papers on Architecture 1 (New York: The Museum of Modern Art in association with the Graham Foundation for Advanced Studies in the Fine Arts, Chicago, 1966), 101.

29. Venturi, "Mannerism and Poetry" (MS), 1.

30. Cleanth Brooks, *The Well Wrought Urn: Studies in the Structure of Poetry* (London: Dobson, 1949), 194.

31. All in the unprocessed folder "UPenn Studio: A Theater for Shakespeare, c.1960–64," VSB Collection, AAUP.

32. Venturi, "Mannerism and Poetry" (MS), 1, 5.

33. Philip J. Finkelpearl, "Contemporary Confrontations," review of *Complexity and Contradiction in Architecture*, 2nd ed., by Robert Venturi; *Learning from Las Vegas: The Forgotten Symbolism of Architectural Form*, rev. ed., by Robert Venturi, Denise Scott Brown, and Steven Izenour; *The Yale Mathematics Building Competition*, edited by Charles W. Moore and Nicholas Pyle; and articles in *Architecture and Urbanism*, *Werk-Archithese*, *Progressive Architecture*, and *L'Architecture d'Aujourd'hui*, in *Journal of the Society of Architectural Historians* 38, no. 2 (May 1979): 203.

34. Ibid.

35. As noted in Aron Vinegar, *I Am a Monument: On "Learning from Las Vegas"* (Cambridge, Mass.: MIT Press, 2008), 186.

36. Draft typescript response by Robert Venturi to a letter from Peter Eisenman, Michael Graves, and Thomas R. Vreeland, October 15, 1964, 255.VI.D.3581, "Princeton Conference Report [1964–65]," VSB Collection, AAUP.

37. Ibid.

38. William Weaver (attr., signed "Bill") to Venturi, July 15 [1947], 255.RV.35, "Correspondence to RV [1949–50]," VSB Collection, AAUP. Venturi's first visit to Rome was in 1948. See Denise Costanzo, "'I Will Try My Best to Make it Worth It': Robert Venturi's Road to Rome," *Journal of Architectural Education* 70, no. 2 (2016): 269–83.

39. Philip J. Finkelpearl, "From Petrarch to Ovid: Metamorphoses in John Marston's *Metamorphosis of Pigmalions Image*," *ELH* [*English Literary History*] 32, no. 3 (September 1965): 333–48; "John Marston's *Histrio-Mastix* as an Inns of Court Play: A Hypothesis," *Huntington Library Quarterly* 29, no. 3 (May 1966): 223–34; "The Use of the Middle Temple's Christmas Revels in Marston's *The Fawne*," *Studies in Philology* 64, no. 2 (April 1967): 199–209; and *John Marston of the Middle Temple: An English Dramatist in his Social Setting* (Cambridge, Mass.: Harvard University Press, 1969).

40. On which, see the biblically scaled *Mongrel Rapture: The Architecture of Ashton Raggatt McDougall*, ed. Mark Raggatt and Maitiú Ward (Melbourne: Uro Publications, 2014).

41. The project's process documents are published in Peta Carlin, "The Kronborg Clinic: The Nether Worlds of a Dionysian Disco," *Transition* 44/45 (1994): 180–89.

Opus 2: Robert Venturi's Metamorphosis of Duke House

Jean-Louis Cohen

The last thirty-odd pages of Robert Venturi's *Complexity and Contradiction in Architecture* are devoted to a portfolio of his work, both built and unbuilt. This juxtaposition of a theoretical argument with examples of the author's own architectural projects had a precedent in Le Corbusier's sandwiching of his designs between the more polemical chapters of his 1923 *Vers une architecture*; it can be seen as a sign of Venturi's ambition to be considered within this lineage. Given Venturi's frequent parodies of the French-Swiss architect's writings, the parallel is no accident. The second project in the chronological sequence of works in the book's appendix is Venturi's first completed design, which is accompanied by five illustrations and here described under the title "Renovations of the James B. Duke House, The Institute of Fine Arts, New York University, Robert Venturi, Cope and Lippincott, Associated Architects, 1959."[1]

On February 10 of that year, *The New York Times* informed its readers that the "first fete . . . since '39" had taken place at "Duke Mansion" upon the occasion of its "dedication as [New York University]'s Fine Arts Center." Under a photograph of a group of students gathered around a circular seminar table,

Fig. 1. Horace Trumbauer (American, 1868–1938). James B. Duke Mansion, New York. 1912. Exterior view. 1959. The Architectural Archives of the University of Pennsylvania, Philadelphia. Gift of Robert Venturi and Denise Scott Brown

reporter Sanka Knox wrote: "Directors of libraries, curators, scholars and students thronged the great hall. . . . It was the first time in twenty years that the classic building at Fifth Avenue and Seventy-eighth street had been opened to a large group."[2] Most likely using copy provided by the designers, she explained: "The eighteenth-century French style of the Duke house has been left intact by the university's architects, Robert Venturi, Paul Cope and Mather Lippincott. New, adjustable lighting and modern tables have been installed in the dining room, but the creamy marble walls were not touched. The ballroom is now a lecture room. A screen for slides has been 'floated' out from a wall to prevent injury to the ivory and gold paneling."

The mansion into which James B. Duke and his wife Nanaline (née Holt), had moved in 1912 still serves as NYU's Institute of Fine Arts today (fig. 1). It was designed in the office of Philadelphia architect Horace Trumbauer, whose firm was responsible for buildings including the Philadelphia Museum of Art, crowning the city's Fairmount Parkway, and scores of palatial mansions on the outskirts of the Pennsylvanian metropolis.[3] The designer in charge of Duke House was Julian Abele, the first African American to graduate from the University of Pennsylvania's School of Architecture;[4] he modeled the building's envelope on the château built in 1770 in Bordeaux by the architect Étienne Laclotte for the printers and booksellers Jacques and Antoine Labottière.[5] In Venturi's "Architect's Notes" on the project, which were written in 1959 for communication purposes (reproduced in an extremely condensed version in the section on Duke House in *Complexity and Contradiction*), he described the mansion as follows: "Its unique characteristics are its enormous scale, a Louis XIV scale in a Louis XVI building, and the fineness and chasteness of these Edwardian-Louis XVI details inside and out."[6] The house caught the attention of Frank Lloyd Wright; Venturi liked to tell an anecdote about the elder architect "riding down Fifth Avenue in an open car when he was designing the Solomon R. Guggenheim Museum, and passing the Duke House and saying, 'Stop! There is a good building.'"[7]

Besides its homothetic inflation, this New York version of the Hôtel Labottière has expanded piers between the windows, reflecting that the interior was extremely different from the original: it was designed to accommodate the grandiose parties Nanaline aspired to host on Millionaire Row. (In this regard, the building reflects the importance of the dichotomy of inside and outside, which would become the subject of the ninth chapter of *Complexity and Contradiction*.) It had a music room, a ballroom, a marble dining room, a wood-paneled corner room for Duke himself, and—one of its most peculiar features—a majestic stairway that did not lead to any grand social room but to the bedrooms, and hence was not meant for a procession of guests but rather for the dignified descent of Nanaline, while Duke, who limped, would have taken the lavish elevator. The decoration was commissioned to the Parisian firms Lucien Alavoine and Carlhian & Cie.

James Buchanan Duke died in 1925, and over time, the place lost its preeminence in the life of the Duke family, as its members spent more time at their other expansive abodes, from Rough Point in Newport, Rhode Island, to Shangri La in Hawaii.[8] Then, in 1958, Nanaline and her scandalous daughter, the world-renowned heiress and socialite Doris Duke, decided to bequeath the mansion to the Institute of Fine Arts.

By this point, the Institute needed the space. It had grown from an initial nucleus of professors, recruited by the art historian Fiske Kimball, who had started teaching in NYU's College of Fine Arts on Washington Square and moved in the late 1920s to the Crystal Building on 250 East Forty-third Street. In 1933 the college's Graduate Division had become an autonomous program under the leadership of its founding director Walter S. Cook, who had begun hiring German scholars, beginning with Erwin Panofsky. It then migrated again, this time to the second floor of the Hotel Carlyle on Madison Avenue, where it stayed for two years, before settling in 1937 in the Paul Warburg House, at 17 East Eightieth Street.[9] By the 1950s, these exiguous premises physically impeded any expansion of the library, and the art historian Craig Hugh Smyth, who succeeded Cook as director of the Institute in 1950, declared that his intention was "to have at least the books you go to first and use the most . . . on our side of the street, not having to go over to the [Metropolitan] Museum or down to the Public Library." He commented, "the move [into the Duke mansion] . . . was very motivated for me by the notion that we should have a decent library and a place to put it."[10] Negotiated with savvy by Smyth, the gift of the Dukes thus came as a blessing.

In order to transform the mansion into a place of research and learning, a project Doris Duke had agreed to support financially, Smyth started looking for an architect.[11] His first contacts with young architects he had met at the American Academy in Rome were unpromising. He tried one, "but he didn't sound to me, when he talked about the house, as if he would be sympathetic with [it]. So I thought that can't be."[12] He then asked Richard

Krautheimer—a professor in the history of architecture at the Institute since 1938—who fondly remembered a young man he had met in Rome: Robert Venturi, whose professional debut in the Dukes' Upper East Side ballroom thus finds its origins on the banks of the Tiber. In his "Note to the Second Edition" of *Complexity and Contradiction*, Venturi insisted on rectifying "an omission in the acknowledgments of the first edition": "I want to express my gratitude to Richard Krautheimer, who shared his insights on Roman Baroque architecture with us Fellows at the American Academy in Rome."[13] Venturi thus called attention to the visits to Baroque churches that the great historian had prescribed he undertake during his time as an Academician in Rome from 1954 to 1956,[14] but he said nothing relating to his mentor's role in steering the Duke House commission to him.

Recommending Venturi in 1960 to Arnold Trueblood, a prospective client, Smyth did credit Krautheimer in this respect, affirming that: "Robert Venturi was suggested by one of the foremost architectural historians of our day, a man profoundly aware of architectural styles of the past and at the same time perceptive with respect to contemporary design. What I saw of Venturi, Cope and Lippincott persuaded me that they were indeed exactly suited. The Board of Trustees of the University initially rejected my recommendation on the ground that the architects were too young. I persuaded them in the end to accept them on my responsibility, and no one concerned had anything but admiration for what they have done."[15] Smyth would admit in a 1990 interview that Venturi had not told him that it was his first independent job.[16]

In a long memorandum to the treasurer of New York University, George F. Baughman, Smyth had written in January 1958 that, rather than hiring a large firm:

> We set out to find a young architect of known talent, great sensitivity and real interest in doing the job, who should be able to give us all his time. Out of a number of possibilities, most of which we discarded without even bringing them to your attention, we chose Robert Venturi. He seems to us to combine the necessary qualifications. As a winner of the Rome Prize, he has proven his ability as a designer; secondly, we were in a very good position to know of his sensitivity to historical monuments; thirdly, his experience has been entirely in the office of what are perhaps the two outstanding architects in the country—Eero Saarinen and Louis Kahn. With Kahn he is still in very close

touch and collaboration. He is now, moreover, associated with Cope & Lippincott, which seemed to us an alert and sound firm. Our lengthy discussions with Venturi have convinced us that he has imagination to think his way into our problems wholly sympathetically and to accommodate the house to our needs while preserving its character—not just in a utilitarian way, but with the positive distinction the building deserves and the University wants. We are aware that Venturi does not have building experience in New York, but as an intelligent man he must be able shortly to learn what it is necessary to know.[17]

Smyth wrote with the same eloquent persuasiveness to Doris Duke, who approved his choice.[18]

Venturi and his partners lost no time in accepting the commission in late January 1958, commenting on their motivation in a letter sent to the university: "We consider this job [as] more than [a] usual, certainly not a typical school or office building alteration; we would not intend merely to paint the walls, renew the wiring and design desk and chairs layouts. The present architectural value of the mansion and its new habitation for a school of art history require special consideration of space and proportion, as well as treatment of lighting, acoustics, and cabinetwork."[19]

The design process was relatively rapid, with the space-planning study and the architectural design running on parallel

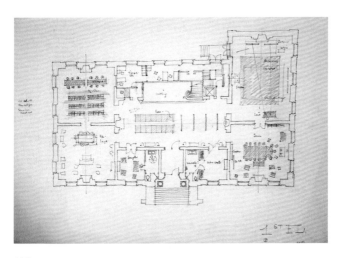

Fig. 2. Robert Venturi (American, 1925–2018). Space planning study for the James B. Duke House, New York. 1958. Plan of first floor. The Architectural Archives of the University of Pennsylvania, Philadelphia. Gift of Robert Venturi and Denise Scott Brown

3.   4.

tracks between February and August 1958, and the contract documents being completed in July of the same year (fig. 2). In their preliminary outline, Venturi and his partners described the scope of the job in the plainest possible terms: "Alteration of interior of former residence for occupancy by private graduate school, to include in general: new stairway, new electric service, wiring and fixtures; new books storage equipment and furnishings; addition to and alteration of certain room finishes; general painting; changes to elevator."[20] In 1990, Smyth would recall a meeting in the building with Venturi and Doris Duke "at a table in what was then the dining room, with Robert putting out his plans for her. His drawings are elegant. . . . They're not your normal architectural drawings. I think she was intrigued. She argued with him, but . . . in the end she approved."[21]

The philosophy of the design is best conveyed in the aforementioned "Architect's Notes": "the Institute desired to respect this distinctive house, maintain its monumentality and character, and yet adapt it in a contemporary and apparently easy way to its new function. We, as the architects, chose in the renovation neither to copy the existing forms nor to ignore them. Our recent prototypes we considered the Genovese and Milanese renovations of Albini, Gardella, and BBPR: the museum in the Palazzo Bianco rather than the wartime headquarters in Caserta."[22] This direct allusion to Italy gives a key to Venturi's design strategy, which consisted of installing contemporary elements in metal that would touch lightly or lean on the existing features without ruining them. The systems used by Franco Albini for carrying the paintings and suspending the lighting features in the Palazzo Bianco in Genoa in 1950–51 (fig. 3), those of Ignazio Gardella's installation at Milan's Padiglione d'Arte Contemporanea in 1949–53 (fig. 4), and the supports of the sculpture at the Castello Sforzesco

Fig. 3. Franco Albini (Italian, 1905–1977) and Franca Helg (Italian, 1920–1989). Renovations of the Palazzo Bianco. Genoa. 1950

Fig. 4. Lodovico Barbiano di Belgiojoso (Italian, 1909–2004), Enrico Peressutti (Italian, 1908–1976), and Ernesto Nathan Rogers (Italian, 1909–1969). Restoration and exhibition design, Castello Sforzesco, Milan, 1954–56. Installation of medieval sculpture

in Milan by Studio BBPR (Lodovico Barbiano di Belgiojoso, Enrico Peressutti, and Ernesto Nathan Rogers) in 1954–56 are not literal models for Duke House, but comparable examples of a radical yet careful way of engaging with an existing building envelope and its materiality.[23]

The Roman parallels confirm Venturi's interest in contemporary Italian architecture, which has been underlined by Martino Stierli in his investigation of the architect's study trips through the peninsula, and his contacts with both Rogers and Luigi Moretti.[24] The latter's Casa del Girasole, built in 1950 in Rome, was used to illustrate the notion of "ambiguity" in *Complexity and Contradiction*.[25] And Rogers's discourse of "environmental preexistences" and the "critical revision" of the modern movement were also not without echoes in Venturi's book.[26] As for the dismissive allusion to the Caserta headquarters outside Naples, used by the American military in a tactless manner in 1944–45 for the accommodation of soldiers, it could be understood as an ironic allusion to Smyth's wartime service in the ranks of the Monuments Men.

In the presentation of the conceptual principles of the Duke House project, Venturi suggested terms that would be further developed in his 1966 book. His technique was "to create harmony through contrast rather than similarity; to employ the principle of juxtaposition rather than integration; to separate visually the joint between the old and new; to change by adding to rather [than] modifying the existing elements; to consider the new elements furniture rather than structural architecture; to use furnishings which, if they were not 18th-century in form, were not of modern design in the fine-arts sense, but rather contemporary objects often industrially produced and designed, perhaps anonymously and not primarily for aesthetic effect."[27] Long before being elaborated in the lectures at the University of Pennsylvania that eventually led to *Complexity and Contradiction*, these fundamental positions were already a guide for Venturi's design strategy.

Venturi's Roman experience was eloquently mobilized in the presentation, too. He wrote that Rome's "tradition of adapting family palazzi to museums, parliaments and banks is a long one which Americans especially, with their cult of obsolescence, should consider. A program which saves worthy monumental buildings from uselessness and employs a harmonious combination of past and contemporary methods and expression is a timely one, since it promotes a sense of contrast and continuity lacking in our cities."[28] To implement this strategy, the academic functions of the Institute were distributed throughout the floors of the mansion, as first described in the space-planning study and then depicted in perspectival line drawings (figs. 5–7). Books were given preeminence, turning the house into an inhabited library of sorts. The grand ballroom became the lecture hall; the music room was turned into a seminar room and the oak parlor into a lounge and boardroom; periodicals invaded the marble dining room, while the library—the chief motivation for the move to new facilities—occupied almost the entire second floor, which also included, in a first version, three small corner offices assigned to Harry Bober, Friedlaender, and Krautheimer. On the third floor, the servants' rooms were replaced with the majority of the faculty offices.

The "contemporary objects" introduced were both fixed and mobile. Partitions were kept low, operating like "undulating curtains" in homage to Ludwig Mies van der Rohe and

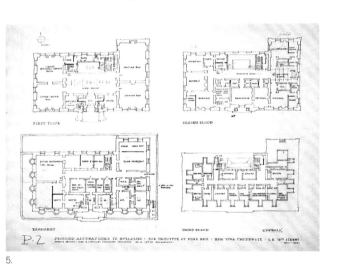

5.

Fig. 5. Robert Venturi (American, 1925–2018). Space planning study for the James B. Duke House, New York. 1958. Plan of the four floors. The Architectural Archives of the University of Pennsylvania, Philadelphia. Gift of Robert Venturi and Denise Scott Brown

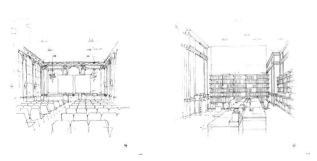

6.   7.

Figs. 6–7. Robert Venturi (American, 1925–2018). Sketches of the lecture hall (left) and library (right) of the James B. Duke House, New York. 1958. The Architectural Archives of the University of Pennsylvania, Philadelphia. Gift of Robert Venturi and Denise Scott Brown

121

Lilly Reich's Café Samt und Seide (Velvet and Silk Café) at the 1927 exhibition *Die Mode der Dame* (Women's Fashion) in Berlin; and they remained visually detached from the box erected by Trumbauer. Essential in an institution that was focused on comparing visual evidence through parallel projections, the screens for the lantern slide projectors were installed in pairs, and, in Venturi's words, "not applied directly to existing panels of the walls, but . . . bracketed out to 'float' beyond the walls, not analogously related in size, shape or position to the older paneling" (fig. 8).[29] The relationship to Albini's solutions at the Palazzo Bianco could not be more explicit.

Ready-made Remington Rand steel shelves—usually deployed in prosaic library stacks—formed a "light, airy framework" and were superposed to create double height storage. The aesthetic intention was deliberate: "The geometry and rhythm of the open shelving, always only partially filled with books, is juxtaposed in a fugued relationship [with] the contrasting patterns of the off-white panels."[30] The only shelving parts designed by the architects were the bases of the posts and the brass brackets anchoring the shelves to the walls. Venturi also designed autonomous elements such as light-tables and desks, however, and he adapted the tables that had been produced in Europe by Thonet. Two categories of chairs were used; because historicist replicas of ancien régime French fauteuils and contemporary steel and plastic

Fig. 8. Robert Venturi (American, 1925–2018). Renovations of the James B. Duke House, New York. 1959. View of the ground floor seminar room with "floating" screens and Windsor chairs. The Architectural Archives of the University of Pennsylvania, Philadelphia. Gift of Robert Venturi and Denise Scott Brown

designs by Knoll International were judged equally unsuitable, the architect specified Windsor chairs to equip the seminar rooms and reading rooms, complemented in the study rooms and offices by "semi-anonymous, cheap, mass-produced" Thonet chairs (fig. 9). The latter were considered to be almost contextual: "These are light and comfortable and, although an industrial product, have a sinuous elegance not dissimilar to French 18th-century chairs and their architectural context here."[31] It is perhaps useful to note that Le Corbusier included the same Thonet chairs in his 1920s interiors, with a similar justification.[32]

As early as January 1958, Lippincott had written to Baughman, saying: "A preliminary analysis of the problem has led us to believe that special consultants on lighting and acoustics might well be used. We have already approached Richard Kelly, probably New York's most eminent specialist in the lighting field, and he is most interested."[33] Kelly had just completed the sophisticated lighting scheme of the Seagram Building, and he had developed systems based on the ones used for his own New York apartment.[34] According to a story published in 1959 by *The New Yorker*, his doctrine combined three categories of light: "a focal, or directed glow, which aims at separating the trivial from the important in interior composition; a play of brilliants, which he says offers an 'aesthetic ocular stimulus,' and . . . ambient luminescence, which is a sort of indirect background lighting that makes one comfortable in relation to one's surroundings."[35]

Fig. 9. Robert Venturi (American, 1925–2018). Renovations of the James B. Duke House, New York. 1959. View of the ground-floor Marble Room with Windsor chairs. The Architectural Archives of the University of Pennsylvania, Philadelphia. Gift of Robert Venturi and Denise Scott Brown

Venturi described the library lighting in his "Architect's Notes": "In the study rooms we did not want bright, overall lighting from high ceiling fixtures [as is] typical of classrooms, but rather several sources of local light for the study tables and illumination for the book shelving. The table fixtures made several individual foci in each room corresponding to the individuals working there. This lighting became four fixtures per room, designed by Mr. Kelly, suspended from movable rings on ceiling tracks. This permitted a limited flexibility of location and height and did away with floor outlets and cord. The shelving lighting features were specially designed metal brackets in the vocabulary of the shelving, shielded, and hooked to the slotted posts in the same manner as the shelving."[36]

All these lighting effects in combination created a calm and focused study atmosphere: a sort of chamber theater, a comfortable machine to study in (fig. 10). Using Venturi's own terms, the renovations featured altogether "banal" and "ordinary" elements and more complex ones, contradicting the existing architecture without negating it. Perhaps his most elaborate contribution to the design was the new staircase required by the fire code, which was made of black painted steel, with handrails composed of folded flat profiles. Venturi's attitude was fully endorsed by Smyth, who, in retrospect, lauded the architect's conception "of what he was doing: juxtaposing his changes to the house in a very different style and loving the juxtaposition, thinking of the effect that this face-to-face would have."[37]

The response of the Institute's community to the design was most positive, as exemplified by Bober's comments in its institutional newsletter: "Thanks to the thoughtful planning and to sympathetic and subtle execution by our architects, the beauty of an elegant home has been preserved in its transformation into a splendid center for teaching, study, and research. The success of the remodeling may be measured by the fact that the additions and changes have merged almost invisibly with the main and unaltered parts of the building. Indeed, in respect for the original architectural character of the Duke House, simplicity and economy were among the primary guiding principles in making the changes."[38]

Venturi would subsequently work on other projects for the Institute. In 1960, he designed the transformation of the basement and subbasement for its Conservation Center, and proposed the creation of a reading room with student carrels under the roof—an unbuilt project that would have modified the building's silhouette. In the following years, he engaged in

Fig. 10. Robert Venturi (American, 1925–2018). Renovations of the James B. Duke House, New York. 1959. View of the library with Remington Rand shelves and lamps by Richard Kelly. The Architectural Archives of the University of Pennsylvania, Philadelphia. Gift of Robert Venturi and Denise Scott Brown

preliminary investigations for the colonization by the Institute of the neighboring building at 3 East Seventy-eighth Street.

As late as 1969 Venturi also continued to monitor changes proposed by New York University's often ill-intentioned or brutal building managers. Under the mandate of Jonathan Brown, who had taken the directorship of the Institute in 1973, the expansion of the library prompted a new cycle of transformations, designed by Richard Foster and Associates and implemented in 1975–77.[39] These consisted mainly of the insertion of a mezzanine, entailing the elimination of the 1958 shelves and the related lighting, and the replacement of the carefully selected furniture by nondescript substitutes.

The friendly relationship Venturi had with Smyth and his wife Barbara continued through the 1960s. He was keen to update his inaugural patron on the most significant events in his life. In a handwritten note dated April 22, 1964, he shared "some good news," namely: "My book *Complexity and Contradiction in Architecture* is to be published by the Museum of Modern Art" (the agreement had been confirmed in March), and he expressed the hope that Smyth could "meet [his] new partner [John Rauch] in New York."[40]

The two pages devoted to Duke House in the appendix to *Complexity and Contradiction* are thus the understated evidence of a defining architectural and human experience. The design ideas that Venturi articulated while engaged with his first executed project laid firm foundations for the book to come.

Notes

1. Robert Venturi, *Complexity and Contradiction in Architecture*, The Museum of Modern Art Papers on Architecture 1 (New York: The Museum of Modern Art in association with the Graham Foundation for Advanced Studies in the Fine Arts, Chicago, 1966), 104–106, figs. 260–64. See also Stanislaus von Moos, *Venturi, Rauch & Scott Brown: Buildings and Projects* (New York: Rizzoli, 1987), 296–98.
2. Sanka Knox, "N.Y.U. Party Held at Duke Mansion: Dedication as School's Fine Arts Center Marks First Fete There Since '39," *New York Times*, February 10, 1959.
3. Rachel Hildebrandt, *The Philadelphia Area Architecture of Horace Trumbauer* (Charleston, S.C.: Arcadia, 2009). Michael C. Kathrens, Richard C. Marchand, and Eleanor Weller, *American Splendor: The Residential Architecture of Horace Trumbauer* (New York: Acanthus, 2011).
4. Bridget Booher, "Stones, Bricks, and Faces: Julian Abele, Mr. Duke's Architect," *Duke Magazine,* November–December 1994, 13–17.

William E. King. "The Discovery of an Architect: Duke University and Julian F. Abele," *Southern Cultures* 15, no. 1 (spring 2009): 6–21.

5. Philippe Maffre, *Construire Bordeaux au XVIIIe siècle: Les frères Laclotte, architectes en société (1756–1793)* (Bordeaux: Société archéologique de Bordeaux, 2013).

6. Robert Venturi, "Architect's Notes on the Renovations to the James B. Duke House," 1959, p. 1, 287.III.84, "Project descriptions and clippings, Robert Venturi and Cope & Lippincott, architects," Cope and Lippincott Collection, Architectural Archives of the University of Pennsylvania, Philadelphia. In subsequent quotations from this source, the punctuation has occasionally been modified for legibility.

7. Craig Hugh Smyth, interview by Blanche Brown and Milton Brown, 1990, *IFA Alumni Newsletter*, no. 28 (winter 2001–2002): 5.

8. Robert F. Durden, *The Dukes of Durham, 1865–1929* (Durham, N.C.: Duke University Press, 1975). Pony Duke and Jason Thomas, *Too Rich: The Family Secrets of Doris Duke* (New York: Harper-Collins, 1996).

9. Harry Bober, "The Gothic Tower and the Stork Club," *Arts and Sciences* 1 (spring 1962): 1–8.

10. Smyth, interview, 5. On Smyth, see Elizabeth Cropper, "Craig Hugh Smyth," *Proceedings of the American Philosophical Society* 153, no. 4 (2009): 496–500.

11. A comprehensive research program, including a chronology of the design and construction work and a catalogue of the archives of the Institute of Fine Arts was conducted by Elizabeth Buhe, in preparation for a seminar I taught on the building in the fall of 2012. She prepared a finding aid: "Field Report: Duke House History," Institute of Fine Arts, New York University, August 2012. See also Lauren Elizabeth Fly, "Historic Preservation and the Institute of Fine Arts: The Adaptive Reuse of 1 East 78th Street," MA qualifying paper, Institute of Fine Arts, New York University, 2005.

12. Smyth, interview, 5.

13. Robert Venturi, "Note to the Second Edition," in *Complexity and Contradiction in Architecture*, 2nd ed., (New York: The Museum of Modern Art in association with the Graham Foundation for Advanced Studies in the Fine Arts, Chicago, 1977), 14.

14. Martino Stierli, "In the Academy's Garden: Robert Venturi, the Grand Tour and the Revision of Modern Architecture," *AA Files*, no. 56 (2007): 46.

15. Craig Hugh Smyth to Arnold Trueblood, April 30, 1959, IFA archives, New York University.

16. Smyth, interview, 5.

17. Craig Hugh Smyth, memorandum to George F. Baughman, January 26, 1958, IFA Archives, New York University.

18. Craig Hugh Smyth to Doris Duke, February 14, 1958, IFA Archives, New York University.

19. Mather Lippincott to George F. Baughman, January 23, 1958, IFA Archives, New York University.

20. Venturi, Cope and Lippincott, "Preliminary Outline Specification and Estimate," April 28, 1958, IFA Archives, New York University.
21. Smyth, interview, 5.
22. Venturi, "Architect's Notes," 1.
23. In addition to his visits, Venturi could have read: Franco Albini, "Galleria di Palazzo Bianco," *Spazio* 7, no. 53 (1952): 31–40 and 106. "Galleria d'arte contemporanea a Milano," *Metron*, no. 37 (1950): 32–33. Lodovico Barbiano di Belgiojoso, Enrico Peressutti, and Ernesto N. Rogers, "Carattere stilistico del Museo del Castello," *Casabella*, no. 211 (June–July 1956): 63–68. "The Castello Sforzesco Museum," *Interiors*, no. 12 (December 1956): 89–93.
24. Stierli, "In the Academy's Garden," 56.
25. Venturi, *Complexity and Contradiction*, 29.
26. Anna Giannetti and Luca Molinari, eds., *Continuità e crisi: Ernesto Nathan Rogers e la cultura architettonica italiana del secondo dopoguerra* (Florence: Alinea, 2010).
27. Venturi, "Architect's Notes," 1–2.
28. Ibid., 1.
29. Ibid., 4.
30. Ibid., 3.
31. Ibid., 5.
32. Le Corbusier, *The Decorative Art of Today* [1925], trans. James I. Dunnett (Cambridge, Mass.: MIT Press, 1987), 17.
33. Lippincott to Baughman, January 23, 1958, IFA Archives, New York University. Richard Kelly was not unknown to the art historians as he had published "Lighting as an Integral Part of Architecture," *College Art Journal* 12, no. 1 (autumn 1952): 24–30.
34. The Kelly Papers at Yale University Library's Manuscript and Archives division contain mostly correspondence relating to billing and fees. See Christie Mitchell, "Systems of Renovation at the James B. Duke House: Richard Kelly and Robert Venturi," seminar paper, Institute of Fine Arts, New York University, 2012.
35. S. H., "On and Off the Avenue: About the House," *The New Yorker*, April 4, 1959, 130. See Dietrich Neumann, ed., *The Structure of Light: Richard Kelly and the Illumination of Modern Architecture* (New Haven, Conn.: Yale University Press, 2010), where the lighting for Duke House is described on p. 171.
36. Venturi, "Architect's Notes," 4.
37. Smyth, interview, 5.
38. H. B. [Harry Bober], editorial, *Institute of Fine Arts News*, fall 1959, 2.
39. "The New York University Institute of Fine Arts: How Do You Re-Use a Jewel Box? Restoration and Re-Use of the Duke Mansion by Richard Foster," *Architectural Record* 164, no. 2 (August 1978): 107–12.
40. Venturi, handwritten note to Smyth, April 22, 1964, IFA Archives, New York University.

Stanley Tigerman in conversation
with David B. Brownlee

DAVID B. BROWNLEE: Can you remember your first impressions of *Complexity and Contradiction in Architecture*? What you were doing, and what did the book look like to you when you first saw it?

STANLEY TIGERMAN: I was back in Chicago at that time, after studying at Yale. It was also at that time the *Forty under Forty* show took place [at the Architectural League of New York, in 1966] with Bob [Robert A. M.] Stern and Bob Venturi, and I got to know him more from the show than the book. I wasn't an aficionado at first. But Bob made us think, as opposed to simply respond to issues, to programs, to buildings, to whatever. And that thinking process has stayed with me all my life. So I undoubtedly was encouraged by him. And I think that I've over time come to understand his work much better than I did early on.

DB: Is that because there wasn't much work to look at back then, or why do you think that is?

ST: The problem is more mine. Bob's words and Bob's built work were dichotomous. They didn't ring true to me. Over time I've changed my mind. He was an outlier. He was an outsider trying to break in, and I understand that position very well.

DB: Because you're an outsider, too?

ST: Because I'm an outsider. So I understand and empathize with him vastly more now than I did initially.

DB: I think many people found the first book more difficult than *Learning from Las Vegas*—drier, less exciting.

ST: It was like a big pill. You needed to take it and it was hard to get to go down your throat. It was the more important of the two books, and ultimately had a gigantic impact on me: in my work, in my understanding of life, and of architecture.

DB: What do you appreciate in the book looking back on it now?

ST: It made me think. I remember reading through the entire book and when I finished it I was puzzled—which is very, very healthy. It was difficult early on to understand completely. It caused me to reflect. Don't forget I come from a town—Chicago, to which I've been committed my entire life—which is a Mies town. It's for type A–personality architects only; others need not apply. And so I was confused, and the confusion was healthy. Bob was good for me, to put it that way.

DB: When you think about your own work—whether architecture or writing—how do you compare or contrast it with his?

ST: He was much more of an intellectual than I was. I admired him predominantly for his writing: I admired the ease by which he conveyed his thoughts. And in all my dealings with him he was a gentleman. He treated me as he treated everyone, kindly and gently. He was a mensch.

Complexity and Complacency in Architecture

Dianne Harris

One of the most frequently quoted lines in Robert Venturi's *Complexity and Contradiction in Architecture* was written not by the book's author but by the architectural historian Vincent Scully—namely, the assertion in his introduction that the book represents "the most important writing on the making of architecture since Le Corbusier's *Vers une Architecture*, of 1923."[1] This sweeping statement, penned by one of the most revered scholars of architecture at the time, paved the way for Venturi's book to be regarded as singular and groundbreaking, as an accomplishment of historical significance. In the years that have passed since, many readers have been hard-pressed to consider the book otherwise; its importance for the profession long went uncontested.

Venturi's work—both his architecture and his writing—has been and is still widely received and accepted as boldly transformational, radical, and even revolutionary.[2] Yet the use of such terms may be surprising, even jarring, for readers outside the architectural profession, especially when we consider the context of genuine social revolutionary activity at the time of the book's publication, in view of the civil rights protests of the 1960s—for example, the Freedom Rides of 1961 or the Selma-to-Montgomery marches of 1965—and the rising tide of demonstrations against the Vietnam War that began to swell in the mid-1960s and were being increasingly violently suppressed by the time Venturi's book was published.

This raises the question of what we might learn from the reception of a book, first published half a century ago, that argued for a historically informed (if eclectically so) understanding of the built environment if we contextualize it within what was happening in culture and society beyond the confines of the profession itself. What does the esteem in which architects have held *Complexity and Contradiction* tell us about the field of architecture, and how might it help us better understand its frequent distance from the most pressing political and social issues of its day?

As a sign of how the times are changing, the anniversary of the book inspired some revisionist takes on its reputation. In a 2016 essay, the architectural historian Jonathan Massey was among the first to assert that *Complexity and Contradiction* should be seen as augmenting "the stock of capital vested in ideas and materials associated with some of the discipline's most privileged people, institutions, and canons." He went on to ask a key question: "What does it mean to dedicate our attention . . . to revisiting *Complexity and Contradiction in Architecture?*"

> *Complexity and Contradiction* is a great book that models a nuanced and rich way of seeing buildings. But how much attention does it merit given the sense many of us have that we are just arriving at a basic understanding of vast areas of the world's architectural production and theory? How can we intersect Venturi's compositional and stylistic approach with analytics that reveal other kinds of architectural complexities and contractions, such as those relating to architecture's imbrication with systems of class and labor, gender and sexuality, ethnicity and race? To the extent that we do keep rereading *Complexity and Contradiction*, we should situate the book within a history of privilege that skews architectural knowledge, excludes a wide range of perspectives, and alienates people who might otherwise engage with our discipline. Intersectional analysis can help us not only to better understand books like *Complexity and Contradiction* . . . but also to challenge the reproduction of power and privilege.[3]

Massey's essay opens the door to a larger set of issues that begin with Venturi's theoretical treatise but extend well beyond it. He points to the struggle many twenty-first-century historians and theorists encounter when examining *Complexity and Contradiction* in an era that insists—far more than Venturi did in his inclusion of literary scholarship alongside architecture—on forms of intellectual inquiry that are based in multi- and even transdisciplinary study, and seldom exclude questions of race, class, gender, sexuality, power, privilege, globalization, neoliberalism, colonialism, and more. It would perhaps be anachronistic to expect such concerns to feature in the book, since their prominence postdated Venturi's education: in the 1960s he was no longer a student, but a Princeton-trained faculty member teaching architecture at a prestigious institution, the University of Pennsylvania. And yet these issues clearly deserve our attention, especially since we are living through another period of intense and dramatic political unrest marked by street protests, riots, and sociopolitical instability in the U.S. and abroad; of innumerable instances of hate crimes, anti-Semitic and anti-Muslim sentiments, racism, and misogyny. Parallels are, indeed, increasingly often drawn between our time and the 1960s, with one writer claiming we are living through "a comparable historical inflection point."[4] But at least with a view to the architectural profession, the post-Obama era should perhaps still—or also—be understood more as an outgrowth of the Reaganomics of the 1980s, which remains an important touchstone for subsequent developments in architectural theory and practice.[5]

An appreciation of how we got to where we are today can also help us register the cognitive dissonance or the sense of cultural disorientation we might feel if a contemporary theoretical text were to be published that completely ignored the shock effect of a rising tide of white supremacist nationalism, xenophobia, and an apparently crumbling judicial system that fails to punish law-enforcement officers who murder black men. Even architecture, a profession that has long been politically quiescent—and that is to some degree always complicit with existing power structures—has shown at least some signs of "getting woke." For example, thousands of members of the American Institute of Architects expressed outrage when the organization issued a statement shortly after the election in November 2016 indicating a willingness to support the policies of the forty-fifth president—including, by implication, his call for the construction of a US/Mexico border wall. Students have also staged Black Lives Matter events at a few prominent architecture schools, and a renewed awareness of life beyond the walls of the architectural studio seems at last to be picking up steam.[6]

Nevertheless, what we might actually experience if confronted by a contemporary book that ignored all these issues is no sense of shock or dissonance whatsoever. We might come across a book like Venturi's today and never wonder why even now nearly everyone in the architectural office or studio is white, why most of the tenured faculty in the department or partners in the firm are still men, why so little has actually changed demographically in architectural practice since 1966.[7] Anyone who has spent time in architecture schools or offices would have little reason to identify political engagement as an intrinsic part of the field: it has never really taken root, grown, become a robust or sustained area of investigation, or found the intellectual ecosystem required to thrive and survive in that professional realm.

It would be unfair, however, not to acknowledge that activism has existed among architects at various moments in history. When activists took to the streets in the 1960s to protest the Establishment and fight for civil rights, this had its corollary in architectural profession. Some architects pioneered socially engaged modes of practice, including participatory design processes that engaged entire communities, sometimes staged as Happenings or informed by New Age therapeutic methods and often focused on the inclusion of disenfranchised groups.[8] Lawrence Halprin's landscape architecture and planning firm modeled such an approach from the late 1960s into the 1970s, creating choreographies of inclusivity—even if trained architects still held the pens and made the final plans. Already in 1965, Californian designers including Sanford Hirshen and Sym Van der Ryn pursued rural housing reform by designing innovative dwellings for migrant farm workers in Indio, California. The architecture historian Gwendolyn Wright has written about young architects of the 1960s who looked to alternatives such as "freeform hippie communes; advocacy groups committed to helping the poor; environmentalist experiments; lighthearted, camp playfulness" as they sought a way out of conventions within which they felt constrained.[9]

Venturi and Denise Scott Brown themselves engaged in the Citizens' Committee to Preserve and Develop the Crosstown Community in 1970, which aimed at the revitalization of the South Street district in Philadelphia as well as to prevent its destruction by the construction of a highway. South Street was in the core of one of the city's African American neighborhoods, and its main shopping street was also home to Jewish, Italian, and other first-generation American merchants (among them Venturi's father).[10] VSB understood the primary focus of their work as the rehabilitation of housing for low-income owners and renters, with corresponding neighborhood improvements and with minimum relocation of households. But at the same time, and more problematically, Scott Brown envisioned turning South Street into "another Greenwich Village," one that could make it into a "model thoroughfare of Negro culture, past and present," a planning vision that assumed all of Black culture could be represented in a single street, designed into existence by white professionals.[11] Although their intervention may have become almost too easy to critique with the benefit of hindsight and the past few decades of critical race theory, the VSB office clearly understood this project in an activist vein.

A progressive social agenda is also apparent in the design of Guild House (1960–63), which provided subsidized, dignified, comfortable, and light-filled housing for elderly men and women who wished to remain in their own neighborhood, which was then undergoing urban renewal.[12] So when Wright describes architects of the period engaging with preservation efforts in impoverished, inner-city neighborhoods, creating community design centers where "dissident professionals worked directly with neighborhood groups," we can count VSB among them, if only episodically so.[13]

It is also true that *Complexity and Contradiction* emphasized an environmental contextualization that valued buildings and landscapes that had previously received little academic attention and fell outside the canon most valued by Venturi's professional colleagues. In this vein, he may also have imagined his embrace of stylistic populism as itself an important political act. But the "establishment" against which he was reacting was largely the world of architectural and urban design, his chief enemy being the restrictive formal purity associated with architectural modernism.

If some radical architects of the time pushed against modernism for more explicitly political reasons—because of its connections to corporate capitalism, for example, or to the military-industrial complex and by extension to the Vietnam war, Venturi's focus on aesthetics was in keeping with Wright's observation that instead of emerging from this tumultuous, experimental, and creative period with a sense of the entire profession's ethical obligation to social and political engagement, the majority of architects exited the fray of the 1960s and early 1970s by retreating to issues of style and discourse.[14] And that discourse—then as now—largely ignored racism, inequality, segregation, homelessness, incarceration, and other pressing political and social-justice issues, despite the fact that all of them have a spatial/design corollary. Along similar lines, Mary McLeod pointed out in 1989 that the "advocacy impulses" of nominally or theoretically rebellious architects (Venturi among them) had already by the early 1970s been channeled into "the formal sphere."[15]

While we might well imagine that Venturi, like many architects of the period, personally supported the free speech, civil rights, and antiwar movements, little sustained effort was made within the walls of VSB or other professional architectural offices to engage in social change, least of all to alter the demographics of its practitioners to include more women and people of color. From this perspective, Venturi's lifelong professional and personal partnership with Scott Brown, a woman whose talents as a designer and as a theoretician matched his own, was not an insignificant political act, even if the architect himself did not always articulate it as such. More generally, however, we might think of Venturi's primary audience of practicing architects as essentially representing the "silent majority" hailed by Richard Nixon in the famous 1969 speech in which he described them as the counterpart to the "vocal minority" which, in his view, was made up of those protesting and demonstrating against the Vietnam War at the time of his election and afterward. The putative existence of those silent Americans served then as now to reinforce the status quo, including structural racism and the deep fissures of inequality with which we continue to struggle.[16]

Architect and writer Jeremy Till has recently sought to understand whether the emergence of the citizen-architect might be possible in the renewed political turbulence of our time. He finds a productive theoretical framework in Anthony Giddens's *The Consequences of Modernity* (1990), with its postulation of four "adaptive reactions" to describe how groups respond to periods of instability. Of these, Till notes that "sustained optimism" perhaps best describes the kind of thinking that allows the architectural profession and its practitioners to remain aloof from the broader political and social situation. Till connects this to contemporary neoliberal economics, whose proponents "claim to be pursuing the higher 'truths' of reason and hence to be beyond direct political motivation." He continues, "This neutrality is a mirage, but a brilliant one; for it allows the neoliberals to sustain the optimistic rhetoric of individual freedom and collective progress and remain seemingly above the messy contingencies of political life. It is just this sort of removal from the political sphere that allows architecture to maintain its own form of sustained optimism." This, in turn, has fostered the idea that "these shiny happy new buildings exist entirely on their own terms. The unmistakable inference is that architecture does not emerge from or exist within the social complexities of politics, culture, and nature."[17]

All this points to the conclusion that the profession's embrace of *Complexity and Contradiction* as "radical" should be understood against the context that most established architects, then and since, have turned inward and away from almost all external realities except for the market. Along related lines, architectural historian Despina Stratigakos has called attention to the field's unfinished (and seemingly unending) "cycles of acknowledging and then abandoning gender issues," that have continued for "a very long time" in what she calls "a hopeless and grim continuity."[18] Indeed, issues of social justice, equality, race, and gender have been briefly taken up by the profession and then abandoned more often than one can count. If such issues received intense attention in the 1960s and 1970s, real change was rare even then and never became widespread. Very few institutions developed a stronger focus on the connections between design and social justice; none currently count that broad subject as a core focus of the curriculum.[19]

In the aforementioned 1989 article, McLeod already pointed to the ways in which the rise of postmodernism—led by the work of Venturi and Scott Brown, Michael Graves, Peter Eisenman, and others—had been instrumental to the demise of socially engaged design: "The image of the architect shifted from social crusader and aesthetic puritan to trendsetter and media star. This change in professional definition had ramifications throughout architectural institutions. In the 1980s most schools stopped offering regular housing studios; gentlemen's clubs, resort hotels, art museums, and vacation homes became the standard programs. Design awards and professional magazine coverage have embodied similar priorities. Advocacy architecture and pro bono work are almost dead."[20] Whatever frustration we may feel about the entrenched and unyielding conservativism of architectural practice, recognizing it helps contextualize the reception of *Complexity and Contradiction*. Indeed, the social conservatism that defined the field is what enabled architects of the 1960s to choose what we would now see as relatively soft targets for their professional rebellions. If a rather small percentage of Venturi's peers chose to reject the corporate elitism that by then had become the norm by focusing on alternative modes of practice involving, for example, community design centers in economically depressed and disadvantaged neighborhoods, Venturi himself chose a different path; his professional rebellion was, above all, against architectural modernism.

This rebellion was, as many have noted, accompanied by an embrace of Pop art, which emerged in the same era as *Complexity and Contradiction.* (With reference to *Learning from Las Vegas*, Dell Upton has noted that in the 1960s "to be in touch with authentic popular values" was—and here he borrows Venturi, Scott Brown, and Steven Izenour's own language—"a way of being revolutionary for an architect.")[21] In his introduction to the book, Scully draws attention to Venturi's engagement with Pop painters, calling him "probably the first architect to perceive the usefulness and meaning of their forms."[22] This assertion was not entirely accurate: it neglected the architects involved in Britain's Independent Group and the work of Peter and Alison Smithson, who had staged their own rebellions against International Style modernism in the 1950s.[23] Nevertheless, Venturi's engagement with Pop art and popular culture (which would emerge somewhat more forcefully in the qualified embrace of Las Vegas and Levittown in *Learning from Las Vegas*) is certainly a reflection of the architect's desire to remove the distance between architecture and the vernacular or the lives of ordinary folk. As McLeod notes, however, 346 of the 350 plates in *Complexity and Contradiction* and most of the book's text contributed to "an elitist appreciation of high art."[24] And the most obvious point of rebellion against the prevailing architectural theory (and theorists) was his embrace of the past, welcoming historical architecture back into the academy from which it had largely been banished. It was his own quiet theoretical counterrevolution—one that might seem small in the cultural and political context of both the present and its own historical moment, but one that was nonetheless perceived by architects of the 1960s as quite daring.

Picking up on Venturi's famous question, "Is not Main Street almost all right?"[25] Upton has also emphasized that the popular landscape was for Venturi and Scott Brown "almost (but *only* almost) all right."[26] Tellingly, Scott Brown herself emphasized "the agony in our acceptance of pop,"[27] noting that "we are part of a high art, not a folk or popular art, tradition. We use these other traditions, as others have before us, for an artistic reason; but for a social reason as well. . . . There is a social need for architectural high art to learn from and relate to folk and pop traditions if it is to serve its real clients and do no further harm in the city. The idea of the everyday forces us to acknowledge that Architecture is part of architecture, that designers are a part of the everyday world, not explorers from a more civilized society or detached doers *for* clients and *to* cities."[28]

In view of these thoughtful comments, it is difficult not to detect an inherent contradiction that runs through Venturi and Scott Brown's work, in which a professed interest in a socially and politically engaged architectural practice exists alongside a record of built work and publications that never quite manage to engage deeply and consistently with the issues that were most pressing for the time and place in which they were made. In the end, their embrace of popular culture, and the politics that it might imply, was always at arm's length. Although they proclaimed a wish to connect to the social and cultural world beyond conventional architectural practice, ultimately this is not backed up by their work. And the two environments they selected to prove their concern for the everyday, the popular, and, by association, the authenticity of American urban life, were overwhelmingly populated by whites—the original Levittown in Pennsylvania notoriously so, as the location for one of the most infamous riots in U.S. postwar history (which began when the residents of this all-white enclave objected to the arrival of an African American family in the 1950s), and then 1970s Las Vegas, whose front-of-the-house whiteness was supported then as now by a back-of-the-house system of workers of color.[29]

In other words, from the standpoint we now occupy, after several decades of advanced neoliberalism, *Complexity and Contradiction* cannot seriously be understood as a work of either political or social rebellion. Venturi's book can today be more productively considered if it opens up a broader question: What would it have meant if the critique of modernism by architects during and after the 1960s had extended beyond considerations of aesthetics and beyond a qualified and selective embrace of popular culture and Pop art? Within architecture theory, Venturi was a generative intellectual force in the production of the field's own version of poststructuralism. The primary accomplishment of Venturi's book was, in Upton's words, that it "inaugurated the period of high theory in architecture. *Complexity and Contradiction*'s reliance on modes of literary criticism and the communications model employed in *Learning from Las Vegas* were instrumental in delivering American architectural theory into linguistic bondage from which it has yet to be liberated."[30] Outside of the sphere of architecture, in the humanities more broadly, poststructuralism was around the same time developing into a theoretical framework that critically examined, critiqued, and even rejected existing cultural structures. The politically engaged and progressive nature of poststructuralist literary criticism—which ultimately led to postcolonial theory, critical race theory, and, more recently, intersectional analysis (to name a few)—was simply not carried over into architectural theory and practice, although it could have been. Instead, poststructuralist theory in architecture focused on a new historicism, regionalism, and a range of aesthetically rather than politically engaged formal concerns.

If we view *Complexity and Contradiction* in the most positive light, we can, however, see it, along with Venturi's later work, as constituting a softly delivered and aesthetically circumscribed rebellion aimed primarily at troubling a profession whose theoretical apparatus had become somewhat fossilized. But the book also leaves us with unsettling questions that extend to the nature of the profession itself, its ongoing modes of practice, and the need for a critical (self-)questioning that it has so far been spared. Above all, *Complexity and Contradiction* may still warrant our attention as a cultural document that points to the ways professional structures are resolutely upheld even in turbulent times. It shines a bright spotlight on the priorities of the field of architecture, on what it has valued, and on the issues from which it has consciously and persistently turned away. It allows us to see the contradictions at play in a sphere that—while it claims to embrace aesthetic and design creativity and new ways of seeing and thinking—remains steadfastly devoted to structural systems that permit it to remain a by-and-large racially homogenous patriarchy. And it helps us understand why the profession of architecture has only episodically embraced alternative modes of practice that would contribute to overcoming the inequalities and injustices that it instead all too often perpetuates.

The author wishes to thank Dell Upton, Sharon Irish, Kathryn Bond Stockton, Stephen Tobriner, and Mabel O. Wilson for conversations that contributed to this essay.

Notes

1. Vincent Scully, introduction to *Complexity and Contradiction in Architecture*, by Robert Venturi (New York: The Museum of Modern Art in association with the Graham Foundation for Advanced Studies in the Fine Arts, Chicago, 1966), 11.
2. For instances of the use of such terminology to describe Venturi or his works, see, for example, Kathleen James-Chakraborty, *Architecture Since 1400* (Minneapolis: University of Minnesota Press, 2013), 458; see also Philip Johnson's remarks in an interview with Barbaralee Diamonstein-Spielvogel, "American Architecture Now: Philip Johnson," 1984, http://www.youtube.com/watch?v=bHb0DB6pnk4, accessed

April 7, 2017, cited in Deborah Fausch, review of *Complexity and Contradiction in Architecture*, by Robert Venturi, in *Journal of Architectural Education* 66, no. 1 (December 2012): 32. See also Deborah Fausch, "Portraits of Influence: Robert Venturi '47 *50. A 'gentle manifesto' created a revolution in architecture," http://www.princeton.edu/paw/archive_new/PAW07-08/07-0123/top25_11.html, accessed April 7, 2017.

3. Jonathan Massey, "Power and Privilege," *Journal of the Society of Architectural Historians* 75, no. 4 (December 2016): 498.

4. Julian Zelizer, "Is America Repeating the Mistakes of 1968?" *The Atlantic*, July 8, 2016, https://www.theatlantic.com/politics/archive/2016/07/is-america-repeating-the-mistakes-of-1968/490568/.

5. For an overview see David Harvey, *A Brief History of Neoliberalism* (New York: Oxford University Press, 2005).

6. For a summary of the AIA controversy, see Nicholas Korody, Amelia Taylor-Hochberg, and Paul Petrunia, "Architects Respond to the AIA's Statement in Support of President-Elect Donald Trump," *Archinect*, November 14, 2016, http://archinect.com/features/article/149978362/architects-respond-to-the-aia-s-statement-in-support-of-president-elect-donald-trump. On the "Design As Protest" movement that started after Trump's election, see Brentin Mock, "Design as Protest During the Trump Era," *CityLab*, January 25, 2017, https://www.citylab.com/design/2017/01/design-as-protest-during-the-trump-era/514313/, both accessed July 18, 2018.

7. Recent data indicates that 91.3 percent of architects identify as white. See, for example, Gregory Walker, "A Profession Almost as White as the Walls," *Archinect*, November 7, 2013, https://archinect.com/news/article/85972778/a-profession-almost-as-white-as-the-walls. According to data published by the American Institute of Architects in 2014, only 18 percent of licensed architects are women; 2 percent of licensed architects are African American; 3 percent of licensed architects are Latino. See the American Institute of Architects report *Diversity in the Profession of Architecture: Key Findings 2015* (Washington, D.C.: American Institute of Architects, 2015), http://www.architecturalrecord.com/ext/resources/news/2016/03-Mar/AIA-Diversity-Survey/AIA-Diversity-Architecture-Survey-02.pdf, accessed July 18, 2018.

8. See, for example, Eve Blau, "This Work is Going Somewhere: Pedagogy and Politics at Yale in the Late 1960s," *Log* 38 (fall 2016): 131–50.

9. Gwendolyn Wright, *USA: Modern Architectures in History* (London: Reaktion Books, 2008), 213, 195; Sym Van der Ryn, *Design for Life* (Salt Lake City, Utah: Gibbs Smith, 2005), 27–30.

10. My thanks to David B. Brownlee for contributing information on this important aspect of the South Street story.

11. Christopher Klemek, *The Transatlantic Collapse of Urban Renewal: Postwar Urbanism from New York to Berlin* (Chicago: University of Chicago Press, 2011), 195, 198.

12. Wright, *USA*, 210.

13. Wright, *USA*, 199.

14. Wright, *USA*, 201.

15. Mary McLeod, "Architecture and Politics in the Reagan Era: From Postmodernism to Deconstructivism," *Assemblage*, no. 8 (February 1989): 29.

16. Richard Nixon delivered what became known as his "Silent Majority Speech" on November 3, 1969. See Richard Nixon, "Address to the Nation on the War in Vietnam," November 3, 1969, online version by The American Presidency Project, http://www.presidency.ucsb.edu/ws/?pid=2303, accessed July 18, 2018.

17. Anthony Giddens, *The Consequences of Modernity* (Stanford, Calif.: Stanford University Press, 1991); Jeremy Till, "Reality in the Balance," *Places Journal*, January 2017, https://placesjournal.org/article/reality-in-the-balance/.

18. Despina Stratigakos, *Where Are the Women Architects?* (Princeton, N.J.: Princeton University Press, 2016), 1–2.

19. Among the university programs that were best known for curricula that focused on architecture and social justice in the 1960s and 1970s were those at the University of California, Berkeley; University of Illinois at Urbana-Champaign; and North Carolina State University.

20. McLeod, "Architecture and Politics," 38.

21. Robert Venturi, Denise Scott Brown, and Steven Izenour, *Learning from Las Vegas: The Forgotten Symbolism of Architectural Form*, rev. ed. (Cambridge, Mass.: MIT Press, 1977), 3; Dell Upton, "Architecture in Everyday Life," *New Literary History* 33, no. 4 (autumn 2002): 707–23.

22. Scully, introduction, 14.

23. My thanks to Dell Upton for providing this helpful insight.

24. McLeod, "Architecture and Politics," 28.

25. Venturi, *Complexity and Contradiction*, 102.

26. Upton, "Architecture," 710.

27. Denise Scott Brown, "Pop Off: Reply to Kenneth Frampton" [1971], in *A View from the Campidoglio: Selected Essays, 1953–1984*, by Robert Venturi and Denise Scott Brown (New York: Harper & Row, 1984), 34.

28. Ibid., 37.

29. For a detailed account of the Learning from Levittown studio and its efforts—and ultimate failure—to tackle the social and political challenges in that suburb, see Jessica Lautin, "More Than Ticky Tacky: Venturi, Scott Brown, and Learning from the Levittown Studio," in *Second Suburb: Levittown, Pennsylvania*, ed. Dianne Harris (Pittsburgh, Penn.: University of Pittsburgh Press, 2010), 324–39. This volume also contains a detailed history of the riot that ensued when the first African American family moved into Levittown in 1957.

30. For more on this, see Dell Upton, "Signs Taken for Wonders," *Visible Language* 37, no. 3 (2003): 349.

Michael Meredith

With phrases such as "calculated ambiguity," "both-and," "double meanings," "messy vitality," and "expressive discontinuity," *Complexity and Contradiction* embraces intellectual relativism and takes us on a historical road trip. Along with its inclusion of artists such as Jasper Johns (Venturi's doppelgänger) and Robert Rauschenberg, this evokes similarities to "The Aesthetic of Indifference," an essay by art historian and critic Moira Roth published in *Artforum* in 1977. Two attitudes, Roth writes, mapped out the poles of national consciousness during the McCarthy period: bigoted, (over-)zealous conviction and embittered passivity. These positions were illustrated, respectively, by crime novelist Mickey Spillane's detective-protagonist Mike Hammer and writer J. D. Salinger's antihero Holden Caulfield.

In this context of political extremism, a cool aesthetic of indifference was taken up by artists such as John Cage, Merce Cunningham, Marcel Duchamp, Johns, and Rauschenberg. This attitude would persist, proving integral to the formation of Pop and Minimal art, not to mention Conceptual art. Art production became playful, ironic, removed, cerebral, and ambiguous through a calculated indifference that rejected established models of art, including Abstract Expressionism, and stopped art's movement toward a "pure," Greenbergian medium-specific condition, instead opening up other possibilities through collecting and mixing objects and mediums, using fragments and theatrical performance, doing things wrong, and generally challenging the institutions of art. Ultimately, Roth's text is a critique suggesting that the work of this group of artists could have been more political and more socially engaged, and less anti-expressionist, less ambiguous, less "cool."

Yet, given our current political climate, this cool approach offers something to think about. Even if one argues that indifference lies at the core of modernism—in Albert Camus, Édouard Manet, Paul Cézanne, Fernand Léger, and so on—it is nonetheless also very much an aspect of our current McCarthyesque environment, in which bigoted conviction and embittered passivity coincide with an exhaustion of technologically progressive models of architecture, which applies to both medium-specific design techniques and the real expansion of analytical, organizational, and technical skills through the computer.

A world of the sort delineated by Hammer and Caulfield is here again, suggesting that *Complexity and Contradiction* and its lessons remain relevant. My sole criticism of Roth's article is that artistic, social, and political agency can indeed come through aesthetics, not solely through direct political or social engagement. An artistic expression of indifference is not necessarily either the avoidance or acceptance of extremist politics. When done well, architecture's complexity and contradiction— its calculated ambiguity or indifference—is a social engine with the ability to produce discussion, reflection, thought, and ultimately action. It is a social engine directed toward something better. In this way, *Complexity and Contradiction* illustrates architecture's truly utopian project. Utopia has never been the impossible, glistening, fictional, perfectly functioning, and sustainable machine that most imagine. Rather, it has always been the much less grandiose sociocultural project of questioning, discussing, and instantiating values that lead us toward a better society—one that is equitable, inclusive, and takes pleasure in difference.

On the Rhetoric of a "Gentle Manifesto"

Peter Fröhlicher

As Venturi seeks to establish the central terms of his conception of architecture in the opening chapters of *Complexity and
Contradiction in Architecture*, he quotes nearly as many writers,
critics, and essayists as he does architects and art historians. He
makes reference to Cleanth Brooks, William Empson, August
Heckscher, Stanley Edgar Hyman, and above all, the poet and
critic T. S. Eliot. Even the programmatic terms of the book's title
are associated with textual analysis or propositional logic and
foreground the rhetorical character of the architectural theory
being expounded here. The text thus invites formal analysis as
a piece of writing and prompts questions such as: Does a manifesto that postulates certain discursive qualities for architecture
also present itself in a corresponding textual form? How does
an architect construct a text about complexity and contradiction? Let us begin by looking again at the book's first chapter,
"Nonstraighforward Architecture: A Gentle Manifesto," which
reads, in full, as follows:

> I like complexity and contradiction in architecture. I
> do not like the incoherence or arbitrariness of incom-
> petent architecture nor the precious intricacies of pic-
> turesqueness or expressionism. Instead, I speak of a
> complex and contradictory architecture based on the
> richness and ambiguity of modern experience, including
> that experience which is inherent in art. Everywhere,
> except in architecture, complexity and contradiction
> have been acknowledged, from Gödel's proof of ulti-
> mate inconsistency in mathematics to T. S. Eliot's anal-
> ysis of "difficult" poetry and Joseph Albers' definition
> of the paradoxical quality of painting.

But architecture is necessarily complex and contradictory in its very inclusion of the traditional Vitruvian elements of commodity, firmness, and delight. And today the wants of program, structure, mechanical equipment, and expression, even in single buildings in simple contexts, are diverse and conflicting in ways previously unimaginable. The increasing dimension and scale of architecture in urban and regional planning add to the difficulties. I welcome the problems and exploit the uncertainties. By embracing contradiction as well as complexity, I aim for vitality as well as validity.

Architects can no longer afford to be intimidated by the puritanically moral language of orthodox Modern architecture. I like elements which are hybrid rather than "pure," compromising rather than "clean," distorted rather than "straightforward," ambiguous rather than "articulated," perverse as well as impersonal, boring as well as "interesting," conventional rather than "designed," accommodating rather than excluding, redundant rather than simple, vestigial as well as innovating, inconsistent and equivocal rather than direct and clear. I am for messy vitality over obvious unity. I include the non sequitur and proclaim the duality.

I am for richness of meaning rather than clarity of meaning; for the implicit function as well as the explicit function. I prefer "both-and" to "either-or," black and white, and sometimes gray, to black or white. A valid architecture evokes many levels of meaning and combinations of focus: its space and its elements become readable and workable in several ways at once.

But an architecture of complexity and contradiction has a special obligation toward the whole: its truth must be in its totality or its implications of totality. It must embody the difficult unity of inclusion rather than the easy unity of exclusion. More is not less.[1]

While the book's title may lead one to expect an abstract theoretical treatise—as also implied in the opening words of Vincent Scully's introduction, "This is not an easy book"— the personal, colloquial tone at the beginning of its first chapter suggests, instead, a conversational relationship of author and reader. The first sentence can be understood as simply a variation on the words of its title, albeit with the author now appearing in the first person, quoting the book's title and proclaiming that he *likes* the concepts named in it.

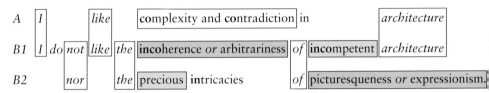

In the similarly constructed second sentence, he contrasts the two positively connoted terms of his title with "incoherence or arbitrariness" (B1) as manifestations of "incompetent architecture." The syntactic parallelism between A and B1 is varied in the subclause B2, and overlaid with a chiasmus of the two adjective/noun constructions and the two pairs of nouns connected by "or." The repetition of the words' initial sounds connects, on the one hand, the positively connoted concepts "**complexity** and **contradiction**" in A, and on the other hand, the negatively connoted "**incoherence** . . . of **incompetent** architecture" in B1, with the echo in the first syllable of "**in**tricacies" in B2. The function of the syllable *in* as a marker of negativity is further strengthened in the contrast between "**complexity**" and "**incompetent**."

This kind of rhetorical composition, which appears often in literature as well as in the language of advertising, was described by the Russian-American linguist Roman Jakobson in a much-quoted study in 1960 as a manifestation of what he called the "poetic function" of language.[1] The formal correspondences between the words suggest a connection on the level of meaning as well, and prompt the reader to understand the corresponding words or concepts through their relationship of reciprocity. The syntactic parallelisms and the accompanying correspondences of sound, moreover, contribute to calling into question conventional meanings and constructing new definitions and value assignments.

As examples of what he disparagingly calls "precious intricacies," Venturi cites "picturesqueness" and "expressionism." These two stylistic tendencies are arguably examples of complexity but have a negative connotation here.[2] Although "contradiction" is semantically close, at least in everyday usage, to "incoherence," the former here has a positive value and the latter a negative one. And a dislike of incoherence would necessitate assigning a positive value to coherence—which, however, seems incompatible with the preference for contradiction here. Defining the two terms used in the title by differentiating them from their negatively connoted opposites proves a complex endeavor that, at least at first glance, itself runs the risk of contradiction. That it is nonetheless effective is thanks to the elegance of the formal rhetorical construction. The first two clauses lay out the pairs of opposites that structure the argument that follows, and they are the point of departure for a discourse on architecture that shifts and redefines the meaning and value accorded to familiar terms by situating them within a complex web of relationships.

The author gives his preference for complexity and contradiction an objective frame by claiming that the two terms are given their due "everywhere, except in architecture," citing their use by Kurt Gödel, T. S. Eliot, and Josef Albers. Venturi backs up his assertion that architecture itself has long been characterized by these qualities by referring to the Vitruvian triad *utilitas, firmitas, venustas*, here translated (following Henry Wotton) as "commodity, firmness, and delight." Unlike earlier commentators such as Leon Battista Alberti, who added other terms to the triad, Venturi understands it as a still valid expression of the increasingly complex and contradictory demands made upon twentieth-century architects and urban planners. "Complexity and contradiction" can thus itself be understood as the essence of the Vitruvian formula and its contemporary interpretation at the same time. In contrast to the champions of modernism, Venturi aspires to a productive engagement with these challenges as part of his striving toward what, at the end of the second paragraph, he calls "vitality as well as validity."

In the first two paragraphs of this opening chapter, then, the first-person speaker stages himself successively as a) an architecture enthusiast ("I like . . .") who justifies his aversions ("I don't like . . .") b) someone taking the perspective of an expert ("incompetent architecture"); c) a manifesto writer in the performative mode ("I speak . . ."), and finally, d) as a practicing architect ("I exploit . . . ," "I welcome . . . ," "I aim for . . ."). This establishes a complex identity for the continually reappearing "I." The credibility of this speaker, which is crucial to the text's persuasive effect, is doubtless based on the combination of professional expertise and the sincerity and intimacy implicit in the colloquial register of a discussion of likes and dislikes.

The case being made is bolstered by the alternations between personal opinion and sweeping statements in these two paragraphs. Forming a chiasmic counterpart to the "I," canonical figures are introduced as experts in complexity and contradiction in different fields of "modern experience." Then Venturi brings in Vitruvius, from whose famous formula complexity and contradiction in architecture allegedly follows as the necessary and logical next step.

After thus laying out his implicit argumentative framework, Venturi proffers two models for this first-person author. On the one hand, as the successor to the founder of architecture theory, and as his exegete, he presents himself as a comparable authority in his own day. On the other, as the harbinger of an architecture of complexity and contradiction, he assumes a role in his own field structurally homologous to that of luminaries such as Eliot, Albers, and Gödel. The first two paragraphs of this chapter hence appear as rhetorical constructions that can be correlated with one another on the basis of their sequential exposition of similar contents, albeit in reversed order.

First paragraph

| "I" | Aficionado of complexity and contradiction |
| Gödel, Eliot, Albers | Experts in complexity and contradiction in different areas |

Second paragraph

| Vitruvius | Expert in complexity and contradiction in the theory of architecture |
| "I" | Expert in complexity and contradiction in modern architecture |

Moreover, the programmatic connection of the formal language of architecture—"complexity and contradiction"—with the "vitality and validity" that is its desired effect continues the series of phonic and graphemic correspondences. The shared initial sound is joined by the identical ending, the homoeoteleuton of classical rhetoric; in addition to which the anagrammatic structure of the two words—barring the small deviation (t/d)— is striking:

v   it a l   i t y

v   a l i d   i t y

In architecture theory, the word *vitality* often invokes associations with the organic and the living. But for Venturi it is not about the return, in a traditional sense, of architectural elements to the human body or its proportions, as it still was for Le Corbusier's Modulor. Rather, it refers to the energy and multiplicity of modern life in general, as they are expressed in the very Main Street of which Venturi famously asks at the end of *Complexity and Contradiction* "is not Main Street almost all right?"[3] It is in this sense that vitality presents an antithesis to modernist purity—which is the subject of the next paragraph.

The author's confident asseveration of the principles of a new architecture is here contrasted with the insecurity of the manifesto's real audience: "Architects can no longer afford to be intimidated by the puritanically moral language of orthodox Modern architecture." The contrast between "I like" and "I do not like" at the beginning of the chapter is then varied here, in that the phrase "I like" pertains to the first element in a series of opposing adjectives in which a positive attribute is paired with a negative one. The quotation marks around most of the second-named elements signal that Venturi is quoting from the "moral language" of modernism. The series achieves a paradoxical effect in that the terms the author prefers, such as "distorted" or "inconsistent," tend to be more pejorative in general usage, while, conversely, most of the spurned terms from the vocabulary of "orthodox" modernism, such as "pure" or "clean," have positive associations, and not only for its adherents.

I like elements which are

hybrid	**rather than**	"pure,"
compromising		"clean,"
distorted		"straightforward,"
ambiguous		"articulated,"
perverse	**as well as**	impersonal,
boring		"interesting,"
conventional	**rather than**	"designed,"
accommodating		excluding,
redundant		simple,
vestigial	**as well as**	innovating,
inconsistent and		
equivocal	**rather than**	direct and clear.

Instead of the absolute rejection of one of these pairs of characteristics, Venturi either proclaims his preference for the first element over the second ("rather than") or the inclusion of the second as an equal to the first ("as well as"). Alongside conventional binary oppositions such as "boring" versus "interesting," there are a number of newly minted antitheses such as "compromising" versus "clean," or "perverse" versus "impersonal"—in this case doubtless inspired by the shared sounds or graphemes.

But while many of these antonyms cannot be found in any dictionary, what may at first glance appear as a somewhat random list can in fact be understood as a theme and variations taking up various formal and semantic elements. The alternating conjunctions "rather than" and "as well as" lend a basic rhythm to the series of contrasting terms, which gain variety through the different numbers of paired concepts (4, 2, 3, 1, as well as a double pair at the end) in each of the five groups.

Juxtapositions that follow a schema of compare-and-contrast—or of parallelism, as in the first two sentences—are here introduced in the context of Venturi's reflections on the commonalities between architecture and poetry. When, later in the book, Venturi introduces the idea of "using convention unconventionally" (with reference to Le Corbusier), he follows it with a paragraph that begins: "Poets, according to Eliot, employ 'that perpetual slight alteration of language, words perpetually juxtaposed in new and sudden combinations.'"[4] In the passage discussed above, the customary meaning of words is systematically called into question through the author's paradoxical preference for terms that normally have negative connotations. A further shift in their lexical definitions comes about through the unconventional binary oppositions: Venturi's new rhetorical framework deconstructs the previous, orthodox discourse, integrating it into a new complex and multifaceted theoretical schema both by incorporating seemingly antithetical terms and through the implication of positive or negative value implied by the oppositions themselves.

The series of deliberately provocative preferences expressed within this carefully elaborated rhetorical structure thus has a precise persuasive function. In the text, it follows—immediately and without any explicit logical connection—the mention of architects who should not be but are intimidated by modernist discourse. Evidently, they should take the author's courage as an inspiration and, thanks to his rhetorical performance of complexity and contradiction, liberate themselves from the shackles of the puritanical language of orthodox modernism. The idea of a new, more inclusive architecture is built upon the foundation of a discursive logic that itself constitutes a complex logical structure that defies existing categories and calls the principle of mutually exclusive oppositions into question—as further exemplified in the author's summary at the end of the paragraph: "I am for messy vitality over obvious unity. I include the non sequitur and proclaim the duality."

This violation of the principles of modernism was very likely a provocation not only for fellow architects who prized concepts such as "clean," "straightforward," or "articulated," but also for readers who remember the pejorative invocation of "arbitrariness" and "incoherence" at the beginning of the manifesto. The apparent contradiction is, however, mitigated if "messy vitality" is understood as the opposite of "obvious unity" at the end of the paragraph. In fact, even what appears to be utterly disordered can ultimately lead to something that can be recognized as unity. Later in the book, Venturi writes (for example): "The seemingly chaotic juxtapositions of honky-tonk elements express an intriguing kind of vitality and validity, and they produce an unexpected approach to unity as well."[5] The process of perception involved in such instances should present a challenge to the viewer and require a certain amount of time: "In the validly complex building or cityscape, the eye does not want to be too easily or too quickly satisfied in its search for unity within a whole."[6]

The idea that the complexity of the train of thought that discovers the unity of a work has value in itself recalls the theory of *obscuritas* in the poetics of the seventeenth century. One might link this to Venturi's predilection for Mannerist and Baroque architecture, which is apparent in the choice of the examples he discusses in the main part of his treatise. In chapter 3, moreover, he refers to the "mannerist" strain in literature, calling particular attention to "contradiction, paradox, and ambiguity."[7] Along such lines, the Spanish writer and theoretician Baltasar Gracián, in his famous treatise *Agudeza y arte de ingenio* (1648), advocates sophisticated rhetoric with paradoxical formulations, emphasizing that seemingly disparate things should be brought into harmony. The delay with which the active reader or viewer eventually discerns the unity itself enhances aesthetic enjoyment.[8]

It is nevertheless notable that Venturi hardly uses any properly aesthetic terms in *Complexity and Contradiction*, except in a few quotations from others. As a value judgment on the part of the author, the adjective "beautiful" appears only once in reference to a building, in a footnote in the second edition, picking up on a passage where Venturi praises Alvar Aalto's Church of the Three Crosses in Imatra, Finland, by contrasting it with Giovanni Michelucci's Chiesa di San Giovanni Battista outside Florence, condemning the "willful picturesqueness of the haphazard structure and spaces" of the latter.[9] The new footnote is a retraction of this criticism: "I have visited Giovanni Michelucci's Church of the Autostrada since writing these words, and I now realize it is an extremely beautiful and effective building. I am therefore sorry I made this unsympathetic comparison."[10] Aside from demonstrating the difficulty of judging buildings on the basis of photographs, the footnote leaves open the question as to why "willful picturesqueness," when reevaluated as a positive attribute, mutates into beauty—rather than, say, an expression of the "validity" or "vitality" that Venturi frequently uses as terms of praise. Perhaps there is some reticence lurking here with respect to the standard vocabulary of aesthetic appreciation—elsewhere, the adjective *exquisite*, likewise used only once, seems to strike an ironic note: "Mies' exquisite pavilions have had valuable implications for architecture, but their selectiveness of content and language is their limitation as well as their strength."[11]

The terms used to express a positive judgment, "validity" and "vitality," with the variant "vividness," and the corresponding adjectives for each of these terms, may occupy a realm beyond traditional aesthetic categories but are nonetheless linked with traditional concepts of architectural theory in the final paragraphs of the book's programmatic first chapter. There, we find the author praising "messy vitality" and the "many levels of meaning and combinations of focus." Such propositions may seem to call totality into question, yet the chapter ends with a postulate of totality. The previously dominant first-person voice speaking of personal predilections now cedes to the deontic mode typical of treatises and manifestos. "An architecture of complexity and contradiction has a special obligation toward the whole," Venturi writes, specifying that "it must embody the difficult unity of inclusion." Nothing less than the "truth" of architecture is at stake. While, in traditional conceptions of architecture, aesthetic categories—what Vitruvius calls *venustas*: beauty, attractiveness, or, as here, "delight"; or what Alberti calls *concinnitas*: the harmonious joining of different parts—were held to ground a building in totality, Venturi formulates an ethical obligation for architecture: "its truth must be in its totality or its implications of totality." As a universal value, truth ennobles "messy vitality," and it ought to be understood as the outcome of the evident labor of bringing together the complexity and contradictions of the demands placed on architecture into a "difficult unity."[12] Venturi opposes the puritanical moral precepts of modernism—which have, he implies, ossified into a belief system—with an ethics based on the constant striving for truth.

If the text switches to a *stilus sublimis* in taking up the ethical imperative, the closing sentence of the chapter—"More is not less"—lays out an ironic counterpoint by inverting Mies van der Rohe's famous motto "less is more," perhaps the quintessence of modernism's "puritanically moral language."[13] The idea that "more is not less" corroborates on the level of content the positive value of the leitmotif of "complexity and contradiction" that is invoked in the chapter's first sentence and repeated throughout. With great rhetorical efficiency, Venturi negates the opposing credo, which is based on a paradox, and parodies it in a tautology that reflects his own standpoint. Such a gesture, which, so to speak, attacks the opponent using his own weapon, would have been seen as a demonstration of the greatest rhetorical skill by the theorists of the Baroque period.[14] A further parody of modernist maxims appears in the subsequent chapter in the form of a paronomasia, when Venturi recasts "less is more" into "less is a bore."[15] Indeed, Mies and Vitruvius together stake out the field that Venturi surveys in the following chapters. The Roman architecture theorist is the representative of a tradition that Venturi here redefines as "complexity and contradiction," while Mies stands, on the opposing side, as one of the icons of modernism.

For Venturi, architecture is also, or even above all, language. His conception of architecture is based on terms—not least "truth" itself—that are defined through the logic of language. In a way that was unprecedented in writing about architecture, it is clearly founded in an analogy with literature and supported by numerous quotations from Eliot and literary criticism of the 1950s, which centers on terms such as "ambiguity," "paradox," "plurality," "tension," "duality," and, above all, "complexity" and "contradiction." But it is not only Venturi's conception of architecture that is distinguished by its affinity with the poetics of literary texts: it also underlies his own writing about architecture, whose meaning is, in essence, determined by its form. In rhetorical figures based on syntactic or phonic structures of repetition—parallelism, alliteration, paronomasia—the poetic capacity of language creates new correspondences and relationships. The compositional principle of this manifesto for an architecture of complexity and contradiction is itself complex and contradictory: the self-reflexive text allows readers to experience the characteristics of the new architecture in the act of reading itself. Venturi's repeated statement of preferences for one or more elements within unconventional pairings undermines conventional binary oppositions, thus expanding the categories of architectural description and interpretation and creatively revealing new dimensions to how we think about architectural practice—that is, about buildings and their effects. This "gentle manifesto" lays the groundwork for the comparative analysis of buildings that comprises the greater portion of Venturi's book—in his own version of a methodology that has been standard practice in art history since Heinrich Wölfflin. The hybrid categories Venturi introduces at the outset place this comparative approach on a new footing that is eminently suitable for the conceptual framing and elucidation of an architecture of complexity and contradiction.

Translated from German by Elizabeth Tucker

Notes

1. Roman Jakobson, "Linguistics and Poetics," in *Style in Language*, ed. Thomas A. Sebeok (Cambridge, Mass.: MIT Press, 1960), 358.
2. Similar problems surrounding the concept of coherence form the basis of an article in which Nikolaus Pevsner defends the picturesque, in the process criticizing Basil Taylor's terminological slippages with respect to "irregularity," "intricacy," and "variation," quoted here with italics added:

   > *The characteristic qualities of the picturesque, according to Mr. Taylor, are "irregularity of form, of colour, of light and shade, of texture," and in addition "intricacy and sudden variation."* It was an excellent touch to link these qualities to the emergence of historicism in architecture, that is, to the admission of various styles of building all acceptable in their place and their mood, and also to the new belief in nature, according to which "nature is virtuous in herself and not only when subject to man's refinements."
   >
   > So far no quarrel. *But Mr. Taylor then almost imperceptibly exchanged such terms as varied and irregular against "accidental" and "disorderly."* Here to my mind lies his fundamental error, an error especially fatal in considering the Picturesque today. Its full implication will only gradually come out.

   Nikolaus Pevsner, "Twentieth Century Picturesque," *The Architectural Review* 115 (April 1954): 227–29, https://www.architectural-review.com/rethink/nikolaus-pevsner-in-defence-of-the-picturesque/8635346.article.
3. Venturi, *Complexity and Contradiction*, 102.

4. Ibid., 51.
5. Ibid., 102.
6. Ibid., 103.
7. Ibid., 28.
8. On the debate about mannerism in Venturi's treatise, see Maarten Delbeke, "Mannerism and Meaning in Complexity and Contradiction in Architecture," *The Journal of Architecture* 15, no. 3 (2010): 267–82. In note 6 on p. 278, Delbeke comments: "My reading of *Complexity and Contradiction* differs from M. Stierli, 'In the Academy's Garden: Robert Venturi, the Grand Tour and the Revision of Modernism,' *AA Files*, 56 (2007), 42–55, esp. 54f., who writes that 'mannerism was, at least explicitly, only marginally present in *Complexity and Contradiction*.' I do believe, however, that the concept of mannerism arrived quite late in the writing process of the book."
9. Venturi, *Complexity and Contradiction*, 26.
10. Robert Venturi, *Complexity and Contradiction in Architecture*, 2nd ed. (New York: The Museum of Modern Art in association with the Graham Foundation for Advanced Studies in the Fine Arts, Chicago, 1977), 19.
11. Venturi, *Complexity and Contradiction*, 25.
12. Before Venturi turns to a discussion of his own works at the conclusion of the extended manifesto of *Complexity and Contradiction*, he comes to speak once again about the relationship of totality and truth in architecture. On p. 89, he quotes August Heckscher and credits him in a footnote, thereby indirectly identifying him as a potential source for the language in the first chapter, too: "I have emphasized the goal of unity rather than of simplification in an art 'whose . . . truth [is] in its totality.'" In Heckscher's book, however, the quoted sentence refers not to buildings but to Shakespeare's plays. Architecture is thus directly analogous to a literary text, also with respect to the artwork's defining qualities. Heckscher writes: "The dramatic form lent itself, even better than Donne's poems, to contrasts and juxtapositions; it could embrace the contrarities of a universe which seemed to be ordered by no single principle and whose only truth was in its totality." August Heckscher, *The Public Happiness* (New York: Atheneum, 1962), 287.
13. Cf. Martino Stierli's observation that "Venturi's catchy formula 'complexity and contradiction' is obviously developed in antagonism to Mies's famous dictum 'less is more.'" See Martino Stierli, "Taking on Mies: Mimicry and Parody of Modernism in the Architecture of Alison and Peter Smithson and Venturi/Scott Brown," in *Neo-Avant-Garde and Postmodern: Postwar Architecture in Britain and Beyond*, ed. Mark Crinson and Claire Zimmerman (New Haven, Conn.: Yale University Press, 2010), 162.
14. In Gracián's terminology, this involves the combination of an "agudeza por alusión" (wit by allusion) and an "agudeza paradoja" (paradoxical wit), which belongs among the "trofeos de la sutileza" (trophies of subtlety). Baltasar Gracián, "Agudeza y arte de ingenio," *Obras completas* (Madrid: Aguilar, 1960), 339, 449.
15. Venturi, *Complexity and Contradiction*, 25.

Sam Jacob

The original manuscript of *Complexity and Contradiction*—all on yellow paper, typed and handwritten, cut up and taped together—suggests it is a text that has been both shredded and composed, as if placing words and sentences together was, for Venturi, an act of composition or construction. One can imagine him working with his scissors on both text and images simultaneously, as he snipped and glued the paper overlays for the interior elevation of his design for Grand's Restaurant in Philadelphia. One recalls, too, the compositional slicing and reassembly that characterized the endless iterations of his "Mother's House." In other words, the manuscript is as much a visual and spatial composition as it is a text.

Even in the phrase used to describe the book in its first chapter, "a gentle manifesto," Venturi's text is both proposition and performance. The phrase first soothes us, but before we get too comfortable, it tugs the rug from under our feet. It works like a gloss on the highfalutin, alliterative title—full of clattering consonants—that precedes it. It is a phrase that is itself both complex and contradictory.

Linguistically the book is a tour de force of structure and form that twists with lithe elegance. Venturi's language is teasing and playful. Like many of his aphorisms, his prose is full of cadences that seem to turn back on themselves: sentences that seem to pause to whisper asides to us while hiding a smile behind an almost straight face, or switch modes while pulling unexpected references as if from a magician's hat. One might even suggest that the narrative path of the writing itself takes the reader on the same kind of journey as the staggered plan at the entrance of Venturi's "Mother's House."

Venturi explores architectural languages and meanings in writing that not only describes these effects but also enacts them. Ideas and the medium of their communication are interwoven throughout the book. Text and image perform a kind of choreography through the pages, creating effects of spatial and elevational juxtaposition and adjacency. As with the Jasper Johns flag painting that features in the book as an illustration, the flatness of the page becomes ambiguously active in the act of representation.

As a formal object, *Complexity and Contradiction* is overtly a book, its layout making the reader hyperaware of both the text and the act of looking at illustrations on a page. Yet this layout also operates spatially, as the images sidle up to the words they illustrate, performing just the kind of adjacencies the Venturi describes. Especially in *Complexity and Contradiction*, but elsewhere, too, Venturi's writing is far more than a functional window onto the world: it is a place where ideas are generated through the use of language. *Complexity and Contradiction* creates its polemic not just through what it says but through how it says it.

Rowe, Scully, Venturi:
Two Forms of Corbusianism

Emmanuel Petit

Robert Venturi's notion of complexity can best be understood through its relationship to the work of Le Corbusier. The links between the two architects were first explored by two of the most idiosyncratic revisionists of Corbusianism in the 1950s and 1960s: Colin Rowe and Vincent Scully. It was they who radically altered the interpretation of Le Corbusier's oeuvre, shifting it from the revolutionary role it had been given in the progressive project undertaken by "operative" historians of modern architecture, especially Sigfried Giedion and Nikolaus Pevsner. Rowe and Scully both saw the meaning of Corbu's work changing as it was received in the United States, and made Venturi into a pivotal character in that history of influence.

On the one hand, Scully made Venturi an heir to an inclusive, humane, and accommodating artistic sensibility that Le Corbusier had rediscovered in the architecture of the Greek polis, and which could now be adjusted to the context of American democracy. Rowe, on the other, thought that Venturi had learned from Corbu's mannerist esprit but lacked the analytical discipline to uphold the distinction between the sophisticated play of forms and the cult of the commonplace. Between these two interpretations of Le Corbusier, the historical role of the search for "complex and contradictory" architecture in the 1950s and 1960s takes on discursive texture.

The notion of complexity has been one of the keystones of the discussion of postmodernity in architecture as well as in the other humanities; the term itself underwent a repurposing through the decades to accommodate new meanings, new techniques, and new philosophical alliances, much like its sister concepts "undecidability" in the 1980s (which is tied to the culture of textuality and the theses of deconstruction) and "intricacy" in the 1990s (which combined the possibilities of digital modeling with the structural effects of biology and zoology in a philosophical climate that foregrounded notions of variation and differentiation).[1] For Venturi, especially in the context of *Complexity and Contradiction in Architecture*, complexity had equally important ties to the discourses of formalism and of art history. What enabled his particular fusion of formal and historical arguments to emerge was the critical category of mannerism, which had entered Anglo-American discourse in the 1950s. It did so primarily as part of a revisionist analysis of the historical precedents of modern architecture—usually, as was the case with both Rowe and Scully, with a special focus on Le Corbusier. Venturi took on particular importance in this discussion (as did James Stirling). Four decades after the publication of *Complexity and Contradiction*, Venturi claimed, "If I were to give the book a new title, I would call it 'Mannerism in Architecture,' because that is what it is about."[2]

Colin Rowe

Rowe had declared his interest in Le Corbusier's formally sophisticated modernism as early as 1950, in "Mannerism and Modern Architecture"—a text whose argument bears many conceptual resemblances with the theses of Venturi's *Complexity and Contradiction* sixteen years later.[3] In the Villa Schwob in La Chaux-de-Fonds, Switzerland—one of Le Corbusier's early projects, completed 1917—Rowe found a remarkable paradox in the tension between the highly articulated, complex, and sculptural volumes of the building and the blank abstraction of the blank and flat panel on its front facade. He linked the formal incongruities of these "*systematically* opposite values"[4] to the broader theme of modernity's "self-division"—a division caused by a desire for clarity of forms that reflected some eternal truth, on the one hand, and the need for individual self-expression and Romantic drama, on the other.[5] Rowe suggested that this ambiguity in Le Corbusier's building could be related to Mannerism, which he described as "an unavoidable state of mind, and not a mere desire to break rules." He continued, "Sixteenth-century mannerism appears to consist in the deliberate inversion of the classical High Renaissance norm as established by Bramante, to include the very human desire to impair perfection when once it has been achieved, and to represent too a collapse of confidence in the theoretical programs of the earlier Renaissance. As a state of inhibition, it is essentially dependent on the awareness of a preexisting order."[6]

Rowe's dehistoricized notion of mannerism was more than the mere designation of a movement and its moment in history—for instance, the time from 1520 to 1600 (as Pevsner had suggested).[7] Instead, it was generalized as a particular mental disposition that could recur at various moments throughout history. In fact, the mannerist impulse to challenge the critical framework of "ideality" was described as a byproduct of all rational thought; Rowe put it in terms of "jeu d'esprit" and argued that the "distinction between the thing as it is and as it appears . . . seems to haunt"[8] the (rhetorical) facades of mannerist buildings, including those of the modernist period. Because of modern architecture's double nature—i.e., its internal schism between the cerebral and the sensuous, between its morale and its physique[9]—Rowe maintained that none of the mannerist buildings then or now could provide immediate visual satisfaction. The meaning of these buildings was not simply and plainly visible, and only an intellectual reconstruction of fragmentary visual episodes could render the structure of mannerist architecture comprehensible in all its complexity.[10] For Rowe, this observation was the beginning of a more mature appreciation of modern architecture, but it was also an assessment that brought to the fore the loose and ambivalent tie between a specific architectural form and its manifold meanings.

Rowe further developed the notion of the double entendre of forms in the "Transparency" essays coauthored with the painter Robert Slutzky in the mid-1950s—the argument of which rested on an analysis of Analytic Cubism. In contradistinction to the "literal" transparency of see-through materials, phenomenal transparency provided "the sensation of looking through a first plane of significance to others lying behind";[11] as in Rowe's earlier portrayal of mannerism, the clarity of modern forms was here described as compromised, and works revealed the complexity of their meaning through multiple alternative readings. Because of his cunning use of Analytic Cubism's techniques of transparency and collage, Le Corbusier became, for Rowe, a model for an alternative or oblique modernism in architecture, which he saw as akin to Pablo Picasso's in painting.[12] Based on this comparison between a modern architect and a modern painter, Rowe proceeded to identify two traditions of modernity: the first, he claimed, had a distaste for art; the second was more "prone" to it but was never very worried about fundamental methods. Both Picasso and Le Corbusier exemplified the second type of modernity, which believed in its foundations in art and, in

Rowe's analysis, relied on the incommensurability of meaning. He argued that Picasso's composite collage techniques made it impossible to understand "what is false and what is true, what is antique and what is 'of today'" and maintained that "the alternative . . . tradition of modernity has always made a virtue of irony, obliquity and multiple reference."[13]

Based on this analytical construction of the meanings of form, Rowe identified a generation of architects for whom the formal inventions of modern architecture were a most appealing project to be revisited, listing them by name: Michael Graves, Aldo Rossi, James Stirling, and Robert Venturi. These figures had all, Rowe explained, "with varying degrees of success, . . . maintained much more of a liaison with the morphological components of Modern architecture. Neo-technological, neo-avant-garde, neo–Art Deco, neo–Belle Epoque; whatever the surface trim, all alike have been unwilling to cut the umbilical cord and to make the ultimate separation. Almost all alike make willful complexity or willful simplicity."[14] The playful engagement with the formal and morphological aspects of modern precedents that characterized the work of these architects testified to their dependence on the inventions of a prior generation while at the same time insinuating the ways they were distancing themselves from it. In particular, they eschewed the positivist and activist correspondence between form and social program, and thus opened the door to a looser and more plural relationship between the spheres of "things" and "ideas."

In the context of his critical text on Venturi's winning design for the Yale Mathematics Building competition in the late 1960s, Rowe discussed in more depth the relationship between Le Corbusier and Venturi's interests in formal complexity. He acknowledged Corbu's "witty and collisive intelligence"[15] in the course of observing that the architect's "normative" formal systems were mostly composed of geometric abstractions, such as the Platonic shapes and the column-grid, and making the case that formal "contradictions" were justified only in terms of the formal normality they disrupted—i.e., in terms of the geometrical system within which the formal disturbance occurred and had to be "read." This sophisticated dialectic play between system and exception was what made Le Corbusier's architecture intellectually rich and challenging.

Rowe's appraisal of Venturi was less positive. He recognized that, unlike Corbu, Venturi made no attempt to rationalize his play with diverse images and metaphors, and argued

that Venturi developed a taste for formal ambiguity per se—
that without any system to contradict, Venturi's work bor-
dered on an esoteric and learned *vers de société*.

Based on the distinction between the two architects,
Rowe sided with Le Corbusier and concluded that Venturi's
"cult of ambiguity could become an excuse for irresolution,"[16]
and that, besides, "blatant failures can become explained as
ironies and total lack of distinction may become exonerated
by asserting the ideal of the average."[17] By the early 1970s,
Rowe's preference for Corbu's tacit formal contradictions over
Venturi's overt proclamations of irony caused him to endorse
the "Five Architects" (i.e., Peter Eisenman, Michael Graves,
Charles Gwathmey, John Hejduk, and Richard Meier) as the
true progeny of a mannered Corbusianism; like Le Corbusier,
the New York Five defended formal deviations on aesthetic
grounds—on the grounds, that is, of their syntactic depen-
dency on a geometric "normalcy." Their rhetorical exegeses
of Le Corbusier's architecture, he claimed, only added to the
esprit of mannerism, which Rowe saw as the defining characteristic of a mature (neo-)modernism in architecture.[18] This
conception of mannerism was premised upon an abstract play
with geometry, and hence distinguished itself from the more
figural ironies Venturi would more and more put to use.

Vincent Scully

In the process of seeking out the suitable heir of Le Corbusier
in the 1960s, and with the intention of constructing a historical pedigree for American architecture, Scully did not side with
Rowe and the Five Architects; instead, he uncovered a different early project by Le Corbusier, the La Scala Movie Theater
(1912–16), also in La Chaux-de-Fonds, and pointed out the
visual similarity between its arched frontispiece and the front
facade of Venturi's Guild House in Philadelphia.[19] In the 1960s,
the qualities of Scully's Le Corbusier (i.e., the architect, not the
urban planner) were strikingly similar to the ones he eventually
saw in the rising figure of Venturi. In this formulation, irony
was the key term with which Scully described the mental disposition of Le Corbusier's (and later Venturi's) inclusionary
and "humanist" modernism. Unlike Rowe, Scully embraced
the term (which Venturi picked up later) to encourage a departure from the technocratic dogmatism of International Style
modernism—most prominently, Walter Gropius's legacy at
Harvard.[20] While his broader goal was not so different from
Rowe's, Scully made Le Corbusier the conceptual link between

the ethic of democracy, descended from ancient Greece (remember Corbu's admiration for the Acropolis) and the architecture of modern America. Irony was to be the "civilizing" agent: it was inextricably linked to the ideals of Greek public life, and acknowledged the irreducible plurality of the public domain, the polis. Corbu had the ability to handle such pluralities, a skill which had been lost since the days of Giorgio Vasari, Baldassare Peruzzi, and, most importantly, Giulio Romano. Ultimately, Scully intended to transmit the virtues of Le Corbusier's sophisticated modernism, itself ultimately derived from a "Greek" sculptural sensibility, to Venturi.

The cultural program of this more humanist attitude would be to relax modern architecture's tenacious "organicism." Scully identified this latter, nonironic strategy with the desire to assimilate every aspect of design into a homogeneous, abstract scheme based on coherent formal principles, which was most visibly realized by such disparate figures as Giambattista Piranesi and Frank Lloyd Wright. Abstraction and continuity, he believed, were Piranesi's and Wright's basic assumptions about the modern world—a postulation that would find expression in the homogeneity of their spaces. Scully argued that the modern quest for formal synthesis sought to resolve the existential cleft between the creator's (inner) imagination and the external realities he had to face; he also maintained that the seamless formal continuity underlying these architectures merely put a veneer over the modern individual's fundamentally divided condition. Any formal reconciliation could only be artificial, precarious, and willful, and as a consequence, this modern understanding of "perfection" was based on a lie.

Piranesi's prints were introduced as a milestone in the evolution toward spatial continuity in Scully's historical review; in Piranesi's depictions of space, man lost orientation in an ongoing spatial flux; no fixed and recognizable point was to be found, and even gravity seemed subsumed under the will of the artist's mind.[21] In particular, Piranesi's subterranean prison vaults, the Carceri (1745–61), epitomized a continuous movement through space, without a baroque anchor, and thus encapsulated the sense of uprootedness that underlay Scully's idea of modernity. Kafkaesque fantasies were contained in the hermeticism of Piranesi's imagination, and were uninflected by gravity or other actualities outside the architect's mind.

Scully saw Wright's Guggenheim Museum in New York, which had been completed in 1959, as the temporary apotheosis

of this modernist evolution toward continuity. The Guggenheim's spatial structure constituted an all-encompassing
environment in which the space of the building was focused
through the help of one continuous spiraling movement grav-
itating only around itself.[22] The Guggenheim was a closed
world, which inverted the "open" (read: democratic) logic of
the New York street grid into a self-contained and autonomous interior. In it, Scully argued, the subject was conceptu-
ally situated in the center: in control, egocentric, and heroic.
The surrounding space was determined by the subject's mind
alone, and acknowledged no resistance from any pressures of
the "outer" world. This space was, in a sense, the symptom
of modernism's naive belief in a utopia of control and dominance. Scully maintained that Wright's strategy of integrative
organicism, like Piranesi's, had created intellectual totalities
that suppressed the juxtaposition of architectural elements
belonging to disparate "systems"—which Scully ultimately
argued was equal to repressing the plurality of the public
sphere. Scully's position was that the architectural totality of
the Guggenheim produced intellectual closure, and that it thus
failed to do justice to the fact that traditional collective beliefs
were in crisis after the war.

Such an understanding of centralized space was opposed
to the ideology of form that Scully admired. He had appropri-
ated it from Henri Focillon's *Life of Forms* (1934), a book that
opens with the observation that "the questions emerging in the
interpretation of the work of art present themselves under the
form of almost obsessive contradictions."[23] Scully's idea of the
"dramatic" and humanist impulse in architecture was also nur-
tured by his study of the psychological art history of Geoffrey
Scott, on the one hand, and of the theory of archetypes of analytical psychologist Carl Gustav Jung, on the other.[24]

Scully described Corbu's only edifice in the United States,
the Carpenter Center for the Visual Arts at Harvard (1963), as
"a building with slender columns of smooth, plywood-molded
concrete, soft as a cloud, sharp-edged as a cigar box, for
America."[25] This building seemed to express all the qualities
that Venturi codified in *Complexity and Contradiction*. Scully's
subsequent quasi-conflation of his description of Le Corbusier,
Venturi's own theoretical lexicon, and the idea of a properly
"American" architecture was strategic, serving to put forward Venturi as the American architect who truly understood
Le Corbusier:

[The Carpenter Center] is ironic, too: complex, contradictory, and full of easy accommodations and Pop asides, a master's sketch, in fact . . . but in all ways more understood, apparently, by Venturi than by any other architect in America.

Few architects anywhere have been able to accommodate contradiction and to suggest irony through their forms. Perhaps Furness could a little, or Maybeck; Wright, not at all, nor Saarinen, nor Rudolph, nor Johnson, who probably understands the principle but cannot embody it. Not Kahn. But with Venturi it is fundamental.[26]

The Carpenter Center's geometric heterogeneity and multiplicity had the reforming qualities necessary for a new "American" architecture and, furthermore, could be perceived as a diatribe against American Puritanism. Scully claimed, "It is undoubtedly because of that very heterogeneity [of the American condition] that Americans have so often preferred 'unifying,' homogenized solutions. The self-righteousness of American Puritanism, which must see alternatives in terms of black or white, also continues to play a part."[27] Delineating a different trajectory, Scully designated Venturi as the heir of the humane sociocultural and artistic sensibility that had sprung from ancient Greece and was transmitted to the New World through Le Corbusier.

Nonjudgmentalism

It was not until *Learning from Las Vegas* (1972) that the importance of a more properly "American" architecture was foregrounded by Venturi himself, not least thanks to his coauthorship with Denise Scott Brown and Steven Izenour. What Scully had interpreted as a particular view of aesthetic form that was "humanist" in orientation and "American" in its formulation was what the book's authors labeled "nonjudgmental."[28] The implication was that "complex form" was less prone to being co-opted by the ideology of a single, "strong" author, and that it served an open, democratic process—albeit one that depended on a certain level of erudition about the history of architecture. And yet, as had been the case with the New Critics a generation previously, their opponents criticized them precisely for this nonjudgmentalism, because for them it meant committing oneself to nothing, and this was a recipe for political inertia.

Giving voice to the heterogeneous and signaling doubt and self-awareness about one's position in historical time and geographical context are defining characteristics of post-modernism. These debates thus also reveal how its cultural themes emerged from the close dialogue between art and architectural discourses in Europe and in the United States, and, more specifically, from the particular formalist and ahistorical spin that theorists such as Rowe and Scully gave them. Venturi acted as a bridge between these worlds, not least because of his fascination with Italian and English architecture as well as with Pop art. And Venturi's book, which at times comes across as a sort of travelogue of an art lover, carries the jubilant exposition of a world filled with those little formal incongruities that make it both aesthetically elaborate and politically inclusive. These are the ingredients of his cultural and political program we have come to call "postmodern."

Notes

1. The notion of undecidability emerges from the influence of deconstruction on architecture—as can for instance be followed in the discussions between Jacques Derrida and Peter Eisenman with Jeffrey Kipnis and Thomas Leeser in *Chora L Works: Jacques Derrida and Peter Eisenman*, ed. Jeffrey Kipnis and Thomas Leeser (New York: Monacelli Press, 1997). The notion of intricacy is here cited in reference to Greg Lynn's 2003 exhibition of that title at the Institute of Contemporary Art, Philadelphia, which gathered work by artists, designers, and architects in order to reflect an emerging sensibility characterized by "highly complex compositions of an almost organic intricacy with macroscopic holism, coherence, and synthesis, and microscopic variation and diversity." Participants included painter Fabian Marcaccio, sculptor Tom Friedman, fashion designer Hussein Chalayan, and architects Peter Eisenman and Preston Scott Cohen. For further discussion of complexity theories with regard to *Complexity and Contradiction*, see Joan Ockman's contribution to this volume, pp. 78–97.
2. Robert Venturi and Denise Scott Brown, interview by Emmanuel Petit, January 2002, in Emmanuel Petit, "Irony in Metaphysics's Gravity: Iconoclasm and Imagination in Architecture, 1960s–1980s" (PhD diss., Princeton University, 2006), 649–77.
3. Colin Rowe, "Mannerism and Modern Architecture," in *The Mathematics of the Ideal Villa and Other Essays* (Cambridge, Mass.: MIT Press, 1982), 31. Originally published in a slightly different form in *Architectural Review* 107 (May 1950): 289–99. Citations refer to the MIT Press edition.
4. Ibid., 31. Italics added. The word *systematically* is of great importance here because Rowe implies that the paradox in the Villa Schwob is not a discrepancy of facade treatments but that the system Le Corbusier's building is dependent on is a principle of "opposite values."

5. Ibid., 42.

6. Ibid., 35.

7. See Nikolaus Pevsner, "The Architecture of Mannerism," in *The Mint: A Miscellany of Literature, Art and Criticism*, ed. Geoffrey Grigson (London: Routledge, 1946), 116–38.

8. Rowe, "Mannerism," 34.

9. In his introduction to *Five Architects*, Rowe discusses the non-simultaneity between thing and idea in the context of modern architecture: "Which is again to establish that the *physique* and the *morale* of modern architecture, its flesh and its word, were (and could) never be coincident; and it is when we recognize that neither word nor flesh was ever coincident with itself, let alone with each other, that, without undue partiality, we can approach the present day. . . . Then do we adhere to *physique*-flesh or to *morale*-word?" Colin Rowe, *Five Architects: Eisenman, Graves, Gwathmey, Hejduk, Meier* (New York: Oxford University Press, 1975), 7.

10. For Rowe, this twist also influences the way the eye sees: "[in the 1920s], it is as though the eye received a decisive twist by which, since it demanded visual ambiguity, it could produce it in contemporary works." He goes on to assert that the 1920s was also when "modern architecture felt most strongly the demand for inverted spatial effects." Rowe, "Mannerism," 51.

11. Colin Rowe and Robert Slutzky, "Transparency: Literal and Phenomenal," in *Mathematics of the Ideal Villa and Other Essays*, by Colin Rowe (Cambridge, Mass.: MIT Press, 1976), 161. Originally published in *Perspecta* 8 (1963): 44–54.

12. See Colin Rowe and Fred Koetter, *Collage City* (Cambridge, Mass.: MIT Press, 1978), 138.

13. Ibid.

14. Colin Rowe, "The Revolt of the Senses," in *As I Was Saying—Recollections and Miscellaneous Essays*, ed. Alexander Caragonne, vol. 3, *Urbanistics* (Cambridge, Mass.: MIT Press, 1996), 275. Originally published in *Architectural Design* 54, no. 7/8 (1984): 8.

15. Colin Rowe, "Robert Venturi and the Yale Mathematics Building Competition," in *As I Was Saying—Recollections and Miscellaneous Essays*, ed. Alexander Caragonne, vol. 2, *Cornelliana* (Cambridge, Mass.: MIT Press, 1996), 88.

16 Ibid., 100.

17. Ibid.

18. See Rowe, "Introduction," *Five Architects*, 3–8.

19. In Vincent Scully's *The Shingle Style, or The Historian's Revenge* (New York: George Braziller, 1974), he cites the similarities between Venturi's "Mother's House" and Le Corbusier's La Scala facade. The revenge of the title relates to his desire to demonstrate that Venturi is, after all, the true heir of Le Corbusier.

20. One significant difference between Scully's and Venturi's use of the term *irony* is apparent in their respective stances vis-à-vis the New Criticism. While Venturi was directly influenced by the way the term was taken up by the New Critics, Scully's dislike of the movement was why he left the English department at Yale, albeit

to return a few years later (after he had served in the US Marines) to study art history.

21. Vincent Scully, *Modern Architecture: The Architecture of Democracy* (New York: George Braziller, 1961), 11.
22. Ibid., 32.
23. Henri Focillon, *Vie des formes, suivi de Éloge de la main* (Paris: Presses universitaires de France, 1943; 7th edition, 1981), 5. Translated by the author from the French: "Les problèmes posés par l'interprétation de l'œuvre d'art se présentent sous l'aspect de contradictions presque obsédantes."
24. I am referring to Geoffrey Scott, *The Architecture of Humanism: A Study in the History of Taste* (London: Constable, 1914).
25. Vincent Scully, *American Architecture and Urbanism*, rev. ed. (New York: Henry Holt, 1988), 230.
26. Ibid.
27. Ibid., 229.
28. Robert Venturi, Denise Scott Brown, and Steven Izenour, *Learning from Las Vegas: The Forgotten Symbolism of Architectural Form*, rev. ed. (Cambridge, Mass.: MIT Press, 1977), xi.

Sharpening Perception

Stanislaus von Moos

The reason for the somewhat insistent presence of the term "Modern Art" on the cover of Robert Venturi's *Complexity and Contradiction in Architecture* is simple enough: the book was meant to inaugurate a series of publications then planned by the museum of that name. Yet it is tempting to speculate about the not so obvious implications of the term, especially since the book is considered to be a key text of post-modernism.[1] Its publication date of 1966, one may note in passing, coincided with Venturi's second stay at the American Academy in Rome (this time as architect in residence). That, in turn, would be a mere coincidence if Venturi's first printed essay had not been about the Campidoglio, and had not, some thirteen years prior to the book, presented an important element of its working hypothesis. That article was published in 1953, i.e., one year before his Rome Prize Fellowship at the American Academy began in 1954 (it lasted till 1956).

Venturi's 1953 essay does not offer a discussion of the Campidoglio's building history. Its exclusive focus is the perceptual conditions that determined how its users and visitors across time saw the piazza and experienced it as a space. The first sentence already seems to reverberate with preoccupations that had been key in modern art, and in particular painting, since the 1860s. Venturi writes: "The architect has a responsibility toward the landscape, which he can subtly enhance or impair, for we see in perceptual wholes and the introduction of any new building will change the character of all the other elements in a scene."[2] He then describes the Campidoglio before, during, and after the Renaissance building campaigns. When the piazza was opened up in the fifteenth century, in order to allow the Palazzo del Senatore to be seen from afar, the effect was one of bigness, magnitude; in the twentieth century, in

buildings, 3, their form and position, that the senatorial palace acquired new value. The contrasting elements of their colour and texture, and the neutral, even rhythm of their columned façades gave emphasis to the palace. Their unique positional arrangement created direction and an illusion of increased size; moreover, it concern itself not so much with its form (which can appeal to one's sense of the grotesque), but with its effect on its architectural neighbours. By its size, scale and colour, it makes the Campidoglio a weak anti-climax. Furthermore, the monument's direction, 5, creates for the Campidoglio a backstage position and causes it to loose any meaningful relation as capitol to the city plan.

Similarly drastic in effect was the sub- circulation system of the city. The vast Parisian spaces and other trimmings have robbed the buildings and their immediate exterior spaces of force. The modern planners' scrupulous respect for a Michelangelo design has caused them to leave the Campidoglio untouched physically, but they have, nevertheless, obscured its meaning and significance. A wrecking crew could hardly have damaged it more.

Robert Venturi

turn, the construction of the Monument to Vittorio Emanuele II as well as, subsequently, the massive "*diradamenti*" carried out under Mussolini completely altered the situation. The result was a radical change in context, and thus a complete "revolution" of the plaza's character in relation to its surroundings "as perceived by the eye" (fig. 1).[3]

Fig. 1. Robert Venturi. "The Campidoglio: A Case Study." 1953. Detail of p. 334 of *The Architectural Review* 113, no. 677

Contrast and Context

As an art historian, I have always been intrigued by the analogy between Venturi's ideas about "context in architectural composition" (the title of his MFA thesis)[4] and one of the most influential concepts in nineteenth-century color theory, Michel-Eugène Chevreul's theory of the *contraste simultané des couleurs* (simultaneous color contrast), published in 1839. Without Chevreul's theory, much of the evolution of painting since Delacroix, not to mention Impressionism, and, in particular, Neo-Impressionism, would be a mere question of abandoning figurative representation in favor of an arbitrary play of colors.[5] A chemist by training, Chevreul demonstrated that the quality and character of colors do not exist "objectively," in so-called reality, but are fabricated by the mind in response to the play of contrasts (including the contrasts of complementary colors), and in response to the colors being modified by their immediate environment. The color white, Chevreul

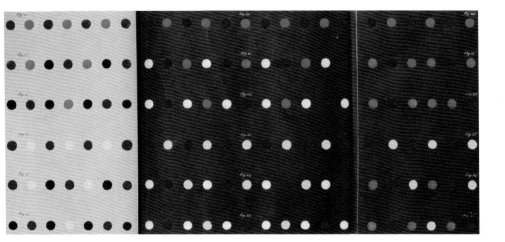

observes, is never absolutely white but changes depending on the neighboring color; nor is a red dot the same red dot when placed near an orange dot, near a white dot, or near a yellow dot, etc. The chromatic environment, in other words, profoundly influences our perception; the relative position of one color in relation to another determines our brain's reaction as to its character. Color, in short (and I am brutally simplifying), depends on the chromatic context (fig. 2).

Fig. 2. Michel-Eugène Chevreul. Detail of plate 8 of *De la loi du contraste simultané des couleurs, et de l'assortiment des objets colorés*. Paris: Pitois-Levrault, 1839

Borrowed from Gestalt theory and not from chromatology, Venturi's ideas about context in urban design assume a similarly structured relativity of perceptual effects.[6] With regard to the role of context in the design of buildings, the problem (for him) is how to realize a satisfactory "perceptual whole." What this requires is for context to be acknowledged critically, though not necessarily imitated: contrast can be as indispensable a means toward this end as mere imitation or paraphrase of what already exists in the immediate environment.[7]

Vitality, Validity, or the Pleasures of Language

Along with the diminutive size of the book's illustrations—"impossible to decipher," as Peter Blake noted in his 1967 review[8]—readers of the first edition have been irritated by the extreme diversity of what they depict: a muddle of buildings, styles, and epochs, pertaining to innumerable types of authorship and photographic representation. A detail from the Palazzo Farnese in Rome, side by side with the University of Virginia, Charlottesville, a mix of medieval and baroque church facades, a plan of the Sanctuary of the Holy Sepulcher in Jerusalem, a Shingle-style house in Manchester-by-the-Sea, a painting by Jasper Johns, etc., are all assembled on one page (p. 63).[9] While the swarming graphic effect created by this rather randomly dumped backpack of art-historical erudition fails to result in a "perceptual whole," the combination of miniature size and diversity of subject matter seems to indicate that what is at stake is not primarily what is shown but the act of looking at architecture, and thus the onlooker: the artistic subject.

Armed with patience and curiosity, the reader who follows up on the author's suggestions on how to look will be repaid by an intensified experience of buildings. Such can be the pleasures of looking at architecture, and since the pleasures of looking thus attained most often depend on the viewer's capacity to mentally engage with the complex functions architecture serves ("functionalist" pleasures), they turn out to be more easily accessible to those engaged in or at least familiar with the design of buildings. Furthermore, as the reader struggles with the text, stumbling over passages that oscillate between information and wordplay, paradox and parody—over language games that exploit the sound of the words while clarifying the issues at hand—one is reminded of just how much *writing* a book may involve the pleasures of language.[10]

Finally, as one keeps running into the author himself ("I like . . . ," "I welcome . . . ," "I am for . . ."), it becomes clear that, indeed, part of the argument is authorship; that what is at stake is the artist's right to understand the world (or at least the given object of inquiry) through personal opinion—in other words, through subjective perception. Thus: "I like elements which are hybrid rather than 'pure,' compromising rather than 'clean,' distorted rather than 'straightforward.'"[11] Or: "I welcome the problems and exploit the uncertainties. By embracing contradiction as well as complexity, I aim for vitality as well as validity."[12] And finally: "I am for richness of meaning rather than clarity of meaning; for the implicit function as well as the explicit function. I prefer 'both-and' to 'either-or,' black and white, and sometimes gray, to black or white."[13]

Some of the plates in the book corroborate the observations made in the text; others are mere placeholders for the works cited. What sticks in the mind are those that belong to the former category: the Cloth Hall in Bruges, which dramatizes the conflict of scales, in that the facade relates to the square while the "violently disproportionate scale of the tower above" relates to the town at large;[14] the detail of Michelangelo's apse of St. Peter's, which highlights the unsettling combination of elements that are "too big," such as the horizontal openings in the attic, with more conventional elements that look "too small"; or the plan of the Hôtel Matignon in Paris, whose irregularities seem absurd as long as one fails to understand their contextual raison d'être. Not to mention Edwin Lutyens's Nashdom, in Taplow, England, and its ambiguous status: Is it two loosely connected buildings, or merely one with a very small main entrance and central entrance hall?[15]

"I" and "We"

In the section of *Complexity and Contradiction* that features Venturi's own (frequently collaborative) designs, the auctorial "I" tends to be replaced by a more collective "we."[16] Unlike Aldo Rossi, Venturi never explicitly invokes "collective memory" in the context of the city—rather, memory is personalized as *experience* and *emotional association*. Nor is it a coincidence that, when speaking about experience and emotional association in architecture, he places "perception" before "creation," thus both establishing a priority for the act of perception on the creator's side while also, by implication, granting the viewer the autonomy she/he needs for the act of "responding." In *Learning from Las Vegas*, a collectively written work to begin with, the "I" is consistently replaced by "we": "We shall emphasize image— image over process or form." Yet when the authors go on to say that "architecture depends in its perception and creation on past experience and emotional association"[17] they do not merely imply that architecture depends on shared references in order to communicate, but also that there is a possibility of shared responsibility in design, once the hermeneutics of complexity and contradiction, the rules of the "difficult whole," are consistently applied.[18]

Imageability and Electronics

The historical references come in great quantity, as the roster of 253 illustrations in *Complexity and Contradiction* suggests. Stored in the archive of memory they may contribute to what Venturi refers to as "richness of meaning" in design, provided this "richness" results not from mere accumulation but from the "difficult unity through inclusion."[19] This process will work (or fail to work) in the architect's mind via accumulated perceptual recordings arrested in time under conditions of imageability— given that, as Venturi had already noted in 1953, "we see in perceptual wholes."[20] Thus it is as a visual unity, due to the finite, framed, and frontal character it shares with the painting in the gallery, that the facade of Guild House reveals its many levels of character and symbolism, that it refers to the classical tradition (if not more specifically to Palladio's Villa Zeno in Cessalto, shown in the book),[21] while at the same time subverting the aura implied by the model through the "cheapness" of the brickwork and the brash "commercial" lettering (fig. 3). It comes as no surprise that the rectangular box with a circular opening à la Kahn, elliptically anticipated as a possibility in the thermal window, is discarded, as it would have turned the facade into its own iconic abstraction. Finally, the antenna sculpture that crowns the facade is emblematic of the project's "ugly and ordinary" as opposed to "heroic" allure.[22] A metal sculpture, it is not abstract but figurative, since it represents an antenna (in fact, on most photographs, the "real" antenna appears behind it): a symbolic antenna that, in its form, and by its commanding position on axis with the facade, resonates both with royal or imperial insignia on palaces of the Baroque era *and* with the commercial reinterpretations of such symbols such as the "imperial" globe on top of the Stardust Casino in Las Vegas. In short: "ironic" monumentality "similar to that at the entrance to Anet."[23]

More importantly, perhaps, the sculpture is also a marker of the "death of architecture"—of what some (Venturi included) have seen as architecture's inevitable marginalization within the visual universe of modernization. Remember, we are advised, the architect would do better to "accept his role as combiner of significant old clichés . . . as his condition within a society which directs its best efforts, its big money, and its elegant

Fig. 3. Venturi and Rauch with Cope and Lippincott. Guild House, Philadelphia. 1960–63. The Architectural Archives of the University of Pennsylvania, Philadelphia. Gift of Robert Venturi and Denise Scott Brown

technologies elsewhere," in order for him, in such a way, to "ironically express . . . a true concern for society's inverted scale of values."[24] Victor Hugo's concept of the death of architecture has often been referred to in this context, except, of course, that Hugo's "*Ceci tuera cela*" suggests that it is the book that will kill architecture—whereas what the antenna stands for is the electronic maelstrom of the global village.

Venturi is extraordinarily up-to-date with his references, even though they are more often implied than explicitly named: with Guild House, we are obviously beyond Hugo, beyond the Gutenberg Galaxy altogether (note that Marshall McLuhan's book of the same title appeared in 1962, when Guild House was about to be completed).[25] When, more than fifteen years later, Hugo's role in nineteenth-century architectural theory became a topical issue in architectural studies (mainly due to Neil Levine's work on Henri Labrouste and the Bibliothèque Ste. Geneviève), McLuhan, in turn, had all but vanished from the architectural radar.[26]

The Responsive Eye

More intriguing, yet not unconnected to these issues, is Venturi's dialogue with Jasper Johns's *Three Flags* (1958; fig. 4). The painter had resolved his struggle with his chosen patriotic iconography by stacking three flag paintings on top of each other, the smallest closest, a bigger one immediately behind it, and the biggest in the back, thus constructing a reverse perspective in which the parts that are closest are smallest and those that are furthest away are biggest. If Johns here combines straightforward imagery in a shrill formal experiment, the same can be said about Guild House, where Venturi used an almost identical principle of reverse perspective for the windows (small on the closest wall plane, bigger on the intermediate plane, very big on the plane that is farthest away). In his case, too, the arrangement is justified both as a means to make the ordinary look extraordinary and to achieve compositional unity, i.e., to force the images together into a "perceptual whole."[27] Of course, reverse perspective is an old "trick" in urban design, and the conspicuously awkward way in which it is engaged here (producing an effect similar to a stereoscopic image seen without a stereoscopic viewer) is perhaps no more than a gratuitous complication in terms of architecture, let alone in the context of a home for retired people. Yet this complication is deeply inscribed in the artistic culture of the 1960s and its rediscovery of the cognitive mechanisms of perception as a prime shaper of artistic practice.

4.

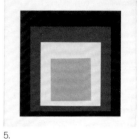

5.

One should not forget that Josef Albers is, after all, one the key witnesses in Venturi's chapter on ambiguity, which explores "the complexity and contradiction that results from the juxta-position of what an image is and what it seems." Albers "calls 'the discrepancy between physical fact and psychic effect' a contradiction which is 'the origin of art,'" Venturi reports.[28] More than about anything else, the painter's many versions of the Homage to the Square are about the disjunction between the convention of linear perspective (evoked by the symmetrical succession of concentric squares) and the "psychic effect" of color, which so blatantly plays *against* the rules of perspectival foreshortening (fig. 5).

Robert Smithson's *Plunge*, which was also made in 1966, may illustrate the fascination with what critics have referred to as "alternating perspective figures," "isometric figures," or "alog-ons." *Plunge* is an installation of cubes. Depending on one's angle of approach, one might first see two parallel ranges of ten identical cubes in perspective foreshortening, only to realize that there are two further rows of cubes between the two ranges, and that those actually merge into the big cubes in the foreground. A small adjustment to one's viewing position is, however, enough to see that the foreshortening is an illusion, and that the further the cubes recede in space, the more their proportions are stretched to produce the appearance of foreshortening; in other words, the actual work and the space that it occupies don't add up.[29] Venturi surely wasn't thinking of Smithson when he designed Guild House, but the book shows that both shared a fascination with

Fig. 4. Jasper Johns (American, born 1930). *Three Flags*, 1958. Encaustic on canvas. 30⅝ x 45½ x 4⅝ in. (77.8 x 115.6 x 11.7 cm). Whitney Museum of American Art, New York. Purchase, with funds from the Gilman Foundation, Inc., The Lauder Foundation, A. Alfred Taubman, Laura-Lee Whittier Woods, Howard Lipman, and Ed Downe in honor of the Museum's Fiftieth Anniversary

Fig. 5. Josef Albers (German, 1888–1976). *Day and Night VIII* from *Day and Night: Homage to the Square*, 1963. One from a portfolio of ten lithographs. Composition: 15¹¹⁄₁₆ x 15⅝ in. (39.9 x 39.7 cm); sheet: 18¾ x 20⅜ in. (47.7 x 51.8 cm). The Museum of Modern Art, New York. Gift of Kleiner, Bell & Co

the kind of ambiguities just described: "The size of Vanbrugh's fore-pavilions at Grimsthorpe in relation to the back pavilions is ambiguous from a distance: are they near or far, big or small?" Or: "Bernini's pilasters on the Palazzo di Propaganda Fide: are they positive pilasters or negative panel divisions?"[30] Indeed, these are typical Albers riddles; and although Venturi does not illustrate any work by him, he does show work by Ellsworth Kelly and Morris Louis. And in fact all three artists—Albers, Kelly, Louis—were included in an exhibition at The Museum of Modern Art in 1965, when Venturi must have been putting his final touches on the manuscript.

That show, curated by William C. Seitz, was titled *The Responsive Eye*.[31] While Venturi's comment on Kelly's *Green, Blue, Red* (1964; since retitled *Blue Green Red*) is disappointing (he is content to range it among his examples of "duality" in art),[32] it is notable that what was at stake in the work for the curator was the "perceptual urge" to make the two vertical elements (or beams) overlap—an impulse that keeps being frustrated by the format of the painting (fig. 6).[33] Like Albers, and even more like Smithson (and the Cubists before them), Kelly creates a work that *stimulates*, or rather *simulates*, the viewer's share in the creation of visual experience—or, indeed, in the creation of a perceptual whole.

Fig. 6. Ellsworth Kelly (American, 1923–2015). *Blue Green Red*. 1964. Oil on linen. 73¼ x 100⅜ in. (186.1 x 255 cm). Whitney Museum of American Art, New York. Gift of the Friends of the Whitney Museum of American Art

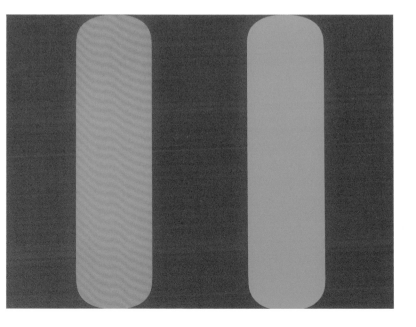

God's Own Junkyard

With documentary photography, by the nature of the medium, the issue is not the dichotomy between the appearance of the object and the space it occupies, but the dichotomy between information and the formal structure in which it is held—a dichotomy which is also a quality of (or a problem in?) *Complexity and Contradiction* as a text. With photography, of course, information can be ambivalent to begin with, as in, for example, Richard Saunders's 1952 picture of the McNulty service station in Camden, New Jersey (fig. 7). For Blake, who uses one of its several versions in his manifesto *God's Own Junkyard* (1964), the picture represents the evils of commercialism and the ways it corrupted the American landscape. For Venturi, who includes the image in *Complexity and Contradiction*, "the pictures in [Blake's] book that are supposed to be bad are often good. . . . The seemingly chaotic juxtapositions of honky-tonk elements express an intriguing kind of vitality and validity, and they produce an unexpected approach to unity as well."[34] In short, by oscillating between information and ornament, the visual mess rescued by photography defines a no-man's land that Venturi and Scott Brown would subsequently colonize with a multitude of signs of their own making. Here too, the information most often lies between the lines, or, indeed, in their simple presence as ornamental variations on the retinal *divertimenti* offered by the contemporary city—especially its postwar shopping strips. In their elaborate "language games," each "ornament" is configured as a "perceptual whole"—as with Jasper Johns's *0 through 9* (1960) or Robert Indiana's *LOVE*, which The Museum of Modern Art

Fig. 7. Richard Saunders (American, 1922–1987). McNulty service station, Camden, N.J. 1952. From p. 108 of Peter Blake, *God's Own Junkyard: The Planned Deterioration of America's Landscape*. New York: Holt, Rinehart and Winston, 1964

8.   9.

initially commissioned as a Christmas card in 1965 (fig. 8).[35]
These oscillations between architecture and typography, erudite
variations on themes of graffiti art (practiced with humor, up to
a few years ago, even on the VSBA website)[36] may be the one
aspect of Venturi and Scott Brown's work that has enjoyed uninterrupted popularity among many of their colleagues—granted
that this popularity also reflects the by now ubiquitous presence
of Pop and Conceptual art tropes in the networks of commercial
communication (fig. 9).

Perception Restrained

The patronage of The Museum of Modern Art did not prevent
Venturi's book from being criticized as either a misunderstanding
of modern art or as a sign of the erosion of its foundations. The
eclecticism of the historic references, not to mention the implication that mimesis was key to artistic creation, was seen as an
offense to the modern dogma of abstraction.[37] The references to
Pop art appeared as mere surfing on the waves of fashionable
gallery talk, while the more serious implications of the priority
of "perception" were largely ignored. Perhaps the smallness
of the illustrations in the book should be understood as a way
of restraining perception in order to focus attention. I am borrowing this notion from Jacques Herzog and Pierre de Meuron;
Perception Restrained was the title of their small exhibition at The
Museum of Modern Art in 2006, forty years after the publication
of *Complexity and Contradiction*. The two architects—the first
to be included in the Museum's Artist's Choice series—decided
to make the act of seeing itself the subject of their exhibition.

Fig. 8. Robert Indiana (American,
born 1928). *LOVE*. 1967. Screenprint.
Composition and sheet: 33 15/16 x
33 15/16 in. (86.3 x 86.3 cm). Multiples,
Inc., New York. Sirocco Screenprinters,
North Haven, Conn. Edition of 250.
The Museum of Modern Art, New
York. Riva Castleman Fund

Fig. 9. Venturi & Short. Grand's
Restaurant, Philadelphia. 1961.
The Architectural Archives of the
University of Pennsylvania,
Philadelphia. Gift of Robert Venturi
and Denise Scott Brown

They did so by transforming the white cube of the gallery into a mysterious black box with only small openings allowing visitors to peer into a brightly lit adjacent space where artworks were arranged at a distance, thus redefining the passive museum visitor as an active treasure hunter seeking out partly hidden objects.[38] In such a way, the perceptive act, or more generally the "image," is once again defined as a matter of subjective choice—much as in Venturi's book ("I like . . . ," "I am for . . . ," etc.). Whereas Venturi's concept of perception still needed the explicitness of the complex and contradictory object in order to be activated, however, the two Swiss architects would progressively separate the act of perception from specific architectural subject matter.[39] As a result, in their design work—their architectural "image building"—the framework of architectural references, which still served as a guardrail for the generation of Venturi and Rossi, gradually moved out of sight.

What sense is to be made of all this in terms of the history of recent architecture? Architecture and art were still discussed separately when *Complexity and Contradiction* appeared. When architects moved closer to fine-art practices in the 1960s and 1970s, this could be seen as a defensive move away from corporate architecture, but it also set in motion larger forces that culminated in the notion of the "starchitect" and ultimately ended up stripping architecture of some of its core competence. Not by coincidence, contemporary architecture thus gradually moved into the focus of art, art criticism, and art history with the new millennium. In *The Art-Architecture Complex* (2011), Hal Foster sees the issue of visuality, the phenomenal as opposed to the literal, as crucial in recent architecture. Indeed, the first chapter is titled "Image Building," and in a section on museums, Herzog and de Meuron are quoted as stating that "architecture is perception."[40] Foster also insists that in recent decades art has, for better or for worse, replaced theory in the making of an architect. When he refers to buildings "that do the looking for us,"[41] it is as if we were catching a glimpse of *The Responsive Eye*. Foster illustrates these phenomena with works by Frank Gehry, Jean Nouvel, Herzog & de Meuron, Renzo Piano, Zaha Hadid, Rem Koolhaas—the usual suspects. He sees Venturi and Scott Brown's contribution primarily as having opened up architecture toward Pop, thus paving the way toward "faux-populist iconicity," the "decorative symbolism of postmodern architecture"—in short, an avant-garde "of most use to the Right" and now thoroughly "discredited."[42] A second look at *Complexity and Contradiction* may suggest more nuanced readings of this historical trajectory.

Notwithstanding an at times disheartening tendency to blur its argument by multiplying references and allowing language to play games of its own—or perhaps precisely for this reason—the book defines a space at the core of the twentieth century's preoccupation with pure visibility, or, better, the grammar of vision in the arts.

Notes

1. The argument explored in this paper has intrigued me since I first read *Complexity and Contradiction in Architecture* on a Greyhound bus from New York to Chicago in 1967, yet much of what follows is an elaboration of ideas proposed long ago by others—with particular insight by Vincent Scully, Alan Colquhoun, and, more recently, Hal Foster. I am grateful to David B. Brownlee, Martino Stierli, and The Museum of Modern Art for granting me this occasion to revisit my earlier, rather preliminary thoughts on Venturi's book (see Stanislaus von Moos, *Venturi, Rauch & Scott Brown: Buildings and Projects* [New York: Rizzoli, 1987], esp. 11–17 and 47–59), and to this book's copy editors and their patient efforts toward bringing this text into publishable form.
2. Robert Venturi, "The Campidoglio: A Case Study," in *A View from the Campidoglio: Selected Essays, 1953–1984*, by Robert Venturi and Denise Scott Brown (New York: Harper & Row, 1984), 12. First published in *Architectural Review* 113 (May 1953): 333–34.
3. The quotation is from Robert Venturi, "Context in Architectural Composition," MFA thesis, Princeton University, 1950, reprinted in *Iconography and Electronics upon a Generic Architecture: A View from the Drafting Room* (Cambridge, Mass.: MIT Press, 1996), 335–61, here 335.
4. See preceding note. For a brief summary, see Stanislaus von Moos, *Venturi, Rauch & Scott Brown*, 79–80.
5. Michel-Eugène Chevreul, *De la loi du contraste simultané des couleurs, et de l'assortiment des objets colorés* (Paris: Pitois-Levrault, 1839). On Cheuvreul's initiatory role in modern art, see the classic study by William Homer, *Seurat and the Science of Painting* (Cambridge, Mass.: MIT Press, 1964) and, more recently, the somewhat pedestrian yet still inspiring Paul G. Vitz and Arnold B. Glimcher, *Modern Art and Modern Science: The Parallel Analysis of Vision* (New York: Praeger, 1984), esp. 71–87, as well as Pascal Rousseau, "Un langage universel. L'esthétique scientifique aux origines de l'abstraction," in *Aux origines de l'abstraction. 1800–1914*, ed. Serge Lemoine (Paris: Musée d'Orsay, 2004), 18–33.
6. See Robert Venturi, *Complexity and Contradiction in Architecture*, The Museum of Modern Art Papers on Architecture 1 (New York: The Museum of Modern Art in association with the Graham Foundation for Advanced Studies in the Fine Arts, Chicago, 1966), 49–50. In his MFA thesis, Venturi summarily indicates "Nelson,

Gestalt Psychology," as his source for the following statement: "Meaning is what one idea is as context of another idea" (Venturi, "Context in Architectural Composition," 338). Venturi was surely referring to Harry Helson, author of one of the founding texts of Gestalt psychology. See Harry Helson, "The Psychology of Gestalt," *American Journal of Psychology* 36 (1926): 342–50 and 494–526; 37 (1927): 26–62 and 189–223. For further discussion of Venturi's relationship to Gestalt theory, see Joan Ockman's contribution to this volume, pp. 78–97.

7. I have discussed Venturi, Scott Brown & Associates' approach to the issue of context in greater detail in Stanislaus von Moos, "Contextual Oscillations," in *Venturi, Scott Brown & Associates: Buildings and Projects, 1986–1998* (New York: Monacelli Press, 1999), 10–71, esp. 29–30.

8. Peter Blake, "Complexity and Contradiction in Architecture," *Architectural Forum,* June 1967, 56–57, 98.

9. Venturi, *Complexity and Contradiction,* 63.

10. I am indebted here to the linguist Peter Fröhlicher's comments on rhyme, allusion, alliteration, phonetic parallelism, and other rhetorical modes used by Venturi in *Complexity and Contradiction.* See Fröhlicher's contribution to this volume, pp. 144–55.

11. Venturi, *Complexity and Contradiction,* 22.

12. Ibid.

13. Ibid., 23.

14. Ibid., 37.

15. Ibid., 31–32 (St. Peter's); 88–89 (Hôtel Matignon); 29 (Nashdom).

16. Ibid., 104–33.

17. Robert Venturi, Denise Scott Brown, and Steven Izenour, *Learning from Las Vegas* (Cambridge, Mass.: MIT Press, 1972), 64.

18. The importance of architects' negotiation of constraints in relation to the "difficult whole" is forcefully made by Enrique Walker in "Scaffolding," *Log* 31 (spring 2014): 59–61.

19. Venturi, *Complexity and Contradiction,* 23.

20. Venturi, "The Campidoglio," 333.

21. Venturi, *Complexity and Contradiction,* 94. See Stanislaus von Moos, "Language Games and Mass Media," in *Venturi, Rauch & Scott Brown,* 47–59, for a tentative inventory of the references implied in the Guild House facade.

22. Venturi, Scott Brown, and Izenour, *Learning from Las Vegas,* 100.

23. Venturi, *Complexity and Contradiction,* 116.

24. Ibid., 52.

25. Marshall McLuhan, *The Gutenberg Galaxy: The Making of Typographic Man* (Toronto: The University of Toronto Press, 1962).

26. See Neil Levine, "The Book and the Building: Hugo's Theory of Architecture and Labrouste's Bibliothèque Ste. Geneviève," in *The Beaux-Arts and Nineteenth-Century French Architecture,* ed. Robin Middleton (London: Thames & Hudson, 1982), 138–73. Venturi's interest in Labrouste was probably stimulated by a lecture given by Levine; see Robert Venturi, "Learning the Right Lessons from the Beaux-Arts, *Architectural Design* 1 (1979): 23–31.

27. Johns's *Three Flags* is referred to in Venturi, *Complexity and Contradiction*, 62–63 and 131 (in connection with Venturi's Copley Square project of 1966), but its importance as a reference for Guild House is only implied in the text devoted to the building (114–17). See also Venturi, Scott Brown, and Izenour, *Learning from Las Vegas*, 86–87.

28. Venturi, *Complexity and Contradiction*, 27.

29. On Smithson's interest in perceptual effects, see Ann Reynolds, *Robert Smithson: Learning from New Jersey and Elsewhere* (Cambridge, Mass.: MIT Press, 2003), esp. 45–46.

30. Venturi, *Complexity and Contradiction*, 29.

31. See William C. Seitz, introduction to *The Responsive Eye* (New York: The Museum of Modern Art, 1965); also Harriet Schoenholz Bee and Michelle Elligott, *Art in Our Time: A Chronicle of The Museum of Modern Art* (New York: The Museum of Modern Art, 2004), esp. 132.

32. Venturi, *Complexity and Contradiction*, 90.

33. Seitz's description of Kelly's work is quoted in Reynolds, *Smithson*, 48.

34. Venturi, *Complexity and Contradiction*, 102; cf. Peter Blake, *God's Own Junkyard: The Planned Deterioration of America's Landscape* (New York: Holt, Rinehart and Winston, 1964), 108. The picture in question is fig. 88 on p. 59 of *Complexity and Contradiction*. Its origin and purpose within a public relations offensive by Standard Oil have been analyzed in detail by Jutta von Zitzewitz in *Die Stadt, der Highway und die Kamera: Fotografie und Urbanisierung in New York zwischen 1945 und 1965* (Berlin: Deutscher Kunstverlag, 2014), 54–56.

35. Indiana's card "proved enormously popular" to the point of compromising the painter's reputation among "serious" art critics. See *Robert Indiana: Hard Edge; Essays by Adrian Dannatt* (New York: Paul Kasmin Gallery, 2008), esp. 14.

36. VSBA's elaborate use of typography as information and ornament is a subject of its own that involves not only the work of Johns, Indiana, and others but also themes in poetry and linguistics as studied by Liz Kotz, *Words to Be Looked At: Language in 1960s Art* (Cambridge, Mass.: MIT Press, 2007).

37. For an early critique of Venturi's alleged return to premodern "mimesis," a key point among modernist caveats against *Complexity and Contradiction*, see Yve-Alain Bois, Christian Bonnefoi, and Jean Clay, *Architecture / arts plastiques* (Paris: Corda, 1972).

38. *Artist's Choice: Herzog & de Meuron; Perception Restrained*, The Museum of Modern Art, New York, June 21–September 25, 2006. No catalogue was published.

39. For an early discussion of this apparent paradox, see Martin Steinmann, "Hinter dem Bild: nichts," in *Herzog & de Meuron: Architektur Denkform* (Basel: Architekturmuseum in Basel, 1988), 14–19.

40. Hal Foster, *The Art-Architecture Complex* (London: Verso, 2011), 124.

41. Ibid., viii, 90.

42. Ibid., 8, 15.

Deborah Berke

Can a book be both revolutionary and reactionary at the same time? This question would likely delight Robert Venturi, whose *Complexity and Contradiction in Architecture* is a curious title to look back on more than fifty years after it was first published. Its observations seem at once totally assimilated and capable of transporting the reader to a long passed era in architectural discourse.

The Museum of Modern Art published *Complexity and Contradiction* in 1966, just two years after mounting Bernard Rudofsky's exhibition *Architecture Without Architects* and publishing the accompanying book. The hegemony of the International Style was beginning to crack, and MoMA, one of its chief promoters, had brought the barbarians (Rudofsky and Venturi) to the gate and then invited them inside. If Rudofsky found wisdom in the naive and unauthored, Venturi looked to architectural history, especially Baroque and Mannerism, for examples of "nonstraightforward architecture." Meanwhile, Aldo Rossi, whose *Architecture of the City* also appeared in Italy in 1966, explored the "collective memory" of the city built over generations. These three stepsons aligned to maim, if not kill, the modernist father, writing three books that share a similar methodology, a sort of alternative architectural history by way of collage and visual association. All three men were masters of collecting, arranging, and cropping images to make visual arguments.

Venturi took modernism on a scenic, and necessary, detour. But today, *Complexity and Contradiction* wears its age. Much of the urgency of Venturi's argument seems quaint, in part because

Venturi is trying to make room for new architectural ideas by arguing against the dogma Le Corbusier had established forty years earlier. In fairness, *Complexity and Contradiction* is far more than a retort to Le Corbusier—in fact, Le Corbusier's late works are held up as models for the kind of architectural ambiguity that Venturi extols. Still, it can often seem as if Venturi is having an extended debate with Le Corbusier, Walter Gropius, and Mies van der Rohe, seeking to vanquish their dated, and, to Venturi, all-too-narrow and simplistic design manifestos.

Complexity and Contradiction established Venturi as a major thinker in architecture, a position he further developed in design studios and books such as *Learning from Las Vegas* (coauthored with Denise Scott Brown and Steven Izenour). Through his work at Yale, Princeton, and the University of Pennsylvania, Venturi took aim at purism to find a new expression, and in so doing was hugely influential on a generation of students and on the profession itself. As a practicing architect, I found inspiration in his impulse to reexamine history and his inclusive view of what merits architectural investigation. This found its way into my own book, *The Architecture of the Everyday* (1977; coedited with Steven Harris), primarily through rereading the American landscape and attempting to widen the conversation on and criticism of the built environment to include a broad range of voices and disciplines.

Venturi's outlook is profoundly American. There is an enthusiasm and an openness in his thinking—with something of the spirit of early Pop art—that embraces whimsy and optimism. His view is expansive, drawing on the many possibilities and cultural threads of American life. Yes, much of *Complexity and Contradiction* was inspired by his time in Europe, specifically Rome; and yes, while he was at Princeton for his bachelor's and master's degrees the course of study was fully immersed in the Beaux-Arts tradition. But as a theorist and as a designer, he is all-American. Smile. Have fun. Let your buildings have fun. Tell an inside joke, and then tell another joke that a passerby can get.

It is challenging to divorce the book from Venturi's architecture, so closely associated is he with the development of postmodern design. Indeed, it also contains a sort of mini-monograph at the end featuring Venturi's early projects, among them the dour, flat-faced Guild House and the charmingly idiosyncratic Vanna Venturi House, for which he used commonplace materials to create spatial ambiguity and even drama within an intimate domestic setting. One sees echoes of Kahn in the better of these early projects, echoes that faded as ornamentation and signage took on greater importance in his work. It can be confounding to see how postmodernism is primarily identified today with a pictorial approach to design, which many students and young architects seem intent on reviving, at least in installations, design fairs, and biennials. In the end, perhaps these questions of style have overshadowed Venturi's interest as thinker and as an urbanist.

Complexity and Contradiction ends with a thoughtful competition entry to redesign Boston's Copley Square. In discussing the urban thinking of the time, he observes, "Another crutch of Modern architecture is the piazza compulsion derived from our justifiable love of Italian towns. But the open piazza is seldom appropriate for an American city. . . . Empty piazzas are intriguing only in early de Chiricos." He concludes the book with a commonsense—if dangling—note that was truly radical at the time: "We are in the habit of thinking that open space is precious in the city. It is not. Except in Manhattan perhaps, our cities have too much open space in the ubiquitous parking lots, in the not-so-temporary deserts created by Urban Renewal and in the amorphous suburbs around." In much of the United States, these are lessons we are still learning.

Contributors

David B. Brownlee is the Frances Shapiro-Weitzenhoffer Professor of the History of Art at the University of Pennsylvania. His books include *Out of the Ordinary: Robert Venturi, Denise Scott Brown and Associates; Architecture, Urbanism, Design* (with David G. De Long and Kathryn B. Hiesinger, 2001).

Jean-Louis Cohen has been a professor at New York University's Institute of Fine Arts since 1994. He is the author of some forty books, including *Architecture in Uniform* (2011) and *The Future of Architecture since 1889: A Worldwide History* (2012), and the editor of *Le Corbusier: An Atlas of Modern Landscapes* (2013).

Lee Ann Custer is a doctoral candidate in history of art at the University of Pennsylvania specializing in the art, architecture, and urbanism of the United States. For the 2018–19 academic year, she is a Luce/ACLS Dissertation Fellow in American Art. Her current research focuses on the development and imaging of the modern metropolis.

Peter Fröhlicher was a professor of Romance literatures at the University of Konstanz and professor of French literature at the University of Zurich and dean of its Faculty of Arts and Social Sciences. He has published work on Spanish Baroque literature, contemporary Latin American fiction, and French poetry of the nineteenth and twentieth centuries, as well as on the theory and practice of literary analysis.

Dianne Harris is a senior program officer in the Higher Education and Scholarship in the Humanities program at The Andrew W. Mellon Foundation in New York. She is the editor of *Second Suburb: Levittown, Pennsylvania* (2010) and the author of *Little White Houses: How the Postwar Home Constructed Race in America* (2013), among other titles.

Andrew Leach is a professor of architecture at the University of Sydney. His recent books include *Crisis on Crisis, or Tafuri on Mannerism* (2017) and *Gold Coast: City and Architecture* (2018). He is the coeditor of *The Baroque in Architectural Culture, 1880–1980* (2015) and *On Discomfort: Moments in a Modern History of Architectural Culture* (2017).

Mary McLeod is a professor of architecture at Columbia University, where she teaches architectural history and theory. Her research and publications focus on contemporary architecture theory and the history of the modern movement. Besides editing and contributing to *Charlotte Perriand: An Art of Living* (2003), she is coeditor of the website Pioneering Women of American Architecture.

Stanislaus von Moos is professor emeritus of modern and contemporary art at the University of Zurich. He has published on Italian Renaissance architecture and on modern architecture and design in Switzerland, and is the author of *Le Corbusier: Elements of a Synthesis* (1968), *Venturi, Rauch & Scott Brown: Buildings and Projects* (1987), and *Venturi, Scott Brown & Associates: Buildings and Projects, 1986–1998* (1999).

Joan Ockman teaches at the University of Pennsylvania School of Design and at The Cooper Union School of Architecture. Among the books she has edited are *Architecture School: Three Centuries of Educating Architects in North America* (2012) and *Architecture Culture, 1943–1968: A Documentary Anthology* (1993).

Emmanuel Petit has taught architectural design and theory at Yale, Harvard, MIT, University College London, and the Federal Institute of Technology in Lausanne. He is the author of *Irony, or, the Self-Critical Opacity of Postmodern Architecture* (2013) and the editor of books on Philip Johnson, Colin Rowe, and Stanley Tigerman, as well as on formalism in architecture.

Martino Stierli is The Philip Johnson Chief Curator of Architecture and Design at The Museum of Modern Art, New York. He is the author of *Las Vegas in the Rearview Mirror: The City in Theory, Photography, and Film* (2013) and *Venturis Grand Tour: Zur Genealogie der Postmoderne* (2011) and the coeditor of *Las Vegas Studio: Images from the Archives of Robert Venturi and Denise Scott Brown* (2008).

Additionally, the architects **Deborah Berke**, **Sam Jacob**, **Stephen Kieran and James Timberlake**, **Rem Koolhaas**, **Michael Meredith**, **Pier Paolo Tamburelli**, and **Stanley Tigerman** have contributed statements or short interviews that address the influence of *Complexity and Contradiction in Architecture* on contemporary practices, including their own.

Photograph Credits

© 2019 The Josef and Anni Albers Foundation / Artists Rights Society (ARS), New York: 83, 176 (fig. 5). Photograph courtesy Waddington Custot, London: 83

© Fondazione Franco Albini: 119 (fig. 3)

Courtesy Christopher Alexander Foundation, Center for Environmental Structure: 88

Photograph David Allison: 22 (fig. 8)

Courtesy American Academy in Rome, Photographic Archive, Fototeca Unione: 86 (fig. 4b)

Courtesy Architect of the Capitol, Washington, D.C.: 33 (figs. 3f–g)

The Architectural Review © EMAP Publishing Limited, London: 170

Photograph George Barrows: 12

© Cambridge University Press: 85

Photograph © Christie's Images / Bridgeman Images: 171

Photograph Jean-Louis Cohen: 119 (fig. 4)

Courtesy Michele Durrant: 178

© Aldo van Eyck. Courtesy Aldo van Eyck archive: 89 (fig. 7)

Courtesy Katherine Finkelpearl: 57, 58

Courtesy Fisher Fine Arts Library Image Collection, University of Pennsylvania: 33, 34

Photograph Leni Iselin: 114

Photograph Steven Izenour: 34 (figs. 4a–b)

Courtesy Charles Jencks: 93

© 2019 Jasper Johns / Licensed by VAGA at Artists Rights Society (ARS), New York: 176 (fig. 4)

© Ellsworth Kelly Foundation: 177

Courtesy © The MIT Press. Cover Jerry L. Meyer: 16

© 2019 Morgan Art Foundation Ltd. / Artists Rights Society (ARS), New York: 179 (fig. 8)

Photograph Mali Olatunji: 23 (fig. 9)

Photograph Peter Papadimitriou: 32

© 1965 Penguin Random House LLC. Used by permission of Random House, an imprint and division of Penguin Random House LLC. All rights reserved. Excerpts from *The American Landscape* by Ian Nairn: 91

Photograph George Pohl: 30

Photograph Josephine Powell: 33 (fig. 3a)

Collection Howard Raggatt, Ashton Raggatt McDougall: 109

Courtesy Royal Melbourne Institute of Technology. Cover photograph Swetik Korzeniewski: 98

Courtesy Denise Scott Brown: 61, 64

Courtesy Katherine Scully: 55

Courtesy Robert C. Smith: 34 (figs. 4d–e)

Courtesy Robert A. M. Stern: 60

© Ezra Stoller/Esto: 20

Courtesy TIME. © 1979 TIME USE LLC. All rights reserved. Used under license: 21

Courtesy Venturi, Scott Brown & Associates, Inc.: 62

Photograph William Watkins: 174

© Whitney Museum of American Art / Licensed by Scala / Art Resource, New York: 176 (fig. 4), 177

Photograph Lawrence S. Williams: 179 (fig. 9)

Major support for this publication is provided by the Graham Foundation for Advanced Studies in the Fine Arts, Elise Jaffe and Jeffrey Brown, and by The Dale S. and Norman Mills Leff Publication Fund.

Produced by the Department of Publications, The Museum of Modern Art, New York
Christopher Hudson, Publisher
Don McMahon, Editorial Director
Marc Sapir, Production Director
Hannah Kim, Business and Marketing Director

Edited by Alexander Scrimgeour
Designed by Amanda Washburn
Production by Matthew Pimm
Printed and bound by Ofset Yapimevi, Istanbul

This book is typeset in Sabon and Akzidenz Grotesk. The paper is 135gsm Magno Gloss

Published by The Museum of Modern Art
11 West 53 Street
New York, NY 10019-5497
www.moma.org

Library of Congress Control Number: 2018968453
ISBN: 978-1-63345-061-5

Distributed in the United States and Canada by
ARTBOOK | D.A.P.
75 Broad Street
Suite 630
New York, NY 10004

www.artbook.com

Distributed outside the United States and Canada by
Thames & Hudson Ltd
181A High Holborn
London WC1V 7QX
www.thamesandhudson.com

Printed and bound in Turkey